AGING

Twelfth Edition

Editor

Harold Cox
Indiana State University

Harold Cox, professor of sociology at Indiana State University, has published several articles in the field of gerontology. He is the author of *Later Life: The Realities of Aging* (Prentice Hall, 1993). He is a member of the Gerontological Society of America and the American Sociological Association's Occupation and Professions Section and Youth and Aging Section.

Annual Editions
A Library of Information from the Public Press
Dushkin/McGraw·Hill
Sluice Dock, Guilford, Connecticut 06437

Visit us on the Internet—http://www.dushkin.com/

The Annual Editions Series

ANNUAL EDITIONS, including GLOBAL STUDIES, consist of over 70 volumes designed to provide the reader with convenient, low-cost access to a wide range of current, carefully selected articles from some of the most important magazines, newspapers, and journals published today. ANNUAL EDITIONS are updated on an annual basis through a continuous monitoring of over 300 periodical sources. All ANNUAL EDITIONS have a number of features that are designed to make them particularly useful, including topic guides, annotated tables of contents, unit overviews, and indexes. For the teacher using ANNUAL EDITIONS in the classroom, an Instructor's Resource Guide with test questions is available for each volume. GLOBAL STUDIES titles provide comprehensive background information and selected world press articles on the regions and countries of the world.

VOLUMES AVAILABLE

ANNUAL EDITIONS
Abnormal Psychology
Accounting
Adolescent Psychology
Aging
American Foreign Policy
American Government
American History, Pre-Civil War
American History, Post-Civil War
American Public Policy
Anthropology
Archaeology
Astronomy
Biopsychology
Business Ethics
Child Growth and Development
Comparative Politics
Computers in Education
Computers in Society
Criminal Justice
Criminology
Developing World
Deviant Behavior
Drugs, Society, and Behavior
Dying, Death, and Bereavement
Early Childhood Education

Economics
Educating Exceptional Children
Education
Educational Psychology
Environment
Geography
Geology
Global Issues
Health
Human Development
Human Resources
Human Sexuality
International Business
Macroeconomics
Management
Marketing
Marriage and Family
Mass Media
Microeconomics
Multicultural Education
Nutrition
Personal Growth and Behavior
Physical Anthropology
Psychology
Public Administration
Race and Ethnic Relations

Social Problems
Social Psychology
Sociology
State and Local Government
Teaching English as a Second
    Language
Urban Society
Violence and Terrorism
Western Civilization,
    Pre-Reformation
Western Civilization,
    Post-Reformation
Women's Health
World History, Pre-Modern
World History, Modern
World Politics

GLOBAL STUDIES
Africa
China
India and South Asia
Japan and the Pacific Rim
Latin America
Middle East
Russia, the Eurasian Republics,
    and Central/Eastern Europe
Western Europe

Cataloging in Publication Data
Main entry under title: Annual Editions: Aging 98/99.
    1. Gerontology—Periodicals. 2. Gerontology—United States—Periodicals. 3. Aged—United States—Periodicals. 4. Aging—Periodicals. I. Cox, Harold, comp. II. Title: Aging.
ISBN 0–697–39296–1   301.43 5'0973   78-645208

Twelfth Edition

Cover image © 1998 PhotoDisc, Inc.

Printed in the United States of America

Printed on Recycled Paper

Editors/Advisory Board

Members of the Advisory Board are instrumental in the final selection of articles for each edition of ANNUAL EDITIONS. Their review of articles for content, level, currentness, and appropriateness provides critical direction to the editor and staff. We think that you will find their careful consideration well reflected in this volume.

EDITOR

Harold Cox
Indiana State University

ADVISORY BOARD

Staff

Ian A. Nielsen, Publisher

To the Reader

In publishing ANNUAL EDITIONS we recognize the enormous role played by the magazines, newspapers, and journals of the *public press* in providing current, first-rate educational information in a broad spectrum of interest areas. Many of these articles are appropriate for students, researchers, and professionals seeking accurate, current material to help bridge the gap between principles and theories and the real world. These articles, however, become more useful for study when those of lasting value are carefully *collected, organized, indexed,* and *reproduced* in a *low-cost format,* which provides easy and permanent access when the material is needed. That is the role played by ANNUAL EDITIONS. Under the direction of each volume's *academic editor,* who is an expert in the subject area, and with the guidance of an *Advisory Board,* each year we seek to provide in each ANNUAL EDITION a current, well-balanced, carefully selected collection of the best of the public press for your study and enjoyment. We think that you will find this volume useful, and we hope that you will take a moment to let us know what you think.

The decline of the crude birth rate in the United States and other industrialized nations combined with improving food supplies, sanitation, and medical technology has resulted in an ever-increasing number and percentage of people remaining alive and healthy well into their retirement years. The result is a shifting age composition of the populations in these nations—a population comprised of fewer people under age 20 and more people 65 and older.

In 1900 approximately 3 million Americans were 65 years old and older, and they comprised 4 percent of the population. In 1990, there were 31 million persons 65 years old and older, and they represented 12.5 percent of the total population. The most rapid increase in older persons is expected between 2010 and 2030 when the "baby boom" generation reaches 65. Demographers predict that by 2030 there will be 66 million older persons representing approximately 22 percent of the total population. The growing number of older persons in the population has made many of the problems of aging immediately visible to the average American. These problems have become widespread topics of concern for political leaders, government planners, and the average citizen.

Moreover, the aging of the population has not only become a phenomenon of the United States and the industrialized countries of western Europe, but it is also occurring in the underdeveloped countries of the world as well. An increasing number and percentage of the world's population is now defined as aged.

Today almost all middle-aged people expect to live to retirement age and beyond. Both the middle-aged and the elderly have pushed for solutions to the problems confronting older Americans. Everyone seems to agree that granting the elderly a secure and comfortable status is desirable. Voluntary associations, communities, and state and federal governments have committed themselves to improving the lives of older persons. Many programs for senior citizens, both public and private, have emerged in the last 15 years.

The change in the age composition of the population has not gone unnoticed by the media or the academic community. The number of articles appearing in the popular press and professional journals has increased dramatically over the last several years. While scientists have been concerned with the aging process for some time, in the last two decades there has been an expanding volume of research and writing on this subject. This growing interest has resulted in this twelfth edition of *Annual Editions: Aging.*

This volume is representative of the field of gerontology in that it is interdisciplinary in its approach, including articles from the biological sciences, medicine, nursing, psychology, sociology, and social work. The articles are taken from the popular press, government publications, and scientific journals. They represent a wide cross section of authors, perspectives, and issues related to the aging process. They were chosen because they address the most relevant and current problems in the field of aging and present a variety of divergent views on the appropriate solutions to these problems. The topics covered include demographic trends, the aging process, longevity, social attitudes toward old age, problems and potentials of aging, retirement, death, living environments in later life, and social policies, programs, and services for older Americans. The articles are organized into an anthology that is useful for both the student and the teacher.

The goal of *Annual Editions: Aging 1998/99* is to choose articles that are pertinent, well written, and helpful to those concerned with the field of gerontology. Comments, suggestions, or constructive criticism are welcomed to help improve future editions of this book. Please complete and return the postage-paid *article rating* form on the last page of this volume. Any anthology can be improved. This one will continue to be—annually.

Harold Cox
Editor

Contents

UNIT 1

The Phenomenon of Aging

Six selections examine the impact of aging on the individual, the family, and society.

The concepts in bold italics are developed in the article. For further expansion please refer to the Topic Guide and the Index.

UNIT 2

The Quality of Later Life

Seven selections consider the implications of living longer, as well as the physiological and psychological effects of aging.

The concepts in bold italics are developed in the article. For further expansion please refer to the Topic Guide and the Index.

UNIT 3

Societal Attitudes toward Old Age

Five selections discuss societal attitudes of discrimination toward the elderly, sexuality in the later years, and institutionalization.

UNIT 4

Problems and Potentials of Aging

Four selections examine some of the inherent medical and social problems encountered by the aged, including the dynamics of poverty and elder abuse.

The concepts in bold italics are developed in the article. For further expansion please refer to the Topic Guide and the Index.

vii

UNIT 5

Retirement: American Dream or Dilemma?

Four selections look at the broad social implications of the continuing trend toward early retirement and examine the necessity of reassessing and reshaping policies to keep valuable elderly employees in the workforce.

The concepts in bold italics are developed in the article. For further expansion please refer to the Topic Guide and the Index.

UNIT 6

The Experience of Dying

Five selections discuss how increased longevity will affect support programs and the family and consider the effects of death and terminal illness in the family.

UNIT 7

Living Environments in Later Life

Five selections examine the problems of mainstreaming a positive living environment for the increasing number of elderly people.

The concepts in bold italics are developed in the article. For further expansion please refer to the Topic Guide and the Index.

UNIT 8

Social Policies, Programs, and Services for Older Americans

Five selections consider the necessity of developing effective and positive support programs and policies.

The concepts in bold italics are developed in the article. For further expansion please refer to the Topic Guide and the Index.

The concepts in bold italics are developed in the article. For further expansion please refer to the Topic Guide and the Index.

Topic Guide

This topic guide suggests how the selections in this book relate to topics of traditional concern to students and professionals involved with gerontology. It is useful for locating articles that relate to each other for reading and research. The guide is arranged alphabetically according to topic. Articles may, of course, treat topics that do not appear in the topic guide. In turn, entries in the topic guide do not necessarily constitute a comprehensive listing of all the contents of each selection. **In addition, relevant Web sites, which are annotated on the next two pages, are noted in bold italics under the topic articles.**

TOPIC AREA	TREATED IN	TOPIC AREA	TREATED IN
Abuse	22. Understanding Elder Abuse and Neglect *(1, 2, 10)*	Euthanasia	27. Euthanasia's Home: What the Dutch Experience 28. Euthanasia in the Netherlands *(22)*
Alzheimer's Disease	33. "Low-Stimulus Alzheimer's Wings" 37. Canada's Health Insurance and Ours *(1, 2, 4, 12, 13)*	Family Relations	19. Three Phases in the History of American Grandparents 21. My Mother Is Speaking from the Desert 22. Understanding Elder Abuse and Neglect 29. Going Home to Die 36. Caring for Aging Loved Ones *(1, 2, 4)*
Attitudes toward Aging	4. Why We Will Live Longer . . . and What It Will Mean 13. New Passages 18. Learning to Love (Gulp!) Growing Old *(6, 7)*	Gender Gap	11. Men and Women Aging Differently *(7, 8)*
Baby Boomers	4. Why We Will Live Longer . . . and What It Will Mean 25. Rethinking Retirement *(6)*	Health Care/Health Problems	5. Mind Connection 6. Caloric Restriction and Aging 9. Roles for Aged Individuals in Post-Industrial Societies 37. Canada's Health Insurance and Ours 39. Final Indignities *(1, 2, 4, 10, 12, 13, 15, 16, 17, 18, 19, 21, 29)*
Biology of Aging	1. Study for the Ages 2. Toward a Natural History of Aging 5. Mind Connection 6. Caloric Restriction and Aging 7. Sexuality and Aging *(1, 2, 4)*		
		Life Expectancy/ Longevity	3. How to Live to 100 4. Why We Will Live Longer . . . and What It Will Mean 6. Caloric Restriction and Aging 8. Live Longer and Prosper? 11. Men and Women Aging Differently *(4)*
Death and Dying	27. Euthanasia's Home: What the Dutch Experience 28. Euthanasia in the Netherlands 29. Going Home to Die 30. Ashes to Ashes, Dust to Dust 31. American Way of Dying *(15, 16, 21, 22, 23, 24, 25, 26)*		
		Living Will	27. Euthanasia's Home: What the Dutch Experience 28. Euthanasia in the Netherlands
Demography	10. Age Boom 20. American Maturity *(4, 28, 30)*	Migration Patterns	20. American Maturity 35. Retirement Migration and Economic Development
Economic Status	26. Economics of Ageing 39. Does Getting Old Cost Society Too Much? *(2)*	Mortality Rate	16. What Doctors and Others Need to Know *(4)*
Employment	26. Economics of Ageing		

TOPIC AREA	TREATED IN	TOPIC AREA	TREATED IN
Physiology of Aging	5. Mind Connection 6. Caloric Restriction and Aging 7. Sexuality and Aging 17. Amazing Greys 20. American Maturity (2, 4, 18)	**Social Policy**	9. Roles for Aged Individuals in Post-Industrial Societies 32. Story of a Nursing Home Refugee 37. Canada's Health Insurance and Ours (1, 2)
Politics	37. Canada's Health Insurance and Ours 40. Unquiet Future of Intergenerational Politics (2, 37)	**Social Security**	26. Economics of Ageing 41. Less Medicare, More Magic (35)
		Social Services	38. Senior Citizens: A New Force in Community Service 39. Does Getting Old Cost Society Too Much? 41. Less Medicare, More Magic (32, 33, 34, 36)
Psychology of Aging	3. How to Live to 100 7. Sexuality and Aging 12. Getting Over Getting Older 18. Learning to Love (Gulp!) Growing Old (1, 2, 4, 8, 9)	**Sociology of Aging**	13. New Passages 14. On the Edge of Age Discrimination 23. Busy Ethic (1, 2, 4)
Retirement	23. Busy Ethic 24. Does Retirement Hurt Well-Being? 25. Rethinking Retirement 26. Economics of Ageing 35. Retirement Migration and Economic Development (20, 30)	**Support**	9. Roles for Aged Individuals in Post-Industrialized Societies 29. Going Home to Die 36. Caring for Aging Loved Ones (1, 2)
Sexuality	7. Sexuality and Aging (8, 9)	**Understanding the Aged**	13. New Passages 18. Learning to Love (Gulp!) Growing Old 32. Story of a Nursing Home Refugee (1, 2, 4)

Selected World Wide Web Sites for *Annual Editions: Aging*

All of these Web sites are hot-linked through the *Annual Editions* home page: *http://www.dushkin.com/annualeditions* (just click on a book). In addition, these sites are referenced by number and appear where relevant in the Topic Guide on the previous two pages.

Some Web sites are continually changing their structure and content, so the information listed may not always be available.

General Sites

1. Eldercare Web—*http://cube.ice.net/~kstevens/docs/*—This site, created by Karen Stevenson Brown, provides numerous links to eldercare resources. Information on health, living, aging, finance, and social issues, can be found at this site.

2. GoldenAge.Net—*http://elo.mediasrv.swt.edu/goldenage/content.htm*—A "super site" with information on aging. Site includes links to listserv, usenet, and resources on aging.

3. Yahoo: Geriatrics and Aging—*http://www.yahoo.com/Health/Geriatrics_and_Aging/*—Links to numerous Geriatric and Aging sites.

The Quality of Later Life

4. The Gerontological Society of America—*http://www.geron.org*—The Gerontological Society of America promotes the scientific study of aging, and it fosters growth and diffusion of knowledge relating to problems of aging and of the sciences contributing to their understanding.

5. The National Council On the Aging—*http://www.ncoa.org*—The National Council on the Aging, Inc., is a center of leadership and nationwide expertise on the issues of aging. A private, nonprofit association committed to enhancing the field of aging through leadership, service, education, and advocacy.

6. Senior-site.com—*http://www.senior-site.com/*—The is a "super Web site" with links to important sites for seniors. An interesting and entertaining Internet Web site for older Americans and their families.

7. WWW Virtual Library for Women—*http://www.nwrc.org/vlwomen.htm#h*—Scroll to Aging for a list of resources focused on the concerns of older women.

Societal Attitudes toward Old Age

8. Adult Development and Aging: Division 20 of the American Psychological Association—*http://www.iog.wayne.edu/APADIV20/APADIV20.HTM*—This group is dedicated to studying the psychology of adult development and aging.

9. Canadian Psychological Association—*http://www.cpa.ca/*—This is the home page of the Canadian Psychological Asso-

ciation. Material on aging and human development can be found at this site.

10. National Center on Elder Abuse—*http://interinc.com/NCEA/indexnf.html*—This is a consortium of four organizations dedicated to providing information and resources on elder abuse.

11. The Robert Wood Johnson Foundation—*http://www.rwjf.org/main.html*—The Robert Wood Johnson Foundation, based in Princeton, New Jersey, is the nation's largest philanthropic organization devoted exclusively to health and health care.

Problems and Potentials of Aging

12. Alzheimer's Association—*http://www.alz.org/*—The Alzheimer's Association is dedicated to researching the prevention, cures, and treatments of Alzheimer's disease and related disorders, and providing support and assistance to afflicted patients and their families.

13. Alzheimer's Page—*http://www.biostat.wustl.edu/ALZHEIMER/*—The Alzheimer's Page is an educational service created and sponsored by Washington University Alzheimer's Disease Research Center and supported by a grant from the National Institute on Aging.

14. A.P.T.A. Section on Geriatrics—*http://geriatricspt.org/*—This is a component of the American Physical Therapy Association. At this site, information regarding consumer and health information for older adults can be found.

15. Caregiver's Handbook—*http://www.acsu.buffalo.edu/~drstall/hndbk0.html*—This site is an online handbook for caregivers. Topics include nutrition, medical aspects of caregiving, and liabilities of caregiving.

16. Caregiver Survival Resources—*http://www.caregiver911.com/*—This site offers information for caregivers. Information on books, seminars, and information for caregivers can be found at this site.

17. International Food Information Council—*http://ificinfo.health.org/*—At this site, you can find information regarding nutritional needs for aging adults. This site focuses on information for educators and students, publications, and nutritional information.

18. MedWeb: Geriatrics—*http://www.gen.emory.edu/medweb/*—A large search engine at Emory University devoted to health issues. Enter the keyword "geriatrics" into the MedWeb search engine for information on the problems facing aging adults in America.

19. Wellness, Nutrition, and Exercise Information for Healthy Aging—*http://www.aoa.dhhs.gov/aoa/webres/wellness.htm*—This U.S. government Web and Gopher site provides infor-

mation on wellness, nutrition, and exercise for aging adults. Receive advice from nutritionists, health care providers, and mental health organizations.

Retirement

20. American Association of Retired People—*http://www.aarp.org/*—The AARP is the nation's leading organization for people 50 and older. AARP serves their needs through information, education, advocacy, and community service.

The Experience of Dying

21. Agency for Health Care Policy and Research—*http://www.ahcpr.gov/*—Information on the dying process in the context of U.S. health policy is provided here, along with a search mechanism. The agency is part of the Department of Health and Human Services.

22. Articles on Euthanasia: Ethics—*http://www.acusd.edu/ethics/euthanasia.html*—This site covers the ethical issues raised by euthanasia. Also included are articles on euthanasia, historical information, philosophical literature, and Web sites dedicated to the ethical issues surrounding euthanasia.

23. Hospice Foundation of America—*http://www.HospiceFoundation.org/*—On this page, you can learn about hospice care, how to select a hospice, and how to find a hospice near you.

24. Hospice Hands—*http://hospice-cares.com/welcome.html*—The Online Hospice Community at Hospice Hands provides information about hospice care in North Central Florida and other states at this award-winning site.

25. Hospice HotLinks—*http://www.teleport.com/~hospice/links.htm*—Links with information about all aspects of hospice care can be found at this site.

26. Yahoo: Disease and Conditions—*http://yahoo.com/health/diseases_conditions/*—Links to numerous sites about diseases and serious health conditions.

Living Environments in Later Life

27. American Association of Homes and Services for the Aging—*http://www.aahsa.org/*—The American Association of Homes and Services for Aging represents a not-for-profit organization dedicated to providing high-quality health care, housing, and services to the nation's elderly.

28. Center for Demographic Studies—*http://cds.duke.edu/*—The Center for Demographic Studies is located in the heart of the Duke Campus. The primary focus of their research is long-term care for elderly populations, specifically, those over 65 years of age and older.

29. Consumer Coalition for Quality Health Care—*http://www.consumers.org/*—This is a nonprofit group dedicated to protecting and improving the quality of health care for elderly Americans and others.

30. Guide to Retirement Living Online—*http://www.retirement-living.com/*—An online version of a free publication, this site provides information about nursing homes, continuous care communities, independent living, home health care, and adult day care centers.

31. The United States Department of Housing and Urban Development—*http://www.hud.gov/*—News regarding housing for aging adults can be found at this site sponsored by the U.S. federal government.

Social Policies, Programs, and Services for Older Americans

32. Administration on Aging—*http://www.aoa.dhhs.gov/*—This site, housed on the Department of Health and Human Services Web site, provides information for older persons and their families. There is also information for educators and students regarding the elderly.

33. American Geriatrics Society—*http://www.americangeriatrics.org/*—This organization addresses the needs of our rapidly aging population. At this site, you can find information on health care and other social issues facing the elderly.

34. Community Transportation Association of America—*http://www.ctaa.org/*—C.T.A.A. is a nonprofit organization dedicated to mobility for all people, regardless of wealth, disability, age, or accessibility.

35. Medicare Consumer Information from the Health Care Finance Association—*http://www.hcfa.gov/*—A site devoted to explaining Medicare and Medicaid costs to consumers.

36. National Institutes of Health—*http://www.nih.gov/*—Information on health issues can be found at this government site. There is quite a bit of information relating to health issues and the aging population in the United States.

37. The United States Senate: Special Committee on Aging—*http://www.senate.gov/~aging/*—This committee, chaired by Senator Chuck Grassley of Iowa, deals with the issues surrounding the elderly in America. At this site, you can download committee hearing information, news, and committee publications.

We highly recommend that you review our Web site for expanded information and our other product lines. We are continually updating and adding links to our Web site in order to offer you the most usable and useful information that will support and expand the value of your Annual Editions. You can reach us at: *http://www.dushkin.com/annualeditions/*.

The Phenomenon of Aging

The process of aging is complex and includes biological, psychological, sociological, and behavioral changes. Biologically, the body gradually loses the ability to renew itself. Various body functions begin to slow down, and the vital senses become less acute. Psychologically, aging persons experience changing sensory processes; perception, motor skills, problem-solving ability, and drives and emotions are frequently altered. Sociologically, they must cope with the changing roles and definitions of self that society imposes on the individual. For instance, the role expectations and the status of grandparents are different from those of parents, and the roles of the retired are quite different from those of the employed. Being defined as "old" may be desirable or undesirable, depending on the particular culture and its values. Behaviorally, aging individuals may move slower and with less dexterity. Because they are assuming new roles and are viewed differently by others, their attitudes about themselves, their emotions, and, ultimately, their behavior can be expected to change.

Those studying the process of aging often use developmental theories of the life cycle—a sequence of predictable phases that begins with birth and ends with death—to explain individuals' behavior at various stages of their lives. An individual's age, therefore, is important only because it provides clues about his or her behavior at a particular phase of the life cycle, be it childhood, adolescence, adulthood, middle age, or old age. There is, however, the greatest variation in terms of health and human development among older persons than among any other age group. While every 3-year-old child can be predicted to experience certain developmental tasks, there is a wide variation in the behavior of 65-year-old persons. By age 65, we find that some people are in good health, employed, and performing important work tasks. Others of this cohort are retired but in good health. Still others are retired and in poor health. Others have died prior to the age of 65.

The articles in this section are written from biological, psychological, and sociological perspectives. These disciplines attempt to explain the effects of aging and the resulting choices in lifestyle, as well as the wider cultural implications of an older population.

In the first article, "A Study for the Ages," Nancy Shute reports on the results of a longitudinal study that followed the lifestyles of a sample of volunteers whose ages ranged from 20 to 90. Many of the losses formerly associated with aging were found to be treatable and sometimes reversible. Next, John Lauerman, in his article "Toward a Natural History of Aging," argues that new scientific findings can now guide older persons into living lives in better health than have any previous generations of Americans. Then, Geoffrey Cowley, in "How to Live to 100," observes the critical factors that allows persons to live with clear minds and bodies well into their later years.

The essay "Why We Live Longer . . . and What It Will Mean," by Richard Kirkland, explains why he believes that the baby boom generation will be the longest-living generation in U.S. history. This generation is expected to have a profound effect on the lifestyles of Americans.

UNIT 1

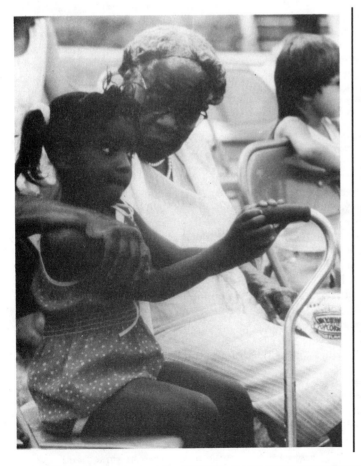

In the next report, "The Mind Connection," Beth Baker takes a holistic approach to the causes and recovery from diverse health problems. She argues that the brain regulates and influences many physiological functions, including immunity, and that mental and physical well-being are inextricably intertwined. The emerging evidence indicates that psychological and emotional factors may influence recovery from everything from heart disease to the common cold. In the final unit article, "Caloric Restriction and Aging," Richard Weindruch observes that numerous studies have shown that reducing calories extends the life of laboratory rats. He suggests that eating less while being sure the individual consumes enough protein, fat, vitamins, and minerals would most likely extend the longevity of humans as well.

Looking Ahead: Challenge Questions

What accounts for most behavior changes during the aging process: biological, psychological, or sociological factors? Explain your answer.

Biological, psychological, sociological, and behavioral researchers usually work independently to explain the aging process. Do you think it would be possible to combine these disparate perspectives into one single theory of aging? Defend your answer.

Will it ever be possible to slow down the aging process? Would this be desirable? Why or why not?

What is meant by the concept of successful aging?

A STUDY FOR THE AGES

Generations of volunteers are helping scientists to comprehend time's toll

BY NANCY SHUTE

JOHN FREDERICK KIRBY IS 87, but the retired engineer still treks the quarter mile to his Scientists Cliffs, Md., mailbox twice a day to get the newspaper and the mail. His 60-year-old daughter, Rosemary Hill, moved nearby last year in case her dad needs help. And her nephew, 30-year-old Sean Kirby, still makes the three-hour drive from his home in Frederick, Md., down to his grandfather's, where he can walk the beach and hunt for fossilized shark teeth, as he did as a child. It's just an average family—but one that by being so very ordinary is helping to decipher a mystery of consuming interest to everyone: What happens as we age?

The Kirby-Hills, along with more than 1,100 other volunteers from their 20s to their 90s, are guinea pigs for the Baltimore Longitudinal Study of Aging. The 39-year-old federal effort has become one of the world's great medical studies—and the first to illuminate in detail how healthy people grow old. By tracking physical and mental changes in a total of 2,438 study participants over the decades, the BLSA has made medical history. BLSA researchers, to cite one noteworthy example, discovered in 1992 that a rise in the blood of a substance called prostate-specific antigen (PSA)

might warn of prostate cancer five years before traditional exams detect it.

On a larger scale, the BLSA's mountain of data confirms the great good news about aging: It may be inevitable, but it's not immutable. Many losses of function once thought to be age related, such as decreased mobility or memory lapses, can be stopped or slowed. And many supposed indignities of aging turn out to be pure misconception. A few examples:

• Only 20 to 30 percent of people over 70 have symptoms of heart disease; an additional 25 percent have heart disease but no symptoms. "If you're in the other 50 percent, you're not going to die of your aging heart" says Jerome Fleg, a BLSA cardiologist. "You're going to be able to function essentially like a healthy 20- or 25-year-old for the activities of daily living."

• People don't get crankier as they age; personality is a constant after age 30. A peevish 80-year-old was a peevish 40-year-old.

• Even into very old age, high blood cholesterol significantly raises the risk

On average, Americans say middle age ends and old age starts at age 64.

of cardiovascular disease. Thus, preventive measures like a low-cholesterol diet may well be worthwhile after age 70, particularly for people with heart disease.

• Senility is not inevitable. Only 10 percent of people over 65 ever develop dementia, and much of the cognitive decline that we associate with old age is due to treatable medical conditions and diseases such as depression, diabetes, and hypertension. The small decline in memory and reaction time that many people experience with age doesn't impair their intellectual ability. "Aging is not a disease," says Paul Costa, chief of the BLSA's Laboratory on Personality and Cognition. "The ravages of aging are somewhat of a myth."

The youthful old. If you don't believe that, check out the nearest octogenarian. John Frederick Kirby's generation is living proof that old age has already moved beyond doddering fogyhood. George Bush is 72. Lena Horne is 79. So is Mike Wallace. George Burns was still cracking vaudeville jokes when he turned 100.

"What was old in the last century is not old anymore," says Robert Butler, chair of New York's International Longevity Center of the Mount Sinai School of Medicine and founding director of the National Institute on Aging (and 70 years old). "Even in my own career I've seen it. In the 1950s, the people coming into the nursing homes were age 65. Now they're in their 80s."

Only relatively recently have enough people lived long enough to warrant nursing homes. In 1900, the average life span was 47. It has zoomed to 79 now, largely because of improved sanitation and nutrition and better medical care, which have effectively eliminated two major causes of death: childbirth and infectious diseases like smallpox and polio. Social Security and Medicare have contributed, too, by granting people over 65 an unprecedented degree of financial security. (Poverty is not a healthful lifestyle.)

But with people living longer and baby boomers streaming into middle age, the nature of old age has become an economic issue as well as a physiological one. By 2040, 21 percent of the U.S. population will be over 65, up from 13 percent now. That fifth of the population is projected to consume half the nation's health care resources, compared with about a third today. In an era of limited government funding, health and independence may be the best insurance a senior citizen can have.

Birth of a notion. In 1958, when the BLSA was launched, researchers trying to grasp the biological factors of aging were frustrated by the paucity of good data. Aging studies then were largely cross-sectional, meaning that they compared people living at the same time: 80-year-olds in a nursing home with college students, say. Differences in experience, education, and affluence between the generations tainted the results.

So in February 1958, when noted National Institutes of Health gerontologist Nathan Shock got a call from William Peter, a physician and retired medical missionary, asking how he could donate his body for medical research after he died, Shock told him he'd be more useful alive than dead. The two men decided to start a longitudinal study that would track the same people over time. They recruited themselves, their families, and their friends. Shock and Peter prodded the NIH to fund the research; longitudinal studies take years before

there's any payoff. Today, the BLSA receives $6 million a year in federal funds as its total budget—surely one of Uncle Sam's better investments. "It's one of the most influential long-term studies in the world," says Caleb Finch, a professor of gerontology at the University of Southern California. "It was the first serious investigation of healthy people from middle age into later life."

The BLSA was more like a men's club at first, and an all-white one at that; women weren't included until 1978. Their numbers now equal the men's, and thanks to extensive recruiting, 13 percent of the participants are African American. These days, volunteers in their 20s and 80s and minorities are most sought after, says James Fozard, chief of the NIA's longitudinal studies branch. (To volunteer, contact the NIA Information Center at 800-222-2225, department 1.)

Since volunteers are self-selected, they tend to be better educated and better off than the average American. No one is paid, and participants make their own way to Baltimore once every two years for a 2½-day visit. Sixty percent live in the Baltimore-Washington region, but others come from Australia, Hawaii, and California. Almost nobody drops out.

John Frederick Kirby was one of the first volunteers; he was recruited by neighbors in Scientists Cliffs, a summer community on the Chesapeake Bay built by researchers in the 1930s. He then signed up his father and, later, his two daughters, two sons, and two grandsons. "The first time I went, I was really nervous," says grandson Michael Hill, 35, like his cousin Sean Kirby the fourth generation of Kirbys in the BLSA. "But I don't feel like a guinea pig. It's more like part of the team." Hill, in turn, recruited his wife. They go to Baltimore's Little Italy neighborhood for dinner after a day of CT scans. "It's kind of a nice romantic time for us" Hill says.

But hardly plush. Study subjects stay at Johns Hopkins Bayview Medical Center, across the street from BLSA headquarters, in a hospital wing so old that the gritty TV series *Homicide* once

41% of Americans ages **30** to **64** say they will exercise regularly when they are old. **95%** of those **65** and older say they do now.

filmed there. After settling in, volunteers get a thorough physical exam and are steered through a gantlet of physical and psychological tests from simple hearing exams to the Guilford-Zimmerman Temperament Survey, a personality test. "It's not the typical physical," says Georgia Burnette, a 68-year-old retired nurse from Buffalo who has been a volunteer since 1991. "You don't have a thallium scan routinely. You don't have Dopplers of your carotids."

Rosemary Hill loathes the treadmill test, in which subjects are run until they're about to drop. "They have you all hooked up to tubes, with a clothespin on your nose." Other volunteers find the psychological tests unnerving. Fred Litwin, the 73-year-old owner of a Washington, D.C., used-furniture store, quit taking a memory test in which words are flashed on a screen; it unearthed a deeply buried fear, he says, of being labeled a "dummy." (Volunteers can refuse any test without being banished.) Despite infirmities that the examination might reveal, Litwin says the rigorous probing also bestows confidence. "Knowing that I'm being studied and that there are no surprises makes me feel good."

Oh, by the way... Sometimes there *are* surprises. "The physician assistant was palpating my belly, and while they do that you secretly wonder what they're looking for," Litwin says of his last visit. "She said, 'You have an aortal aneurysm.'" Such weak spots in the wall of the aorta, the body's major artery, can balloon and burst; Litwin's mother had died of an aneurysm 12 years before. The BLSA reported the finding to Litwin's personal physician (study doctors do not treat participants), and Litwin had surgery that successfully repaired the artery. "That was really a lifesaver for me," Lutwin says.

Many volunteers cite the world-class medical work-up as reason enough to put up with the inconvenience—and the expense. (They get room and board but are not otherwise compensated.) Just as many participants say they like contributing to the research. "I really believe in what they're doing," says Jamie Netschert, a 46-year-old veterinarian from Northern Virginia who has been in the study for 23 years, following in the footsteps of his father. "I saw how much it meant to my dad."

Such devotion yields a rich investigative harvest. In the case of the prostate-cancer research, for instance, researchers pulled blood samples taken as long as 25 years ago, then drew fresh samples from the same participants. BLSA data—thousands of blood and tissue samples stashed in 22 freezers and results stored in a mainframe computer and dozens of file cabinets stacked to the ceiling—are open to scientists around the world, awaiting questions not yet posed.

From the outset, the study's mission was to see if aging follows a predictable pattern. As results have built up, the BLSA researchers realized that while most people associate aging with gray hair, Medicare, and early-bird specials, it really starts in the mid-30s. Muscles begin to shrivel. Bones lose mass. Hearing and vision become less acute. The immune system loses some of its punch. Hormone levels drop. Lung capacity contracts. And the body gets a bit shorter every year.

Wrinkled but running. But these insults aren't meted out monolithically. Different people age at very different rates, and the variation expands with age. Even within the same person, organ systems seem to have individual internal clocks. While one person feels her age in an aching, arthritic back, another develops shortness of breath due to heart disease. A third may be balding and wrinkled but still running marathons. Aging is infinite in its variety. There is no single pattern.

The *why* of the aging process remains one of science's great unresolved questions. Theories fall into two camps: the "program" camp, in which genes, hormones, or the immune system is thought to be programmed to follow a biological clock to self-destruction to make room for the next generation, and the "error" camp, in which cells and organs are thought to wear out or to suffer environmental damage. Most gerontologists now think that we age because of complex interactions that involve all of these. And they do know one thing for sure: So far, no one has figured out how to push the human life span beyond 120 years or so. Most of us will barely make it two thirds of the way, and we want

to make it as far as we can, eking out every last day.

Realizing that aging varies widely from person to person prompted BLSA researchers to search out characteristics that lead to a healthy, satisfying, successful old age. Reubin Andres, an expert in obesity and diabetes who has spent most of his career at the BLSA, determined that it's healthier to gain some weight, as much as a pound a year from about age 40 on, and that those famous Metropolitan Life height/weight charts were set too low for older people. "We published that, and that led to a controversy that continues," Andres says, smiling. Indeed: In other studies, rats fed an extremely low-calorie diet lived up to twice as long as their well fed peers. Studies are underway with monkeys to see if a low-calorie diet will have the same life-extending effect on primates. In the meantime, Andres stresses that he's not advocating obesity, a major risk factor for heart disease and diabetes. "But for such a large fraction of the American population, and women more than men, to be concerned about losing 5 pounds, even 10 pounds, is trivial. All they're doing is removing some of the pleasure of living."

Disbelief. The BLSA finding that personality doesn't change after age 30 challenged such a deeply held stereotype of old age that even the researchers didn't believe it at first. So they ran five different personality tests. And they extended the study over 18 years. And they polled friends and spouses of participants, in case people were deluding themselves. "Quite amazingly, we got the same picture of stability from spouses and peers," says Costa, chief of the BLSA's personality laboratory. "When we do see significant change, it's often a sign of disease, like Alzheimer's disease."

Of late the BLSA has put more resources into Alzheimer's, for many people the most terrifying curse of age. In March, BLSA researchers reported that participants who took ibuprofen for as little as two years had half the risk of contracting Alzheimer's as did those who took aspirin or acetaminophen.

Many researchers believe inflammation plays a key role in Alzheimer's ability to damage brain tissue; if so, ibuprofen, a nonsteroidal anti-inflammatory, may reduce or prevent the damage. At this point no one knows what dose works best, so the BLSA isn't telling people to start downing ibuprofen, says Jeffrey Metter, a physician and the study's medical director. But if you're already taking ibuprofen for arthritis or another reason, he says, "reap the wealth of the benefits."

By looking at decades' worth of results of tests that measure mental acuity, Costa's laboratory found that BLSA participants who developed Alzheimer's showed subtle changes, particularly in memory, 10 to 20 years before the debilitating symptoms came to light. The researchers are now performing MRI (magnetic resonance imaging) and PET (positron emission tomography) scans of participants' brains to try to detect signs of early changes in the hippocampus and other structures, and are investigating suspected links between Alzheimer's and changes over the years in the way the body metabolizes glucose. By attacking the same question from different angles within the same population, the investigators hope to find early markers for Alzheimer's and, eventually, a way to treat people before the disease irrevocably damages the brain.

BLSA researchers also are continuing their landmark research on prostate-specific antigen and prostate cancer, which is newly diagnosed in 334,500 men a year. Just this spring, they reported that the ratio of two forms of PSA in a man's blood can reveal cancer up to 10 years before a manual exam would. The sophisticated test also identifies the cancer as aggressive or slow growing, making it possible to determine a man's level of risk, eliminate unnecessary PSA tests, and more reliably decide when surgery is necessary.

No more roast. While it can take years for researchers to sift through the BLSA data and reach conclusions, the individuals studied have more immediate—and personal—reasons to be interested in the results. Burnette, the retired

> **71%** of Americans expect to be in good health when they are old. But **28%** say they won't be able to drive.

How time takes its toll

Even if you're already 40 or 50, it could be decades before you fully realize you're aging. The loss of 40 percent of lung capacity by age 80, say, is so gradual that most people never sense the difference. Besides, the signposts on this page are population averages. As car people say, your mileage may vary.

Your 40s

- At 40, the body burns 120 fewer calories a day than at age 30, making weight control harder.
- The body is $5/8$ of an inch shorter at 40 than at 30 and will continue to shrink by about $1/16$ of an inch a year because of changes in posture, bone loss, and compression of the spongy disks that separate the vertebrae.
- Changes in the inner ear erode the ability to hear higher frequencies for men, who lose hearing more than twice as fast as women do.
- The eyes begin to have trouble focusing on magazines and other close objects as the lenses become thicker.

Your 50s

- With menopause, fertility ends, and lower estrogen speeds bone loss and raises the risk of heart disease.
- As the eye's sensitivity to contrast declines, the ability to see in dim light or under conditions of glare, or to catch sight of moving objects, diminishes.
- Loss of strength becomes measurable as muscle mass diminishes.
- Vulnerability to infections and cancer increases; the thymus, a gland that plays a key role in the immune system, has shrunk by 90 to 95 percent.

Your 60s

- Making out conversations becomes harder, especially for men, as high-frequency hearing deteriorates further. (Consonants, which carry most of the

meaning of speech, largely consist of higher frequencies.)
- The pancreas, which processes glucose, works less efficiently. Blood-sugar levels rise and more people are diagnosed with adult-onset diabetes.
- Joints are stiff in the morning, particularly the knees, hips, and spine, because of wear and tear on the cartilage that cushions them.
- Men's sexual daydreams all but vanish after age 65. Researchers don't know why.

Your 70s

- Blood pressure is 20 to 25 percent higher than in the 20s; the thicker, stiffer artery walls can't flex as much with each heartbeat.
- Reaction to loud noises and other stimuli is delayed as the brain's ability to send messages to the extremities slows.
- Short-term memory and the ability to learn spoken material, like a new language, decline with changes in brain function.
- More than half of men show signs of coronary-artery disease.
- Sweat glands shrink or stop working in both men and women, raising the risk of heatstroke (but reducing the need for deodorant).

Your 80s

- Women become particularly susceptible to falling and to disabling hip fractures. They are generally weaker than men and by now have lost over half the bone mass in the hips and upper legs.
- Almost half of those over 85 show signs of Alzheimer's disease.
- The heart beats, at maximum exertion, about 25 percent slower than it did at age 20—but compensates by expanding and pumping more blood per beat.
- The stereotype notwithstanding, personality *doesn't* change with age. A cranky 80-year-old was a cranky 30-year-old.

Buffalo nurse, learned she had extremely high cholesterol and slightly elevated blood sugar. So she took up mall walking with a friend. "Walking six or seven days a week, 3 miles in an hour, has lowered my cholesterol by half," she says. The 16 pounds she lost didn't hurt, either. Sister Mary Pauline Hogan, a 57-year-old participant from Boston, likes a nice piece of roast beef. But she's a little overweight and has a family history of heart problems; her mother died at age 54. So Sister Pauline

is eating more chicken, fish, and vegetables. That can be a challenge because as administrator of a convent for retired nuns of the Sisters of Charity of St. Elizabeth, she cooks supper for 20 people. "I'm doing a lot of stir-fry," she says. "We have a grill, and I'm getting really fancy with it."

Of course, heredity has a lot to do with how we age, and nobody has figured out how to pick his or her parents. But as a result of efforts like Burnette's and Sister Pauline's, over the years BLSA

participants have markedly improved the group's overall cholesterol levels, blood pressure, and smoking rates. They're also eating less fat and more fiber. "On the negative side, we have more obesity [among participants), and there's not a lot of exercising," Metter says. "But we do see more people walking."

It would be easy to dismiss these behavior changes, arguing that BLSA participants are unnaturally dutiful when it comes to healthy behavior. But the BLSA participants aren't the only ones changing. Nationally, the death rate from heart disease, the No. 1 cause of death in the United States, dropped 50 percent between 1950 and 1990, and it wasn't just due to better medical care. Diet and lifestyle have changed, too.

The point is not that lifestyle changes can affect the aging process—no one has yet devised an antiaging elixir, despite claims touted in tabloids and in health-food stores—but that they can fend off or slow age-related diseases such as arthritis, diabetes, heart disease, and stroke. BLSA researchers and others agree that moderate, regular physical activity, whether it's walking, gardening, bicycling, or golf, lowers blood pressure, cholesterol, and glucose; helps relieve the pain and stiffness of arthritis; and recently was shown to be a powerful antidepressant in the elderly. Weight training is proving remarkably useful in combating age-related loss of strength, even in women in their 90s.

And older people are indeed more active than their counterparts were just 10 years ago. Fitness participation by people over 55 rose 73 percent from 1987 to 1995, according to a study commissioned by the Sporting Goods Manufacturers Association. If this trend continues, increasing numbers of old people will avoid the invalidism that many people still presume to be the penalty of old age.

Before joining the BLSA research team 10 years ago, Metter worked as a neurologist at a Veterans Administration hospital, where "you had the impression that getting old was really bad for your health." The patients were infirm, impaired by strokes and other ailments. Coming to the BLSA was an awakening. "You saw those people who were really aging for the most part successfully or were managing their illnesses" well. The BLSA participants' ability to negotiate the aging process, Metter says, "has major implications in terms of how we can live into our older age more healthy and productive."

Pushing the limits. And many BLSA participants are healthy and productive well past 65. Fred Litwin, at 73, rides his Honda 450 motorcycle to work every day, where he hauls furniture up four stories in a hand-hoisted elevator. His wife, Evelyn, 74, also a BLSA volunteer, is the director of an outdoor nursery school where she has worked for 35 years. "I've been outdoors more than indoors," Evelyn Litwin says. "I feel like quite a vigorous person." Lee Canfield, an 83-year-old retired national security analyst, spends hours chopping wood and tilling his 1-acre Falls Church, Va., garden. "I like to push myself fairly close to the limits," Canfield says. "I'm not as young as I was, so my limits are closing. But I get a heck of a lot done, and in the process I enjoy it immensely."

None of these people feels like a teenager. Litwin concedes a loss of strength and short term memory, and Canfield's back is so stiff he can hardly bend over. But they adjust and move on. "I didn't think I was aging until last week," says Maurine Mulliner, a Washington, D.C. resident who was one of the first women to join the BLSA and, at 92, is among its oldest volunteers. (A few others are also in their 90s.) "It's a great surprise."

Mulliner was in bed with painful spinal arthritis at the time. The flare-up was playing havoc with her calendar, usually thickly penciled with meetings to alleviate the District of Columbia's financial crisis, lunches at the tony Cosmos Club (she was the third female member), church events, and her daily hatha yoga session (she danced with the Chicago Opera ballet in the 1930s, until the Depression did it in). A Mormon childhood taught her good values and a healthy diet, Mulliner says. Sturdy stock helped, too; a grandmother who was a frontier doctor and a mother who was a politician taught her that women could do whatever they wanted. Mulliner did,

including a long career as an official with the Social Security Administration, political activism (she helped found the Americans for Democratic Action), and a World War II posting to the U.S. Embassy in London.

"If we learn to accept change, that's key," Mulliner says of growing old. "The people who can accept what comes along and know that they're not going to be able to change much of it and make a reasonable adjustment are the ones who can do it best."

TOWARD A NATURAL HISTORY OF
AGING

SCIENTISTS PROBE BEYOND DISEASE TO IDENTIFY THE PARAMETERS OF AN ENERGETIC LATER LIFE.

BY JOHN LAUERMAN

IT'S THE SAME EACH TIME WE MEET. I'm conversing with Henrietta Aladjem at her condominium just outside Boston. Trading ideas across her dining-room table is an elaborate game of confidences, intimidation, braggadocio, hopes, some gloating, and laughter. We start by deploring the assassination of a foreign leader, move to the violence of the inner cities, briefly touch on the nature of learning, and then return, as we so often do, to a discussion of the power of human strength, of the unfathomable reasons why one person flourishes while another flounders.

It's a familiar resting point for us, and as we revisit oft-repeated views, I discern signs of another familiar pattern. Once again, the "elderly" woman I'm talking with has worn me out. Not with shouting, pestering, or shrill demands for attention, but with energy. With persistence, idea-making, and curiosity.

Chances are that you already know of Henrietta, or have even made her acquaintance. The former Widener librarian is one of those ubiquitous personalities who turn up in Hollywood, at the Massachusetts State House, at Congressional offices, at the National Institutes of Health, even the White House.

The revered Canadian physician Sir William Osler once said that if you want to live a long life, get a chronic disease and take good care of it. For better or worse, Henrietta has followed this advice for more than 30 years, since her diagnosis with an autoimmune disease, systemic lupus erythematosus. Her energy seems inexhaustible. She's written five books about lupus. Two weeks ago, she was the featured speaker at the annual meeting of Lupus Canada. This morning, she drove herself to Framingham and bought a couch.

Now she sighs and rests heavily in the dining-room chair where she writes each day, surrounded by old-world furnishings that have accompanied her throughout a lifetime—a mirror-backed china cabinet in which her stationery resides, a couple of

dark wood sideboards topped with ornamental plates. She is working on her sixth book. It won't be her last. There's frequent talk of a screenplay, or sometimes a romance novel. Those who have tried to push her toward retirement have underestimated her. For 14 years, Henrietta was editor of *Lupus News*, published by the Lupus Foundation of America, which she established. In March, she sent out the first copies of *Lupus Letter*, a new publication for patients with the disease. Henrietta's in her eighth decade of life, and it's utter, hectic chaos.

"I know I am old, but I have taken care of my skin," she says in a strong Bulgarian émigré's accent, only slightly slurred by the Bell's palsy that affects one side of her face. "I do not have the skin of a 79-year-old woman. And you know, inside I am bounding with enthusiasm. There are many, many things that I am deeply interested in, and I have the enthusiasm of a 30-year-old...of a child."

PIONEERS OF A NEW KIND OF AGING

IN HIS LATER YEARS, BERTRAND RUSSELL SAID THAT HE NEVER FELT like an old man, but rather like a young man who had something not quite right with him. What is age? A synonym of infirmity and frailty? A number? A pattern? A risk factor? When we say that someone is aging, what exactly does that imply? When someone says, "I feel old," we assume the person is fatigued and dispirited. But there are plenty of people whose experience of aging belies that image, people who continue to thrive, without or in spite of illness and disability.

Take the number 65. It's a number commonly associated with slowing down, retirement, a desire for warmer climes and fewer responsibilities...and increased susceptibility to disease. For many Americans, these associations are well founded. The elderly do consume more health services than any other age group.

They visit more doctors, take more drugs, spend more days in hospitals and nursing homes, and in general need more care than other people.

But that doesn't accurately reflect the real diversity of the elderly in terms of health and mental status. As the over-65 population blossoms, hidden vitality and energies among these people will surface. Like "old Father William," stereotypes of the helpless, frail elderly are about to be stood on their heads. The Baby Boom countdown to 65 is at 13 years, and as it gets closer, expect the unexpected, because what is about to happen has never happened before on this earth.

As much as any fresh wave of immigrants, the elderly are about to become a much more visible component of our national scene. Daily, 3,000 people turn 65, and only 2,000 above that age die, leaving 1,000 new members of the elderly population. In the 30 years between 1990 and 2020, the over-65 American population will grow by 71 percent, more than twice the rate of growth in the general population. By the year 2020, one out of six Americans will be over 65. The term "retirement community" will describe just about any neighborhood in the United States.

Public health measures introduced in this century—advances in nutrition, hygiene, and vaccination—have redefined old age. One hundred years ago, it wasn't unusual to become a sage grandparent before your fortieth birthday, or to die soon afterward. In 1900, average life expectancy for American women was 49, for men 46. Since then, we've seen average length of life climb by about 50 percent, to 78.8 for girls and 72.1 for boys. This means that half the people now alive in this country will live past 75.

Needless to say, change like this doesn't occur very often; the previous 25-year increase in life expectancy took approximately the length of recorded history, or about 4,000 years. By the year 2050, average American life expectancy will climb further, to a projected 82.6 years.

"Aging is a new field driven by demographics as much as by scientific discovery," observes Ken Minaker, M.D., chief of a new geriatric medicine unit at Massachusetts General Hospital and associate professor at Harvard Medical School. "Today's elderly are pioneers of a new kind of aging. The next century will be dominated by the concerns of the elderly."

A STUDY IN FRUSTRATION

ONLY RECENTLY HAVE HUMAN AGING STUDIES ENTERED THE REALM OF serious science. The National Institute on Aging was formed just 20 years ago. Models for studying human aging were rare until recently.

"In the animal world, aging is almost nonexistent," says Jan Vijg, director of the molecular genetics section of Beth Israel Hospital's gerontology division, in Boston. "Most animals die of infectious diseases or accidents or are killed long before they become adults, let alone get a chance to age."

This is not to say that animals do not have long lifespans: some tortoises may live 150 years. Consider the saga of Scottish ornithologist George Dunnet and the fulmar, told in two photographs. In the first, taken by a shoreline in 1950, Dunnet is in

> LIKE "OLD FATHER WILLIAM," STEREOTYPES OF THE HELPLESS, FRAIL ELDERLY ARE ABOUT TO BE STOOD ON THEIR HEADS.

the act of tagging a young adult female bird. Dunnet looks fit, in his twenties or thirties, and sports a full head of dark, wavy hair. The second picture, taken in 1992, shows an older, sagging Dunnet, with thinning grey hair, while the fulmar looks almost identical to its 1950 picture.

Why not study these long-lived animals to further understand human aging? Because, although they can rack up years, in an important physiological sense they are not aging. There's nothing to distinguish the fulmar from its younger fellows but a 42-year-old leg band. Females of this species, and some others, remain fertile at a point in their lifespans long after humans would have undergone menopause. By the same token, there are species that age very quickly after reproduction. For example, take the rapid physical deterioration that occurs in sockeye salmon as they make their way upstream to spawn. One sees bone deformity, muscle weakness, reduced immunity, and finally an exhausted death. A decline that takes decades in humans is compressed into days. Extrapolations from these species to ours would be fraught with misgivings.

"Rodent aging is well characterized," says Beth Israel gerontology division chief Jeanne Y. Wei, M.D., "and there are transgenic mouse models that can give valuable insights. But there are many ways in which we can never extrapolate from the rodent to the human. Unfortunately, it's extremely difficult to do longitudinal aging studies in humans.

"There are all kinds of obstacles," Wei continues. "One of the problems of studying the elderly is that the techniques change over time. For instance, blood glucose measurement techniques have changed significantly over the past few years. Means of data analysis change. People and groups change. There are mass lifestyle changes, such as the recent focus on exercise, or the exodus from farming communities. Something can be added to the drinking water, like fluoride, that has the potential to skew your sample enormously. Or people may change their dietary habits in very subtle ways.

"Another confounding aspect of studying aging is that you're usually studying only survivors; you're finding out a lot about the diseases that certain subjects have died from and others have managed to survive or avoid. For example, you may see a drop in cholesterol at a certain age. That drop could be due to changes in measurement technique, which have changed over the last few years, or to dietary intake, which has also changed drastically due to improved awareness of the importance of diet, or it could be simply that most of the study subjects with high cholesterol have died by this age. And none of this would really tell us anything about aging."

Wei is director of Harvard's division on aging, a consortium that brings together researchers and clinicians throughout the University's affiliates. The division was born in 1979 out of a collaboration between doctors Jack Rowe and Richard Besdine. Rowe, a Beth Israel nephrologist who had trained at the National Institute on Aging, believed that geriatricians needed to begin working with subspecialists from all disciplines to answer basic questions about aging: how it affects functioning of major systems and what implications it has for disease prevention and treatment.

Besdine, who came from the Hebrew Rehabilitation Center for Aged, promoted research into so-called "geriatric syndromes": falls, incontinence, and dehydration, to list just a few. Researchers who trained under Besdine have gone to extraordinary lengths to investigate the multiple causes of these syndromes and develop imaginative treatments (see "Make Me Dry").

"Aging is so complex that we probably can't study it with the same methodological techniques we have used for other diseases," concedes Wei. "We need new methods, new paradigms, a new way of looking at things to find out what happens to people as they get older."

YOUR GENES AND THE OXYGEN MENACE

OSCAR WILDE'S DYING WORDS IN A CHEAP, POORLY APPOINTED Paris hotel were supposed to have been, "Either this wallpaper goes or I do." Wilde's nonchalance is not widely shared; intrinsic to the way we think about life is that it is worth holding on to at all costs, to the point that we refuse to acknowledge death. Why else would so many people put off for so long important decisions about health-care proxies, do-not-resuscitate instructions, inheritance and funeral plans?

Our genes point to a different set of priorities. Their only goal and measure of success is reproduction. If you die without reproducing, your individualized collection of genes dies, too. Any genetic features interfering with reproduction are automatically unlikely to survive in future generations, while genes that abet mating are preserved. But so are the genes that undoubtedly play a role in all the chronic diseases of aging—Alzheimer's disease, heart disease, diabetes, osteoporosis, cancer, and others.

"Aging occurs after you've had your children," Jan Vijg says. "Consequently, there is no selection for successful aging genes. . . . Genes with negative effects in old age have a tendency to stick, because they've been passed along before they've had the chance to affect reproduction."

Many experts on aging agree that genes determine who ages successfully. That's too bad, because when it comes to aging, genes can be notoriously bad decision-makers. For example, Vijg says, choices our genes made millenia ago made us reliant on oxygen. A highly reactive element, oxygen bonds to almost anything in the environment, including important biomolecules like DNA. This reactivity renders oxygen highly toxic; the element deactivates enzymes, contorts protein, and compromises the DNA sequence perhaps as often as 100,000 times a day in each human body.

Long ago in our evolution, however, genes were selected that acknowledged that the competitive advantage of metabolizing oxygen, which can produce lots of energy quickly, was worth the long-term risk of chronic oxygen toxicity. Animals developed highly specialized red blood cells for transporting oxygen safely through the bloodstream in ways that temporarily prevent it from reacting with other molecules.

Just the fact that we breathe oxygen is evidence of our genes' ambivalence toward longevity. Oxygen's toxicity seldom becomes an issue until we age. Vijg thinks that oxidative damage may be one of the major causes of the aging process, and went to the trouble of developing a complicated mouse model to look further

into the question. The model enabled him to measure for the first time the "mutation load" that accumulates in specific tissues—heart or liver, for instance—as mice age or develop tumors.

Vijg was surprised to find that there were widespread mutations in adult mouse brain and liver. Because both these tissues have stopped growing in the adult mouse, they should have been less vulnerable to mutations. Presumably, the majority of the mutations could have been caused by oxidative damage.

"It's quite possible that the major defense mechanism against this type of damage is simply cell death," Vijg says. "Now we need to find out how frequent these mutations are. Are they mutations or deletions? Could it be that these are just background mutations in an aging genome? Although this is still a rough methodology, it may enable us to look for ways to improve the DNA defense system."

AGING VERSUS ALZHEIMER'S: LISTENING TO CENTENARIANS

LIKE ALMOST EVERY OTHER PERSON OVER THE AGE OF 100 WITH WHOM I've spoken, Ruth McShane chuckles briefly almost every time she speaks. It's not confused laughter, more like a quick preface to her reply that seems to warn, "This sounds silly even to me, but I'm going to say it anyway."

McShane is doing her best to "pass" a battery of tests put to her by Dr. Tom Perls, M.P.H. '93, and Margery Silver, Ed.D. '82, collaborators in a study of centenarians initiated by Perls, a gerontologist at Beth Israel Hospital and director of geriatrics curriculum development at Harvard Medical School. The tests, which assess cognition, are administered by Silver in McShane's kitchen. Ten years ago, her daughter's family bought this Victorian house in a middle-class South Boston community and renovated the first floor, allowing McShane to move from a senior housing facility in Maine.

She's an extremely fortunate woman at her age, surrounded by loving relatives and living in a state of near independence with considerable privacy. Somewhat deaf, she avoids watching television, but despite failing vision enjoys reading books by Horatio Alger and Zane Grey. After breaking a hip several years ago, she began using a walker. Otherwise, there's little to distinguish her from people 20 or 30 years her junior.

While Perls tapes the kitchen-based testing scene with a camcorder, McShane listens intently as Silver, a neuropsychologist on staff at the New England Deaconess and Beth Israel hospitals, slowly reads a series of random digits. With little hesitation, McShane repeats the eight-digit sequence flawlessly. Then Silver reads an absurd story about Will Rogers and his dog, and McShane laughingly answers questions about it with virtually no mistakes. Finally, there's a page of multiplication and long division problems. McShane hesitates, seemingly stumped. As we wait, tension prickles up slightly in the small kitchen.

"I'm having trouble seeing your numbers," she says after a few minutes. The numbers are a bit faint on the page. Silver quickly takes the sheet back and retraces the figures with a marker. Mrs. McShane clears her throat with a Mainebred *ayuh*, and resumes calculating. Within a few minutes, she has solved all the problems flawlessly. Her daughter informs us that McShane worked as a bookkeeper into her 80s. After a few more problems, the researchers pack up their materials and leave, with many thanks to McShane and her family.

"There's nothing clinically wrong with her," Perls says a few minutes later, outside the home. There was only one part of the assessment in which McShane had real difficulty: drawing hands on a clock's face to read ten-to-eleven. Many centenarians stumble on this one, Perls noted, suggesting that it may be an early indicator of impending mental dysfunction. Or it may just be a by-product of poor vision. But nowadays, most clocks are digital, anyway. There's no reason McShane couldn't go back to balancing the books tomorrow. "So the question we're left to grapple with," Perls says, "is what is disease and what is normal cognitive pathology at this age?"

In the same way that urinary incontinence was once thought to be part of normal old age, it was assumed that dotage and aging were synonymous. Today, we realize that these cognitive deficits result from bona fide disease: the destructive neuritic plaques and tangles of Alzheimer's disease or the oxygen-depriving brain damage caused by stroke. Depression, also pathological, can also interfere with clear thinking. It appears that healthy centenarians like Ruth McShane are not lucky aberrations, but rather what is to be expected from the human body and mind in the absence of disease. Today, researchers like Perls are focusing on a "natural history" of aging that does not necessarily include such illnesses. Although aging certainly is accompanied by change in capacity, it's not clear that age imposes illness or frailty, as has been so commonly assumed.

Several older studies have indicated that electroencephalograms (EEGs), a measure of brain electrical activity, slow down in the elderly. Slowed EEGs also appear in people with Alzheimer's disease. Many people drew the conclusion that aging and Alzheimer's disease might represent different points on a single continuum, reinforcing the notion of a close relationship between aging and Alzheimer's. Perhaps Alzheimer's was simply the cognitive decline that would take place in all of us, should we be unlucky enough to live that long.

However, research by two associate professors at Harvard Medical School, Marilyn Albert, a Massachusetts General Hospital neuropsychologist, and Dr. Frank Duffy, a Children's Hospital neurologist, bolsters the idea that Alzheimer's is not a natural part of aging. These researchers chose as their study population healthy elderly people who had been enrolled in the Boston Normative Aging Study.

"We didn't want to fall into the trap of studying sick people," Albert recalls. "We wanted to study aging, not disease."

Their studies showed that—at least in healthy adults—brain activity does not slow down, but rather speeds up. "Alzheimer's is not just a logical consequence of aging," says Albert, "and age-related changes may be quite different from those caused by Alzheimer's. There is obviously some overlap, but that overlap is what everyone focused on before; now we're focusing more on the differences."

The popular assumption is that the odds of anyone maintaining a well-burnished brain for an entire century are extremely slim. But Perls thinks that is probably a necessity for anyone to survive that long. "A few years ago, when I was a fellow at the Hebrew Rehabilitation Center for Aged," Perls recounts as we head back from Ruth McShane's house to Beth Israel, "there were two residents living there who were over 100. The amazing

THE BRAIN, IT WOULD APPEAR, REMAINS COGNITIVELY INTACT AND REJECTS MANDATORY RETIREMENT AT AGE 65.

thing was that I never saw them because they were never on the floor. They were always off somewhere doing activities; they were very busy people. Now, this flew in the face of everything I'd learned as a medical student. We were taught that very elderly people were ill and frail and in constant need of assistance and accommodation. But I think there's a demographic selection, a 'survival-of-the-fittest' phenomenon in deciding who lives into old age. For instance, you find that on average, men in their 90s are more likely to be cognitively intact than men in their 80s. People who have lost their cognitive capacity can't make the cut; you have to be extremely smart and assertive to live to be 100."

Perls's own research lends credence to these conjectures. A study he published recently shows that, at least in the hospital setting, individuals over age 70 cost less to take care of than younger people. Perls believes that the reason is that the very elderly are actually on average healthier than the "younger elderly."

But if there's so much pressure on our genes to maximize the vim and vigor of our younger years while ignoring our post-childbearing era, if our genes really don't care about us when we're old, why are steadily increasing numbers of people surviving well into their 80s and 90s?

"It may turn out that there's some genetic pressure to age slowly," Perls says. "It certainly would confer a reproductive advantage in terms of extending the childbearing years. In fact, we've seen some centenarians who were born late in their parents' lives. One of our centenarians was born when her mother was 54."

Perls's study will aid in the demarcation of the mind's lifespan, the boundaries of which are still far from clear. Jeanne Calment, a 121-year-old French woman whom Perls refers to as "the Michael Jordan of aging," appears to remain cognitively intact, despite failed eyesight and hearing. The brain, it would appear, rejects mandatory retirement at age 65.

TOWARD SUCCESSFUL AGING

"I OFTEN TELL PEOPLE THAT MY GRANDMOTHER LIVED TO BE 99," SAYS Marilyn Albert. "They would sometimes ask me if that was the reason I decided to study aging and I would say, 'No.' I've since realized that that's not true, that she probably was the reason."

Albert's grandmother, Rose Silbermann, was mentally intact until the day she died. She was interested in the world, Albert recalls, liked to talk about everything that was going on in her family, and determinedly and admirably independent. Albert remembers the home-cooked food her grandmother would un-pack after bringing it from the Bronx to Manhattan on the subway. After her husband died, she lived on her own until three months before her own death. "I always felt comfortable with her," Albert says. "She looked very old but she was comfortable with herself and that comfort put me at ease. This ingrained in me that aging was something positive."

More and more researchers are looking to the Rose Silbermanns of the world for information about successful aging. She, Henrietta Aladjem, and Ruth McShane sound so unusual because they defy our notions about aging. Although about 1.7 million Americans live in nursing homes, they constitute only 4.5 percent of the over-65 population. The rest of the elderly live in homes: houses, apartments, retirement communities, with in-laws, or in assisted-living facilities. However you count them, the vast majority of elderly are noninstitutionalized participants in society, albeit with widely varying degrees of independence.

In the early 1980s, when the MacArthur Foundation decided to devote funding to studies of successful aging, Albert, Jack Rowe, and Lisa Berkman (now Norman professor of health, social behavior, and epidemiology at the Harvard School of Public Health), were some of the first researchers to become involved. The results of a recently released collaborative study draw strong connections between preserved cognitive function—an important component of successful aging—and education, physical activity, and lung function.

PEOPLE WITH NO CLOSE TIES TO FRIENDS, RELATIONS, OR THE COMMUNITY WERE THREE TIMES MORE LIKELY TO DIE.

Although the link between education and successful aging seems firm, its implications are not entirely clear. It is possible that higher education could substitute for environmental factors the study didn't measure, such as better health care. Or perhaps formal schooling enables people to perform better on tests. The explanation Albert feels is most plausible is that mental activity produces lasting change in the brain itself—proliferation of nerve cells, for example—that may serve the brain in good stead in years to come. "Just having more synapses may make the brain more resilient to stress, even the stress of cognitive degeneration," she says. "This change may be produced by education early in life, but we hope it also is effected by lifelong habits of mental activity."

That's a small piece in a larger puzzle. "Normal, successful aging is an interesting and vital way to study the aging process," says the medical school's Ken Minaker. "We're focused on provoking the system, stressing it, and then watching it recover. For example, in the elderly, there's an erosion of ca-

pacity to tolerate extremes of too much or too little salt. Older patients are frequently on the brink of over- or under-hydration. Under these conditions, simple illnesses such as a mild fever can precipitate severe dehydration."

In one set of experiments, Minaker looked at the capacity of elderly people to regulate fluid and electrolyte balance in their bodies. This is a common source of problems; dehydration costs some $400 million to $600 million in hospitalization and treatment each year, primarily among the elderly. In some cases, people become disoriented and may temporarily appear demented. "What we've found," says Minaker, "is that in adapting to different conditions, elderly people 'get there'—they make the adjustment—but it takes them more time and they do it by different mechanisms than younger people."

If you've ever watched an older tennis player on the court, you can visualize what he is talking about. Lost mobility encourages restraint. Players learn that if they take fewer chances, they stand a much better chance of returning the next volley. Likewise, the body learns that recovery from stress is a process best undertaken cautiously, with one eye toward what's coming next.

"There's a tendency to muddle through," Minaker says. "I think that advancing age means adapting to limits on maximum capacities that allow people to adjust, but without doing self-damage. Physiologically, age is a time of adaptation, when compensatory mechanisms adjust in order to fight off challenges and keep self-regulated. You can't tolerate severe challenges, but for little hits you manage pretty well."

As a result, the aging body seems capable of much more than has been widely acknowledged. In many cases, it's not the depredations of aging itself that cause disease, but factors outside the body: infection, behaviors like diet, smoking, lack of exercise, and the social environment. And most of these factors can be modified; they don't bear the permanent stamp of genetic birthright.

More signs on the route to successful aging come from the interface of social sciences and medicine. It's now becoming clear that keeping up social connections and interpersonal contacts—friends, family, and community—matters as much as mental and physical fitness. Lisa Berkinan began thinking about this issue when she worked at a family-planning clinic in San Francisco. She observed what she was later to call "a protective web of social networks."

"It struck me that those people who were most disconnected and socially isolated were vulnerable, and were in trouble across a lot of domains," recalls Berkman. "On the other hand, people who were really connected to their communities were doing really well."

She decided to investigate the connection further, despite the obvious pitfalls of looking for connections between health and such hard-to-define variables as social support. Her research demonstrated that people with no close ties to friends, relations, or the community were three times more likely to die over a nine-year period than those with at least one source of social support.

"It's clearly a two-way street," says Berkman, now chair of the School of Public Health's department of health and social behavior. "It's clear that people by the nature of their illness undergo social and psychological changes that are consequences of illness, like the loss of social contacts. However, it also seems that social circumstances like isolation precede and predict the onset and course of illness. My question was, how could something that's 'outside' your body—like social support—get 'inside,' and what are the pathways through which it could get inside?"

Berkman is forging the next link by looking for the biochemical effects that social contacts might have. She's focusing on levels of hormones that increase in response to stress; repeated exposure to these hormones may leave elderly people more vulnerable to all types of illnesses, such as heart disease. She is also testing interventions to see if prognoses may be improved with alterations in social support.

"People thought it was normal to experience health and functional declines with age and that it was all determined by genes," Berkman says. "Today, more people recognize that the key to aging is in large part related to conditions we can do something about, like the social environment, behaviors, health practices, and kinds of experiences we have in midlife. The key to extending life lies in genes *and* in how we're living."

SURVIVING WITH CHAOS

THE TRADITIONAL MEDICAL MODEL OF AGING ENCOURAGES US TO THINK in terms of degenerating organs—a bad heart, a failing liver, a cancerous pancreas. But in the aging body, problems are often interconnected; the aging process puts pressure on all these systems, resulting in geriatric syndromes like incontinence, falls, depression, and dementia. None of these can be considered the domain of a single hospital unit or organ-based specialty.

"The geriatric syndromes are complex problems that can't be boiled down to one molecule or one cell," says Dr. Lewis Lipsitz, Usen director of medical research at the Hebrew Rehabilitation Center for Aged and an associate professor at Harvard Medical School. "We need better clinical tools to predict a person's vulnerability to disabling illness and to measure their frailty—that is, their impaired ability to adapt to stress."

Lipsitz is one of several Harvard researchers looking into the possibility that one of the body's most important defenses against stress has an unlikely name: chaos. On the face of it, the statement sounds absurd. Common English usage maligns chaos, with associations of disorganization and disarray. In fact, there's considerable beauty and structure in chaos. Chaos and the fractal patterns it produces trace the irregular outlines of seashores, mountains, and trees.

Likewise, the human body's organs and processes abound with chaotic fractal patterns. Chaos is an important component of a healthy heartbeat, of strong bones, of the branching structures of blood vessels, and of our natural walking stride. This built-in irregularity expands our repertoire of responses and allows us to adapt to the exigencies of everyday life. To remove the element of chaos from human physiology would reduce our resiliency and adaptive capacity; it would be about as productive as paving a coastline.

"MAKE ME DRY"

OF ALL THE GERIATRIC SYNDROMES, MANY PEOPLE FIND URInary incontinence one of the most socially isolating. It's embarrassing, it occurs without warning, and often leaves sufferers and their families with the feeling that, if only the patient were "paying attention," wet episodes could be avoided.

"Elderly people come to me with problems ranging from cancer to their hearts," says Neil Resnick, chief of gerontology at Brigham and Women's Hospital and assistant professor at Harvard Medical School. "But all they say to me is, 'Please, doctor, make me dry.' It's an ego insult. They won't shop, they won't go to church, they won't do anything because of their trouble with bladder control."

A geriatrician by training, Resnick pursued special training in urodynamics to better investigate urinary incontinence. Unexpectedly, he encountered continuing resistance from both funding agencies and ethical oversight boards. Urinary incontinence was so completely identified with aging and dementia that no one thought it was abnormal in the elderly. "The summary statement on our first grant questioned the value, interest, or utility of studying questions such as these in a population this old," Resnick recalls. "The reviewers took the step of filing an ethical objection to the study. They said 'How can you involve normal elderly people in this study and subject them to detailed urodynamic testing? Everyone knows that the elderly have physical and cognitive problems that make them wet, and your study will only prove it.' But we knew that nobody had ever looked at this problem."

And he was convinced that there was much more to the incontinence story. He was particularly interested in why some demented patients were able to stay continent, while so many others were wet. Most researchers had tended to look to lost bladder control as the root cause of urinary incontinence. But Resnick found that while nearly all immobile demented patients were incontinent, only half of mobile demented patients were, suggesting that there was much more to incontinence than defects in the urinary tract.

Resnick's team also found that "simple" cases of incontinence frequently included a cause that had never before been recognized. Further studies showed that this condition—termed DHIC, or detrusor hyperactivity with impaired contractility—was actually the single most common cause of incontinence. "As it turned out, incontinence was even more multifactorial than we had thought," Resnick says, "because we had been so focused on finding a single cause in the urinary tract."

Despite resistance from doubtful funding agencies and review boards, research on DHIC eventually demonstrated that different types of bladder dysfunction were associated with distinctive cellular abnormalities. This was a dramatic step forward in understanding and suggesting treatment strategies for a condition that, incidentally, affects some 15 million Americans. Preliminary results from Resnick's latest work call into question our entire understanding of the role of the urinary tract in geriatric incontinence.

The repercussions of Resnick's study are widely felt and appreciated among older nursing-home residents. Legislation enacted by Congress in 1992 requires that all nursing homes assess and treat geriatric incontinence according to a strategy he and his colleagues developed. No longer would incontinence be summarily dismissed as a foregone conclusion.

Lipsitz is also part of a group of researchers who have broken ground in combining chaos and geriatrics. He and Beth Israel cardiologist Ary Goldberger '70 have observed that as people age, heart function becomes much more regular and predictable (see "Arias from the Heart," March-April, page 22). Chaos may be the basis of new, sensitive tools to study aging and disease.

"Most of medicine is very reductionist," Lipsitz says. "You add up blood pressure, cholesterol, and throw in heart rate, and say someone's going to get heart disease. It's an incomplete picture. But that's the way we think.

"Now we're on the verge of using the underlying principles of chaos theory to look at all areas of physiological functioning. For example, a grandmother needs to go to surgery. We may be able to quantify her vulnerability to complications through measurements of chaos. A loss of chaos in the heartbeat's behavior might increase her risk of heart attack during surgery. Structural patterns in bone are also chaotic, and the breakdown of these patterns may tell us how fragile bones are, as opposed to how thin they are."

Gerontologist Jeanne Wei and Jeff Hausdorff, a Beth Israel bioengineer, have already designed a system for measuring irregularities in the length of walking strides that may predict the course of congestive heart failure. The applications of chaos to the study of aging may tell us a great deal more about the durability of people like Henrietta Aladjem and Ruth McShane, or the many other people whose extended lifespans bear witness to their ability to adapt.

All of us are going to learn a lot more about aging in the years to come—or die trying. For most of us, the knowledge will come from personal experience, and from those gone into the breach before us. The perceptions we build and acquire will have tremendous influence on our futures. As Tom Perls remarks, myths and generalizations about older people affect everything about their lives. He's particularly concerned about the provision of adequate medical care for chronic diseases of aging.

"Prostate cancer can take years to cause any serious problems," Perls says, "so some people tell their older patients, 'Look, you've got prostate cancer, but you'll probably die of something else before it kills you, so don't worry about it.' Well, if the patient's healthy and lives into his 90s with the malignancy, he'll wish he'd had it taken care of earlier. Everyone knows people in their 70s, 80s, and 90s who are in great shape, and it's those people that you better take care of. You can't fall into the paternalistic trap of thinking that you don't need to give someone complete, aggressive care, just because he or she is old."

Now that researchers have begun to shine a light down the dark hallway of aging, they are finding unexpected strength and resiliency in the elderly. They are relaying the message that we need not acquiesce in the imagined decrees of senility, that aging demands activity, participation, interaction, exertion. The next century's beginning will be well stocked with elderly people like Henrietta Aladjem, Ruth McShane, and Rose Silbermann. If we wish to emulate their longevity, productivity, and durability. we need to start listening and paying attention while we can.

Author John F. Lauerman, a freelance writer living in Brookline, Mass., is also the co-author of Diabetes: Understand Your Condition, Make the Right Treatment Choices, and Cope Effectively, *published in 1997 by Times Books.*

A LEADING LADY

AT AGE 103, ANGELINA STRANDAL LOOKS AND ACTS YEARS younger than chronology would dictate. Even she was surprised, though, when a postcard arrived a couple of weeks before her most recent birthday inviting her to come—free of charge—to the local Discovery Zone. Apparently their database accommodated only meager two-digit ages, rendering her a perky three-year-old. Still, what could be more fun than to climb through the gerbil's cage of kids' amusements they offer and finish off with a game of "Spin-Out"?

"It's very kind of them to offer," she says, "but I don't think I'll be going. I think they need to take a look at their computer."

Not that Strandal fears center stage; as one of the most humorous and engaging subjects in Dr. Tom Perls's study of Massachusetts centenarians, she's been featured on Channel 5's *Chronicle* and NBC's *Nightly News*, and in articles in the *Boston Herald* and *Quincy Patriot Ledger*.

Strandal was born on Prince Edward Island in 1893 and moved to the Boston area in 1917. After seven years of marriage, her husband died in 1931, and she began raising her children, Philip and Barbara, on her own. She worked at department stores and supermarkets to support her family, but never admitted to being overwhelmed by the challenge. "The money was clean," she says proudly. "I didn't mind working for it."

Strandal attributes her longevity to healthy personal habits, like eating vegetables. She doesn't watch television, but maintains her interest in poetry and still follows politics closely through the newspapers. She has even come close to endorsing a candidate. "I'm not voting for Dole," she says with a smile. "He's too old."

Decrepitude isn't inevitable. New research shows we all have the tools to live longer lives and die faster deaths. BY GEOFFREY COWLEY

HOW TO LIVE TO

100

At 104, Angeline Strandal doesn't place much stock in doctors. "If they start poking around you," she says, "they'll only make you sick." The Massachusetts centenarian does go in for a physical once in awhile, but she hasn't been seriously ill since the time she came down with appendicitis—in 1925. "People ask me what I eat," she says. "I'm a vegetarian, more or less. I never smoked. I don't drink either. That's one of my good qualities. And I keep my bedroom window open 365 days a year." Strandal has outlived 11 siblings and a husband, who died back in 1931, but she still cooks every day except Sunday for her 67-year-old daughter and her 69-year-old son. She also catches a daily mass on TV, roots faithfully for the Boston Red Sox and loves nothing more than a good heavyweight fight. "Every day I ask God to give me one more day," she muses. "And believe it or not, he does."

We baby boomers may soon find ourselves emulating Angeline Strandal, or someone like her, as devoutly as we once did Jim Morrison. We've watched our parents or grandparents die in their 70s—often sick, lonely and helpless—and we're beginning to sense that life should be longer and richer than that. "when the boomers started turning 50, it was like the start of the Oklahoma land rush," says Dan Perry, director of the Washington-based Alliance for Aging Research. Surveys by Perry's organization suggest that today's 50-year-olds are suddenly serious about living to 100, and keen

to get there in reasonably good health. "They don't want to spend any time at all in a nursing home," he says. "The fear of losing independence and the ability to fend for oneself is overwhelming."

Well, it turns out we may have a say in the matter. A growing body of research suggests that chronic illness is not an inevitable consequence of aging, as we've long believed, but more often the result of lifestyle choices that we're perfectly free to reject. "People used to say, 'Who would want to be 100?' " says Dr. Thomas Perls, an instructor at Harvard Medical School and director of the New England Centenarian Study. "Now they're realizing it's an opportunity." So are booksellers and magazine publishers. "Live long, die fast," the dust jackets urge us. "Dare to be 100." Many of us will fall short of that number simply through bad genes or bad luck. And high-tech medicine isn't likely to change the outlook dramatically; drugs and surgery can do only so much to sustain a body once it starts to fail. But there is no question we can lengthen our lives while shortening our deaths. The tools already exist, and they're within virtually everyone's reach.

Life expectancy in the United States has nearly doubled since Angeline Strandal was a kid—from 47 years to 76 years. And though centenarians are still rare, they now constitute the fastest-growing segment of the U.S. population. Their ranks have increased 16-fold over the past six decades—from 3,700 in 1940 to roughly 61,000 today. And

People 100 or older are the fastest-growing segment of the U.S. population. There are now 61,000 members of the 100-plus club; by 2020, there will be an estimated 214,000.

Anselmo Medina, 102

DENVER, COLO.

His family calls him 'Mr. Party' because he never misses a birthday, wedding or anniversary celebration. He lives alternately with two of his daughters, moving back and forth across the street. Medina 'eats everything' and likes an occasional drink of Jim Beam bourbon. He stays fit by shoveling snow and moving the furniture when it's time to vacuum the house.

Women make up 79% of the over-100's. That gender gap is expected to widen.

Lenore Schaeffer, 100

PHOENIX, ARIZ.

She took up dancing after being widowed at 82 and hasn't stopped since. Her home is filled with trophies for the fox trot, the rumba and the merengue. 'I've danced from Santa Monica to Miami,' says Schaeffer, who learned to waltz at Jane Addams's Hull House, the famous turn-of-the-century school. 'Ballroom dancing gave me a whole new life.'

---

the explosion is just getting started. The Census Bureau projects that one in nine baby boomers (9 million of the 80 million people born between 1946 and 1964) will survive into their late 90s, and that one in 26 (or 3 million) will reach 100. "A century ago, the odds of living that long were about one in 500," says Lynn Adler, founder of the National Centenarian Awareness Project and the author of "Centenarians: The Bonus Years." "That's how far we've come."

If decrepitude were an inevitable part of aging, these burgeoning numbers would spell trouble. But the evidence suggests that Americans are living better, as well as longer. The disability rate among people older than 65 has fallen steadily since the early 1980s, according to Duke University demographer Kenneth Manton, and a shrinking percentage of seniors are plagued by hypertension, arteriosclerosis and dementia. Moreover, researchers have found that the oldest of the old often enjoy *better* health than people in their 70s. The 79 centenarians in Perls's New England study have all lived independently through their early 90s, taking an average of just one medication. And when the time comes for these hearty souls to die, they don't linger. In a 1995 study, James Lubitz of the Health Care Financing Administration calculated that medical expenditures for the last two years of life—statistically the most expensive—average $22,600 for people who die at 70, but just $8,300 for those who make it past 100.

These insights have spawned a revolution in the science of aging. "Until recently, there was so much preoccupation with disease that little work was done on the characteristics that permit people to do well," says Dr. John Rowe, the New York geriatrician who heads the MacArthur Foundation's Research Net-

work on Successful Aging. Over the past decade, Rowe's group and others have published hundreds of studies elucidating the factors that help people glide through their later years with clear minds and strong bodies. The research confirms the old saw that it pays to choose your parents well. But the way we age depends less on who we are than on how we live—what we eat, how much we exercise and how we employ our minds.

The Magic of Exercise

Suppose there was a potion that could keep you strong and trim as you aged, while protecting your heart and bones; improving your mood, sleep and memory; warding off breast and colon cancer, and reducing your overall risk of dying prematurely. Respectable studies have shown that exercise can have all those benefits—even for people who take it up late in life. Experts now agree that most of the physical decline that older people suffer stems not from age but from simple disuse. When we sit all day, year after year, our bones, muscles and organ systems atrophy. But exercise can preserve and even revive them.

When Dr. Ralph Paffenbarger started tracking the health of 19,000 Harvard and University of Pennsylvania alumni back in the early 1960s, many experts thought vigorous exercise was downright dangerous for people over 50. But by monitoring the volunteers' activity levels and health status over the years the Stanford epidemiologist turned

Hitting a Century

If increases in life expectancy continue, people may routinely live to be 100 by the end of the next century.

LIFE EXPECTANCY AT BIRTH, IN YEARS

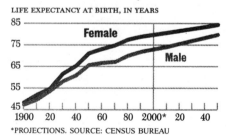

*PROJECTIONS. SOURCE: CENSUS BUREAU

that wisdom on its head. In a landmark 1986 study, Paffenbarger showed that the participants' death rates fell in direct proportion to the number of calories they burned each week. Those burning 2,000 a week (roughly the number it takes to walk 20 miles) suffered only half the annual mortality of the couch potatoes, thanks mainly to a lower rate of heart disease.

The alumni study wasn't set up to gauge the benefits of any particular exercise regimen, but subsequent studies have shown that different activities bring different rewards. Everyone now agrees that aerobic exercise

preserves the heart, lungs and brain. And researchers at Tufts University have recently shown that weight lifting can do as much for the frail elderly as it does for high-school jocks. When Dr. Maria Fiatarone got 10 chronically ill nursing-home residents to lift weights three times a week for two months, the participants' average walking speed nearly tripled, and their balance improved by half. Two had the audacity to throw away their canes.

Miriam Nelson, another Tufts researcher, has since shown how a series of simple strength-training exercises could help keep women from resorting to canes in the first place. She recruited 40 volunteers—all past menopause, none taking estrogen—and split them into two groups. Half continued life as usual, while the other half went to Tufts twice a week to pump iron. Over the course of a year, the women in the control group suffered a predictable loss of bone density, but the weight lifters enjoyed slight increases. They didn't lose weight (that wasn't the goal), but they lost fat, and many ended up measurably stronger than their daughters, who were 30 to 40 years younger. Dorothy Barron, who was 64 when she joined Nelson's experiment, says the experience not only remodeled her body but gave her more energy and confidence than she had had since her youth. Five years later, she still lifts weights—and she has added power walking, horseback riding and white-water rafting to her hobbies. When people ask why she pushes herself so hard, she replies, "I'm too old not to."

Eating to Nourish Long Life

We all know that living on fat, salt and empty calories can have a range of nasty consequences, from obesity and impotence to hypertension and heart disease. Yet we seem to forget that there are other ways to eat, and that people who adopt them stay younger longer. George and Gaynel Couron will never forget that lesson. The Sacramento, Calif., couple gave up eating meat back in the early 1920s, when they became Seventh-day Adventists. They eventually strayed from the church and its dietary edicts, but they returned to both in 1943, when George suffered a heart attack. Today he's 100 years old, and Gaynel is 98. They've been married for 81 years and have 14 kids ranging in age from 58 to 80. They have slowed down a bit (they're not planning any more children), but George still takes great delight in growing and eating his own tomatoes, melons, beets, squash and black-eyed peas. As he puts it, "We're still perking along."

No one can say exactly what role food has played in the Courons' good fortune, but the age-reversing effects of a plant-based diet are not in question. In controlled studies, San Francisco cardiologist Dean Ornish has shown that a diet based on low-fat, nutrient-rich foods not only prevents heart disease—

the Western world's leading cause of early death—but can help reverse it. And other studies suggest that dietary changes could virtually eliminate the high blood pressure that places 50 million older Americans at high risk of stroke, heart attack and kidney failure. "Hypertension is not an inevitable part of aging," says Dr. Boyd Eaton, an Atlanta-based radiologist who has written extensively on nutrition and chronic illness. "It's a disease of civilization."

You wouldn't know that from watching people age in this country. Hypertension afflicts a third of all Americans in their 50s, half of those in their 60s and more than two thirds of those over 70. But preindustrial people don't follow that pattern. Whether they happen to live in China or Africa, Maska or the Amazon, people in primitive settings experience no change in blood pressure as they age, and the reason is fairly simple: they don't eat processed foods. Dr. Paul Whelton of Tulane University's School of Public Health has spent the past decade tracking 15,000 indigenous Yi people in southwestern China. As long as they eat a traditional diet—rice, a little meat and a lot of fresh fruits and vegetables—these rural farmers virtually never develop hypertension. But when they migrate to nearby towns, their blood pressure starts to rise with age. "Their genes don't change when they move," Whelton says. "Their diet does."

What makes processed food so harmful? Salt is one key suspect. When you subsist mainly on fresh plant foods—as our ancestors did for roughly 7 million years—you get 10 times more potassium than sodium. That 10-to-one ratio is, by Eaton's reasoning, the one our bodies are designed for. But salt is now showered on foods at every stage of processing and preparation (a 4-ounce tomato contains 9 mg of sodium, 4 ounces of bottled tomato sauce nearly 700 mg), while potassium leaches out. As a result, most of us now consume more salt than potassium. "Modern humans are the only mammals that do that," says Eaton, "and we're the only ones that develop hypertension."

Correcting that imbalance takes some effort, but it doesn't require moving to the bush. In fact a recent clinical study suggests that dietary changes can reduce blood pressure as markedly as drug treatment, and can produce results in as little as two months. In the study (known as DASH, or Dietary Approaches to Stop Hypertension), researchers at several institutions placed volunteers on one of three diets. Those on a low-fat menu that included 10 daily servings of fresh fruits and vegetables, plus two servings of calcium-rich dairy products, reduced their systolic and diastolic readings by 5.5 mm and 3.0 mm, respectively. And those suffering from hypertension got reductions of twice

that magnitude. "We suspected this was possible," says nutritionist Eva Obarzanek of the National Heart, Lung and Blood Institute, the federal agency that sponsored the study. "Now we know the size of the effect."

Researchers have since shown that a simple potassium supplement can bring similar if less dramatic benefits. That's worth knowing, but keep in mind that potassium is just one of countless age fighters found in real food. The antioxidant vitamins in a tomato or a green leaf can help boost immunity and slow the corrosion of aging cell membranes, and the B vitamins may help protect your heart. By eating plants, you also bathe yourself in cancer-fighting phytochemicals, bone-

---

Exercise is a key to living longer, but it's also important to keep an active mind

Philip Carret, 100
SCARSDALE, N.Y.

Last year, he cut back to a three-day week at Carret & Co., the money-management firm he founded in 1963. He's written three books on investments; a widower, he plans another on marriage. 'Keep active and keep a positive outlook on life,' he says. 'Pessimism is a deadly poison. I have known several pessimists. They all died prematurely.'

---

saving calcium and the fiber needed to maintain the colon and modulate blood sugar. Best of all, you can down them by the bushel without getting fat.

Staying Connected and Engaged
Exercise and good food may help keep you going, but successful aging is also a psychological feat. Loneliness, for example, can speed your demise no matter how conscientiously you care for your body. "We go through life surrounded by protective convoys of others," says Robert Kahn, a University of Michigan psychologist who has studied the health effects of companionship. "People who manage to maintain a network of social support do best." One study of elderly heart-attack patients found that those with two or more close associates enjoyed

twice the one-year survival rate of those who were completely alone.

Companionship aside, healthy oldsters seem to share a knack for managing stress, a poison that contributes measurably to heart disease, cancer and accidents. Researchers have also linked successful aging to mental stimulation. An idle brain will deteriorate just as surely as an unused leg, notes Dr. Gene Cohen, head of the gerontology center at George Washington University. And just as exercise can prevent muscle atrophy, mental challenges seem to preserve both the mind and the immune system. But what most impresses researchers who study the oldest old is their simple drive and resilience. "People who reach 100 are not quitters," says Adler of the National Centenarian Awareness Project. "They share a remarkable ability to renegotiate life at every turn, to accept the inevitable losses and move on."

Merle McEathron knows all about accepting losses. She's 102 today, but she was just 7 when she found her mother dead on the floor at her childhood home in Vincennes, Ind., felled by a heart attack. As the oldest girl in the family, Merle had to raise her baby sister and take over cooking and cleaning for her father and two older brothers ("I stood on a box to reach the range," she recalls). She married at 15, but her man left her at 25, so she started a general store and worked there long enough to put both of her sons through college. The boys were grown by the time World War II came along, but she found other ways to stay busy. She worked as a house mother at the Cadet Club, a military social center, where young airmen took her flying in small warplanes after hours. And when the war ended, she got in her Buick and headed for Arizona.

She was 51 years old by the time she hit Phoenix, but the move brought many adventures, including three more husbands. After dumping one (a dance hall sax player with a roving eye) and outliving the others, she moved herself into the Eastern Star retirement center to avoid getting lonely. A doctor assured her she would never walk again when she broke her leg four years ago, but she got herself a walker, made her way down to the exercise room and worked the injured limb until she could get around on a cane. Then she threw away the cane. She now walks a mile and a quarter each day, and every September she travels to Indiana for a reunion at the Cadet Club. When she gets there, she climbs over the wing of a restored World War II training plane, crawls into the cockpit behind the pilot and rides that baby into the sky.

With ANNE UNDERWOOD *and* MARY HAGER

WHY WE WILL LIVE LONGER...
AND WHAT IT WILL MEAN

The one-two punch of healthier habits and biomedical breakthroughs could push life expectancy past 90. Get ready for a brave new world.

Richard I. Kirkland Jr.

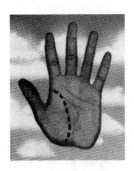

Hope I die before I get old.
PETE TOWNSHEND
1966

The generation that once rocked to that mocking line from the Who is within bifocal range of 50. And guess what? Baby-boomers have to find a new tune. The 76 million Americans born between 1946 and 1964 not only are the largest generation, but are set to become the longest-lived in U.S. history as well. No other change due in the 21st century will so profoundly alter the way we live.

This upheaval-in-the-making didn't begin with the boomers, of course. The two age cohorts just ahead of them will push the old limits too. In 1900, average life expectancy from birth in the U.S. was a mere 47 years. By 1970 it had climbed to around 71. Since then, while most of us were looking elsewhere, it has gone up again, to 76. To be precise, that's 72.7 years for American men and 79.6 for women.

Even if this remarkable upward trajectory ended tomorrow, more than half of you

REPORTER ASSOCIATE *Rosalind Klein Berlin*

reading these words could still expect to live past 81. That's because the longer you live, the better your odds. But it's not going to flatten out. Among experts on aging, even the most conservative agree we should be able to add three or four years to life expectancy over the next five decades. Others think we can do far better than that. Says Dr. Edward Schneider, 53, who heads the Andrus Gerontology Center at the University of Southern California: "If we do things right over the next few decades, at least half the baby-boomers might expect to live into their late 80s and 90s."

A few wild-eyed optimists even contend that by cracking the secrets of our genetic code we can live much, much longer. For all you restless baby-busters and aspiring fortysomethings with one eye on the corner office, here's a terrifying illustration of the sort of paradigm-shattering change they have in mind. Four words: *100-year-old CEOs*!

How many oldsters? Social Security projections are the most conservative. Epidemiologist Jack Guralnik at the National Institute on Aging assumes recent big gains in life expectancy will continue. Kenneth Manton, a demographer at Duke University, thinks they may well accelerate.

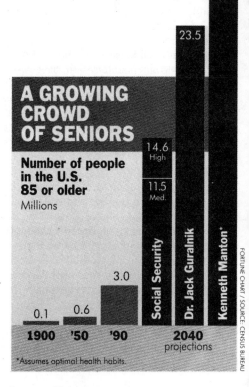

A GROWING CROWD OF SENIORS

Number of people in the U.S. 85 or older
Millions

					43.0
				23.5	
			14.6 High		
			11.5 Med.		
		3.0			
0.1	0.6				
1900	'50	'90	2040 projections		

Social Security · Dr. Jack Guralnik · Kenneth Manton*

*Assumes optimal health habits.

FORTUNE CHART / SOURCE: CENSUS BUREAU

Who's right? In FORTUNE's view, the way to bet is on lives that will increasingly stretch out toward 90 and beyond in the years ahead—with considerable potential on the upside. A host of consequences adhere to that extraordinary prospect. Many are already beginning to be felt, though the biggest shocks are a few decades away.

Among them: Inheritances will get smaller, as long-lived elders consume capital that once flowed to the next generation. (Priced a nursing home for your folks lately? One upscale nursing home in Westchester County, New York, prefers to see that Mom or Dad has $500,000 in liquid assets before it considers taking one of them in.) Extended and multiple careers will become the norm, and the prevailing retirement age (now around 60) will creep back toward 70 as a growing number of older workers choose—some from necessity, some for fulfillment—to remain in the labor force. When Social Security was enacted in 1935 and the retirement age was set at 65, average life expectancy was around 61. The system won't stay afloat unless it is rebuilt into a means-tested welfare program for only the poorest of the elderly.

Are we ready for this? Are you kidding? According to recent polls, most Americans do not expect to live into their 80s. So far, the age at which most of us retire continues to go down, not up. Most taxpayers are acutely aware that America's aging will impose a huge burden on Social Security—after all, isn't that one of the main reasons payroll taxes have been rising steadily since the late 1970s? What they don't realize—as the chart reveals—is that if life expectancy reaches 80 in the next few decades and keeps on climbing, Social Security's bean counters will have woefully underestimated the future size of America's older population. Richard Suzman, the respected chief of demography at the National Institute of Aging (NIA), believes that by 2040 the number of Americans over 85 could top 30 million, up from 3.3 million today.

For an upbeat glimpse of what could be in store, consider the long and still unfolding career of John Marks Templeton, 81: author (eight books), father (five children), grandfather (16 grandkids, so far), great-grandfather (two), and world-beating stock-picker. Sixteen months ago, after 53 years in the investment business, he finally retired, selling his wildly successful Templeton fund group and its $21 billion in assets under management to Franklin Resources of San Mateo, California, for $913 million. His share: $400 million.

Now the Tennessee-born Templeton, who became a British citizen in 1963 after he moved permanently to Lyford Cay, Nassau, and collected a knighthood for his philanthropic work, jets around the globe supervising more than 30 charitable projects backed by the four foundations he has established. "I'm working as hard as I ever did," he reports, with no plans to slow down. Last year Templeton edited and contributed to a collection of essays, by various experts, called *Looking Forward: The Next Forty Years.* "It's such a joy to learn about the new things going on in the world," he says. "This is the most exciting era in history I wake up every morning fairly sizzling with enthusiasm."

MOST OF US will enter our 80s with considerably less capital than Sir John—and simmering, not sizzling. But since most of us *will* enter them, we'd better start thinking hard about how we aim to spend that extra time. Because the whole world is rapidly aging, this adjustment will ultimately pose a global challenge. When it comes to average life expectancy, the U.S. is outpaced by more than 15 countries, led by Japan, where at birth it's now 79 years. Still, two things put America in the vanguard of the longevity revolution: the unrivaled vigor and duration of its postwar birth explosion, which guarantees it an unrivaled cohort of octogenarians, nonagenarians, and centenarians four decades from now; and its role as planetary hotbed for the biomedical and genetic research that's likely to produce major breakthroughs in our ability to add years to life and—most important—quality to those extra years.

What are the advances that will make us live longer and healthier? They range from the marvelous to the mundane.

■ **More targeted medical weaponry.** "Many who used to get sent to heart transplant centers can now be put on medical management and handled outside a hospital without surgery," says Kenneth Manton, director of Duke University's Center for Demographic Studies. "That's the difference biomedical research is delivering and will continue to deliver." No group will benefit from this difference more than older persons, since 80% of fatal heart attacks occur among those over 64 and 80% of cancers appear after age 50.

Take hypertension. The diuretics of the 1950s lowered blood pressure and deaths from cardiovascular disease by draining the body of salt. This often had nasty side effects, such as raising the risk of diabetes. Each subsequent advance in treatment—beta-blockers in the 1960s, calcium channel blockers in the 1970s, and so-called ACE inhibitors in the 1980s, which work by blocking the kidney's production of the hormone that causes blood vessels to constrict—has improved the treatment of hypertension with fewer side effects.

Like those first diuretics, most cancer treatments are still the medical equivalent of using carpet bombing rather than smart bombs. But over the next two decades, rather than blast patients with massive overdoses of radiation or chemotherapy—killing healthy cells as well as malignant ones—doctors will learn how to fire computer-designed compounds directly into affected organs. That should translate into lower doses and longer, higher-quality life.

■ **Better brains through chemistry.** For most people, the greatest terror old age holds is the fear of losing one's mind. It's most cheering then to hear this prediction from Zaven Khachaturian, who directs the lion's share of the $200-million-a-year research program on Alzheimer's disease at the NIA: "Within six years we should come up with treatments that will slow the brain's deterioration enough to enable Alzheimer's victims to function for another decade. In ten to 15 years, we might even be able to prevent this disease."

According to the NIA, some four million Americans today are afflicted with Alzheimer's, a virulent form of dementia that riddles the brain with clumps of protein plaques and tangles and brings on a relentless slide into mental oblivion. This epidemic could explode as America ages. According to recent estimates, 6% of people ages 65 to 74 have the disorder, and nearly half of those over 85 show signs of it. More than 100,000 Americans die of Alzheimer's each year, putting it right up there with the nation's major killers: heart disease (800,000 annual deaths), cancer (200,000), and strokes (150,000). Lucky sufferers expire within five years; the unfortunate stay alive up to two decades. "If curing heart disease and cancer means we get to stick around and die of Alzheimer's," says medical researcher Roderick

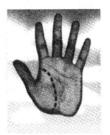

"If curing heart disease and cancer means we get to die of Alzheimer's, we'll look back on them as our friends."

Bronson of Tufts University, "we'll look back on them as our friends."

The war against Alzheimer's is progressing on two fronts. Warner-Lambert has just begun marketing Cognex, a limited treatment that works in a handful of cases and then succeeds only in allowing the patient to function for an extra six to nine months. But several major drugmakers, notably Bayer, are testing in animals a more effective second-generation treatment that works by blocking the accumulation in neurons of toxic levels of calcium—one of the ways those tangles are formed. Researchers in Sweden are even testing on humans what may become the third-generation treatment, compounds that stimulate nerve-cell growth.

Geneticists in the mid-1980s pinpointed the location of the genes connected to an inherited form of Alzheimer's, which tends to strike much earlier, in the 40s and 50s. And last fall a team led by Dr. Allen Roses of Duke University Medical Center announced it had identified a gene—called ApoE 4 and ensconced on human chromosome 19—that is strongly linked with the onset of late-stage Alzheimer's. Doctors will use such genetic markers to identify people most at risk and start them on preventive treatments as these become available. Eventually, healthy nerve cells may be injected directly into the brain, where they will grow make the right connections, and replace dead neurons. 'That's pretty futuristic stuff," says Khachaturian. "But it's definitely coming down the pike, perhaps in 20 years."

Such treatments, along with new memory-enhancing drugs, would also benefit stroke victims and those suffering from spinal injuries or Parkinson's disease and other neurologic disorders. In the not-too-distant future, people may chew pills to fend off dementia the way middle-aged men now munch baby aspirin to prevent heart attacks.

■ **Beefed-up bug fighters.** Body parts don't age at the same rate. But one universal characteristic of getting older—and the reason we become increasingly vulnerable to everything from cold viruses to cancer—is a steady falloff, starting around age 30, in the effectiveness of our immune systems. Part of the problem seems to reside in a class of lymphocytes, known as T-cells, that attack infected cells directly and also serve as messengers to mobilize the rest of the immune system. As we age, the number of T-cells produced by the thymus gland declines, while the percentage of them already in the bloodstream but no longer functioning rises. Getting rid of these so-called effete T-cells, one theory holds, should encourage the thymus to get cracking and put the immune system back in fighting trim.

Gerontologist Edward Schneider believes a drug to do that will be developed in five years—and he's hoping to get there first. Schneider and some colleagues launched a biotech startup, Rejuvon, last year and are currently chasing venture capital.

■ **Hormone cocktails.** Remember hormones? These are the body's chemical messengers that turn genes on or off and regulate how tissues and organs grow and repair themselves. They're also what, in our early teens, made our shoe sizes surge from eight to 11, our pores gush oil, and even not-so-close encounters with the opposite sex a dizzying experience.

As the years accumulate, many of us stop pumping out enough of this bodacious stuff. Levels of human growth hormone, which helps keep us lean as well as make us taller, decline with age in about half of all adults. Researchers have also learned that, just as women during menopause experience a sharp drop in production of the female sex hormone estrogen, most men

aged 60 and older manufacture markedly lower amounts of the male sex hormone testosterone.

The linkage between hormone levels and health, though still poorly understood, is formidable. Estrogen replacement therapy dramatically slows the bone thinning that develops into osteoporosis and cripples millions of older women. It also significantly reduces in most females the risk of heart attack and stroke. In men, testosterone injections can strengthen muscles and counter anemia, while a related hormone, known as DHEA, has been shown in animal tests to revive aging immune systems and even deter cancer.

In the most dramatic display yet of hormonal firepower, Daniel Rudman of the Medical College of Wisconsin in 1990 injected human growth hormone into elderly men whose levels of it were unusually low. Within months their fat shrank by 14%, their lean body mass expanded by 9%, and their skin increased in thickness by 7%. The overall effect on physique, he reported, was equal to shedding ten to 20 years. These remarkable results have since been confirmed by other researchers. They have also spawned a cottage industry of Mexican longevity clinics that supply American and European clients with doses of the high-priced drug, which costs $13,000 for a year's supply.

The real problem with hormone treatments, however, isn't their expense; it's their potentially devastating side effects. Use of growth hormone over long periods—and to be effective it must be taken continually, or else the magical results vanish in a Dorian Gray–style reversal—often results in carpal tunnel syndrome, other kinds of joint inflammation, and diabetes-like symptoms. Estrogen and testosterone may increase the risk of cancer in some recipients.

Still, as more research leads to a better understanding of what dosages are proper—and how best to deliver them—such therapies could become more widespread. Within five years Rudman believes that physicians may be allowed to use growth hormone for short-term therapies—to accelerate healing of wounds, say, or to enhance the ability of some underweight elderly to absorb nutrients. Further down the road, he says, older patients in 20 years may well visit doctors to have their hormone levels checked and get prescriptions for "custom-tailored cocktails" that will help them stay fit.

■ **New, improved, fat- and smoke-free lifestyles.** "No drug in current or prospective use holds as much promise for sustained health as a lifetime program of physical exercise," says Dr. Walter Bortz of Stanford University Medical School, a 20-miles-a-week jogger at age 63. That view, backed by a growing body of evidence, can no longer be dismissed as the raving of fanatics on perpetual endorphin overdoses. "Exercise is one of the real breakthrough areas in the research," agrees Dr. John Rowe, 49, president of Manhattan's Mount Sinai Medical School and Hospital, who was a 1988 recipient of a MacArthur Foundation grant to develop ways to encourage successful aging.

Studies have shown, for example, that in addition to its familiar cardiovascular benefits, working out stimulates the body's production of growth hormone and improves the functioning of the immune system, especially among older people. Says Bortz: "Exercise for young people is an option, but for older people it is an imperative."

In addition to lacing on those jogging shoes, don't neglect to eat your spinach—and your carrots, kale, broccoli, oranges, and bananas as well, all of which are high in vitamins E and C, as well as beta-carotene. Why? It has long been known that as the human body merrily goes about its basic business of converting glucose and oxygen to energy, it spews out a torrent of so-called free-radical molecules. These cause damage to proteins, membranes, and ultimately the DNA in cell mitochondria—the place where the energy we run on is generated. Free radicals have been implicated in many of the changes that accompany aging and appear to play a role in cancer, arteriosclerosis, cataracts, and nerve damage. To defend against such wanton self-destruction, however, the body also produces antioxidants that react with and disarm free radicals. Some are enzymes. The other natural antioxidants are, yes, good old vitamins C and E, and beta-carotene. (For more on what *you* can do to live long and well, see box on next page.)

A final arresting fact for anyone still skeptical about the efficacy of this get-a-lifestyle mumbo jumbo: Since the mid-1960s, the death rate from heart disease in the U.S. has plummeted by 50%. And do we owe this boon to the huge increase over that time in the balloon angioplasties and triple bypasses performed by gifted, dedicated, and highly compensated surgeons? No. Instead, almost every medical and epidemiological expert credits three sweeping changes. First and most important is the sharp decline in smoking—the single most effective, legal way to shorten your life, and now practiced by only 25% of the adult population, vs. 40% in 1965. Second is the rise in exercise, especially among men. Third are dietary changes that have lowered the typical American's cholesterol count.

■ Putting on new pairs of genes. "I'm not interested in adding three or four years to life expectancy," says evolutionary biologist Michael Rose, 38, a professor at the University of California's Irvine campus. "I'm interested in 200-year-old humans."

Say what? Since our ancestors got up off their four feet a couple of million years ago, the longest any human has ever lived, depending on which old coot or cootess you believe, is between 115 and 120 years. That barrier is our species' maximum life span. Breaking it, as Rose contemplates, will require more than simply fighting the manifold disorders of aging one disease at a time, as we now do. It will take nothing less than what gerontologists call "a magic bullet," a fundamental assault at the molecular level on the upward sweep of mortality itself.

If such a bullet is ever made, genetic engineering will supply the ordnance. Consider the lowly roundworm. By manipulating the genes of a species of nematode, Thomas Johnson of the University of Colorado has already doubled its puny 30-day life span. Michael Rose's lab has successfully doubled the maximum and mean life spans of a species of fruit fly.

A series of fairly mundane experiments that seemingly do not involve genetics are helping scientists in their quest. So far, only one technique has consistently extended the life span of short-lived mammals, such as mice—and it requires practically starving them. Caloric restriction, as it's known, adds health as well as years. In the most important such experiment yet, the NIA in 1987 began testing it on primates, our closest relatives in the animal kingdom. Because these animals have a maximum life span of 40 years, vs. 2½ years for mice, the final results won't be in until many baby-boomers are wearing dentures. But already the animals on diets are reaching puberty a year or two later than their brethren who chow down as much as they please.

The goal isn't to persuade us all to go on truly draconian diets (though let's face it, it does seem one more reason to shed a few pounds). Explains Richard Sprott, head of the NIA's biology of aging program: "If we could understand how caloric restriction produces its effects, then we'd understand a great deal more about the basic biological mechanism of aging. And that would give us a way to intervene. It could provide that magic bullet we talk about."

Michael Rose draws a parallel with the success of the U.S. space program after World War II: "Sending men to the moon and back by the end of the 1960s seemed impossible too, until we decided to commit enough resources. Then the science developed. I know we can extend life span for a far smaller sum than the Apollo project cost. I'm doing it on a toy-model scale now." Consultant Kenneth Dychtwald, 43, whose firm Age Wave, in Emeryville, California, advises corporations like Johnson & Johnson, Kmart, and General Motors on what the graying of America means to their markets, believes such an investment is inevitable. Says he: "Breakthroughs that humans have dreamed about for thousands of years are right around the corner."

Exuberant prophecies like those, however, are still a minority. Most scientists, including the NIA's Sprott, suspect there may be hundreds of genes, rather than a handful, that interact to affect human longevity. That complexity, they argue, makes reaching into the genome and resetting the cellular clock a pretty remote possibility.

What we will see fairly soon is genetic repair of flaws that give rise to specific diseases. In the past year researchers—aided by the monumental Human Genome Project, which aims to map our genetic code by early next century—have identified a number of troublesome genes. Among the mala-

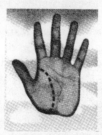

The paradox is that the longer we live, the more urgent it will become to learn how to die.

HOW YOU CAN LIVE WELL AND LONG

First, a brief disclaimer from one of the country's top experts on aging. "Life's a crapshoot," says the NIA's Dick Sprott. "There aren't any guarantees."

The odds get better, though, the longer you stick around. Based on current mortality rates, if you're 40 and male, you're already a good bet to make it to 75, three years beyond an American's average life expectancy at birth. A man who's 65—an age more than 70% of the population now reaches—can expect to live until 80. Women can expect to make 85.

The real way to beat the house is by extending your health span, not just your life span. Personal example: My paternal grandfather quit professional life at 60 to go home to Mississippi and farm. He worked hard and happily every day of the rest of his life and died at 82 of a heart attack while picking his beloved blueberries. My maternal grandmother, on the other hand, lives on at 92 in a north Alabama nursing home. For the past six years she's been unable to recall—within seconds after we depart—whether anyone has visited her. Grandpa won, hands down.

But isn't our fate simply in our genes? No. It's true that a strong genetic predisposition to, say, lung cancer can bring you down no matter how virtuous your habits, just as the reverse may permit you to puff three stogies a day until age 100. But much recent research, notably a study of Danish identical twins by American demographer James Vaupel, suggests that genetic factors account for no more than 30% of variance in life spans. What *you* do matters.

So what's the program? Rule No. 1: Don't smoke, or if you do, quit. A 40-year-old male with a pack-a-day cigarette habit can expect to die seven years before his nonsmoking peer. Anyone who still thinks this issue is debatable is smoking something, all right—but it's not tobacco.

Next, fasten that seat belt. Doing this regularly extends life expectancy by 69 days. That may not sound like a lot, but it's one of the most significant remaining ways to improve your odds on longevity. By comparison, a healthy man at 40 who lowers his cholesterol count from 280 to 240 adds, on average, just seven days to his life.

So if the prospect of too much virtue makes you sick, stick with the steak and hold the smokes. And while you're at it, have a glass of wine. Heck, have two! Heavy boozing is definitely not recommended, but various studies conclude that people who have one to two drinks daily live longer than those who never drink at all.

If you're over 40, you should also consider consuming a little extra vitamin E. Physicians have been reluctant to endorse nutrient supplements, fearing that Americans would assume they could pop a few pills and then keep pigging out on Cheetos and French fries. It *is* important to eat right. Your best guide is the bushman's diet now promoted by the U.S. government: loads of fruit (four servings daily) and vegetables (five), plus lots of whole grains and some lean meat. Even that, though, won't deliver the high levels of vitamin E that have been linked in epidemiological studies to lower risk of heart disease, and shown by scientists with the Department of Agriculture's research center on aging and nutrition at Tufts University to improve functioning of the immune system in older men and women.

How much E is enough? Official guidelines are still a few years away. But many experts interviewed by FORTUNE have, in the past year or so, begun taking a daily pill containing 400 international units—more than 12 times what's in the typical multivitamin. Some also take 15 to 25 milligrams of beta-carotene and 1,000 milligrams of vitamin C—though the consensus on their efficacy is less strong.

Finally, there's exercise. Yes, you need it, and, no, you don't have to train for a triathlon to reap large benefits. Half an hour of vigorous walking three times a week—shoot to cover a mile in under 15 minutes—can cut the risk of heart attack, stroke, diabetes, and even cancer by 55%. You might also consider a little twice-weekly weight-lifting. Aerobics has many virtues, but it doesn't fight the fall in bone density and rise in muscle weakness that accompany aging.

Most important, and contrary to received medical opinion until fairly recently, the case for working out strengthens as we grow older. One Stanford University study tracked the health of some 500 runners ages 50 and over against a comparable group of nonrunners. When the eight-year study began, the runners had a 2-to-1 advantage over the others in various measures of health. At the end, their edge had increased to five times. The gap was widest among 75- to 79-year olds. As Bob Butler of Mount Sinai Medical School says, "Two of the worst pieces of advice an older person can receive, we've learned, are: What do you expect at your age? and Take it easy."

That goes for mental exercise as well. Consultant Joseph Juran is one of the godfathers of the postwar quality movement and, at 89, a man with considerable standing on this subject as well. Says he: "My personal theory is that the key to aging successfully comes down to keeping your mind active." Indeed, the biochemistry of the brain, neurologists agree, supports the notion that it may well function better—and longer—when we keep those nerve cells firing.

Have we mentioned happiness? That's definitely one of the essentials too, as are friends, offspring, a spouse, and other reasons to live. Smile, hug your kids, be silly sometimes, and smell those darn roses whenever possible.

If all this leaves you thinking that a remarkable amount of the latest aging research seems aimed at elaborately and objectively verifying what most of us already thought we knew, well, you're right. "Our grandmother always said, 'People don't wear out, they rust out,'" recalls Don Feigenbaum, 67, who along with older brother Val, 73, runs a thriving systems engineering company that numbers Tenneco and Ford among its clients. Grandma Feigenbaum gets the last word: Use it or lose it.

—R.I.K.

HOW MUCH TIME IS LEFT?

Average life expectancy

Age	Female	Male
Birth	79.6	72.7
40	41.3	36.0
65	19.6	15.8
85	7.2	5.7

FORTUNE TABLE / SOURCE: CENSUS BUREAU

dies they cause are Huntington's disease, amyotrophic lateral sclerosis (Lou Gehrig's disease), a form of colon cancer, and severe combined immunodeficiency, or SCID (a rare condition, better known as "the bubble boy disease," in which the immune system virtually ceases to function). By injecting several children suffering from SCID with a healthy copy of the defective gene that causes it, doctors have succeeded, for now, in revitalizing the immune system. More than 40 other trials are being conducted to test this sort of gene therapy's efficacy on cystic fibrosis, cancer, and AIDS.

EVEN WITH ALL THIS, lifting average life expectancy toward 90 and beyond will require solving some daunting arithmetic. Here's the problem: Because we've already conquered most of the infectious diseases that once killed large numbers of children and young adults, the gains we're making now come from adding a few extra years to an already long-in-the-tooth crowd's lives—and not six or seven decades to the lives of kids. As a result, future victories over disease—even major triumphs—will inevitably deliver small gains in life expectancy compared with those won earlier in this century.

Demographer Jay Olshansky of the University of Chicago Medical School calculates that completely wiping out cancer in the U.S. would add only 3.2 years to average life expectancy from birth. Eliminating heart disease would lift it by just three years for women and 3.6 years for men. "There's a large element of wish fulfillment in these optimistic projections about extending life expectancy," argues Dr. James Fries of Stanford University, who along with Olshansky is a leading proponent of the view that there's a ceiling on average life expectancy of around 85. Indeed, the way Duke's Ken Manton gets life expectancy to 100 is by assuming that the entire U.S. population adopts and maintains optimum health habits throughout their lives. Wanna bet?

On the other hand, neither camp takes into account the enormous wild card of genetic engineering because its potential is impossible to model. And yet, most experts agree breakthroughs will happen—and have a sizable effect on longevity. Says the NIA's Dick Sprott: "Over the next 25 to 30 years, we're going to produce a tremendous change in the number of humans who will make it to something close to the species maximum."

The social and economic consequences of this acceleration in life span will be far greater than anything now contemplated by most American policymakers and institutions. Take inheritance. A few years ago, economists Lawrence Kotlikoff and Lawrence Summers calculated that 80% of the country's capital stock has been piled up through intergenerational bequests. What happens to capital formation if tomorrow's long-lived woopies (well-off older people) consume that seed corn and leave almost nothing behind?

Consider Social Security. As life expectancy rises toward 90, many Americans will spend almost as many years drawing a check from the government as they did working. This cannot stand—not when, even on a conservative demographic forecast, the number of workers per retiree shrinks from 3.3 to fewer than two after 2010. How will Social Security survive then except as a pared-down, straightforward welfare program for the poorest of the very old? But how and when will we transform it?

A society with more than 20% of its citizens over 65 will have to reengineer its physical as well as its fiscal landscape. Example: America's roadways—their signage, the distance to off ramps, and the like—seem optimally designed for 25-year-old males with excellent vision, quick reflexes, and high testosterone levels. But they can be deathtraps for the elderly. Since the mid-1970s, as the number of drivers over 70 rose sharply, deaths from car crashes among this group jumped 30% even though total fatalities among all drivers fell by 12%.

Finally, a paradox. The longer we live, the more urgent it will become to learn how to die. In Greek myth, Tithonus is the pitiful soul who won from the gods the gift of eternal life but, lacking eternal youth, was condemned to live—shrinking, shriveling, and longing for oblivion. Our nursing homes and hospital wards are filled with Tithonuses. There are many more who fear his fate. That grim fact is confirmed by brisk sales of books like *Final Exit*, the growing popularity of living wills, the record number of suicides among 65-and-olders, as well as the awkward career of Jack Kevorkian. Can't we as a society in the years ahead finally agree on better ways to decide—among families and physicians and not by government diktat—when it's worth fighting and when it's time to go?

Hard questions, easier to pose than to answer. One obvious answer, though, is to at least stop doing things that make matters worse. Right now, the Social Security system appears to treat the fraction of over-65s who still draw a paycheck the way America's welfare system treats low-income working mothers. It encourages dependency. If you're 65 to 69 and earn more than $11,160 a year, your monthly benefits get cut by one-third. Since interest and dividends don't count as earned income for this calculation, this disincentive is aimed not at the well-off but at those who could most benefit from a little extra money.

THE CULTURE still too often patronizes and stigmatizes its elderly citizens—a phenomenon for which Dr. Robert Butler, 67, the NIA's founding director, coined the word *ageism* back in the late 1960s. Many corporations continue to push older employees out the door as fast as you can say "early-retirement package." Few yet follow the example of Travelers Insurance, which created a job bank of temporary employees from a pool of retirees and younger workers and found their higher productivity saved it $1.5 million a year, or the Days Inn hotel chain, which began a concerted drive to hire people over 55 as reservation agents when it found that, compared with younger employees, they cost 64% less to train and recruit.

The thumb rule offered by economist Larry Kotlikoff is that to keep the economy from slowing down, we should offset every 10% increase in life span with a 10% increase in the retirement age. Here's John Templeton's advice: "Don't retire until 75."

By all means, though, don't feel compelled to slog away at the same old grind unless you really love it. One large advantage of longer lives should be that they expand our opportunities for change. Such change may not involve highly paid work, unless you're self-employed. For some years yet, it will be difficult to find decent corporate jobs after age 65. But volunteerism can be personally rewarding and produce huge benefits for society. "The key is to have a real purpose to your life," says Bob Butler, now chairman of geriatrics at Mount Sinai Medical School. "Numerous studies confirm that when people have goals and a structure to their lives, they actually live longer and also enjoy better health." If you're not working or volunteering, take a course. Take a trip. Take a chance. Old men ought to be explorers, as the poet T.S. Eliot once observed. Old women too.

Perhaps the most critical question raised by the longevity revolution is how healthy tomorrow's outsize elderly population will be. About seven million Americans today require long-term care because they are too mentally or physically frail to fend for themselves. The annual cost is more than $54 billion. But that figure doesn't begin to reflect the cost of treating the disabling infirmities and diseases of old age. According to the most recent estimates, Americans over 65, though just 12% of the population, account for 36% of personal health care spending. Unless we can shrink both the level of disability among older Americans and the time they spend in poor health during their final years—compress morbidity, in the jargon of gerontology—we may eventually have to choose between bankruptcy and health care rationing on a distressingly large scale.

S THIS compression occurring? Various surveys confirm what our eyes tell us daily: The average 70-year-old today is considerably healthier than his or her counterpart 50 or even 20 years ago. In an important study last fall, Duke's Manton found that the rate of chronic disability among Americans over 65 may have declined by 5% between 1982 and 1989. But none of the evidence is conclusive. Says Laurence Branch, director of long-term-care research at Abt Associates, a Cambridge, Massachusetts, consulting firm: "We're increasing life expectancy, but it's still not clear if we're increasing most people's *active* life expectancy—the percentage of their lifetime they can expect to enjoy good health and independence. What is clear, however, is that we know we can do it."

That upbeat attitude is worth keeping in mind, since in some ways the biggest hurdle an aging America faces may be psychological. The U.S. has never stopped thinking of itself as a young country, a frontier country—a new world, not an old one. For such a people, growing up is hard to do. It's worth remembering, then, that alongside its many discomforts, long life has always been thought to bring with it large rewards—among them, perspective, maturity, insight. William Butler Yeats said it best in his poem "The Coming of Wisdom With Time":

Though the leaves are many, the root is one:
Through all the lying days of my youth,
I swayed my leaves and flowers in the sun:
Now I may wither into truth.

Maybe we will too.

The Mind Connection

Scientists finding more evidence of link between mind and health

Beth Baker

Beth Baker is a Washington-based free-lance writer.

When Gene Craft, 42, of Columbus, Ohio, badly twisted his back at work, he received physical therapy to ease the pain and prevent further injury. But when the pain recurred, he knew he needed something more.

"I had learned about the body mechanics, but now I'm covering the other part," he says. "I'm learning that when you have pain, you can control it and not let it totally stress you out."

The "other part" to which Craft refers is the mind, the uncharted realm that science now believes has a powerful role in healing. For Craft, who sought help at the health psychology division of the state's Industrial Rehabilitation Center, this means learning how stress worsens his pain, participating in group therapy and mastering relaxation techniques.

Craft is benefiting from a holistic approach to medicine popularly referred to as mind-body healing. The "new" thinking holds that the mind and body are one, and influences our views of health and recovery from illness.

Questions about the extent of this interplay form an ongoing debate in the scientific community.

"No thinking person believes the mind has no effect on the body. It's all part of the same organism," says Edward Campion, M.D., deputy editor of the New England Journal of Medicine. "But it would be unrealistic to expect that . . . medical problems can be solved by thinking or feeling differently."

Other experts see a deeper connection. "The mind and body cannot be separated," says psychiatrist George F. Solomon, M.D., of the University of California at Los Angeles (UCLA). "The mind is the brain, and the brain is part of the body. The brain regulates and influences many physiological functions, including immunity. Mental and physical well-being are inextricably intertwined."

Solomon, who coined the term "psychoimmunology" in 1964 (later expanded by Robert Ader to psychoneuroimmunology or PNI), has spent 25 years studying the biological mechanisms by which emotions, stress, attitudes and behavior affect resistance to disease. "We have studied people with a variety of illnesses, and people with very good coping skills tend to have a greater speed of recovery," he says.

While uncertainties abound, there is intriguing evidence that psychological factors may influence recovery from everything from heart disease to hip fractures, to the common cold and even some types of cancer. Some examples:

- David Spiegel, M.D., psychiatry professor at Stanford University, studies 86 women with advanced, metastatic breast cancer. All the women received standard medical treatment, but half also had group therapy and were taught self-hypnosis for pain. To Spiegel's surprise, the women in group therapy lived twice as long as their counterparts—an average of 37 months compared to 19 months. Of the three women who survived, all had group therapy. Spiegel is now seeking to replicate the study.
- Janice Kiecolt-Glaser and Ronald Glaser, psychologists at Ohio State University, have been studying spousal caregivers of Alzheimer's patients. Lab tests revealed that over time, caregivers had a decrease in cellular immunity; they were also ill more often from respiratory tract infections than noncaregivers. Evidence suggests chronic psychological stress may lower the body's immune function.
- In a study of older patients who were admitted to a New York hospital with hip fractures, two groups were followed. Both received identical medical treatment, but one group also received mental health consultations. This group's hospital stay was 30 percent shorter, an average of 30 days compared to 42 days for the other group.

"I've followed a group of older adults for 22 years and what I think is apparent, both from the literature and from my own research, is the very significant interplay between mental and physical factors," says Gene Cohen, a geriatric psychiatrist at the National Institutes of Health.

While many physicians remain skeptical of the significance of psychological factors in illness and health, some researchers believe they have made significant progress in identifying the mechanisms of communication between the mind and the body.

Neuroscientist Candace Pert discovered that neuropeptides and other molecules are found not only in the brain but throughout the body, acting as messengers to the cells. Through millions of tiny receptors, each cell receives instructions about growing, producing protein and other activities. Her work also led to the discovery of endorphins, the chemicals that produce emotions when released from the brain.

Other researchers for the first time found nerve fibers in the immune system, further evidence that the mind—or central nervous system—is involved in the immune system's ability to ward off disease.

"The implications of these discoveries are really profound," says Pert. "How you feel, how you react to stress, the emotions that you repress are all going to play a role in your health. This is very radical. It has the potential to change the face of medicine."

Pert and other researchers believe that a "new medicine" is on the horizon. "The boundaries between psychology, medicine, endocrinology, immunology are getting blurred, because of the discoveries that all of the body systems use the same messenger molecules," she says. "This will lead to much more holistic therapies, not just treating one system or another."

One big unanswered question is the precise relationships among stress, emotions, the immune system and illness. "We know that stress can affect immunity and can affect disease," says Solomon. "It's like A, B, C. We know A-C, we know A-B, but what we need to know better is A-B-C."

To learn more, Solomon is following a group of healthy older people, doing periodic tests to see if emotional stress brings out immune changes before the subjects become ill. "Unfortunately for our research, our healthy old people refuse to be sick!" he says. "So I don't have any answers for you yet."

Contributing to the complexity is the fact that the mind may play a bigger role in some medical problems than others. For example, there is wide agreement that "type A" people—aggressive, competitive types—are more vulnerable to heart disease. It is also recognized that those under stress may be more prone to infections, such as cold viruses.

But other diseases, such as cancer, are murkier. Some cancers, like melanoma and breast cancer, may be more influenced by the immune system than others, such as lung and prostate cancer. What part emotions play in this remains controversial.

"The link is very weak that personality contributes to the onset of cancer," says Margaret Kemeny, assistant professor of psychiatry at UCLA. "Cancer is not one disease. It's a very diverse group of tumors, each of which has a different biological context."

Researcher Lydia Temoshok believes she has found a link between the way some cancer patients cope with stress and the course of their illness. "There is a style of coping with having cancer that seems to be involved with an immune system response and may contribute—and I underline contribute—to the medical prognosis," says Temoshok, a psychologist with the Henry M. Jackson Foundation for the Advancement of Military Medicine in Rockville, Md.

Temoshok's book, "The Type C Connection: The Behavior Links to Cancer and your Health," identifies a "type C" coping style (at the opposite end of the spectrum from type A), in which patients are obliging, extremely nice and generally at a loss to express their emotions, especially anger.

Temoshok asserts that one's emotional style, along with diet, age, genetic inheritance and environmental factors, contributes to disease and recovery. Constantly repressing emotions may wreak havoc on the immune system, she says, and if the immune system is impaired, it may not be able to defend against disease.

While some have criticized psychological links with cancer, saying it fosters a "blame the victim" mentality, Temoshok disagrees. "If by changing emotional and coping factors you might make a difference in your recovery, this is empowering," she says.

Kemeny is more cautious. "There are pathways in the body for relationships to exist, but they don't prove that psychological factors contribute to the development of diseases like cancer," she says. "When we can show that, it will have a profound impact."

Bruce Naliboff, chief of psychophysiology at the Veterans Administration Medical Center in Sepulveda, Calif., agrees: "Just because there's a connection doesn't mean that emotions are an important thing in most diseases—or in any disease.

"There's a potential, but that doesn't mean it's actually true," he adds.

While unanswered questions remain, many researchers feel enough evidence exists for medicine to change, to become more interdisciplinary and to focus more on psychological intervention. "There's so much known in practical terms, I would hate to see science invoked to stem the tide and hold it back—and I'm speaking as a scientist," says Candace Pert.

Practitioners like psychologist Nancy Noble, who works with Gene Craft at Ohio's Industrial Rehabilitation Center, are moving forward with common sense techniques to help patients with chronic medical problems.

'The idea is to find out what healthy things work for you.'

NANCY NOBLE

"The whole idea is to find out what healthy things work for you," says Noble. "Taking a bath or a walk, talking to a friend, doing relaxation exercises, deep breathing—these are all positive ways to deal with stress."

James Stacey, spokesman for the American Medical Association, doesn't deny the value of a holistic approach, but doesn't see what all the fuss is about. "Family physicians are acutely attuned to the emotional side of their patients," he says. "The important thing is to have a single advocate, a general physician, and to establish an excellent relationship."

Candace Pert believes the change is more fundamental. "The U.S. has gone off on this high-tech, mindless, unemotional kind of medicine," she says. "There's going to be a new medicine that will be much more in touch with the realities of how the body is constructed and the important role that people's attitude plays. This involves taking responsibility for your health, diet, stress reduction and exercise. The evidence is overwhelming. And it's common sense."

Caloric Restriction and Aging

Eat less, but be sure to have enough protein, fat, vitamins and minerals. This prescription does wonders for the health and longevity of rodents. Might it help humans as well?

Richard Weindruch

RICHARD WEINDRUCH, who earned his PH.D. in experimental pathology at the University of California, Los Angeles, is associate professor of medicine at the University of Wisconsin-Madison, associate director of the university's Institute on Aging and a researcher at the Veterans Administration Geriatric Research, Education and Clinical Center in Madison. He has devoted his career to the study of caloric restriction and its effects on the body and practices mild restriction himself. He has not, however, attempted to put his family or his two cats on the regimen.

Sixty years ago scientists at Cornell University made an extraordinary discovery. By placing rats on a very low calorie diet, Clive M. McCay and his colleagues extended the outer limit of the animals' life span by 33 percent, from three years to four. They subsequently found that rats on low-calorie diets stayed youthful longer and suffered fewer late-life diseases than did their normally fed counterparts. Since the 1930s, caloric restriction has been the only intervention shown convincingly to slow aging in rodents (which are mammals, like us) and in creatures ranging from single-celled protozoans to roundworms, fruit flies and fish.

Naturally, the great power of the method raises the question of whether it can extend survival and good health in people. That issue is very much open, but the fact that the approach works in an array of organisms suggests the an-

LIFE HAS BEEN EXTENDED, often substantially, by very low calorie diets in a range of animals, some of which are depicted here. Whether caloric restriction will increase survival in people remains to be seen. Such diets are successful only if the animals receive an adequate supply of nutrients.

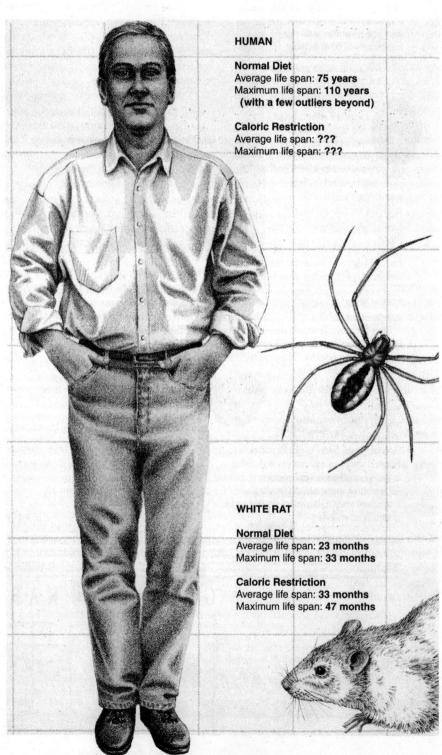

HUMAN

Normal Diet
Average life span: **75 years**
Maximum life span: **110 years**
 (with a few outliers beyond)

Caloric Restriction
Average life span: **???**
Maximum life span: **???**

WHITE RAT

Normal Diet
Average life span: **23 months**
Maximum life span: **33 months**

Caloric Restriction
Average life span: **33 months**
Maximum life span: **47 months**

swer could well be yes. Some intriguing clues from monkeys and humans support the idea, too.

Of course, even if caloric austerity turns out to be a fountain of youth for humans, it might never catch on. After all, our track record for adhering to severe diets is poor. But scientists may one day develop drugs that will safely control our appetite over the long term or will mimic the beneficial influences of caloric control on the body's tissues. This last approach could enable people to consume fairly regular diets while still reaping the healthful effects of limiting their food intake. Many laboratories, including mine at the University of Wisconsin–Madison, are working to understand the cellular and molecular basis of how caloric restriction retards aging in animals. Our efforts may yield useful alternatives to strict dieting, although at the moment most of us are focused primarily on understanding the aging process (or processes) itself.

Less Is More for Rodents

Research into caloric restriction has now uncovered an astonishing range of benefits in animals—provided that the nutrient needs of the dieters are guarded carefully. In most studies the test animals, usually mice or rats, consume 30 to 50 percent fewer calories than are ingested by control subjects, and they weigh 30 to 50 percent less as well. At the same time, they receive enough protein, fat, vitamins and minerals to maintain efficient operation of their tissues. In other words, the animals follow an exaggerated form of a prudent diet, in which they consume minimal calories without becoming malnourished.

If the nutrient needs of the animals are protected, caloric restriction will consistently increase not only the average life span of a population but also the maximum span—that is, the lifetime of the longest-surviving members of the

group. This last outcome means that caloric restriction tinkers with some basic aging process. Anything that forestalls premature death, such as is caused by a preventable or treatable disease or by an accident, will increase the average life span of a population. But one must truly slow the rate of aging in order for the hardiest individuals to surpass the existing maximum.

Beyond altering survival, low-calorie diets in rodents have postponed most major diseases that are common late in life [see box on next page], including cancers of the breast, prostate, immune system and gastrointestinal tract. Moreover, of the 300 or so measures of aging that have been studied, some 90 percent stay "younger" longer in calorie-restricted rodents than in well-fed ones. For example, certain immune responses decrease in normal mice at one year of age (middle age) but do not decline in slimmer but genetically identical mice until age two. Similarly, as rodents grow

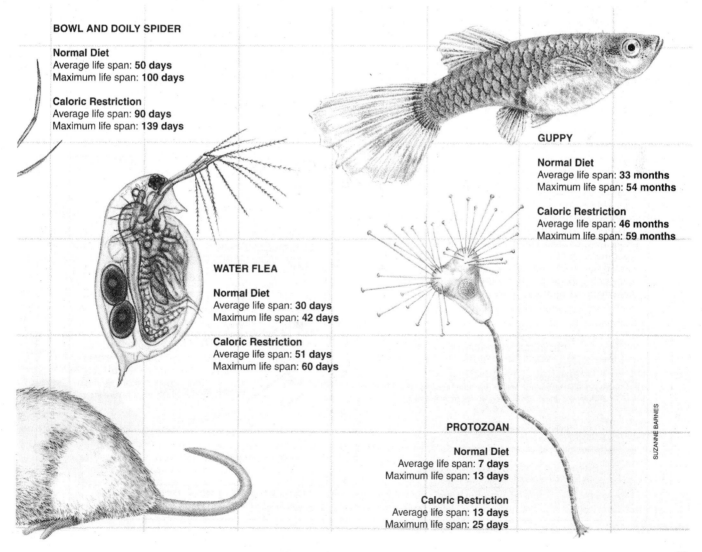

BOWL AND DOILY SPIDER

Normal Diet
Average life span: **50 days**
Maximum life span: **100 days**

Caloric Restriction
Average life span: **90 days**
Maximum life span: **139 days**

GUPPY

Normal Diet
Average life span: **33 months**
Maximum life span: **54 months**

Caloric Restriction
Average life span: **46 months**
Maximum life span: **59 months**

WATER FLEA

Normal Diet
Average life span: **30 days**
Maximum life span: **42 days**

Caloric Restriction
Average life span: **51 days**
Maximum life span: **60 days**

PROTOZOAN

Normal Diet
Average life span: **7 days**
Maximum life span: **13 days**

Caloric Restriction
Average life span: **13 days**
Maximum life span: **25 days**

SUZANNE BARNES

older they generally clear glucose, a simple sugar, from their blood less efficiently than they did in youth (a change that can progress to diabetes); they also synthesize needed proteins more slowly, undergo increased cross-linking (and thus stiffening) of long-lived proteins in tissues, lose muscle mass and learn less rapidly. In calorie-restricted animals, all these changes are delayed.

Not surprisingly, investigators have wondered whether caloric (energy) restriction per se is responsible for the advantages reaped from low-calorie diets or whether limiting fat or some other component of the diet accounts for the success. It turns out the first possibility

is correct. Restriction of fat, protein or carbohydrate without caloric reduction does not increase the maximum life span of rodents. Supplementation alone with multivitamins or high doses of antioxidants does not work, and neither does variation in the type of dietary fat, carbohydrate or protein.

The studies also suggest, hearteningly, that caloric restriction can be useful even if it is not started until middle age. Indeed, the most exciting discovery of my career has been that caloric restriction initiated in mice at early middle age can extend the maximum life span by 10 to 20 percent and can oppose the development of cancer. Further, al-

though limiting the caloric intake to about half of that consumed by free-feeding animals increases the maximum life span the most, less severe restriction, whether begun early in life or later, also provides some benefit.

Naturally, scientists would be more confident that diet restriction could routinely postpone aging in men and women if the results in rodents could be confirmed in studies of monkeys (which more closely resemble people) or in members of our own species. To be most informative, such investigations would have to follow subjects for many years—an expensive and logistically difficult undertaking. Neverthe-

Benefits of Caloric Restriction

Since 1900, advances in health practices have greatly increased the average life span of Americans (*inset in a*), mainly by improving prevention and treatment of diseases that end life prematurely. But those interventions have not substantially affected the maximum life span (*far right in a*), which is thought to be determined by intrinsic aging processes. (The curves and the data in the inset show projections for people born in the years indicated and assume conditions influencing survival do not change.) Caloric restriction, in contrast, has markedly increased the maximum as well as the average life span in rodents (*b*) and is, in fact, the only intervention so far shown to slow aging in mammals— a sign that aging in humans might be retarded as well.

Although severe diets extend survival more than moderate ones, a study of mice fed a reduced-calorie diet from early in life (three weeks of age) demonstrates that even mild restriction offers some benefit (*c*). This finding is potentially good news for people. Also encouraging is the discovery that caloric restriction in rodents does more than prolong life; it enables animals to remain youthful longer (*table*). The calorie-restricted mouse lived unusually long; most normally fed mice of her ilk die by 40 months. She was 54 months old when she died of unknown causes.

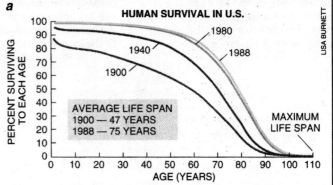

SOURCE: U.S. Bureau of the Census; National Center for Health Statistics

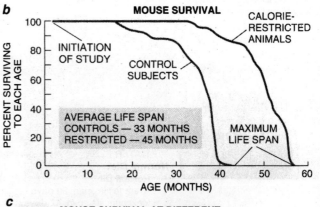

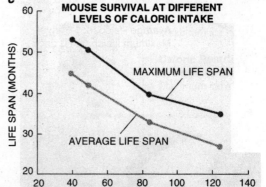

RESTRICTION IN RODENTS: SELECTED EFFECTS

Postpones age-related declines in:
Blood glucose control; female reproductive capacity; DNA repair; immunity; learning ability; muscle mass; protein synthesis

Slows age-related increases in:
Cross-linking of long-lived proteins; free-radical production by mitochondria; unrepaired oxidative damage to tissues

Delays onset of late-life diseases, including:
Autoimmune disorders; cancers; cataracts; diabetes; hypertension; kidney failure

less, two major trials of monkeys are in progress.

Lean, but Striking, Primate Data

It is too early to tell whether low-calorie diets will prolong life or youthfulness in the monkeys over time. The projects have, however, been able to measure the effects of caloric restriction on so-called biomarkers of aging: attributes that generally change with age and may help predict the future span of health or life. For example, as primates grow older, their blood pressure and their blood levels of both insulin and glucose rise; at the same time, insulin sensitivity (the ability of cells to take up glucose in response to signals from insulin) declines. Postponement of these changes would imply that the experimental diet was probably slowing at least some aspects of aging.

One of the monkey studies, led by George S. Roth of the National Institute on Aging, began in 1987. It is examining rhesus monkeys, which typically live to about 30 years and sometimes reach 40 years, and squirrel monkeys, which rarely survive beyond 20 years. Some animals began diet restriction in youth (at one to two years), others after reaching puberty. The second project, involving only rhesus monkeys, was initiated in 1989 by William B. Ershler, Joseph W. Kemnitz and Ellen B. Roecker of the University of Wisconsin–Madison; I joined the team a year later. Our monkeys began caloric restriction as young adults, at eight to 14 years old. Both studies enforce a level of caloric restriction that is about 30 percent below the intake of normally fed controls.

So far the preliminary results are encouraging. The dieting animals in both projects seem healthy and happy, albeit eager for their meals, and their bodies seem to be responding to the regimen much as those of rodents do. Blood pressure and glucose levels are lower than in control animals, and insulin sensitivity is greater. The levels of insulin in the blood are lower as well.

No one has yet performed carefully controlled studies of long-term caloric restriction in average-weight humans over time. And data from populations forced by poverty to live on relatively few calories are uninformative, because such groups generally cannot attain adequate amounts of essential nutrients. Still, some human studies offer indirect evidence that caloric restriction could be of value. Consider the people of Okinawa, many of whom consume diets that are low in calories but provide needed nutrients. The incidence of cen-

tenarians there is high—up to 40 times greater than that of any other Japanese island. In addition, epidemiological surveys in the U.S. and elsewhere indicate that certain cancers, notably those of the breast, colon and stomach, occur less frequently in people reporting small caloric intakes.

Intriguing results were also obtained after eight people living in a self-contained environment—Biosphere 2, near Tucson, Ariz.—were forced to curtail their food intake sharply for two years because of poorer than expected yields from their food-producing efforts. The scientific merits of the overall project have been questioned, but those of us interested in the effects of low-calorie diets were fortunate that Roy L. Walford of the University of California at Los Angeles, who is an expert on caloric restriction and aging (and was my scientific mentor), was the team's physician. Walford helped his colleagues avoid malnutrition and monitored various aspects of the group's physiology. His analyses reveal that caloric restriction led to lowered blood pressure and glucose levels—just as it does in rodents and monkeys. Total serum cholesterol declined as well.

The results in monkeys and humans may be preliminary, but the rodent data show unequivocally that caloric restriction can exert a variety of beneficial effects. This variety raises something of a problem for researchers: Which of the many documented changes (if any) con-

tribute most to increased longevity and youthfulness? Scientists have not yet reached a consensus, but they have ruled out a few once viable proposals. For instance, it is known that a low intake of energy retards growth and also shrinks the amount of fat in the body. Both these effects were once prime contenders as the main changes that lead to longevity but have now been discounted.

Several other hypotheses remain under consideration, however, and all of them have at least some experimental support. One such hypothesis holds that caloric restriction slows the rate of cell division in many tissues. Because the uncontrolled proliferation of cells is a hallmark of cancer, that change could potentially explain why the incidence of several late-life cancers is reduced in animals fed low-calorie diets. Another proposal is based on the finding that caloric restriction tends to lower glucose levels. Less glucose in the circulation would slow the accumulation of sugar on long-lived proteins and would thus moderate the disruptive effects of this buildup.

A Radical Explanation

The view that has so far garnered the most convincing support, though, holds that caloric restriction extends survival and vitality primarily by limiting injury of mitochondria by free radicals. Mitochondria are the tiny intracellular structures that serve as the power

NORMAL DIET	REDUCED DIET
■ **Food intake:** 688 calories per day	■ **Food intake:** 477 calories per day
■ **Body weight:** 31 pounds	■ **Body weight:** 21 pounds
■ **Percent of weight from fat:** 25	■ **Percent of weight from fat:** 10
MEASURES OF HEALTH	**MEASURES OF HEALTH**
■ **Blood pressure:** 129/60 (systole/diastole)	■ **Blood pressure:** 121/51 (systole/diastole)
■ **Glucose level:** 71 (milligrams per deciliter of blood)	■ **Glucose level:** 56 (milligrams per deciliter of blood)
■ **Insulin level:** 93 (microunits per milliliter of blood)	■ **Insulin level:** 29 (microunits per milliliter of blood)
■ **Triglycerides:** 169 (milligrams per deciliter of blood)	■ **Triglycerides:** 67 (milligrams per deciliter of blood)

RESULTS FROM ONGOING TRIAL of caloric restriction in rhesus monkeys cannot yet reveal whether limiting calories will prolong survival. But comparison of a control group (*left*) with animals on a strict diet (*right*) after five years indicates that at least some biological measures that typically rise with age are changing more slowly in the test animals. Blood pressure is only slightly lower in the restricted group now, but has been markedly lower for much of the study period.

plants of cells. Free radicals are highly reactive molecules (usually derived from oxygen) that carry an unpaired electron at their surface. Molecules in this state are prone to destructively oxidizing, or snatching electrons from, any compound they encounter. Free radicals have been suspected of contributing to aging since the 1950s, when Denham Harman of the University of Nebraska Medical School suggested that their generation in the course of normal metabolism gradually disrupts cells. But it was not until the 1980s that scientists began to realize that mitochondria were probably the targets hit hardest.

The mitochondrial free-radical hypothesis of aging derives in part from an understanding of how mitochondria produce ATP (adenosine triphosphate)—the molecule that provides the energy for most cellular processes, such as pumping ions across cell membranes, contracting muscle fibers and constructing proteins. ATP synthesis occurs by a very complicated sequence of reactions, but essentially it involves activity by a series of molecular complexes embedded in an internal membrane—the inner membrane—of mitochondria. With help from oxygen, the complexes extract energy from nutrients and use that energy to manufacture ATP.

Unfortunately, the mitochondrial machinery that draws energy from nutrients also produces free radicals as a by-product. Indeed, mitochondria are thought to be responsible for creating most of the free radicals in cells. One such by-product is the superoxide radical ($O_2^{\cdot-}$). (The dot in the formula represents the unpaired electron.) This renegade is destructive in its own right but can also be converted into hydrogen peroxide (H_2O_2), which technically is not a free radical but can readily form the extremely aggressive hydroxyl free radical ($OH^{\cdot-}$).

Once formed, free radicals can damage proteins, lipids (fats) and DNA anywhere in the cell. But the components of mitochondria—including the ATP-synthesizing machinery and the mitochondrial DNA that gives rise to some of that machinery—are believed to be most vulnerable. Presumably they are at risk in part because they reside at or near the "ground zero" site of free-radical generation and so are constantly bombarded by the oxidizing agents. Moreover, mitochondrial DNA lacks the protein shield that helps to protect nuclear DNA from destructive agents. Consistent with this view is that mitochondrial DNA suffers much more oxidative damage than does nuclear DNA drawn from the same tissue.

TYPICAL MEAL

Lettuce 1/5 head
Tomatoes 1/2 cup
Salad dressing 2 tablespoons
Carrots 1 cup
Peas 1/2 cup
Apple strudel 1 piece
Sparkling water 8 ounces
Baked potato 7 ounces
Sour cream 1 tablespoon
French bread 2 slices
Butter 1 1/2 tablespoons
Beef sirloin 6 ounces (before broiling)

Calories: 1,268
From fat: 33%; from protein: 22%; from carbohydrate: 45%

CALORIE-RESTRICTED MEAL

Plain yogurt 3 ounces
Brewer's yeast 2 tablespoons
Broccoli 1 stalk
Summer squash 1 cup
Salmon 3 ounces (before broiling)
Fruit salad 1/2 cup
Skim milk 8 ounces
Sweet potato 4 ounces
Brown rice 1/2 cup
Spinach 1 cup
Soybeans 1/5 cup

Calories: 940
From fat: 18%; from protein: 32%; from carbohydrate: 50%

KARL GUDE; SOURCE: ROY L. WALFORD *University of California, Los Angeles*

DINNER of a person on a roughly 2,000-calorie diet (*top*) might be reduced considerably—by about a third of the calories (*bottom*)—for someone on a caloric-restriction regimen. To avoid malnutrition, people on such programs would choose nutrient-dense foods such as those shown.

Proponents of the mitochondrial free-radical hypothesis of aging suggest that damage to mitochondria by free radicals eventually interferes with the efficiency of ATP production and increases the output of free radicals. The rise in free radicals, in turn, accelerates the oxidative injury of mitochondrial components, which inhibits ATP production even more. At the same time, free radicals attack cellular components outside the mitochondria, further impairing cell functioning. As cells become less efficient, so do the tissues and organs they compose, and the body itself becomes less able to cope with challenges to its stability. The body does try to counteract the noxious effects of the oxidizing agents. Cells possess antioxidant enzymes that detoxify free radicals, and they make other enzymes that repair oxidative damage. Neither of these systems is 100 percent effective, though, and so such injury is likely to accumulate over time.

Experimental Support

The proposal that aging stems to a great extent from free-radical-induced damage to mitochondria and other cellular components has recently been buttressed by a number of findings. In one striking example, Rajindar S. Sohal, William C. Orr and their colleagues at Southern Methodist University in Dallas investigated rodents and several other organisms, including fruit flies, houseflies, pigs and cows. They noted increases with age in free-radical generation by mitochondria and in oxidative changes to the inner mitochondrial membrane (where ATP is synthesized) and to mitochondrial proteins and DNA. They also observed that greater rates of free-radical production correlate with shortened average and maximum life spans in several of the species.

It turns out, too, that ATP manufacture decreases with age in the brain, heart and skeletal muscle, as would be expected if mitochondrial proteins and DNA in those tissues were irreparably impaired by free radicals. Similar decreases also occur in human tissues and may help explain why degenerative diseases of the nervous system and heart are common late in life and why muscles lose mass and weaken.

Some of the strongest support for the proposition that caloric restriction retards aging by slowing oxidative injury of mitochondria comes from Sohal's group. When the workers looked at mitochondria harvested from the brain, heart and kidney of mice, they discovered that the levels of the superoxide radical and of hydrogen peroxide were markedly lower in animals subjected to long-term caloric restriction than in normally fed controls. In addition, a significant increase of free-radical production with age seen in the control groups was blunted by caloric restriction in the experimental group. This blunted increase was, moreover, accompanied by lessened amounts of oxidative insult to mitochondrial proteins and DNA. Other work indicates that caloric restriction helps to prevent age-related changes in the activities of some antioxidant enzymes—although many investigators, including me, suspect that strict dieting ameliorates oxidative damage mainly through slowing free-radical production.

By what mechanism might caloric restriction reduce the generation of free radicals? No one yet knows. One proposal holds that a lowered intake of calories may somehow lead to slower consumption of oxygen by mitochondria—either overall or in selected cell types. Alternatively, low-calorie diets may increase the efficiency with which mitochondria use oxygen, so that fewer free radicals are made per unit of oxygen consumed. Less use of oxygen or more efficient use would presumably result in the formation of fewer free radicals. Recent findings also intimate that caloric control may minimize free-

radical generation in mitochondria by reducing levels of a circulating thyroid hormone known as triiodothyronine, or T_3, through unknown mechanisms.

Applications to Humans?

Until research into primates has progressed further, few scientists would be prepared to recommend that large numbers of people embark on a severe caloric-restriction regimen. Nevertheless, the accumulated findings do offer some concrete lessons for those who wonder how such programs might be implemented in humans.

One implication is that sharp curtailment of food intake would probably be detrimental to children, considering that it retards growth in young rodents. Also, because children cannot tolerate starvation as well as adults can, they would presumably be more susceptible to any as yet unrecognized negative effects of a low-calorie diet (even though caloric restriction is not equivalent to starvation). An onset at about 20 years of age in humans should avoid such drawbacks and would probably provide the greatest extension of life.

The speed with which calories are reduced needs to be considered, too. Early researchers were unable to prolong survival of rats when diet control was instituted in adulthood. I suspect the failure arose because the animals were put on the regimen too suddenly or were given too few calories, or both. Working with year-old mice, my colleagues and I have found that a gradual tapering of calories to about 65 percent of normal did increase survival.

How might one determine the appropriate caloric intake for a human being? Extrapolating from rodents is difficult, but some findings imply that many people would do best by consuming an amount that enabled them to weigh 10 to 25 percent less than their personal set point. The set point is essentially the weight the body is "programmed" to maintain, if one does not eat in response to external cues, such as television commercials. The problem with this guideline is that determining an individual's set point is tricky. Instead of trying to identify their set point, dieters (with assistance from their health advisers) might engage in some trial and error to find the caloric level that reduces the blood glucose or cholesterol level, or some other measures of health, by a predetermined amount.

The research in animals further implies that a reasonable caloric-restriction regimen for humans might involve a daily intake of roughly one gram (0.04 ounce) of protein and no more than about half a gram of fat for each kilogram (2.2 pounds) of current body weight. The diet would also include enough complex carbohydrate (the long chains of sugars abundant in fruits and vegetables) to reach the desired level of calories. To attain the standard recommended daily allowances for all essential nutrients, an individual would have to select foods with extreme care and probably take vitamins or supplements.

Anyone who contemplated following a caloric-restriction regimen would also have to consider potential disadvantages beyond hunger pangs and would certainly want to undertake the program with the guidance of a physician. Depending on the severity of the diet, the weight loss that inevitably results might impede fertility in females. Also, a prolonged anovulatory state, if accompanied by a diminution of estrogen production, might increase the risk of osteoporosis (bone loss) and loss of muscle mass later in life. It is also possible that caloric restriction will compromise a person's ability to withstand stress, such as injury, infection or exposure to extreme temperatures. Oddly enough, stress resistance has been little studied in rodents on low-calorie diets, and so they have little to teach about this issue.

It may take another 10 or 20 years before scientists have a firm idea of whether caloric restriction can be as beneficial for humans as it clearly is for rats, mice and a variety of other creatures. Meanwhile investigators studying this intervention are sure to learn much about the nature of aging and to gain ideas about how to slow it—whether through caloric restriction, through drugs that reproduce the effects of dieting or by methods awaiting discovery.

Further Reading

THE RETARDATION OF AGING AND DISEASE BY DIETARY RESTRICTION. Richard Weindruch and Roy L. Walford. Charles C. Thomas, 1988.
FREE RADICALS IN AGING. Edited by Byung P. Yu. CRC Press, 1993.
MODULATION OF AGING PROCESSES BY DIETARY RESTRICTION. Edited by Byung P. Yu. CRC Press. 1994.

The Quality of Later Life

Although it is true that one ages from the moment of conception to the moment of death, children are usually considered to be "growing and developing" while adults are often thought of as "aging." Having accepted this assumption, most biologists concerned with the problems of aging focus their attention on what happens to individuals after they reach maturity. Moreover, most of the biological and medical research dealing with the aging process focuses on the later part of the mature adult's life cycle. A commonly used definition of senescence is "the changes that occur generally in the post-reproductive period and that result in decreased survival capacity on the part of the individual organism" (B. L. Shrehler, *Time, Cells and Aging*, New York: Academic Press, 1977).

As a person ages, physiological changes take place. The skin loses its elasticity, becomes more pigmented, and bruises more easily. Joints stiffen, and the bone structure becomes less firm. Muscles lose their strength. The respiratory system becomes less efficient. The individual's metabolism changes, resulting in different dietary demands. Bowel and bladder movements are more difficult to regulate. Visual acuity diminishes, hearing declines, and the entire system is less able to resist environmental stresses and strains.

Increases in life expectancy have resulted largely from decreased mortality rates among younger people, rather than from increased longevity after age 65. In 1900 the average life expectancy at birth was 47.3 years; in 1988,

it was 74.9 years. Thus, in 88 years the average life expectancy rose by 27.6 years. However, those who now live to the age of 65 do not have an appreciably different life expectancy than did their 1900 cohorts. In 1900, 65-year-olds could expect to live approximately 12 years longer, while in 1988 they could expect to live approximately 17 years longer, an increase of 5 years. Although more people survive to age 65 today, the chances of being afflicted by one of the major killers of older persons is still about as great for this generation as it was for their grandparents.

While medical science has had considerable success in controlling the acute diseases of the young—such as measles, chicken pox, and scarlet fever—it has not been as successful in controlling the chronic conditions of old age, such as heart trouble, cancer, and emphysema. Organ transplants, greater knowledge of the immune system, and undiscovered medical technologies will probably increase the life expectancy for the 65-and-over population, resulting in longer life for the next generation. Although persons 65 years of age today are living slightly longer than 65-year-olds did in 1900, the quality of their later years has greatly improved. Economically, Social Security and a multitude of private retirement programs have given most older persons a more secure retirement. Physically, many people remain active, mobile, and independent throughout their retirement years. Socially, most older persons are married, involved in community activities, and leading productive lives. While they may experience some chronic ailments, most are able to live in their own homes, direct their own lives, and involve themselves in activities they enjoy.

The articles in this section examine health, psychological, social, and spiritual factors that affect the quality of aging. All of us are faced with the process of aging, and by putting a strong emphasis on health, both mental and physical, a long, quality life is much more attainable.

The first unit essay, "Sexuality and Aging: What It Means to Be Sixty or Seventy or Eighty in the '90s," examines ways of remaining sexually active throughout a person's life.

In the article "Live Longer and Prosper?" the issues regarding how much longer the working population will be willing to pay the taxes necessary to continue the social service programs that support older persons are examined.

Older persons experience a number of role losses and must adjust to a variety of new roles. Harold Cox, in "Roles for Aged Individuals in Post-Industrial Societies," sees emerging recreational, leisure, educational, and volunteer roles as enriching the lives of older people. Jack Rosenthal, in "The Age Boom," observes that increased longevity is a phenomena of the last century. The realities of old age as the final stage of life are examined by the author. "Men and Women Aging Differently," by Barbara Barer, illustrates how the timing of life course events differs among men and women and the different problems they are confronted with as a result of these factors. Susan Scarf Merrell, in her article "Getting Over Getting Older," examines the effect of money and lifestyle choices that older persons make in order to lead satisfying lives in their later years.

Finally, Gail Sheehy, in "New Passages," contends that because of increasing longevity, the various stages of life must be pushed back by 10 years or more. Age 30 is now what age 20 used to be like, age 40 is what age 30 used to be like, and age 50 is now what age 40 used to be like. No longer are persons viewing the age of 50 and over as a downhill road to death.

Looking Ahead: Challenge Questions

While medical science has increased life expectancy at birth by controlling diseases of the young, there has been relatively little success in controlling the diseases of old age and increasing life expectancy after age 65. Can we expect new breakthroughs in medical technology that will increase the life expectancy of 65-year-olds?

While many people expect that they will live well into their eighties and nineties, very few imagine living to be 120 years old. Do many Americans really want to live beyond their hundredth birthday? Why or why not?

What changes in business, government, social services, and the economy will be produced by an increasing number of older Americans?

Sexuality and Aging

What it means to be sixty or seventy or eighty in the '90s

"It's the awfulness of it, " Harry said when asked how he was getting along after his wife died. It was the way he said the "awe"—with a stunned sound, as if he hadn't expected the blow to be so crushing.

Pounder of pianos, designer of great, black locomotives, father of five, this new fragility was a surprise. But it wasn't his last surprise.

After a year of bridge parties with old friends, Harry and his new fiancée turned up at a family dinner.

Their only worry was that the children would think Martha too young for him. She was 69. He was 78.

When they left for their honeymoon, the family still had questions. No one, including Harry and Martha, knew quite what to expect.

Three trends, longer life expectancy, early retirement and better health, are stretching the time between retirement and old age. These trends are redefining our image of aging for the 31 million Americans older than age 65. If you are in your 60s or 70s, you are probably more active and healthy than your parents were at a similar age. Many people are retiring earlier. This opens a whole new segment of your life.

Like everyone of every age, you probably want to continue sharing your life with others in fulfilling relationships. And, you may want to include sex in an intimate relationship with someone you love.

WHAT IS SEXUALITY?

The sexual drive draws humans together for biological reproduction, but it goes beyond this. Your sexuality influences your behavior, speech, appearance; indeed, many aspects of your life.

You might express your sexuality by buying an attractive blouse, playing a particular song or holding hands. Some people express their sexuality through shared interests and companionship. A more physical expression of sexuality is intimate contact, such as sexual intercourse.

Sexuality brings people together to give and receive physical affection. Although it's an important form of intimacy, sexual intimacy isn't the only one. For many people, sexual intimacy isn't an available or desired form of closeness. A close friendship or a loving grandparent-grandchild relationship, for example, can provide rewarding opportunities for non-sexual intimacy.

For some older people, though, sexual intimacy remains important. Despite this importance, sexuality in people after age 60 or 70 is not openly acknowledged.

From *Mayo Clinic Health Letter,* February 1993, pp. 1-8. © 1993 by the Mayo Foundation for Medical Education and Research, Rochester, MN 55905. Reprinted by permission.

Health and sexuality

Sex, like walking, doesn't require the stamina of a marathoner. It does require reasonably good health. Here are some guidelines:

■ *Use it or lose it* — Though the reason is unclear, prolonged abstinence from sex can cause impotence. Women who are sexually active after menopause have better vaginal lubrication and elasticity of vaginal tissues.

■ *Eat healthfully* — Follow a balanced, low-fat diet and exercise regularly. Fitness enhances your self-image.

■ *Don't smoke* — Men who smoke heavily are more likely to be impotent than men who don't smoke. Smokers are at an increased risk of hardening of the arteries, which can cause impotence. Similar studies for women are needed.

■ *Control your weight* — Moderate weight loss can sometimes reverse impotence.

■ *Limit alcohol* — Chronic alcohol and drug abuse causes psychological and neurological problems related to impotence.

■ *Moderate coffee drinking may keep sex perking* — A recent study reported that elderly people who drank at least one cup of coffee a day were more likely to be sexually active than those who didn't. The reason for this association is unknown; further studies are needed.

■ *Protect against AIDS and other STDs* — The best protection against AIDS and other sexually transmitted diseases (STDs) is a long-standing, monogamous relationship. Next best: Use a condom.

MYTHS AND REALITIES

The widespread perception in America is that older people are not sexually active. Try to remember the last time the media portrayed two seniors in a passionate embrace. In America, sex is considered the exclusive territory of the young.

Comedian Sam Levinson expressed it well when he quipped, "My parents would never do such a thing; well, my father—maybe. But my mother—NEVER!"

This is a myth.

Realities

The reality is that many older people enjoy an active sex life that often is better than their sex life in early adulthood. The idea that your sexual drive dissolves sometime after middle age is nonsense. It's comparable to thinking your ability to enjoy good food or beautiful scenery would also disappear at a certain point.

In now famous studies, Dr. Alfred C. Kinsey collected information on sexual behavior in the 1940s. Drs. W. B. Masters and V. E. Johnson continued this research in the 1970s. Little of their research looked at people over 60. But in the last decade, a few telling studies show the stark difference between myth and reality.

In a 1992 University of Chicago study, Father Andrew Greeley, author and professor of sociology, released "Sex After Sixty: A Report." According to Greeley, "The happiest men and women in America are married people who continue to have sex frequently after they are 60. They are also most likely to report that they are living exciting lives."

Greeley's report, an analysis of two previous surveys involving 5,738 people, showed 37 percent of married people over 60 have sex once a week or more, and 16 percent have sex several times a week.

A survey of 4,245 seniors done by Consumers Union (*Love, Sex, and Aging*, 1984), concludes that, "The panorama of love, sex and aging is far richer and more diverse than the stereotype of life after 50. Both the quality and quantity of sexual activity reported can be properly defined as astonishing."

These surveys are helping today's seniors feel more comfortable acknowledging their sexuality. A 67-year-old consultant to the Consumers Union report wrote:

"Having successfully pretended for decades that we are nonsexual, my generation is now having second thoughts. We are increasingly realizing that denying our sexuality means denying an essential aspect of our common humanity. It cuts us off from communication with our children, our grandchildren and our peers on a subject of great interest to us all—sexuality."

SEX AFTER SIXTY: WHAT CAN YOU EXPECT?

Once you've reshaped your idea of what society should expect of you, you're faced with the sometimes more worrisome obstacle of what you can expect of yourself. Sex, something you've taken for granted most of your life, may suddenly be "iffy" at sixty.

Changes in women

Many women experience changes in sexual function in the years immediately before and after menopause. Contrary to myth, though, menopause does not mark the end of sexuality.

Generally, if you were interested in sex and enjoyed it as a younger woman, you probably will feel the same way after menopause. Yet menopause does bring changes:

• *Desire*—The effects of age on your sexual desire are the most variable of your sexual responses. Although your sex drive is largely determined by emotional and social factors, hormones like estrogen and testosterone do play a role.

Estrogen is made in your ovaries; testosterone, in your adrenal glands. Surprisingly, sexual desire is affected mainly by testosterone, not estrogen. At menopause, your ovaries stop producing estrogen, but most women produce enough testosterone to preserve their interest in sex.

• *Vaginal changes*—After menopause, estrogen deficiency may lead to changes in the appearance of your genitals and how you respond sexually.

The folds of skin that cover your genital region shrink and become thinner, exposing more of the clitoris. This in-

Sex after a heart attack: Is it safe?

If you can climb a flight of stairs without symptoms, you can usually resume sexual activity. Ask your doctor for specific advice. Here are some guidelines:

■ *Wait after eating* — Wait three or four hours after eating a large meal or drinking alcohol before intercourse. Digestion puts extra demands on your heart.

■ *Rest* — Make sure you are well rested before you have intercourse, and rest after.

■ *Find comfortable positions* — Positions such as side-by-side, or your partner on top, are less strenuous.

creased exposure may reduce your sensitivity or cause an unpleasant tingling or prickling sensation when touched.

The opening to your vagina becomes narrower, particularly if you are not sexually active. Natural swelling and lubrication of your vagina occur more slowly during arousal. Even when you feel excited, your vagina may stay somewhat tight and dry. These factors can lead to difficult or painful intercourse (dyspareunia = DYS - pa - ROO - nee - ah).

• *Orgasm*—Because sexual arousal begins in your brain, you can have an orgasm during sexual stimulation throughout your life. You may have diminished or slower response. Women in their 60s and 70s have a greater incidence of painful uterine contractions during orgasm.

Changes in men

Physical changes in a middle-aged man's sexual response parallel those seen in a postmenopausal woman.

• *Desire*—Although feelings of desire originate in your brain, you need a minimum amount of the hormone testosterone to put these feelings into action. The great majority of aging men produce well above the minimum amount of testosterone needed to maintain interest in sex into advanced age.

• *Excitement*—By age 60, you may require more stimulation to get and maintain an erection, and the erection will be less firm. Yet a man with good blood circulation to the penis can attain erections adequate for intercourse until the end of life.

• *Orgasm*—Aging increases the length of time that must pass after an ejaculation and before stimulation to another climax. This interval may lengthen from just a few minutes at the age of 17, to as much as 48 hours by age 70.

Changes due to illness or disability

Whether you're healthy, ill or disabled, you have your own sexual identity and desires for sexual expression. Yet illness or disability can interfere with

After age 60, intercourse may require some planning

Problems	Solutions	
Decreased desire	■ Use mood enhancers (candlelight, music, romantic thoughts). ■ Hormone replacement therapy (estrogen or testosterone).	■ Treatment for depression. ■ Treatment for drug abuse (alcohol). ■ Behavioral counseling.
Vaginal dryness; Vagina expands less in length and width	■ Use a lubricant. ■ Consider estrogen replacement therapy.	■ Have intercourse regularly. ■ Pelvic exercises prescribed by your doctor.
Softer erections; More physical and mental stimulation to get and maintain erection	■ Use a position that makes it easy to insert the penis into the vagina. ■ Accept softer erections as a normal part of aging.	■ Don't use a condom if disease transmission is not possible. ■ Tell your partner what is most stimulating to you.
Erection lost more quickly; Takes longer to get another	■ Have intercourse less frequently. ■ Emphasize quality, not quantity.	■ Emphasize comfortable sexual activities that don't require an erection.

how you respond sexually to another person. Here's a closer look at how some medical problems can affect sexual expression:

• *Heart attack*—Chest pain, shortness of breath or the fear of a recurring heart attack can have an impact on your sexual behavior. But a heart attack will rarely turn you into a "cardiac cripple." If you were sexually active before your heart attack, you can probably be again. If you have symptoms of angina, your doctor may recommend nitroglycerine before intercourse. Most people who have heart disease are capable of a full, active sex life (see "Sex after a heart attack: Is it safe?").

Even though pulse rates, respiratory rates and blood pressure rise during intercourse, after intercourse they return to normal within minutes. Sudden death during sex is rare.

• *Prostate surgery*—For a benign condition, such as an enlarged prostate, surgery rarely causes impotence. Prostate surgery for cancer causes impotence 50 to 60 percent of the time. However, this type of impotence can be treated (see next page).

• *Hysterectomy*—This is surgery to remove the uterus and cervix, and in some cases, the fallopian tubes, ovaries and lymph nodes. A hysterectomy, by itself, doesn't interfere with your physical ability to have intercourse or experience orgasm once you've recovered from the surgery. Removing the ovaries, however, creates an instant menopause and accelerates the physical and emotional aspects of the natural condition.

When cancer is not involved, be sure you understand why you need a hysterectomy and how it will help your symptoms. Ask your doctor what you can expect after the operation. Reassure yourself that a hysterectomy generally doesn't affect sexual pleasure and that hormone therapy should prevent physical and emotional changes from interfering.

• *Drugs*—Some commonly used medicines can interfere with sexual function. Drugs that control high blood pressure, such as thiazide diuretics and beta blockers, can reduce desire and impair erection in men and lubrication in women. In contrast, calcium channel blockers and angiotensin converting enzyme (ACE) inhibitors have little known effect on sexual function.

Other drugs that affect sexual function include antihistamines, drugs used to treat depression and drugs that block

Sex and illness

Changes in your body due to illness or surgery can affect your physical response to sex. They also can affect your self-image and ultimately limit your interest in sex. Here are tips to help you maintain confidence in your sexuality:

■ *Know what to expect* — Talk to your doctor about the usual effects your treatment has on sexual function.

■ *Talk about sex* — If you feel weak or tired and want your partner to take a more active role, say so. If some part of your body is sore, guide your mate's caresses to create pleasure and avoid pain.

■ *Plan for sex* — Find a time when you're rested and relaxed. Taking a warm bath first or having sex in the morning may help. If you take a pain reliever, such as for arthritis, time the dose so that its effect will occur during sexual activity.

■ *Prepare with exercise* — If you have arthritis or another disability, ask your doctor or therapist for range-of-motion exercises to help relax your joints before sex.

■ *Find pleasure in touch* — It's a good alternative to sexual intercourse. Touching can simply mean holding each other. Men and women can sometimes reach orgasm with the right kind of touching.

If you have no partner, touching yourself for sexual pleasure may help you reaffirm your own sexuality. It can also help you make the transition to intercourse after an illness or surgery.

secretion of stomach acid. If you take one of these drugs and are experiencing side effects, ask your doctor if there is an equally effective medication that doesn't cause the side effects. Alcohol also may adversely affect sexual function.

• *Hardening of the arteries and heart disease*—About half of all impotence in men past age 50 is caused by damage to nerves or blood vessels to the penis. Hardening of the arteries (atherosclerosis) can damage small vessels and restrict blood flow to the genitals. This can interfere with erection in men and swelling of vaginal tissues in women.'

• *Diabetes*—Diabetes can increase the collection of fatty deposits (plaque) in blood vessels. Such deposits restrict the flow of blood to the penis. About half of men with diabetes become impotent. Their risk of impotence increases with age. Men who've had diabetes for many years and who also have nerve damage are more likely to become impotent.

If you are a woman with diabetes, you may suffer dryness and painful intercourse that reduce the frequency of orgasm. You may have more frequent vaginal and urinary tract infections.

• *Arthritis*—Although arthritis does not affect your sex organs, the pain and stiffness of osteoarthritis or rheumatoid arthritis can make sex difficult to enjoy. If you have arthritis, discuss your capabilities and your desires openly with your partner. As long as you and your partner keep communications open, you can have a satisfying sexual relationship.

• *Cancer*—Some forms of cancer cause anemia, loss of appetite, muscle wasting or neurologic impairment that leads to weakness. Surgery can alter your physical appearance. These problems can decrease your sexual desire or pleasure.

Cancer may also cause direct damage to your sexual organs or to their nerve and blood supplies; treatment can produce side effects that may interfere with sexual function, desire or pleasure. Discuss possible effects of your treatment with your doctor. If cancer has disrupted your usual sexual activity, seek other ways of expression. Sometimes cuddling or self-stimulation can be enough.

TO REMAIN SEXUALLY ACTIVE, WHAT CAN A WOMAN DO?

Long-term estrogen replacement therapy (ERT) can not only prevent osteoporosis (bone thinning) and heart disease, it can help prevent changes in vaginal tissue, lubrication and desire as well.

Testosterone enhances sexual desire in women. But, it also can produce unwanted, sometimes irreversible side effects such as deepening of the voice and increased facial hair.

Your doctor may prescribe estrogen cream which, applied to your genital area, can prevent dryness and thinning of vaginal tissue. You can also use over-the-counter lubricants just before sexual activity. It's best to use a water-based lubricant, such as K-Y jelly, rather than oil-based mineral oil or petroleum jelly.

If you have problems reaching orgasm, talk to your physician. Your doctor might adjust your medications or offer other options, including counseling, if the problem is non-medical; or, your doctor may refer you to a specialist.

What can a man do?

Only a few years ago doctors generally thought that about 90 percent of impotence was psychological. Now they realize that 50 to 75 percent of impotence is caused by physical problems. There is a wide range of treatments. Keep in mind that the success of any treatment depends, in part, on open communication between partners in a close, supportive relationship. Here are some treatment options:

• *Psychological therapy*—Many impotence problems can be solved simply by you and your partner understanding the normal changes of aging and adapting to them. For help in this process, your doctor may recommend counseling by a qualified psychiatrist, psychologist or therapist who specializes in the treatment of sexual problems.

• *Hormone adjustment*—Is testosterone a magic potion for impotence? No. Although testosterone supplementation is used in rare instances, its effectiveness for aging men experiencing a normal, gradual decline in testosterone is doubtful.

• *Vascular surgery*—Doctors sometimes can surgically correct impotence caused by an obstruction of blood flow to the penis. However, this bypass procedure is appropriate in only a small number, less than 2 percent, of young men who have impotence problems. The long-term success of this surgery is too often disappointing.

• *Vacuum device*—Currently one of the most common treatments for impotence, this device consists of a hollow, plastic cylinder that fits over your flaccid penis. With the device in place, you attach a hand pump to draw air out of the cylinder. The vacuum created draws blood into your penis, creating an erection.

Once your penis is erect, you slip an elastic ring over the cylinder onto the base of your penis. For intercourse, you remove the cylinder from your penis. The ring maintains your erection by reducing blood flow out of your penis. Because side effects of improper use can damage the penis, you should use this device under your doctor's care.

• *Self-injection*—Penile injection therapy is another option. It involves injecting a medication directly into your penis. One or more drugs (papaverine, phentolamine and prostaglandin-E1) are used. The injection is nearly painless and produces a more natural erection than a vacuum device or an implant.

• *Penile implants*—If other treatments fail or are unsatisfactory, a surgical implant is an alternative. Implants consist of one or two silicone or polyurethane cylinders that are surgically placed inside your penis. Implants are not the perfect solution. Mayo experts say there is a 10 to 15 percent chance an implant will malfunction within five years, but the problem almost always can be corrected. Many men still find the procedure worthwhile.

There are two major types of implants: one uses malleable rods and the other uses inflatable cylinders. Malleable rods remain erect, although they can be bent close to your body for concealment. Because there are no working parts, malfunctions are rare.

Inflatable devices consist of one or two inflatable cylinders, a finger-activated pump and an internal reservoir, which stores the fluid used to inflate the tubes. All components—the cylinders, pump and reservoir—are implanted within your penis, scrotum and lower abdomen. These devices produce more "natural" erections.

• *Medications*—Neurotransmitters are chemicals in your brain and nerves that help relay messages. Nitric oxide is now recognized as one of the most important of these chemicals for stimulating an erection. Unfortunately, there is as yet no practical way to administer nitric oxide for treatment of impotence. Other drugs have not proven effective.

SEX IN SYNC

You might wonder how sex can survive amidst tubes, pumps and lubes that can make you feel more like a mechanic than a romantic.

Actually, many people discover that late-life sexuality survives in an increased diversity of expression, sometimes slow, tender and affectionate, and sometimes more intense and spontaneous.

In some ways, middle- and late-life sex are better than the more frantic pace of your younger years. Biology finally puts sex in sync. As a young man, you were probably more driven by hormones and societal pressure. You may find that now desire, arousal and orgasm take longer and aren't always a sure thing. You may find setting and mood more important. Touch and extended foreplay may become as satisfying as more urgent needs for arousal and release.

As a woman, you were probably more dependent on setting and mood when you were younger. You may feel more relaxed and less inhibited in later life. You may be more confident to assert your sexual desires openly.

COMMUNICATION

It can be difficult to talk to another person about sex—doctor, counselor or even a lifetime lover. But, good communication is essential in adapting your sex life to changes caused by aging. Here are three cornerstones of good communication:

• *Be informed*—To start the process, know the facts. Gather as much reliable information as you can about sex and aging and share the facts with your partner.

• *Be open*—If there are unresolved problems in your relationship, sex won't solve them. Be sensitive to the views and feelings of your partner. Work out the differences that are inevitable—before you go to bed. Appropriate sexual counseling can help you and your partner work out problems and enhance your relationship.

• *Be warned*—Most likely, your physician will be willing to discuss questions concerning sexuality with you, but it would be unusual if he or she were a specialist in treating sexual problems. Ask your doctor to refer you to a specialist in this area.

ADAPTING TO CHANGES

As your sexual function changes, you may need to adapt not only to physical changes but to emotional changes as well, perhaps even to changes in your living arrangements.

Lovemaking can lose its spontaneity. Adapting may mean finding the courage to experiment with new styles of making love with the same partner. It may mean trying alternatives to intercourse. You may feel self-conscious about suggesting new ways to find pleasure. But, by changing the focus of sex, you minimize occasional erectile failures that occur.

And, adapting may mean having the flexibility to seek a new partner if you're single. Because women outlive men an average of seven years, women past 50 outnumber unmarried men almost three to one. Older women have less opportunity to remarry.

Families also need to be flexible. Children may need to deal with issues such as inheritance and acceptance of the new spouse.

Another factor that often limits sexual activity is the status of your living arrangements. If you live in a nursing home, you may face an additional problem. Although there are a few nursing homes that offer the privacy of apartment-style living, most do not. Fortunately, this problem is becoming more widely recognized. In the future, nursing homes may offer more privacy.

If you live independently, getting out and around may be a chore. Yet, many older men and women do find new partners. And, they report the rewards of sharing your life with someone you care for may be well-worth the extra effort.

THE NEED FOR INTIMACY IS AGELESS

It takes determination to resist the "over-the-hill" mentality espoused by society today. Age brings changes at 70 just as it does at 17. But you never outgrow your need for intimate love and affection. Whether you seek intimacy through non-sexual touching and companionship or through sexual activity, you and your partner can overcome obstacles. The keys are caring, adapting and communicating.

Live Long and Prosper?

Burgeoning elderly populations threaten to overwhelm government benefit programs in the developed nations, but demographers differ on how great the challenge will be

Is there such a thing as living too long? Czech science fiction writer Karel Čapek thought so. He cut to the heart of the issue in the final scene of his 1926 play *The Makropulos Case*, about a 337-year-old woman, Elina Makropulos, who seeks an elixir that will renew her life for three more centuries. To one hard-headed character, the lawyer Kolenaty, living so long is "an absurd idea. . . . Our social system is based completely on the shortness of life. Take for example contracts, pensions, insurance, wages, probate, and the Lord knows what else."

Although Čapek was a writer of startling clairvoyance—he invented the term "robot" in his 1920 play *R.U.R.*—he couldn't have foreseen how soon Kolenaty's complaint would take on urgent, and very real, dimensions. The industrialized nations' investments in improved nutrition, medical technology, and public health have paid off handsomely, raising the average life expectancy in Europe and the United States from less than 47 years in 1890, the year of Čapek's birth, to a ripe 75.5 in 1993. Japan has done even better, leading the world with an average life expectancy of 76.6 years for men and 83 for women (see box *Japan: Feeling the Strains of an Aging Population*). And more recently, the developing countries have been showing similar gains. Says Eileen Crimmins, a demographer at the University of Southern California (USC), "The lengthening of life expectancy for the population has been one of the greatest triumphs of humanity."

But the triumph could turn to ashes as societies struggle to support their graying populations with proportionally fewer working-age people to pay for the burgeoning costs of old-age assistance programs. Social Security, Medicare, and Medicaid benefits to the elderly already account for more than a third of U.S. federal spending, a major reason the projected 1996 budget deficit is still some $130 billion. If unchecked, spending on

these entitlement programs plus interest on the national debt could consume the entire federal budget by 2012, a bipartisan congressional commission warned in 1994. Other industrialized nations face similar burdens. Member states of the Organization for Economic Cooperation and Development spend an average of 9% of their gross domestic product on old-age pensions—compared to only 6.5% in the United States—and in nations such as Germany, France, Italy, and Japan, this figure is set to rise to between 14% and 20% early in the next century.

Life expectancies will also continue to rise, although there are sharp disagreements about how fast. But even if the increase levels off, the U.S. baby boom generation will swell the elderly population as the boomers begin turning 65 in 2011, and a similar population wave will wash over Europe. The U.S. Census Bureau predicts that by 2030, the elderly's ranks will grow to between 59 million and 78 million, or about one-fifth of the total U.S. population, up from only one-eighth in 1990. The group expanding the fastest is also the frailest, the so-called "oldest old": those aged 85 and over, whose numbers are expected to nearly triple to 8.8 million by 2030. At these rates of growth, programs such as Medicare and Social Security "will bankrupt the next generation," says Laurence Kotlikoff, an economist at Boston University. Indeed, the Department of Health and Human Services calculates that the Medicare Hospital Insurance trust fund will be empty by the year 2001.

But political leaders and economists planning for this coming onslaught of elderly will find they have another problem as well. They will need detailed forecasts of the future size, health, and wealth of the elderly population, and those answers are elusive. While demographers predict that lengthening life expectancy will put severe stresses on public-sector institutions and on the adult children of the elderly, for example, they can't say just how

great those stresses will be, or whether there might be countervailing savings as longer lived citizens retire later or suffer fewer health problems. Says Richard Suzman, director of the National Institute on Aging's (NIA's) Office of Demography of Aging: "Anyone who gives you firm prognostications about what is going to happen is either a liar or a fool, because the uncertainties over trends in life expectancy, health and disability, and retirement age are quite high."

A biological limit to life expectancy?

These uncertainties are keenest when social scientists and biomedical researchers confront the question of human longevity. By some estimates, the practical limit to life expectancy is about 85 years. But by others, the average child born today may survive to age 95 or 100, with no inherent limit to human longevity in sight. The outcome of this dispute is far from academic, for even slight underestimates of the number of people who will become eligible for old-age benefits in the next century could mean huge unanticipated costs to taxpayers. Ronald Lee, a demographer at the University of California, Berkeley, calculates that for every 1-year increase in average life expectancy, everyone's yearly consumption must shrink by 0.9%—or labor effort must increase 0.9%—to pay for the increased benefits to retirees.

Longevity forecasts from the U.S. Social Security Administration (SSA) are among those coming in on the low side. They assume that the easy gains in longevity—those primarily due to conquering many infectious diseases—have already been made. And because SSA actuaries expect that additional progress against the diseases that are today's big killers in developed countries, such as heart attacks, cancer, and strokes, will come only slowly, they project that the average life expectancy in the United States will increase to no more than 83 years by 2050.

A 'Big Science' Survey for the Social Sciences

Rocket builders had the Apollo moon program, molecular biologists have the Human Genome Project, and demographers and economists studying aging have the Health and Retirement Study (HRS). One of the most ambitious and expensive social science projects ever undertaken, the survey is the first to track both the medical and economic conditions of middle-aged Americans as they move closer to retirement and, ultimately, the grave. So far, it has cost $30 million. Says HRS principal investigator Thomas Juster, an economist and survey research specialist at the University of Michigan's Institute for Social Research: "HRS is 'big science' for the social sciences."

The goal of the project, which began in 1992, is to provide information that will help researchers and political leaders gauge the resources that are likely to be required by the generation born during the Great Depression as its members enter old age. The information is collected in a 70- to 180-minute questionnaire administered every 2 years to a representative cohort of 12,654 workers born in the years 1931 to 1941 and their spouses. Included are questions on health and disability, as well as on income and net worth, housing status, family structure, work history, retirement plans, insurance coverage, and even cognitive skills and expectations for the future.

With its comprehensive scope and large sample size, the HRS "will allow us to study things we couldn't study before," says Michael Hurd, an economist at the State University of New York, Stony Brook, and one of the researchers analyzing the first two waves of data produced by the project. He cites as an example the need to know more about how workers make a key decision: determining when to retire.

A better understanding of what goes into that decision is needed because government planners want to encourage later retirements to help lessen the burden on the Social Security system. While researchers know that workers, when choosing to retire, may take into account such factors as their estimated life expectancy and the prospects for inflation that might erode their pensions, a detailed understanding of their decision-making has so far been elusive. But Hurd says, "With HRS we're now getting the data about worker expectations that we need." One remarkable observation so far: Respondents tend to be very good judges of their own life expectancy, giving estimates that closely match actuarial predictions.

HRS should also teach researchers more about the motivations behind "intergenerational transfers," the giving within families that may become increasingly critical to the elderly if government benefit programs shrink. Are the middle-aged motivated to provide for their elderly parents by simple altruism, as some predict, or to encourage their own children to take care of them when they are old? If the latter is correct, then middle-aged adults should be more likely to provide time, space, or money to their elderly parents if they have children of their own, and HRS data should pick up a pattern like that, say economists Donald Cox of Boston College and Oded Stark of the University of Vienna, Austria.

Ultimately, understanding how families cope with the aging of their own members may help political leaders tailor realistic responses to the graying of the population. "You can shape policy concerning aging on the basis of your gut feelings and instincts, or you can base it on the best scientific evidence," Juster says. "If HRS helps us do that, it will be worth its weight in gold." **–W.R.**

That estimate fits neatly with the view of biodemographers S. Jay Olshansky of the University of Chicago and Bruce Carnes of Argonne National Laboratory in Illinois, who calculate that human life expectancy has a practical upper limit of about 85 years. They came to this conclusion partly by tallying up the reductions in current mortality rates that would be needed to achieve a life expectancy of, say, 95 or 100 years. What they found is startling: Even eliminating most of the major killers—including cancer, cardiovascular disease, and diabetes—won't do the trick (*Science*, 2 November 1990, p. 634).

Now Olshansky and Carnes have gone a step further, arguing that a biological "law of mortality" determines how many individuals in a species will survive beyond a given age. They did this by following up on the observation, originally made in 1825 by British actuary Benjamin Gompertz, that human death rates roughly double with every decade of life from age 20 to 80. Ever since, biologists and demographers have been unsuccessfully searching the animal king-

dom for equivalent mortality patterns, which might indicate that the orderly thinning of the old is a natural byproduct of evolution. Now Olshansky and Carnes may have finally uncovered such parallels.

They have found that lab mice and beagles that are less exposed to exogenous causes of death, such as infection and predation, tend to die at the rate Gompertz found for humans. "The only species where you can see the common [Gompertzian] pattern are those protected from these 'extrinsic' causes of death, including humans, lab animals, zoo

animals, and pets," Olshansky observes.

Even if Olshansky and Carnes's conservative estimates of human life expectancy are right, the developed nations will have a tough time meeting the costs of supporting the elderly. In 1990, there were 20 net consumers aged 65 and older for every 100 net economic producers—workers aged 18 to 64. By 2050, however, the Social Security and Medicare taxes of each 100 workers will have to support 36 retirees, according to U.S. Census Bureau projections, which assume future life expectancies only a fraction of a year greater than the SSA figures.

But some researchers paint a far more alarming picture—and are marshaling their own data to back it up. "The Social Security Administration would prefer it if the low-cost future were true," says James Vaupel, a mathematical demographer with appointments at Duke University and Odense University in Denmark. "But the result of our research is that there does not appear to be any genetic barrier to a substantially increased life expectancy."

Using government records on

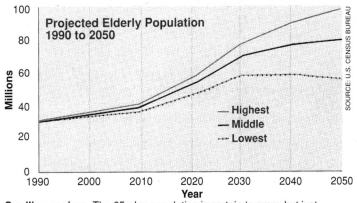

Swelling seniors. The 65-plus population is certain to grow, but just how much depends on assumptions about future life expectancies, fertility rates, and migration.

Japan: Feeling the Strains of an Aging Population

For many researchers and policy-makers trying to figure out how societies will take care of the ever-increasing numbers of the old and very old in their midst, Japan has seemed to provide a glimpse of a future that works. The Japanese currently have the world's longest life expectancy, but the problems of growing old in Japan are eased by a tradition of children taking care of their parents, as well as highly developed pension and health care systems. Yet, beneath the surface, all is not well.

As in most countries the demand for care for the elderly in Japan is far outstripping its availability. Family support structures are breaking down under the strain of wider demographic trends. And pension and health care systems—which provide an average pension for a retired employee of 168,000 yen (about $1600) a month and unlimited outpatient care for people over age 70 for a copayment of ¥1020 (about $10) a month—are already under financial stress. "My preconception was that filial piety would minimize many problems for the elderly," says demographer Linda Martin of the RAND Corp. "But putting such ideals into practice is difficult, even in Japan, when there is rapid aging and social and economic change." Says Keiko Higuchi, a professor of family relations at Tokyo Keizai University, "Elderly-care service is still far less than adequate."

Higuchi, who is also a member of the Council for Health for the Aged, an advisory panel to the health and welfare minister, can speak from personal as well as professional experience. In the mid-1970s, when her mother developed senile dementia, she searched in vain for either a nursing home or home care service and "ended up sending her to a hospital two-and-half hours away from home," Higuchi recalls. Now she is worried about finding care for her husband, who at age 66 has been hospitalized after having a stroke. And Higuchi's plight is far from unusual.

The proportion of people age 65 and older in Japan, now about 14%, is no higher than in Western countries. But according to the

Ministry of Health and Welfare, that percentage is double what it was just 25 years ago. And Japan has more of the "oldest old," who tend to need the most care. Since the mid-1980s, the Japanese life expectancy at birth has been the highest in the world: It is now 76.6 years for males and 83 years for females.

As more and more Japanese enter the ranks of the very old, a declining proportion can count on their children for support. While 55% of the elderly lived with their children in 1994, this number is down from more than 80% in 1957. One reason for the drop is increased mobility of the population. In a 1992 survey by the Management and Coordination Agency, 42% of the elderly living separately from their children cited job-related reasons for the separation. Also, more Japanese women—the traditional caregivers—are working outside the home. In 1960, 22% of women over age 15 were employed, but by 1994, that figure had increased to 38%.

At the same time, the higher life expectancy means a high incidence of disability. Figures compiled by the Ministry of Health and Welfare show that in 1991, nearly half the nation's disabled were over 65, with one of every five people over age 80 needing some kind of care. On top of that, the elderly's children are now elderly. "The situation is that 70-year-old children now look after 90-year-old parents, and they themselves collapse," Higuchi says.

Social services, whether public or private, can't fill the gap left by the decline in family support. The Japanese press reports that some 60,000 elderly people are on waiting lists for the country's 3000 nursing homes, which only take people who are bedridden or have senile dementia. Requests for home care providers, by the Ministry of Health and Welfare's own estimate, also outpaced the supply by 12 to 1 in 1991.

To try to avoid these problems, the government launched a project in 1990 to provide expanded home care and institutional services for the elderly through local governments. "If each

identical twins born in Denmark, for example, Vaupel and his colleagues have found that heredity accounts for only about one-quarter of the variation in human life-spans. "Danish monozygotic [identical] twins die a little bit closer together than dizygotic [fraternal] twins, who die closer together than unrelated individuals," says Vaupel. "But there was no evidence whatsoever that genes operated by fixing the life-span. Rather, they raised or lowered the relative risk of death, by making it more likely that one would get heart disease or Alzheimer's or cancer."

Vaupel and fellow Duke University demographers Kenneth Manton and Eric Stallard further argue that science has repeatedly shown that such diseases are subject to delay, if not prevention. To estimate the impact of such changes on life expectancies, Manton, Stallard, and Yale University epidemiologist Burton Singer have developed a multivariate mathematical model, based on the Gompertz function but including terms that allow for the effects of periodic health advances—such as new drugs or diet and lifestyle modifications—on the risk of death.

They have used the model to calculate, for example, that if the 5209 participants in the well-known Framingham Heart Study, conducted from 1950 to 1984 in Framingham, Massachusetts, had somehow been able to hold their levels of 11 different risk factors—such as blood pressure and serum cholesterol levels—to those of a typical 30-year-old, the men would have survived to an average age of 99.9 years and the women to 97.0 years.

Olshansky counters that the interventions needed to achieve the life expectancies Manton and his colleagues predict are implausible. "The assumptions are that everyone in the U.S. will adopt a perfect lifestyle," Olshansky says. "How realistic is that?"

In response, however, Manton points to recent history. Mortality from heart disease declined 71% between 1958 and 1992, he points out. Further reductions in old-age mortality may be difficult, "but you can't say they are unprecedented," Manton maintains. And while research by Manton, Vaupel, and their collaborators challenges the traditional wisdom about longevity, it's won wide publication and funding, including a $668,000 NIA

grant last year for a multicomponent biodemography project analyzing mortality trends in Denmark, Sweden, and the United States, as well as among laboratory fruit flies.

Realistic or not, the consequences for old-age benefits programs if average life expectancy does approach triple digits are ominous. While SSA's most generous forecasts peg the 65-plus population at 75.5 million in 2040, Manton, Stallard, and Singer's risk-factor-control model produces an estimate of 127.5 million, more than half again as big. How the Social Security and Medicare programs could accommodate an elderly population this large is a question no U.S. political leader has yet dared to broach.

Disagreeing over disabilities

Whether death can be delayed indefinitely or whether longevity researchers come up against a biological brick wall, life expectancy is only one of the important unknowns in the future of the elderly. Unless longer life is accompanied by better health, for example, the years added to people's lives could be both unpleasant and expensive. In 1993, according

municipality accomplishes the elderly-care project plan, every-one who wants nursing services can have them," says Nobukatsu Shinozaki, an official at the Ministry of Health and Welfare. But a Japanese lawyers' group reported last year that 70% of local governments would not be able to fulfill their goals because of the budget strain. "The serious problem is not the aging of the population; it is the lack of substantial measures [to care for the elderly]," says Saburo Nishi, an expert on health and welfare planning at Aichi Mizuho College.

One consequence of the lack of services is that in 1992, 80,000 people, primarily women, were forced to quit their jobs to take care of an elderly relative, according to the Management and Coordination Agency. What's more, the shortage of community care and nursing homes may be part of the reason people age 65 and over average 71 days per hospital stay, compared to 18 days for those between 15 and 34. By some estimates, these "social admissions" cost ¥1 trillion to ¥2 trillion ($10 billion to $20 billion) per year. "This is a big waste of public resources," Nishi says.

And the need for services will continue to grow. By 2025, the number of elderly who need care will increase, from 2 million in 1993 to more than 5 million. This means that the proportion of health care costs going to the elderly, about 30% of Japan's ¥24 trillion ($240 billion) health care budget in 1993, is projected to increase to

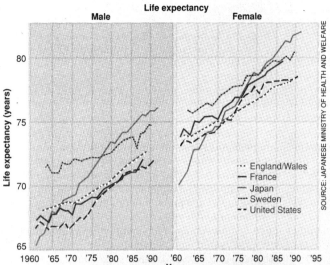

Going up. Life expectancies have been increasing in all the developed countries, but since about 1980 Japan has been leading the pack.

50%. Also, the work force paying into the public employee pension system will outnumber the pensioners by only about 2.4 to 1, compared to 6 to 1 in 1993. As a result, workers' insurance costs for pensions will double, consuming a third of their income.

To reduce the anticipated burden on the pension system, the government plans to raise the pensionable age gradually from 60 to 65. But that could mean trouble for workers, unless the normal retirement age, which is now 60, is also raised to 65.

To pay for the projected demand for elderly services, the Ministry of Health and Welfare, following Germany's lead, has also proposed Care Insurance, a public insurance plan to pay for home care workers and nursing homes. As currently formulated, the costs will be split between the people to be insured and the national and municipal governments. Ministry officials hope to start the system by 2000. However, many analysts argue that, without adequate services for the elderly, workers will be required to pay for "insurance without care." Japan may, indeed, be giving other countries a glimpse of the future, but it is looking less and less like a future that works.

–Sumiko Oshima

Sumiko Oshima is a Knight Science Journalism Fellow at the Massachusetts Institute of Technology.

to the National Health Interview Survey, some 14% of Americans aged 70 and older needed help with routine activities such as household chores and shopping, and 6% needed help eating, bathing, or dressing. In 1990, nearly a quarter of those aged 85 and over lived in nursing homes, a circumstance that can empty the deepest pockets. Nursing-home charges now average $38,000 per year in Florida, for example. How fast the group needing such services can be expected to grow is another area where the experts disagree.

Stanford University physician James Fries, who, in 1980, was one of the first to argue that human life expectancy will peak at about 85, also predicted that the approach to this limit would be accompanied by a "compression of morbidity," or an increase in the proportion of one's lifetime spent free of disease and disability. As more and more "extrinsic" causes of death are eliminated, Fries argued, only deaths due to old age will remain. And indeed, Manton, although he disagrees with Fries's idea that life expectancy will peak at 85, believes he has found evidence of such a compression. Data Manton

analyzed from the National Long-Term Care Survey showed that the proportion of elderly who were chronically disabled or institutionalized decreased from 23.7% to 22.6% over the years 1982 to 1989.

Other researchers, unfortunately, have failed to confirm this promising pattern. USC's Crimmins, for example, says she finds no clear trend in the prevalence of disability in the elderly in either the Longitudinal Study on Aging over the period of 1984 to 1990 or the National Health Interview Survey from 1982 to 1993.

And while some people may indeed be reaping the benefits of a healthier old age, those benefits are by no means equally distributed across the U.S. population, according to Mark Hayward, a demographer at Pennsylvania State University's Population Research Institute. He found, for example, that 20-year-old white non-Hispanic men can expect to live another 54.6 years, with only 14.5% of those years "inactive" ones due to disability. Black 20-year-olds, on the other hand, can expect to live 47.4 years, 18.6% of them inactive, and Native Americans 53.1

years, a whopping 24.8% of them inactive. "We know that longer life means better health for some groups in the population ... but it's more complicated than we heretofore have been thinking about," Hayward says.

Concludes Crimmins, "The U.S. government would like to feel that for its Medicare dollars it's getting a healthy older population. But I think that's the wrong thing to expect. ... Longer life doesn't come without the cost of having more years with diseases unless you prevent people from getting disease."

Family finances

Trimming old-age medical and retirement benefits—or at least capping their rate of growth—is one obvious way to keep health and longevity trends from depleting government coffers. But whether such limitations in public transfers can be put in place without reversing this century's gains against poverty among the elderly hinges largely on the answer to another unresolved question: whether families would help to make up the difference through private transfers.

Analysts who examined this question in

the 1970s, including University of Chicago economist Gary Becker, believed that middle-aged parents' spending on adult children and on their own elderly parents is altruistic, motivated by the donor's perceptions of the recipient's need. As a result, reductions in public transfers to the elderly would be offset to some extent by increases in private transfers. In the eyes of some scholars, including economists Kathleen McGarry of the University of California, Los Angeles, and Robert Schoeni of the RAND Corp., the altruism model has not yet been ruled out. McGarry and Schoeni found that the less well-off an elderly parent, the more likely he or she was to receive a transfer from a middle-aged child. "To some degree," they write, "the middle generation acts like a government entitlement program by buffering elderly parents and adult children against economic hardship."

But other economists, including Boston University's Kotlikoff, have used survey data to test whether, as altruism-based models would predict, well-off family members share their wealth, helping to equalize household consumption throughout an extended family. They don't, Kotlikoff finds: Instead, each household's consumption depends mainly on its own income. "Without Social Security and Medicare, there would be some higher level of private transfers from young to old, but nothing near the magnitude of what we have the government forcing us to do," he says.

Beth Soldo, a demographer at Georgetown University, points out that the magnitude of transfers within families must be considered within a broad demographic context. The baby boomers have fewer children than previous generations to support them when they retire, for example, a trend that will be further exaggerated by the greater labor participation rate of their daughters, she notes: "Unless you model death and disability rates of the coming generation of retirees together with labor supply and other factors, you have an incomplete account of the benefits and burdens accruing to any one generation."

It will be years, Soldo and other researchers say, before demographers, economists, and policy-makers gain much confidence in their answers to all the thorny social and political questions raised by population aging. And in the end, as some of their work indicates, it may be better not to hope for too much longevity too soon. Consider the perspective of Elina Makropulos, who, at the end of Capek's play, chooses death over another 300 years of life. "You cannot go on hoping, creating, gazing at things for 300 years," she admits to Kolenaty. "You fools, how happy you are! And it's simply due to the ridiculous coincidence that you're going to die soon."

–Wade Roush

ROLES FOR AGED INDIVIDUALS IN POST-INDUSTRIAL SOCIETIES

Harold G. Cox

Department of Sociology and Social Work
Indiana State University

ABSTRACT

Cowgill and Holmes in their book *Aging and Modernization* predicted an inverse relationship between industrialization and status accorded older persons. They argued that the more industrialized a country becomes the lower the status accorded older persons. A more careful examination of historical and anthropological work suggests that if we look at the status of the old over the course of history and make projections into the future an S curve is a more realistic pattern. The pattern projected would be one in which the old were accorded a low status in early nomadic tribes, a high status in settled agricultural communities, a low status in industrialized society and ultimately will receive a somewhat higher status in the post-industrial period.

Historically we find a wide variety of patterns of treatment of the aged in different societies. Fischer traced the statements of Herodotus which indicated that at one extreme were the Issedones who gilded the heads of their aged parents and offered sacrifices before them [1]. They seemed to worship their oldest tribal members. At the opposite extreme were the Bactria who disposed of their old folk by feeding them to dogs. Similarly, the Sardinians hurled their elders from a high cliff and shouted with laughter when they fell on the rocks. In traditional China the old men were granted a privileged position. In politics and in family the aged men occupied the top positions of power in a hierarchical society that lasted for thousands of years. This was a value of the prevalent Confucian ideology. Thus we can find diverse patterns of how the aged were treated in different societies and in different historical eras.

An attempt will be made in this article to trace the changing status of aged individuals in different historical periods and to make some educated guesses about what roles aged persons will occupy in post-industrial society.

CRITICAL VARIABLES DETERMINING THE STATUS OF THE AGED

There are a number of variables, often interrelated, which either separately or in combination seem to relate to the status accorded older persons in various cultures. These include: family form, religion, knowledge base of the culture, harshness of the environment, the means of production, and the speed of social changes.

In the consideration of cultural type and status of the aged person, the general rule has been that in the nonindustrial, settled, agricultural societies aged individuals exercise considerable power and are granted a high status. In industrial societies, on the other hand, aged individuals exercise relatively little power and are granted less status. Cowgill and Holmes, in their work on aging and modernization, found an inverse relationship between the degree of modernization and the status accorded old persons [2]. In other words, the more industrialized the system became, the lower the status of the older person. While this is generally the case, a closer look reveals differential treatment of the elders even in the traditional societies. Sheehan, in a study of forty-seven traditional societies, found three different patterns of treatment of aged individuals [3]. Approximately one-fifth of the traditional societies were geographically unstable, as semipermanent bands of people periodically relocating their villages or, in some cases, perpetually mobile. The lowest esteem for seniors was often found in these small and nomadic societies. They have the fewest material resources for seniors to accumulate, thereby gaining respect in the eyes of the youngest person; they are usually located in harsh environments which favor youth and vigor. Food is often in short supply and individual existence is precarious. Elderly individuals may have to be sacrificed to insure the survival of the entire group. Among the societies studied, a plurality were comprised of various forms of tribes which were basically permanently settled, inhabiting fairly large villages, and governed according to a belief in their common ancestry or kinship. Another group of the traditional societies was comprised of small peasant communities whose economic base centered around agriculture or animal husbandry. The most highly developed social organizations were the ones with large landed peasantries; there, the highest esteem was enjoyed by older persons.

It appears that once traditional societies become located in a permanent place with stated residence and property rights, the old began to exercise considerable power over the young by the ownership of the property and the ability to pass it on to their children. Fisher pointed out that [1, p. 6]:

Nearly to our time, the story goes, western society remained nonliterate in its culture, agrarian in its economy, extended in its family structure, and rural in its residence. The old were few in number, but their authority was very great. Within the extended family the aged monopolized power: within our agrarian economy they controlled the land. A traditional culture surrounded them with an almost magical mystique of knowledge and authority.

Where property is the only means of production, by controlling property aged individuals are able to control younger generations. The future occupations and chances for success of the younger generation are tied to seeking the favor of their elders, who control all the resources. While one's parents are alive they are of critical importance because they provide employment and means of survival in the form of resources. After they die, the heirs inherit shares of their lands and control of these resources for themselves and their children. Therefore, in traditional societies that are permanently located, the individual is directly dependent upon his own senior generation for the acquisition of the means of production. The anticipated transfer of the property at the death of the parent provides the children with an incentive that encourages respect for their older family members. It is easy to see why the young defer to their elders and attempt to seek their special favor. Similarly, it is easy to understand how the old, by the development of stable institutions and the control of property, are able to maintain their power and privilege in the social system. This may also explain the higher value placed on the family in rural America where the transmission of land to the next generation may secure that generation a livelihood and a secure position in the social structure.

Thus, rather than Cowgill and Holmes's prediction of an inverse relationship between the degree of modernization and the status accorded old persons [2], we find a curvilinear one in which the old are accorded a low status in simple nomadic societies, a high status in settled agricultural communities, and a low status in modern industrial nations.

Sheehan equates what happens to older persons in the nomadic tribes to what happens to them in modern industrial societies [3]. Sheehan believes that with the development of modern technology, social and geographic mobility become goals and individual autonomy reemerges as a primary value. The young forfeit the security of the village or family to work in factories and offices. They attain financial and social separation from many traditional restraints. Lifestyles turn away from extended family ties. There is no special reason for younger family members to secure the favor of their parents and grandparents. The older family members lose their status, decision-making power, and the security they once had in earlier cultural settings. The result is that the old are considered much less valuable in modern contemporary states. In both the simple nomadic and modern industrial societies the old quickly become dependent on the young for their well-being and survival.

The form of the family is often related to the kind of culture and structural relations among institutions in a particular society. In traditional societies that are primarily agricultural in nature, the extended form of the family (most often comprised of mother, father, their sons and their wives and children) is the prevalent one. The extended family is most often patriarchical, which means that power and lineage are traced through the males of the family. The wife, upon marriage, moves in with the husband's family. When their children are old enough to marry, the parents arrange for their marriages; expect the wives of their sons to move into their household and their daughters to move into the households of their husbands. This family arrangement is one in which the oldest male member of the family exercises the greatest power, privilege, and authority. Individualism is discouraged. The individual is always subservient to the demands of the group. The concept of romantic love (strong, intense emotional attachment between members of the opposite sex) is nonexistent. The criterion for the success of the marriage is the amount of family disruption caused by the entrance of the new bride. If she gets along well with her in-laws and does not cause difficulty it is considered a good marriage. The son's happiness is secondary to the good of the group. The extended family works best in stable cultures which are primarily agriculturally based. This culture is one in which the older members exercise the greatest power and maintain the highest status.

Industrialization leads to the breakup of the extended family. One no longer depends upon land as the principle means of production. New jobs, careers, resources, and opportunities become available. Modern industry requires mobile labor which can be moved from place to place as needed. Extended family ties are broken in order to move the labor force where it is most needed; if not, the industrial system itself would break down. The nuclear family—husband, wife, children—is dominant. The influence of the father and mother over adult children is weakened. The size of the family declines as children become units of consumption rather than production and thereby become less desirable.

The difference between extended and nuclear families for the status of the aged persons can best be seen in Israel. Weihl observed that the older people among the migrants from the Orient are given a relatively high status in comparison to the relatively low status accorded older immigrants from the Western countries [4]. The migrants from the Orient evidence considerable commitment to the extended family concept in contrast with the commitment to nuclear family evidenced by migrants from the West.

The religions of the Far East have generally supported the extended family and higher status of elder members by the moral and ethical codes that they espouse. The Confucian concept is one in which the aged are to be given tender loving care. They are to be exempt from certain responsibilities when they reach old age. Pre-World War II families in China and Japan were ones in which children cared for their elders, and older family members exercised the most authority. This meant also that the elders were the most respected members of the family.

While Christianity clearly admonishes the individual to honor his father and mother, this religious principle has probably had less impact in the Western world than one might expect. The pressure of industrialization results in the educational functions being gradually removed from the family socialization process to formal training outside the home. The nature of wealth changes from land to tangible property. The emphasis shifts to productivity. The young are always seen as more productive and the old as less productive. Degradation generally occurs for the older, and supposedly slower, workers.

Another aspect of modern industrial society is the location of knowledge. In traditional agricultural societies, the old are the reservoirs of knowledge—of past problems and their solutions, of old customs and the appropriate religious rituals. In industrial societies, books, libraries, universities, and current research enterprises are a base for the generation and transmittal of knowledge. The freshly trained college student is often more valuable in the business and industrial world than the older and more experienced employee whose knowledge and expertise may have become obsolete. The inability to maintain control of critical knowledge in modern society has been another factor that has contributed to the general loss of status of older persons.

American society has a well-developed and sophisticated educational system which prepares young people to enter an occupation, but it is ill equipped to retrain older workers when new technologies require additional schooling.

The harshness of the environment in which the culture is found and the amount of physical labor required for survival are also factors that can reduce the usefulness and thereby the status of the older members of a culture.

Holmberg noted that among the Sirono of the Bolivian rain forest, it is the general belief that [5, pp. 224–225]:

> Actually the aged are quite a burden; they eat but are unable to hunt, fish or collect food; they sometimes hoard a young spouse, but are unable to beget children; they move at a snail's pace and hinder the mobility of the group. When a person becomes too ill or infirm to follow the fortunes of the band, he is abandoned to shift for himself.

Cowgill and Holmes noted that there is some difficulty in adjusting to reduced activity in old age when a society is so strongly dedicated to hard physical labor [2]. Kibbutz society in Israel is one example; there, older persons may arrive at an ambiguous status because of their inability to physically keep up with younger counterparts.

Related to the changing knowledge base in modern society is the speed with which social change occurs within the system. Cowgill and Holmes believe that rapid social change in modern societies tends to undermine the status of older persons [2]. Change renders many of the skills of older Americans obsolete. Not only can they no longer ply their trade, there is also no reason for them to teach it to others. In a rapidly changing society younger people are nearly always better educated and possess more knowledge of recent technology than their elders; thus, the latter lose their utility and the basis of their authority.

Referring to both the speed of social change in modern society and the location of the knowledge base in the system, Watson and Maxwell hypothesized that societies can be arranged along a continuum whose basis is the amount of useful information controlled by the aged individuals [6]. They believe the greater the elders are in control of critical information, the greater is their participation in community affairs. Their participation is, in turn, directly related to the degree of esteem in which they are held by other members of the community. Watson and Maxwell believe this control of information and consequent social participation declines with industrialization and its rapid sociocultural change [6, pp. 26–29].

Watson and Maxwell argued that one of the most fruitful models developed for the investigation of human societies has relied heavily on the information storage and exchange model and is described as systems theory [6]. Goffman has demonstrated that groups which share secret information will tend to be more integrated and unified than those which do not [7]. All stored information, according to Goffman, involves a stated arrangement of elements in the sense that they are a record of past events [7, p. 70].

In traditional societies, one of the main functions of old people is to remember legends, myths, ethical principles, and the appropriate relations that should be arranged with the supernatural, and they are frequently asked about these matters.

Elliott described this pattern among the Aleuts in northern Russia [8, pp. 170-171]:

> Before the advent of Russian priests, every village had one or two old men at least, who considered it their special business to educate the children, thereupon, in the morning or evening when all were home these aged teachers would seat themselves in the center of one of the largest village courts or oolagumuh; the young folks surrounded them and listened attentively to what they said.

Watson and Maxwell believe that the printing press was to end this kind of arrangement in the social system [6, p. 20]. In industrialized societies the information that is important is written down, printed, and sold in bookstores.

Some historians have argued that economically, politically, and socially older people are more conservative than younger people and tend to have a stabilizing effect on any social system. The young, being much more changeable in their view, offer adaptability and in some ways may increase the changes for survival in the social system.

One final factor which may in some way explain the declining status of aged individuals in modern industrial countries is the relative proportion of the entire population that they comprise. In most of the ancient and traditional societies they comprised less than 3 percent of the total population. It is easy to reserve a special status for a group of people that comprise a very small percent of the total. In modern society the old have come to comprise between 8 to 15 percent of the total population. Cox observed that it may become increasingly difficult to preserve privileged status for a group that comprises such a large percentage of a total population [9]. Cowgill's book, *Aging Around the World* indicates how rapidly the older age populations are now expanding in even the underdeveloped countries [10]. This is a phenomenon that neither the anthropologists nor the gerontologists had earlier anticipated.

ROLES FOR THE ELDERLY IN POST-INDUSTRIAL SOCIETY

While historically we find a curvilinear relationship with the old being accorded a low status in nomadic tribes, a high status in settled agricultural communities and a low status in modern industrial societies one wonders what roles and status older persons will be granted in post-industrial society. An educated guess would be that there will be a wider variety of roles to choose from and a slight upturn in the status of older persons in post-industrial society. Thus the pattern would be one of an S curve in which the status of the older adults improves following the low that was experienced by them during the industrial period.

Everett Hughes, Daniel Bell, and other social scientists have speculated on what life will be like in post-industrial society [11, 12]. The consensus of the social scientists seems to be that the post-industrial period will see a shift away from expansion in manufacturing and industry to the expansion of social services, entertainment, athletics, recreation and leisure enterprises. The basic argument of the scientists is that as the industrial development of a nation peaks and as an ever efficient manufacturing technology emerges, less of the population will be required to produce the nation's goods. This will make a surplus of manpower available which will ultimately be employed by the expanding service occupations, the entertainment industry, and industries catering to recreation and leisure activities. The post-industrial period will also bring reduced working hours, the advent of a four-day work week which will result in larger amounts of free time for the average citizen. For both the younger and the older members of the society this will mean greater opportunity for entertainment, athletic events, recreation, and leisure pursuits as well as opportunity for education and cultural enrichment. The Protestant ethic which admonished the person to be totally committed to the work role and view recreation and leisure roles as at best a waste of one's time and at worst as sinful will undoubtedly be altered. Recreation, leisure, education and a variety of other emerging roles will be seen as legitimate means of enriching the quality of one's life. They should do two things for the older members of society; first, it will provide a wide range of nonwork roles in which they may choose to participate; and second, these roles will be more highly valued and provide them with a higher status and more respected position in society.

Older persons upon retirement will be deciding whether or not to invest greater time and energy in family roles, recreation and leisure roles, volunteer roles, educational roles, political roles, or perhaps a second career. Post-industrial society will undoubtedly offer a wider range of roles for the elderly to choose whether they will or will not participate.

In all probability they will not have had this much freedom to choose among the different roles they wish to enter at any other time in their lives. Moreover, changing values in post-industrial society will include less emphasis on the importance of productivity and greater emphasis on the quality of life. Volunteer and leisure roles will be more highly valued, giving older persons who occupy them greater respect. In short it would seem that older persons will have a wide variety of roles to choose from in their retirement years and that these roles will bring them greater status than retirees have been accorded in the past.

REFERENCES

1. D. H. Fischer, *Growing Old in America*, Oxford University Press, New York, 1978.

2. D. O. Cowgill and L. D. Holmes, *Aging and Modernization*, Appleton Century Crofts, New York, 1972.

3. T. Sheehan, Senior Esteem as a Factor of Socioeconomic Complexity, *The Gerontologist, 16:5*, pp. 433–444, 1976.

4. H. Weihl, Aging in Israel, in *Aging in Contemporary Society*, E. Shanas (ed.), Sage Publications, Inc., Beverly Hills, California, pp. 107–117, 1970.

5. A. R. Holmberg, *Nomads of the Long Bow*, Natural History Press, Garden City, New York, pp. 224–225, 1969.

6. W. H. Watson and R. T. Maxwell, *Human Aging and Dying: A Study in Sociocultural Gerontology*, St. Martin's Press, New York, pp. 2–32, 1977.

7. E. Goffman, *The Presentation of Self in Everyday Life*, Doubleday, Garden City, New York, 1959.

8. H. W. Elliott, *Our Arctic Province: Alaska and the Sea Islands*, Scribner's, New York, pp. 170–171, 1887.

9. H. Cox, *Later Life: The Realities of Aging*, Prentice-Hall, Inc., Englewood Cliffs, New Jersey, 1988.

10. D. O. Cowgill, *Aging Around the World*, Wadsworth Publishing Company, Belmont, California, 1986.

11. E. Hughes, *Men and Their Work*, Free Press, New York, 1964.

12. D. Bell, *The Coming of Post Industrial Society*, Basic Books, New York, 1973.

The Age Boom

America discovers a new stage of life as many more people live much longer— and better. By Jack Rosenthal

When my father died at 67, leaving my mother alone in Portland, Ore., I thought almost automatically that she should come home with me to New York. Considering her heavy Lithuanian accent and how she shrank from dealing with authority, I thought she'd surely need help getting along. "Are you kidding?" she exclaimed. Managing her affairs became her work and her pride, and it soon occurred to me that this was the first time that she, traditional wife, had ever experienced autonomy. Every few days she would make her rounds to the bank, the doctor, the class in calligraphy. Then, in her personal brand of English, she would make her telephone rounds. She would complain that waiting for her pension check was "like sitting on pins and noodles" or entreat her granddaughter to stop spending money "like a drunken driver." Proudly, stubbornly, she managed on her own for 18 years. And even then, at 83, frustrated by strokes and angry at the very the thought of a nursing home, she refused to eat. In days, she made herself die.

Reflecting on those last days, I realize that the striking thing was not her death but those 18 years of later life. For almost all that time, she had the health and the modest income to live on her own terms. She could travel if she chose, or send birthday checks to family members, or buy yet another pair of shoes. A woman who had been swept by the waves of two world wars from continent to continent to continent — who had experienced some of this century's worst aspects — came finally to typify one of its best. I began to understand what people around America are coming to understand: the transformation of old age. We are discovering the emergence of a new stage of life.

The transformation begins with longer life. Increased longevity is one of the striking developments of the century; it has grown more in the last 100 years than in the prior 5,000, since the Bronze Age. But it's easy to misconstrue. What's new is not the number of years people live; it's the number of people who live them. Science hasn't lengthened life, says Dr. Robert Butler, a pioneering authority on aging. It has enabled many more people to reach very old age. And at this moment in history, even to say "many more people" is an understatement. The baby boom generation is about to turn into an age boom.

Still, there's an even larger story rumbling here, and longevity and boomers tell only part of it. The enduring anguish of many elders lays continuing claim on our conscience. But as my mother's last 18 years attest, older adults are not only living longer; generally speaking, they're living better — in reasonably good health and with enough money to escape the anxiety and poverty long associated with aging.

Shakespeare perceived seven ages of man — mewling infant, whining schoolboy, sighing lover, quarrelsome soldier, bearded justice, spectacled wheezer and finally second childhood, "sans teeth, sans eyes, sans taste, sans everything." This special issue of the Magazine examines the emerging new stage, a warm autumn that's already altering the climate of life for millions of older adults, for their children, indeed for all society.

Longer Life

In 1900, life expectancy at birth in America was 49. Today, it is 76, and people who have reached 55 can expect to live into their 80's. Improved nutrition and modern medical miracles sound like obvious explanations. But a noted demographer, Samuel Preston of the University of Pennsylvania, has just published a paper in which he contends that, at least until mid-century, the principal reason was neither. It was what he calls the "germ theory of disease" that generated personal health reforms like washing hands, protecting food from flies, isolating sick children, boiling bottles and milk and ventilating rooms. Since 1950, he argues likewise, the continuing longevity gains derive less from Big Medicine than from changes in personal behavior, like stopping smoking.

Jack Rosenthal is the editor of The New York Times Magazine.

> I go out and play 18 holes in the morning and then three sets in the afternoon.
> **Bob Cousy, 68**
> Sports Commentator

I still thrive on competition, and when I feel those competitive juices flowing, I've got to find an outlet. Of course, at 68, it's not going to be playing basketball. Basketball's not a sport you grow old with. Sure, I can manage a few from the free-throw line, but being in shape for basketball's something you lose three months after you retire. I stay in shape by doing as little as possible. I play mediocre golf and terrible tennis. My wife calls it my doubleheader days, when I go out and play 18 holes in the morning and then three sets in the afternoon. Now I'm working in broadcasting and schmoozing the corporates. I'm a commentator for the Celtics' away games. I like it because I'm controlling my own destiny. Everything I've done since I graduated from Holy Cross in 1950 has been sports-related, and it's all because I learned to throw a little ball into a hole. A playground director taught me how to play when I was 13. To me it'll always be child's game.

The rapid increase in longevity is now about to be magnified. The baby boom generation born between 1946 and 1964 has always bulged out — population peristalsis — like a pig in a python. Twice as many Americans were born in 1955 as in 1935. Between now and the year 2030, the proportion of people over 65 will almost double. In short, more old people. And there's a parallel fact now starting to reverberate around the world: fewer young people. An aging population inescapably results when younger couples bear fewer children — which is what they are doing almost everywhere.

The fertility news is particularly striking in developed countries. To maintain a stable population size, the necessary replacement rate is 2.1 children per couple. The United States figure is barely 2.0, and it has been below the replacement rate for 30 years. The figure in China is 1.8. Couples in Japan are typically having 1.5 children, in Germany 1.3 and in Italy and Spain, 1.2.

To some people, these are alarming portents of national decline and call for pro-natalist policies. That smacks of coarse chauvinism. The challenge is not to dilute the number of older people by promoting more births. It is to improve the quality of life at all ages, and a good place to start is to conquer misconceptions about later life.

Better Health

"This," Gloria Steinem once said famously, "is what 40 looks like." And this, many older adults now say, is what 60, 70 and even 80 look like. Health and vitality are constantly improving, as a result of more exercise, better medicine and much better prevention. I can't imagine my late father in a sweatsuit, let alone on a Stairmaster, but when I look into the mirrored halls of a health-club gym on upper Broadway I see, among the intent young women in black leotards, white-haired men who are every bit as earnest, climbing, climbing, climbing.

Consider the glow that radiates from the faces on today's cover, or contemplate the standards maintained by people like Bob Cousy, Max Roach, Ruth Bernhard and others who speak out in the following pages.

That people are living healthier lives is evident from the work of Kenneth G. Manton and his colleagues at Duke's Center for Demographic Studies. The National Long-Term Care Survey they started in 1982 shows a steady decline in disability, a 15 percent drop in 12 years. Some of this progress derives from advances in medicine. For instance, estrogen supplements substantially relieve bone weakness in older women — and now seem effective also against

strength of the quadriceps, the major thigh muscle. For many, that meant they could walk, or walk without shuffling; the implications for reduced falls are obvious. Consider what this single change — enabling many, for instance, to go to the bathroom alone — means to the quality and dignity of their lives.

Just as old does not necessarily mean feeble, older does not necessarily mean sicker. Harry Moody, executive director of Hunter College's Brookdale Center on Aging, makes a telling distinction between the "wellderly" and the "illderly." Yes, one of every three people over 65 needs some kind of hospital care in any given year. But only one in 20 needs nursing-home care at any given time. That is, 95 percent of people over 65 continue to live in the community.

Greater Security

The very words "poor" and "old" glide easily together, just as "poverty" and "age" have kept sad company through history. But suddenly

---

After 10 weeks of leg-extension exercises, the participants, some as old as 98, typically doubled the strength of the quadriceps, the major thigh muscle. For many, that meant they could walk. Consider what this single change—the ability among other things to go to the bathroom alone—means to the quality and dignity of their lives.

---

other diseases. But much of the progress may also derive from advances in perception.

When Clare Friedman, the mother of a New York lawyer, observed her 80th birthday, she said to her son, "You know, Steve, I'm not middle-aged anymore." It's no joke. Manton recalls survey research in which people over 50 are asked when old age begins. Typically, they, too, say "80." Traditionally, spirited older adults have been urged to act their age. But what age is that in this era of 80-year-old marathoners and 90-year-old ice skaters? As Manton says, "We no longer need to accept loss of physical function as an inevitable consequence of aging." To act younger is, in a very real sense, to be younger.

Stirring evidence of that comes from a 1994 research project in which high-resistance strength training was given to 100 frail nursing-home residents in Boston, median age 87 and some as old as 98. Dr. Maria Fiatarone of Tufts University and her fellow researchers found that after 10 weeks of leg-extension exercises, participants typically doubled the

that's changing. In the mid-1960's, when Medicare began, the poverty rate among elders was 29 percent, nearly three times the rate of the rest of the population. Now it is 11 percent, if anything a little below the rate for everyone else. That still leaves five million old people struggling below the poverty line, many of them women. And not many of the other 30 million elders are free of anxiety or free to indulge themselves in luxury. Yet most are, literally, socially secure, able to taste pleasures like travel and education that they may have denied themselves during decades of work. Indeed, many find this to be the time of their lives.

Elderhostel offers a striking illustration. This program, begun in 1975, combines inexpensive travel with courses in an array of subjects and cultures. It started as a summer program with 220 participants at six New Hampshire colleges. Last year, it enrolled 323,000 participants at sites in every state and in 70 foreign countries. Older Americans already exercise formidable electoral force, given how many of them vote. With the age boom bearing down, that influence is growing. As a result, minutemen like the investment banker Peter G. Peterson are sounding alarms about the impending explosion in Social Security and Medicare costs. Others regard such alarms as merely alarmist; either way a result is a spirited public debate, joined by Max Frankel in his column on page 30 and by the economist Paul Krugman in his appraisal of the future of Medicare and medical costs on page 58.

Politicians respect the electoral power of the senior vote; why is the economic power of older adults not understood? Television networks and advertisers remain oddly blind to this market, says Vicki Thomas of Thomas & Partners, a Westport, Conn., firm specializing in the "mature market." One reason is probably the youth of copywriters and media buyers. Another is advertisers' desire to identify with imagery that is young, hip, cool. Yet she cites a stream of survey data showing that householders 45 and over buy half of all new cars and trucks, that those 55 and over buy almost a third of the total and that people over 50 take 163 million trips a year and a third of all overseas packaged tours.

How much silver there is in this "silver market" is Jerry Della Femina's subject, on page 74. It is also evident from Modern Maturity magazine, published by the American Association of Retired Persons. Its bimonthly circulation is more than 20 million; a full-page ad costs $244,000.

Sure, someone's probably saying: 'Oh, my God! What's this old bag doing in that suit?'
Ann Cole
Age: "Between 59 and Forest Lawn"
Swimsuit Designer

Everyone has certain features that they hate, and that doesn't change much as you get older—it just gets closer to the ground, as Gypsy Rose Lee once said. So you do just grin and bear it, unless you want to sit indoors and grump about it. I get a lot of women who come in and say, "You wouldn't wear that." And I say, "Why, yes I would." I haven't become more comfortable with my body. I've just taken an attitude that it's easier not to care or worry. Just do it. Sure, someone's probably saying: "Oh, my God! What's this old bag doing in that suit?" I've always been a great advocate of people not listening to their children. There used to be a lot of children who weren't happy unless their mother wore a skirted suit down to her knees. They'd say. "Oh, Mom, you can't wear that." I tried to get people over that in the 60's and 70's, because what do they know? You can't be worried about every bump and lump.

All this spending by older adults may not please everyone. Andrew Hacker, the Queens College political scientist, observes that the longer the parents live, the less they're likely to leave to the children — and the longer the wait. He reports spotting a bumper sticker to that effect, on a passing Winnebago: "I'm Spending My Kids' Inheritance!" Even so, the net effect of generational income transfers remains highly favorable to the next generation. For one thing, every dollar the public spends to support older adults is a dollar that their children won't be called on to spend. For another, older adults sooner or later engage in some pretty sizable income transfers of their own. As Hacker observes, the baby boomers' children may have to wait for their legacies, but their ultimate inheritances will constitute the largest income transfer to any generation ever.

Longer years, better health, comparative security: this new stage of life emerges more clearly every day. What's less clear is how older adults will spend it. The other stages of life are bounded by expectations and institutions. We start life in the institution called family. That's soon augmented for 15 or 20 years by school, tightly organized by age, subject and social webs. Then follows the still-more-structured world of work, for 40 or 50 years. And then — fanfare! — what? What institutions then give shape and meaning to everyday life?

Some people are satisfied, as my mother was, by managing their finances, by tending to family relationships and by prayer, worship and hobbies. Others, more restless, will invent new institutions, just as they did in Cleveland in the 1950's with Golden Age Clubs, or in the 1970's with Elderhostel. For the moment, the institutions that figure most heavily for older adults are precisely those that govern the other stages of life — family, school and work.

FAMILY: The focus on family often arises out of necessity. In a world of divorce and working parents, grandparents are raising 3.4 million children; six million families depend on grandparents for primary child care. And that's only one of the intensified relationships arising among the generations. Children have many more years to relate to their parents as adults, as equals, as friends — a fact demonstrated firsthand by the Kotlowitz-to-Kotlowitz letters on page 46.

SCHOOL: Increasingly, many elders go back to school, to get the education they've always longed for, or to learn new skills — or for the sheer joy of learning. Nearly half a million people over 50 have gone back to school at the college level, giving a senior cast to junior colleges;

adults over age 40 now account for about 15 percent of all college students. The 92d Street Y in New York has sponsored activities for seniors since 1874. Suddenly, it finds, many "New Age seniors" want to do more than play cards or float in the pool. They are signing up by the score for classes on, for instance, Greece and Rome. At a senior center in Westport, Conn., older adults, far from being averse to technology, flock to computer classes and find satisfaction in managing their finances on line and traversing the Internet.

WORK: American attitudes toward retirement have never been simple. The justifications include a humane belief that retirees have earned their rest; or a bottom-line argument that employers need cheaper workers; or a theoretical contention that a healthy economy needs to make room for younger workers. In any case, scholars find a notable trend toward early retirement, arguably in response to pension and Social Security incentives. Two out of three men on Social Security retire before age 65. One explanation is that they are likely to have spent their lives on a boring assembly line or in debilitating service jobs. Others, typically from more fulfilling professional work, retire gradually, continuing to work part time or to find engagement in serious volunteer effort. In Florida, many schools, hospitals and local governments have come to depend on elders who volunteer their skills and time.

FAMILY, SCHOOL, WORK — AND INSTITUTIONS yet to come: these are the framework for the evolving new stage of later life. But even if happy and healthy, it only precedes and does not replace the last of Shakespeare's age of mankind. One need not be 80 or 90 to understand that there comes a time to be tired, or sick, or caught up by the deeply rooted desire to reflect on the meaning of one's life. For many people, there comes a moment when the proud desire for independence turns into frank, mutual acknowledgment of dependence. As the Boston University sociologist Alan Wolfe wrote in The New Republic in 1995, "We owe [our elders] the courage to acknowledge their dependence on us. Only then will we be able, when we are like them, to ask for help."

That time will come, as it always has, for each of us — as children and then as parents. But it will come later. The new challenge is to explore the broad terrain of longer, fuller life with intelligence and respect. One such explorer, a woman named Florida Scott-Maxwell, reported her findings in "The Measure of My Days," a diary she began in her 80's. "Age puzzles me," she wrote, expressing sentiments that my mother personified. "I thought it was a quiet time. My 70's were interesting and fairly serene, but my 80's are passionate. I grow more intense as I age. To my surprise I burst out with hot conviction. ... I must calm down."

MEN AND WOMEN AGING DIFFERENTLY

Barbara M. Barer

University of California, San Francisco

ABSTRACT

Gender differences in health, socio-economic status, and social resources persist into advanced old age and result in variations in life trajectories and responses to the challenges of longevity. The implications of these differences are examined in a sample of 150 community-dwelling white men and women. The majority are women, a high proportion of whom are unmarried, living alone, functionally impaired, and have reduced financial resources. Men, in contrast, have fewer decrements, they are more independent, and they exercise more control over their environment. However, their well-being may be undermined by some unanticipated events such as widowhood, caregiving, and relocation. Case examples illustrate how the timing of life course events differs among men and women and results in differences in the problems they face in late-late life.

At the turn of the century, when the average life expectancy in the United States was forty-nine years of age, only 5 percent of white men and 7 percent of white women could expect to survive to eighty-five years old. Now life expectancy has increased to seventy-six years, with 18 percent of white men and 38 percent of white women projected to live to eighty-five years [1]. One striking change in the older population is the widening gender gap, as proportionately more women than men live longer. Among the population age sixty-five to sixty-nine there are eighty-one men for every 100 women, but the gender ratio drops to thirty-nine men for every 100 women over the age of eighty-five [2]. Today in our country, there are 841,000 men and 2.2 million women of that age or older [3].

This article will explore the implications of gender differences in the lives of men and women in advanced old age. Based on data from our initial sample of 150 white respondents, men and women will first be compared on their demographic characteristics, physical status, and social networks. Second, men and women will be compared by how they manage their daily activities and adapt to the typical problems encountered in advanced old age. Then case examples will illustrate how gender-specific events lead to differing responses among the oldest-old. These case studies will illustrate how such events as widowhood, caregiving, and relocation are timed at different periods over the life course, so that men and women face quite different kinds of problems in late-late life.

BACKGROUND

The New York Times [4] recently reported that the prospects for elderly men are brighter than those for elderly women. Men who survive beyond the age of eighty-five are more likely than women to be in better health and to have more remaining years of independent life. While men are prone to acute and fatal diseases, women are subject to the disabling effects of chronic conditions [3]. National surveys also find that more men than women, aged eighty-five and over, are still married, 48.7 percent of white men in comparison to only 10.3 percent of white women [1]. The tendency of women to marry men older than themselves compounds the likelihood of their being widowed at a younger age. As a consequence, more women live alone in late-late life, two-thirds compared to one-third of men [1].

A further disadvantage for women in this age group is their relatively poor economic status. Twenty-three percent of women aged eighty-five and over live at the poverty level, compared to 16 percent of men [5]. This cohort of women either did not work outside the home or had discontinuous work patterns that excluded them from pensions and related benefits in old age. Hence the nation's oldest and fastest growing population today is dominated by a disproportionately large number of unmarried women who not only suffer from increased functional impairment but also are most likely to live alone and to have economic problems.

While very old women are more impaired than men, they may be better equipped to handle the physical and social losses usually encountered with longevity. Some researchers [6, 7] suggest that widows are better able than widowers to develop and sustain intimate relationships. They tend to form confidante relationships with other widowed women, whereas widowed men, who had relied on their wives for their emotional needs, are left with no one [8, 9]. Moreover there is a great difference in the meaning of friendship to men and women. Women place more importance on friendships and engage in trusted relationships, while men usually have more superficial, less emotionally close relationships [10]. Furthermore when a man is widowed, other men his age are most likely to still be married [11].

Gender differences over the life course also influence the daily lives of the very old. For example, women of this cohort were encouraged to be more passive and family oriented, an orientation that, along with unchanging domestic roles, results in continuities in late-late life [10]. In contrast, male roles throughout life place a premium on competency, activity, productivity, independence, and self-reliance, all characteristics that are difficult to sustain with the increased disability that occurs in late-late life [12]. As a consequence, very old men and women are likely to differ not only in how they manage their daily routine, but also how they adapt to continuities and discontinuities.

Help seeking behavior also varies by gender and is predictable among the oldest-old. Women are usually more willing to acknowledge their need for assistance and to seek or accept help from others [12]. Since men do not like to see themselves as dependent, they may actually accept less formal support than they need [13]. Therefore, as men's needs increase with age, current gender norms may inhibit their adaptation. These variations suggest that men and women who survive into advanced old age have quite different demands placed upon them as well as varied resources and competencies.

SAMPLE CHARACTERISTICS BY GENDER

The mean age of the sample is 88.1 for men and 89.2 for women (Table 1). Consistent with national surveys, one-half of the men in the *85+ Study* are currently married, in comparison to only 10 percent of the women. Household composition also replicates national data, with less than one-half of the men living alone in contrast to two-thirds of the women. Economically, most women report less financial security than men. Men's income tends to be more substantial since more of them receive a pension in addition to social security.

Men are further advantaged in their health status, with over one-fourth perceiving their health to be excellent. They have significantly fewer problems with functional limitations and are less restricted in their mobility. Significantly more women than men have some impairment in their basic activities involving personal care (ADL), and the difference is even greater for the activities of daily living (IADL).

Table 1. A Profile of the White Oldest Old by Gender (Percentages (n + 150))

	Women n = 111 (73%)	Men n = 39 (27%)
Demographic Profile		
Mean age	89.2	88.1
Married	10	49
Living alone	62	46
Economic Status		
Income from pension	38	53
Income from social security	90	100
Income from SSI	9	3
Income from savings	75	85
Income from work	5	11
Income Adequacy		
Good	52	74**
Fair	42	23
Poor	6	3
Perceived Health Status		
Excellent	14	28*
Good	56	51
Fair	24	21
Poor	6	—
Activity Restriction		
None	28	47*
Some	41	23
A great deal	31	18
ADL		
No impairment	69	92*
Impaired 1–3 tasks	22	3
Impaired 4+ tasks	9	5
IADL		
No impairment	18	64***
Impaired 1–3 tasks	12	23
Impaired 4+ tasks	70	13

*p < .05
**p < .01
***p < .001

In contrast to men's advantages physically and economically, women have more extensive social networks (Table 2). While similar numbers have a child in proximity, twice as many women receive some instrumental support from children. Both men and women enjoy expressive or emotional support from children. Forty-seven percent of the women, but only 11 percent of the men had a child functioning as a caregiver. These significant differences could be related to women's greater needs, or to the fact that more men still have a spouse and do not have to turn to children for help [14].

Not only do women receive more support from children, but they also maintain more contact with them (Table 2). Although not statistically significant, over two-thirds of the women report weekly or more contact with a child, compared with less than one-half of the men. They also maintain closer ties with children and are more likely than men to name a child as a confidante. Men more typically respond, "I only share problems with my wife." The difference be-

Table 2. Social Supports by Gender
(Percentages)

	Women	Men
Family Structure		
Those with children	68	70
Child in proximity	58	46
Social Supports from Children		
Instrumental supports	60	30**
Expressive supports	80	74
Child as caregiver	47	11**
Weekly or more contact	69	48
Child as confidant	25	19
Friends		
Instrumental support	41	18
Expressive support	96	25
Friend as confidant	38	10
Formal Supports		
Choreworker	50	23*
Senior/community association	40	46
Transportation services	15	5
Unmet needs	24	10

*$p < .05$
**$p < .01$
***$p < .001$

tween men and women in their receipt of expressive support from friends is also significant. The greater propensity among women to name a friend as a confidante, also reflects women's continuing ability to maintain intimate relationships outside of the family.

These findings indicate that gender differences in social resources persist into late life, with women continuing to be better able than men to rally social supports to meet their greater needs. Furthermore, since women experience more disability in late life, they also use significantly more formal supports than men; twice as many women as men regularly use household assistance. Finally, one-fourth of the women, compared to only a few men, have unmet needs for social services.

Managing Daily Routines

Table 3 reports on how men and women differ in managing their daily activities in advanced old age. Global measures point to significant gender differences. Women do more socializing on a daily basis, but men rated significantly higher in all other categories. Specifically, men maintained a higher level of activity, they were more involved in hobbies and household maintenance, they

participated more in organizational activities and they exercised more independence.

Three types of competencies required to adapt to community living (as described in the Introduction) were also coded into global measures that are reported in Table 3. These are competencies in exercising control over the physical environment, maintaining social integration, and sustaining a sense of well-being and motivations. Again men were significantly more able than women to exercise control over their environment and maintain their motivations (Table 3). Gender differences in maintaining social integration were not significant, however, nor was there significant variation in maintaining a sense of well-being.

In keeping with their better physical status, men in their advanced years are more apt to retain some characteristics as younger men. For example, eighty-six-year-old Mr. Bascomb maintains an active daily program. In describing his typical day as being "rather busy," he indicated his datebook was filled with daily entries. As a still productive member of several committees, he attends four or five luncheon meetings a week. In his own words, he elaborated, "I have a number of civic assignments. I keep up quite a correspondence, writing five to eight letters a day. I also have a number of projects going and spend time in my workshop repairing or making furniture. I play the piano after a fashion, jazzing it up in the evening." Keeping up an active correspondence was not unique to Mr. Bascomb. In fact, political activism in the form of letter-writing was a major

Table 3. Adaptation to Daily Living by Gender (Time 2)
($n = 111$)

	Women ($n = 85$)		Men ($n = 26$)		
	M	S.D.	M	S.D.	Sig.
Daily Routine:					
Sociability	2.92	1.03	2.58	1.10	
Active	2.76	1.18	2.12	.864	*
Hobbies	3.23	1.35	2.31	1.19	**
Home maintenance	2.98	1.36	2.31	1.29	*
Organizations	3.37	1.50	2.62	1.29	*
Independence	2.46	.936	1.92	.796	*
Adaptive Responses					
Control of environment	1.93	.946	1.42	.578	*
Social integration	2.53	1.25	3.15	1.29	
Well-being	2.41	1.08	2.42	1.14	
Maintain motivation	2.12	1.12	1.58	.758	*
Mood					
Affect balance	17	5.00	16	4.18	

*$p < .05$
**$p < .01$

motivating force in the life of Mr. Atkins. "I sit down every day and write to big shots. What's keeping me alive is the pursuit of Reagan!"

With fewer physical restraints men are significantly more able to sustain their independence and devote time and energy to maintaining their hobbies and interests. These covered a wide range of activities, including stamp collecting, carpentry, gardening, and "playing my fiddle." Like eighty-eight-year-old Mr. Walsh, men also participated more in organizational activities outside the home. "I'm a member of two Mason lodges. That gives me things to do, luncheons, meetings, outings." As others summarized their days, "I look at my calendar to find out what to do today. I belong to organizations and I follow plans." "I don't have anything to do in a business way. Now it's all centered around senior activities."

Not surprisingly men with their better health are better able to exercise more control over their environment. A precisely timed day was outlined by an energetic eighty-seven-year-old musician who, unsolicited, gave a minute-by-minute account of his morning schedule. He was meticulous in describing not only what he ate, but when he ate, eating the same thing at the same hour every day—6:45 a.m., 10 a.m., 12 p.m., 4:30 p.m., and 7:30 p.m. He was emphatic about the need for regularity in all activities. Similarly, Mr. Logan controlled his daily routine. "At 7 a.m. I listen to the news for an hour. At 8 a.m. I get up and have coffee and read the paper until 9 a.m. From 9 to 9:30 I take a shower and shave. At 10 o'clock we eat. At 10:30 I go to the office and stay until 1. After lunch I walk in Golden Gate Park for one or two hours."

Women usually described a more passive approach to their daily activities, most likely compatible to their current disabilities. "I'm very free to do what I want, but I just don't get out. When you get to my age, you're glad to rest more." "Mostly I stay home and just spend the day sitting around. I sleep a little. Unfortunately I can't do the things I used to do." "I'm more or less an observer of life now." Women were prone to talk about their limitations and the time and energy consumed in performing basic tasks. Specifically, a ninety-year-old woman explained, "What used to take me three hours to do, now takes me three days. And then I need a two hour nap in the middle of the day, so I lose those hours." Continuities were also evident. "When the children were small, I never went out much. I was never a gadabout so it comes natural for me to stay home."

Life Course Trajectories

Because of marked differences in their life trajectories, men and women usually experience events at different ages and thus require differing types of adaptation. Not uncommonly, men who survive into advanced old age might have to adapt to widowhood, the caregiver role, and relocation, transitions that women experienced at younger ages. The shift in roles required of men is particularly challenging at the age of eighty-five, ninety, or ninety-five, at a time when disability and social losses are more likely. In contrast, the life course for women of this generation was traditionally timed to family events so there was greater role continuity as they aged.

Timing of Widowhood

Recently widowed very old men experience this loss at an age when they are most vulnerable. Although many more women are widowed, they have been widowed for a much longer time (a mean of 25 years in comparison to 10 years for men). As a consequence, they have had time to build networks that substitute for the sociability in marriage. Most men in advanced old age had not expected to outlive their wives, and thus they were not prepared for their bereavement. Many express feelings of inadequacy and abandonment. In the words of one eighty-eight-year-old widower, "We were like two peas in a pod. Now I'm just one man in this big house. I'm helpless here!" Others say, "I am alone with no support. I'm losing confidence in myself and my strength," "I've got nothing without my wife," or, "I have nobody and I am nobody!"

This cohort usually socialized in couples—the men relied on their wives to arrange social activities. Left on their own, few demonstrated resourcefulness in planning social get-togethers. Since these men were unaccustomed to establishing social relationships, they often resist forming new relationships to substitute for their loss. Widowers frequently remarked on their social isolation, "Since my wife passed away, I've drifted away from friends." "When my wife was alive we saw people jointly. She arranged everything. Now I don't bother." "I'm not at an age where I can make friends again."

Eighty-five year old Mr. Long lamented that the death of his wife four years previously was the worst thing that had ever happened to him. "When my wife died, I didn't know what to do with myself—the aloneness, the empty apartment, everything. We had a good marriage and an ordinary life. Now I can't find any suitable companions. I don't visit anybody and nobody visits me. I'm not the least bit interested in sitting and listening to strangers tell me their life story, and they must feel the same way about me! This is the worst kind of life."

Mr. James, at ninety-five, was widowed two years before our first contact. Even though he is the father of four sons, he conveyed a profound sense of loss and desolation. "Before my wife passed away, I was feeling very, very good. Since she died, I've hated living alone. I miss Ginny so much that I almost cry. We had closeness, intimacy, and interest in each other. It was something to live for. Now I've got nothing. Even the last years of looking after Ginny were better than being alone. I haven't the will or mind to engage in anything. All I know is that I'm goddamn lonesome."

Among this generation of oldest-old, women who have been widowed for several years may be better adapted to independent living than widowers. Their prior involvement in domestic and community activities often continues in the absence of a spouse. Eighty-seven year old Mrs. Granger, who has been widowed for half of her life, still lives in the family home, a residence she has maintained for forty-nine years. In addition to her weekly volunteer work serving meals to the homeless, Mrs. Granger is involved in numerous church projects and social activities with her friends and neighbors. Her five children and eleven grandchildren further occupy her energies and time. She reports she never gets depressed or lonely, and she feels good about being able to accomplish so much on her own.

Generally women have had more years than men to adapt emotionally to their losses. For example, Mrs. Richards, now aged ninety, lost her husband when she was only forty-two years of age. Now she lives alone in a high rise apartment building with mostly other older residents. Her only complaint is, "I'm not able to go out as much as I used to." When asked about her marriage, Mrs. Richards responded, "It was a beautiful marriage. I miss him very much but I really don't remember too much about my married life. It was too long ago." Similarly, ninety-three-year-old Mrs. Scott lost her husband thirty-nine years ago. "He died suddenly of a cerebral hemorrhage. He was just found dead. It was horrible but people have had worse things happen. I had a good marriage. He was a lovely gentleman and a marvelous father. I can't imagine wanting anything else. I have no concerns."

Anticipatory socialization may serve to ease the burden of grief for women who, unlike men, had expected to be widowed. Ninety year old Mrs. Billings had outlived two husbands and viewed her status as being the norm. "We were a family of widows, three girls in my family. My mother buried three husbands, and my sisters buried two each. Maybe we all loved our men to death. Burying a husband is no fun, but what good does it do to let it get you down?"

Men as Caregivers

Elderly men who must assume a caregiving role are particularly vulnerable to stress. Typically these men, born at the turn of the century, had not been socialized to a more androgenous gender role, so that they are ill-prepared to tackle domestic chores. In addition, men in their late eighties and nineties may have to contend with their own disabilities that complicate the difficulties of caregiving. Mr. Watts, an eighty-seven-year-old retired banker, recounted his recent experience of caring for his impaired wife. "I took care of her for three years at home and went through Hell. I did it all myself, I did everything, bathed her, everything. I'd do it again, but it was rough. I had never done a darn thing around the house before. I did my own cooking, shopping, cleaned the best I could. Finally I ran out of strength."

Another eighty-seven-year-old retired executive confessed that his life had been much easier running a large corporation than managing his household. He said, "I didn't become a housewife until I was eighty. The hardest thing is taking care of my wife. I help her dress, undress, and take a bath. Although we have nurses, she won't let anyone help her but me. I wish I didn't have to do it. There's no explaining it, you just do it." A similar situation was described by Dr. Chalmers, aged eighty-nine and married fifty-eight years, who was coping with his wife's

recent stroke. "I've become a full-time husband. I shop, cook, clean up. I'm a little housebound now. My life is much more lived around my wife these days. She is confused sometimes. I encourage her and read to her. I'm lucky it happened so late in life though. A year ago we still hiked for miles."

Relocation

A problem common to both men and women in advanced age is the potential "threat" of relocation, but the responses are quite divergent. Men, more than women, tend to be less accepting of relocation to senior or "retirement" housing. Their responses to such a move ranged from outright resistance to resignation. In the words of one eighty-eight-year-old widower, "I can't get enthusiastic about a retirement home. It would bother me to be cooped up in one room. It's confining and restrictive. You have to be on time for meals, be dressed, shaved, cleaned up. I plan to stay where I am." An eighty-seven-year-old former engineer described his reaction to life in a senior residence as follows. "I don't like living like this, but it's the lesser of two evils. Being here I don't have any problems. It's just a matter of getting up and going through the day and going to bed. It's like a jail. If you added bars and threw away the key, it would be the same. I'm stuck with it. No sense in getting upset about it." Another man expressed even greater discontentment. "Senior housing is the end of the line. Before I was busy all the time. Now I have nothing special to live for."

With longer life expectancy, earlier widowhood, and usually reduced financial resources, women more often leave their family dwelling at a younger age and move to an apartment or senior housing. Changes in living arrangements may also be related to women's increasing levels of impairment and their need for more instrumental supports. Like widowhood, relocation usually occurs at an earlier age for women than for men. Some respondents had resided in senior residences for a long time. Ninety-three-year-old Mrs. Dixon bought into a senior residence at the age of seventy-four. "As I think back, I've come to a happy conclusion here. We're well cared for. I came nineteen years ago when they didn't expect us to live this long. I still pay only $550 a month."

Mrs. Hall, aged ninety, is also a long-term resident of senior housing. In spite of her breathing difficulties and painful

arthritis, she maintains active involvement in her building. "This is a lovely place to live. I've had four houses of my own, but when I was in my 70's, I had the chance to come in here. There's always something to do, visit someone, help someone, play cards. Whenever someone is ill, I help them. I enjoy every day. I like the activities, and I like to visit."

CONCLUSION

Among the oldest-old, gender-based disparities are evident in functional status, socioeconomic status, and social resources. While these differences favor men, other differences appear to favor women. Consistent with national data, one-half of the men in our sample are married and thus living with someone. Only 10 percent of the women are married, two-thirds live alone, and many experience economic problems. These women also have greater physical disability because of chronic health conditions. With depleted energy and limited mobility, women are less able to independently manage their activities of daily living. Most often they need help with household maintenance. Their physical limitations further restrict their ability to exercise control over their environment and to maintain motivations. Typically women in advanced old age demonstrate a more passive orientation.

An analysis of gender variations in life trajectories, however, illustrate some advantages for women. Many of them had experienced widowhood at a younger age, so they had time to adjust to their loss and form substitute relationships with other widows. Sex role socialization also benefits these women's adjustment to old age. Having been socialized to domesticity and family responsibilities, they experience greater role continuity in their late life activities and relationships. Although very old women, more than men, have gone from strength to frailty, from self-sufficiency to some degree of dependency, from marriage to widowhood, and from independent living to group living, their problems are in part counteracted by their increased social supports from children and friends.

As an aggregate, men are at an advantage physically and have less need for social supports. However, as their needs increase, cultural norms and the timing of events may threaten their well-being. Widowhood, caregiving, and relocation are off-time events and rarely anticipated in the lives of very old men, so they usually have difficulty in coping with them. These men have been ill-prepared to handle the domestic chores and emotional stresses of living alone or caring for an impaired spouse. Case studies also reveal that men are not particularly amenable to age-segregated living situations, a relocation that is increasingly likely in late life. Our findings also indicate that men in advanced old age have a high risk of social isolation when confronted with widowhood in late late life.

An examination of the daily lives of these men and women, as told in their own words, offers us a unique opportunity to enrich our understanding of the problems they face. These conclusions have implications for policy and further research. Women's ability to sustain community living in advanced old age would be enhanced by the greater availability of quality home care help. With the prolongation of life, more attention must also be given to gender differences and the potential risks faced by very old men.

REFERENCES

1. C. M. Taeuber and I. Rosenwaike, A Demographic Portrait of America's Oldest Old, in *The Oldest Old*, R. M. Suzman, D. P. Willis, and K. G. Manton (eds.), Oxford University Press, New York, 1992.
2. B. Hess, The Demographic Parameters, *Generations*, Summer, pp. 12–15, 1990.
3. C. M. Taeuber, *Sixty-Five Plus in America*, Current Population Reports, United States Department of Commerce, Bureau of the Census, P23-178, 1992.
4. *The New York Times*, November 10, 1992.
5. U.S. Bureau of the Census, *Money, Income and Poverty Status in the United States 1988* (Advance Data), Washington, D.C.: United States Department of Commerce, Current Population Reports, Series P-60, No. 166, U.S. Government Printing Office, 1989.
6. P. M. Keith, The Social Context and Resources of the Unmarried in Old Age, *International Journal of Aging and Human Development*, 23, pp. 81–96, 1986.
7. J. A. Kohen, Old but not Alone: Informal Social Supports among the Elderly by Marital Status and Sex, *The Gerontologist, 23*, pp. 57–63, 1983.
8. C. E. Depner and B. Ingersoll, Employment Status and Social Support: The Experience of the Mature Woman, in *Women's Retirement: Policy Implications for Recent Research*, M. Szinovacz (ed.), Sage, Beverly Hills, pp. 61–76, 1982.
9. G. Peters and M. Kaiser, The Role of Friends and Neighbors in Providing Social Support, in *Social Support Networks and the Care of the Elderly*, W. Sauer and R. Coward (eds.), Springer, New York, pp. 123–158, 1986.
10. J. A. Levy, Intersections of Gender and Aging, *The Sociological Quarterly, 29*:4, pp. 479–486, 1988.
11. R. A. Kalish, Death and Dying in a Social Context, in *Handbook of Aging and the Social Sciences*, R. H. Binstock and E. Shanas (eds.), Van Nostrand Reinhold, New York, pp. 483–510 1976. (publisher . . .) 1976.
12. P. A. McMullen and A. E. Gross, Sex Differences, Sex Roles, and Health-Related Help-Seeking, in *New Directions in Helping*, J. D. Fisher, A. Nadler, and B. M. Depaulo (eds.), vol. 2, Academic Press, Inc. 1983.
13. C. Longino and A. Lipman, Married and Spouseless Men and Women in Planned Retirement Communities: Support Network Differentials, *Journal of Marriage and Family, 43*, pp. 169–177, 1981.
14. C. L. Johnson and L. Troll, Family Functioning in Late Late Life, *Journal of Gerontology, 47*:2, pp. 566–572, 1992.

Getting Over Getting Older

Forget about trying to reverse the process. It's never been a

better time to face up to aging. In fact, getting older truly does mean getting

better. By Susan Scarf Merrell

Baby boomers: We were supposed to be the generation that turned aging into a bedroom act, making it sexy to grow old and gray, and get laugh lines. If 76 million of us wrinkled into middle age with style and verve, well, wow, the entire Western World might rethink the need to search for a fountain of youth. Most of us, however, don't seem to have found that sense of contentment with our aging bodies that we expected to. Instead, baby boomers have both masterminded—and fallen victim to—an anti-aging epidemic far more virulent than the average case of mass hysteria. It isn't simply that we're trying to exercise and eat our way to longer, healthier lives. Sales are up dramatically across the gamut of age-fighting weaponry, from wrinkle creams to collagen injections to cosmetic surgery. Nor are the warriors only women. According to a recent Roper Starch Worldwide survey, six percent of men nationwide actually use such traditionally feminine products as bronzers and foundation to create the illusion of a more youthful appearance.

What is it about aging that makes our sagging skin crawl? Are we frightened of looking and feeling old because it reminds us that we're mortal? That we might become infirm? What, in fact, does older age bring and how will it be different for us boomers than for the generations that came before?

The first surprise is that those of us entering the middle years en masse are truly lucky to be hitting our thirties, forties, and fifties now, in the 1990s. Because the state of a civilization has a very real impact on the inevitable path to getting older, every generation experiences aging differently. According to aging expert Helen Kivnick, Ph.D., a psychologist at the University of Minnesota, the experience of later life is determined partly by biology, partly by history, and partly by society and culture. Never before in history has the phase of later life had the potential to be so long and fruitful. "Old age as we now know it is very new, and doesn't look at all like it used to," Kivnick says. "Because people live longer and with greater independence, they can plan their futures more actively. Elders today [those over 65] are breaking new ground."

OLD AIN'T WHAT IT USED TO BE

If those who are old today are stepping onto untrodden ground, we boomers are about to create a stampede. And chances are we'll be extremely skilled at making old age into an interesting and fruitful time of life. We know how to explore and plumb possibility. We have already been enjoying far fewer societal constraints in our middle years than has ever previously been the norm. Renee Garfinkel, Ph.D., a psychologist and aging expert from Silver Springs, Maryland, says across the board we have fewer age-based limitations to hinder us. "It's not simply that we tend to keep our health longer; it's that we also aren't subject to generational restrictions on behavior, career choices, or clothing." If you decide to go to medical school—or rollerblading—tomorrow, you might just do so. If I pick out similar dresses for my five-year-old daughter and me, neither one of us will seem out of place: She won't be dressed "old," and I won't be dressed "young." Our tastes are actually fairly alike. In blue jeans and sweaters—particularly from the back—one often can't tell a fit 55-year-old from his or her fit adolescent kid.

As recently as twenty or thirty years ago, society was much more hierarchical. When a woman's children left home, she struggled to make sense of a future in which her life's task was done, even though she herself remained healthy and alert and capable of making further—and even greater—contributions. In the 1970s, when women in their thirties and forties ventured out to colleges and universities in large numbers, they were breaking norms and redefining their roles. Certainly, I myself would have been extremely aware of the oddity of an older man or woman—even a person so aged as to be in his or her late twenties—sitting in a lecture hall back when I was in college. Nowadays, that's almost laughable: The student in the next chair in the lecture hall could just as easily be a grandparent as an 18-year-old. In fact, if those "non-traditional" students weren't filling seats, many institutions of higher learning would be struggling to keep their doors open.

Middle age doesn't mean what it used to. Mid-lifers aren't ossified and set in their ways; they tend to be open to new ideas and new experiences; the tastes of childhood

have matured but the sense of potential and of discovery is still deep and real. A former newspaper editor, who had her first child at the age of forty and recently completed her doctoral dissertation at the age of forty-five, says, "I know how old I am. I'm not in denial about the fact of the years. I simply reject the fears, stereotypes, and caricatures of aging. If you ask me my age, I'll tell you, but I don't think it's the most relevant fact about me."

"I think young," says a globe-trotting artist in his early eighties. "I won't allow myself to feel old, or act old, until they cart me out in a box." Does attitude make a difference? Are we truly only as old as we feel?

Yes and no, says Garfinkel, who heads Gerontology Service, a consulting practice for institutions that deal with the elderly. She finds that we associate aging with dysfunction. A young person in poor health tends to report feeling old, while an old person in good health feels young and active. "It's a two-way street," says Garfinkel. "If you aren't in good health, it's very hard to think young. But if you think young, have good genes, and take care of yourself, you'll probably feel and seem younger than you are."

Believing yourself to be in better than normal condition for your age is typical for healthy people in general. It's not that we're deluding ourselves, it's simply that the interplay of chronological age and physical health is much stronger than we tend to realize. That's why the following statistical impossibility can exist: According to "The Wrinkle Report," a national survey of more than 1,200 people ages 30 to 50, three in four baby boomers think they look younger than their actual years, and eight in ten say they have fewer signs of facial aging than other people their age. "People in their forties and those in their eighties actually say quite similar things," Garfinkel reports. "It's more an indication of physical health than of anything else. If we don't feel bad, we feel great. We're a little bit like the people in Lake Woebegon, whose children are all above average."

AM I OLD YET?

People tend not to feel downright old, no matter what their age. They just get more and more surprised when they look in the mirror and see the ways in which they're changing physically. The fact is that aging tends to be subtle and most losses come hand in hand with small, new rewards. For example, one's first gray hairs may arrive around the same time one earns a major promotion—somehow the equation of loss and gain nets out in a surprisingly satisfying manner. In some way, we continue to expect that the next milestone will be the one that makes us suddenly feel old.

I'm reminded of a birthday luncheon I went to recently for a friend who's just rounded the hump of thirty. Call her Sally. Sally had anticipated the event with a great deal of fear and anxiety, and was surprised at how little change the actual big day had wrought. I mentioned that I'd felt very few negative changes during my thirties, and said that I felt surer of myself and much happier than I'd been in my twenties. Then Kim, our 43-year-old friend, smiled broadly at both of us and said that the thirties were a wonderful decade. We continued eating for a moment. After a bit, Sally turned to me and said, "How old are you again? Thirty-eight?"

"Thirty-seven," I snapped. Kim's smile drooped—to her, my quick reaction meant that though I was happy to be getting older, I didn't want to be as old as she was. In fact, she's right. I'm enjoying each year far more than I might have imagined possible as a teenager, but that doesn't mean I want my life to pass any more quickly. As much as I like my thirties, I'm not giving up a single year before it's time.

Paradoxically, I do know that, on most levels, the future looks promising. Given all the fear we seem to have of it, the wondrous news is that getting older is a generally positive thing. We don't just accumulate years, we also gain wisdom which enables us to make decisions with less of the fussing and wheel-spinning that marked our teens and twenties. "I often think the excess energy of youth is nature's way of compensating for a lack of wisdom," says Garfinkel. "All that zip means you don't collapse from all the work of chasing your own tail."

As we get older, we know more not only about the world but about ourselves. We have better attention spans and an increased ability to focus. "In general, most non-neurotic older people are content with what they've done with their lives, are happy, have high self-esteem, and a sense of well-being," says clinical psychologist Forrest Scogin, Ph.D., of the University of Alabama. "We become more adaptable and flexible, and have a greater understanding of our own resilience."

Conventional thinking has always emphasized the miserable, crotchety older person, Scogin adds, but in fact unhappiness is far from the norm. Rates of depression tend to decline after the age of 45, for both men and women. (There's a slight—but temporary—blip in men's rates around the time of retirement.) Other research shows that our sense of what we deem most important for happiness tends to alter appropriately as we age, a sign of the true resilience of the human spirit: We may not look as fresh-faced, but we like ourselves more. We actually think fewer negative thoughts. Life becomes simpler.

Our priorities shift in a healthy and adaptive fashion. "We care less about our appearance and more about our emotional well-being, our character, and our involvements in the world at large and with those we love," says clinical psychologist Betsy Stone, Ph.D., of Stamford, Connecticut.

One other rosy aspect to the future is that as physical attributes become a little less stunning, sex roles begin to blur. Men become more accommodating and emotionally expressive; women more assertive and active in meeting their own needs. With a little less passion, a little less division of roles, and an increase in contentment and openness with one another, relationships in later life tend to become far more important, satisfying, and mutual.

On the down side—and, of course, there had to be one—we begin to slow on all fronts. It becomes increasingly difficult to keep up with the energies of a two-year-old, or to add up a series of numbers in one's head. Memory grows less efficient as well. In fact, it's a process that begins between the ages of 18 and 20 but is so slow and subtle that it doesn't become noticeable until around the age of 35. And when we first face the fact that memorizing what we need to do that day is getting difficult, we adapt. We start making lists and otherwise reorder our approach to retaining information. "You tell yourself it's not so important to remember things," says Garfinkel.

In truth, the worst part of getting older appears to be ageism—the intolerant attitudes of younger people. According to Scogin, "People grow impatient with you for your slowness, even though that decline in speed is appropriate. Think of that driver who makes you crazy when you're trying to get some place. That person isn't being oppositional, as it appears to you. His or her reactions are slower, so it's natural that he or she would drive more cautiously." Of course, older people are as heterogeneous as any other population, Scogin adds: "Some are hot-rodding down the highway, some are doddering along. One can't ever generalize."

BETTER, NOT OLDER

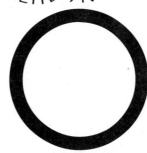

kay, so if we're supposed to be satisfied with our aging selves, does that mean it's wrong to help nature along, to try and slow down the ravages of time? According to Stone, author of the forthcoming *Happily Ever After: A Guide for Newlyweds*, "Dying your hair or having collagen injections doesn't really have anything to do with avoiding getting older per se; it's about wanting to feel good about yourself and feel attractive. It's like wearing beautiful lingerie: Nobody else knows you're doing it, but you feel indulged and valuable. That's a reasonable thing to do."

But such self-improvement can go too far, Stone explains. For example, if a person values his or her attractiveness to the exclusion of other personal characteristics, then the person is loving him or herself from the outside-in rather than the inside-out. "That's a problem," she says.

According to Kivnick, who researches how the lives of very frail elders can be improved, the most important thing we can do to ensure a comfortable and interesting old age is to plan for one. Not simply financially, although that's obviously important. Most of us will spend a good twenty years or more in healthy, active post-retirement, and just expecting to sit on one's heels and rest is hardly a realistic plan for happiness. Don't just daydream about planting a garden, says Kivnick. Learn about gardening, and be ready for the day you'll be free to spend all afternoon with your hands in the dirt. Plan to stay involved in your community, with your family, with whatever has interested and intrigued you thus far. "Perhaps the most important and neglected aspect of getting older is the need to continue giving to others," Kivnick says. "The most unhappy people in the world are those who use retirement to withdraw from involvements, expecting that using their time to concentrate on themselves alone will make them happy. They end up miserable."

Researchers at the Duke University Center for the Study of Aging and Human Development concur. Having family and friends isn't the answer to a happy life, but engaging actively with them is. And it seems possible that this involvement can help you live even longer.

It's also essential to know yourself. Your personality isn't likely to change so much that it becomes unrecognizable as you get older. Thus you can begin to speculate about

the future in practical ways. It's never too early to start considering the basic questions: What's important to me? What life do I most want to live? With whom and where? Would I prefer to stay near my own family or to be in an elder community? Do I want to travel? How will I remain connected to the greater world? What contribution should I make? Once you're no longer bound by the structure of a formal paid job, the whole world can be your oyster.

There's no time better than the present for beginning to imagine an enjoyable, wise, active, and fruitful later life. Such planning can only add richness to the middle years as well. Says Kivnick, "How we are old depends very much on how we are young."

Susan Scarf Merrell is the author of The Accidental Bond: The Power of Sibling Rivalry, *out in paperback this January. She has just completed her first novel.*

New Passages

Author Gail Sheehy hails the advent of a Second Adulthood after age 45

In the space of one short generation, the whole shape of the life cycle has been fundamentally altered. Since the publication of my book *Passages* in 1976, age norms have shifted and are no longer normative.

Consider: Nine-year-old girls are developing breasts and pubic hair; 9-year-old boys carry guns to school; 16-year-olds can "divorce" a parent; 30-year-old men still live at home with Mom; 40-year-old women are just getting around to pregnancy; 50-year-old men are forced into early retirement; 55-year-old women can have egg donor babies; 60-year-old women start first professional degrees; 70-year-old men reverse aging by 20 years with human growth hormone; 80-year-olds run marathons: 85-year-olds remarry and still enjoy sex; and every day, the "Today" show's Willard Scott says "Happy Birthday!" to more 100-year-old women.

What's going on? There is a revolution in the adult life cycle. People today are leaving childhood sooner, but they are taking longer to grow up and much longer to die. That is shifting all the stages of adulthood ahead—by 10 years. Adolescence is now prolonged for the middle class until the end of the 20s. Today, our First Adulthood only begins at 30. Most baby boomers don't feel fully "grown up" until they are into their 40s. When our parents turned 50, we thought they were old!

But today, women and men I've interviewed routinely feel they are five to 10 years younger than the age on their birth certificates. Fifty is what 40 used to be; 60 is what 50 used to be. Middle age has already been pushed far into the 50s—in fact, if you listen to boomers, there is no more middle age. So what's next?

Welcome to Middlescence. It's adolescence the second time around.

The territory of the 50s, 60s and beyond is changing so radically that it now opens up whole new passages leading to stages of life that are nothing like what our parents experienced. An American woman who today reaches age 50 free of cancer and heart disease can expect to see her 92nd birthday. The average man who is 65 today—an age now reached by more than 70 percent of the U.S. population—can expect to live until 81. That amounts to a second adult lifetime.

Stop and recalculate. Imagine the day you turn 45 as the old age of your First Adulthood. Fifty then becomes the youth of your Second Adulthood. First Adulthood just happens to you. Second Adulthood, you can custom design. It's a potential rebirth that offers exhilarating new possibilities. But only for those who are aware and who prepare.

For those who are approaching 50, the question increasingly becomes, "How shall we live the rest of our lives?" And the tantalizing dynamic that has emerged in our era is that the second half of adult life is not the stagnant, depressing downward slide we have always assumed it to be.

In the hundreds of interviews I have done with men and women in middle life, especially pacesetters in the educated middle class I have discovered that people are beginning to see there is the exciting potential of a new life to live: one in which they can concentrate on becoming better, stronger, deeper, wiser, funnier, freer, sexier and more attentive to living the privileged moments—even as they are getting older, lumpier, bumpier, slower and closer to the end. Instead of being a dreary tale of decline, our middle life is a progress story, a series of little victories over little deaths.

We now have not one but three adult lives to anticipate: Provisional Adulthood from age 18 to 30, First Adulthood from 30 to 45 and Second Adulthood from 45 to 85 and beyond. The most exciting development is that Second Adulthood contains two new territories—an Age of Mastery from 45 to 65 and an Age of Integrity from 65 to 85 and beyond. The startling life changes awaiting all of us are now being charted by path breakers from the World War II generation and the "silent" generation of those who came of age in the 1950s, who are writing new maps for everyone else to follow.

THE FLOURISHING FORTIES

The two generations of baby boomers—the Vietnam generation of the 1960s and the "me" generation of the 1970s—are set to become the longest-living humans in American history. The first of them will officially turn 50 in 1996. A million of them, the Census Bureau predicts, will live past 100. Having indulged themselves in the longest adolescence in history, they betray a collective terror and disgust of aging.

Early in life, baby boomers got used to having two things: choice and control. That means that when life's storm clouds threaten, people in their 40s today are likely to feel more out of control than ever. Wally Scott, a participant in one of many "Midlife Passages" group discussions I've attended in recent years, put it this way: "All of a sudden, you have to start listening to the little voices inside: What do I really want to invest my life in? How can I construct a life that fits the me of today as opposed to the me of 15 years ago?"

The Flourishing Forties can be complicated for women by the storms of perimenopause and menopause. Men may face their own version of biological meltdown. Although it is not strictly a male menopause, many men in middle or later life do experience a lapse in virility and vitality and a decline in well-being. About half of American men over 40 have experienced middle-life impotence to varying degrees. This decline can definitely be delayed. It can even be corrected. In the near future, it may even become preventable. But first a man must understand it.

The social arena contains its own challenges as women in their 40s continue to explore new roles, struggle with late child rearing or mourn their lack of children. As couples are forced to renegotiate traditional relationships and medical crises intrude on well-laid plans, men and women in this age group begin to feel their mortality.

Today, smart men and women will use their early 40s as preparation for a custom-designed Second Adulthood. What do you need to learn to maximize your ability to respond quickly to a fluid marketplace? A single, fixed identity is a liability today. Recent research also suggests that developing multiple identities is one of the best buffers against mental and physical illness. When a marriage blows up or the company shuts down or the whole nature of a profession is changed by technology, people with more than one identity can draw upon other sources of self-esteem while they regroup. Such resilience is essential.

SECOND ADULTHOOD

John Guare has been doing exactly what he most loves since he was 9 years old—writing plays. But even the brilliant creator of *Six Degrees of Separation* and *House of Blue Leaves* knows he cannot rest on his laurels. He was 56 when I mentioned to him that I was exploring our Second Adulthood. "I was just saying to my wife, 'I've got to reinvent my life, right now!'" he exploded. "Or we'll be dead. Worse than dead—the walking dead."

That is the challenge of making the passage to Second Adulthood. This new life must be precipitated by a moment of change—the "Aha!" moment. It forces us to look upon our lives differently and to make a transition from survival to mastery. In young adulthood we survive by figuring out how best to please or perform for the powerful ones who will protect and reward us—parents, teachers, lovers, mates, bosses, mentors. It is all about proving ourselves. The transformation of middle life is to move into a more stable psychological state of mastery, where we control much of what happens in our life and can often act on the world rather than react to whatever the world throws at us. Reaching this state of mastery is also one of the best predictors of good mental and psychological functioning in old age.

Second Adulthood takes us beyond the preoccupation with self. We are compelled to search for a greater significance in our engagement in the world. "We are all hungry for connection," said James Sniechowski, a

51-year-old men's group leader in Santa Monica, Calif. *Connection* was a word that came up again and again in my discussions with groups of middle-aged men.

Increasingly, women who have mastered the silent passage through menopause feel a power surge—post-menopausal zest. As family obligations fade away, many become motivated to stretch their independence, learn new skills, return to school, plunge into new careers, rediscover the creativity and adventurousness of their youth and, at last, find their own voices.

THE FLAMING FIFTIES

By the time they reach their Flaming Fifties, most educated women have acquired the skills and self-knowledge to master complex environments and change the conditions around them. Over and over, women who have crossed into their 50s tell me with conviction, "I would not go back to being young again." They remember vividly what it was like to wake up not knowing exactly who they were, to be torn between demands of family and demands of career, to be constantly changing hats (and hairstyles) in the attempt to fit many roles and often losing focus in the blur of it all.

In three major national opinion surveys I have done in the past seven years, I have learned that by Second Adulthood, the dominant influence on a woman's well-being is not income level or social class or marital status. The most decisive factor is age. Older is happier.

"Fifty for me was a time when I really, for the first time, owned my body," said Ginny Ford, a Rochester, N.Y., businesswoman, whose blond hair and dimpled smile evoke Doris Day movies. "I had been very ashamed of my body, and now I love it. Now, there's all this inner stuff going on. I'm probably 10 pounds heavier, my thighs are a little rumply, my arms have flab. Fifteen years ago I would have starved myself. But now I'm enjoying my husband's pasta. I exercise every day, I enjoy myself sexually and I'm proud of this body. It really works!"

For men entering their 50s today, there is no script. It has traditionally been assumed that aging is kinder to men, but a different truth comes out in personal interviews. I found far more uncertainty among men in middle life than among women; indeed, they often appear to be going in opposite directions. Overall, the over-50 men in my surveys don't experience the great transformation from First to Second Adulthood that women do. Most appear to be more resigned to accepting life as it is: Two thirds are not anticipating any major change, and one third feel more concerned about just getting by. Half of these men feel tired and like they're "running out of gas." Their greatest worry is that they can no longer take their health for granted.

Intimate attachments. But among those men I have studied who are well educated, particularly those with an entrepreneurial temperament, a good many are enjoying a sense of mastery. They say the best things about being over 45 are being able to rely on their experience and being clearer about what is truly important in life. Still others find new richness in forging closer, more intimate attachments with their wives or in becoming start-over dads.

How can we make this passage more positively? Find your passion, and pursue it. How do you know where to look? You can start by seeing if it passes the time-flies test. What activity do you do in which time goes by without your even knowing it? What did you most love to do when you were 12 years old? Somewhere in that activity there is a hook to be found that might pull up your dormant self.

Men and women who emerge psychologically healthiest at 50 are those who, as their expectations and goals change with age, "shape a 'new self' that calls upon qualities that were dormant earlier." This was the principal finding of longitudinal studies at the University of California at Berkeley. Men have always been able to start over, and not once but more than once. What is really new is that women now have the option of starting second lives in their mid-40s or 50s, and increasingly they are doing so.

For some that will lead to intellectual pursuits. A remarkable surge is already occurring in higher education among older women. Only 3.2 percent of the women in the World War II generation went back to post-high-school education between the ages of 40 and 54. But fully 11 percent of the "silent" generation of the 1950s went back for some college education in those middle years. In 1991, nearly 1 million women over 40 were enrolled in college nationwide.

This stage brings with it much greater emotional and social license, and a majority of these women have claimed it, becoming more outspoken and less self-conscious. After interviewing 14 women from my national survey who emerged in their 50s with optimum well-being, I learned that they see themselves as survivors. That is not the same as seeing themselves as former victims of terrible physical or emotional abuse, although some do describe overcoming such situations in their lives. What they have "survived" are the economic biases and stereotypical sex roles that threatened to inhibit their development as fully independent adults. They are so strong that they do not expect to feel "old" until they are about 70.

One striking finding among researchers is that men over 50 are becoming somewhat more dependent on their wives, emotionally and financially, and less certain about their future goals. The special stresses of an economy in transition, with its punishing wage declines for non-college-educated workers and corporate downsizing that now robs many college-educated men of identity and meaning, have been added to classic biological stresses, especially the decline of men's physical prowess and, for many, the sagging of their sexual performance. Given this new set of conditions, men at middle life probably face the roughest patch of all in mapping the new adult life across time.

"Men over 45 are becoming the new at-risk population for significant problems with anxiety and depression," says Ellen McGrath, a psychologist and author of *When Feeling Bad Is Good.* "And for the first time ever, some of them are acknowledging it and reaching out for help. This is a brand-new trend."

Making a passage to the Age of Mastery often means men are giving up being the master. Alan Alhadeff, a Seattle lawyer of 45, described his "Aha!" moment on a basketball court: "This 20-year-old kid was checking me real hard in the back court. I'm then about 20 pounds heavier than people my height should be. So I pushed him away, somewhat aggressively. I said, 'C'mon. I'm old enough to be your dad.'" The young man looked the older man straight in the eye: "Then get off the court."

"After that day on the basketball court, I mellowed. I realized I don't have to prove myself in physical contests anymore. I don't see that as a negative at all." Indeed, this freed Alhadeff to try other forms of expression he had never entertained before: art, music, gardening, gourmet cooking. "And they're all a lot easier on the knees!"

The real winners among men in middle life do make this shift. Nearly all have developed passions or hobbies that happily occupy and challenge them outside their workaday routines. Such occupations are crucial in offsetting the disenchantment with their profession that polls show is now felt by large numbers of doctors, or the boredom of the accountant defending yet another tax audit of a rich client, or the weariness of the dentist who cannot expect to be wildly stimulated by drilling his billionth bicuspid.

THE SERENE SIXTIES

The 60s have changed just as dramatically as the earlier stages of middle life. What with beta blockers and hip replacements, you're as likely to run into a man of 65 rollerblading in the park as to see him biking with his youngest child, enjoying the adolescent boy in himself as well as the recycled father. Only 10 percent of Americans 65 and over have a chronic health problem that restricts them from carrying on a major physical activity.

Clearly the vast majority of American women and men now in their 60s have reached the stage where maximum freedom coexists with a minimum of physical limitations. And another passage looms: the one from mastery to integrity. Experts in gerontology make a clear distinction between passive aging and successful aging. To engage in successful aging is actually a career choice—a conscious commitment to continuing self-education and the development of a whole set of strategies.

Resilience is probably the most important protection one can have entering the Age of Integrity. An impressive study of the sources of well-being in men at 65 found that the harbinger of emotional health was not a stable childhood or a highflying career. Rather, it was much more important to have developed an ability to handle life's accidents and conflicts without passivity, blaming or bitterness. "It's having the capacity to hold a conflict or impulse in consciousness without acting on it," concludes George Vaillent, a psychiatrist now at Harvard Medical School, who has been scrutinizing—in the Grant Study—the same 173 Harvard men at five-year intervals since they graduated in the early 1940s.

A related finding in the Grant Study: Time does heal. The research shows that even the most traumatic events in childhood had virtually no effect on the well-being of these men by their mid-60s, although severe depression earlier in life did predispose them to continuing problems. Traits that turned out to contribute to happiness in the golden years were not the same ones that had influenced people back in their college days: spontaneity, creative flair and easy sociability. Instead the traits important to smooth functioning as we get older are being dependable, well organized and pragmatic.

The major predictable passage in this period for most people is retirement, though many consider part-time work to help pay for their longer lives and perhaps to handle other family cares like aged parents or the needs of grandchildren. Forty-one percent of retirees surveyed in New York City in 1993 said the adjustment to retirement was difficult. The younger the retiree, the harder the transition. And the higher the status one's work conferred, the steeper the slide to anonymity.

The comfort of mature love is the single most important determinant of older men's outlook on life. Continued excitement about life is the other factor in high well-being for men at this stage. My research with members of the Harvard Business School class of 1949 shows that those who enjoy the highest well-being had reached out for new adventures in half a dozen new directions *before* retiring. They see semi- or full retirement as an enticing opportunity to add richness to their lives.

Grandparenthood can jump-start the transition to the Age of Integrity. For women or men who had to learn, painfully, in First Adulthood how to compartmentalize their nurturing selves and achieving selves, grandparenthood is a particularly welcome second chance to bring all the parts of their lives into harmony.

THE SAGE SEVENTIES

Those who thrive into their 70s and beyond "live very much in the present, but they always have plans for the future," argues Cecelia Hurwich in her doctoral thesis at the Center for Psychological Studies in Albany, Calif. The seventysomethings Hurwich studied had mastered the art of "letting go" of their egos gracefully, so they could focus their attention on a few fine-tuned priorities. These zestful women were not in unusually good physical shape, but believing they still had living to do, they concentrated on what they could do rather than on what they had lost. Every one acknowledged the need for some form of physical intimacy. They found love through sharing a variety of pleasures: music, gardening, hiking, traveling. Several spoke enthusiastically of active and satisfying sex lives.

After that life stage, the most successful octogenarians I have come across seem to share a quality of directness. Robust and unaffected, often hilariously uninhibited in expressing what they really think, they are liable to live with a partner rather than get married or to pick up an old sweetheart and marry despite their kids' disapproval. They have nothing left to lose.

The Age of Integrity is primarily a stage of spiritual growth. Instead of focusing on time running out, we should make it a daily exercise to mark the moment. The present never ages. And instead of trying to maximize our control over our environment, a goal that was perfectly appropriate to the earlier Age of Mastery, now we must cultivate greater appreciation and acceptance of that which we cannot control. Some of the losses of Second Adulthood are inconsolable losses. To accept them without bitterness usually requires making a greater effort to discern the highest spiritual truths that shape the changes and losses of the last passage of life.

Societal Attitudes toward Old Age

There is a wide range of beliefs regarding the social position and status of the aged in American society today. Some people believe that the best way to understand the problems of the elderly is to regard them as a minority group, faced with difficulties similar to those of other minority groups. Discrimination against older people, like racial discrimination, is believed to be based on a bias against visible physical traits. Since the aging process is viewed negatively, it is natural that the elderly try to appear and act younger. Some spend a tremendous amount of money trying to make themselves look and feel younger.

The theory that old people are a minority group is weak, however, because too many circumstances prove otherwise. The U.S. Congress, for example, favors senior members of the Congress, and it delegates considerable prestige and power to them. The leadership roles in most religious organizations are held by older persons. Many older Americans are in good health, have comfortable incomes, and are treated with respect by friends and associates.

Perhaps the most realistic way to view the aged is as a status group, like other status groups in society. Every society has some method of "age grading," by which it groups together individuals of roughly similar age. ("Preteens" and "senior citizens" are some of the age grade labels in American society.)

Because it is a labeling process, age grading causes members of the age grade, as well as others, to perceive themselves in terms of the connotations of the label. Unfortunately, the tag "old age" often has negative connotations in American society.

The readings included in this section illustrate the wide range of stereotypical attitudes toward older Americans. Many of society's typical assumptions about the limitations of old age have been refuted. A major force behind this reassessment of the elderly has been the simple fact that there are so many people living longer and healthier lives, and in consequence playing more of a role in all aspects of our society. Older people can remain produc-

tive members of society for many more years than has been traditionally assumed.

Such standard stereotypes of the elderly as frail, senile, childish, and sexually inactive are topics discussed in this section. Marianne Lavelle, in "On the Edge of Age Discrimination," believes that as the baby boom generation enters the middle years there will be numerous challenges to the Age Discrimination Act by persons laid off or fired. This could result in a considerable reduction in age discrimination in the workplace. Then, the authors of "Children's Views on Aging: Their Attitudes and Values" expound on the idea that children are affected positively by their interactions with older persons and have a realistic perception of aging.

The essay "What Doctors and Others Need to Know: Six Facts on Human Sexuality and Aging" examines the myths that deny the sexuality of older persons and makes suggestions on how to eradicate them. Mary Nemeth, in "Amazing Greys," indicates how well-known public figures who have remained active are improving the image of older persons. Finally, in "Learning to Love (Gulp!) Growing Old," Jere Daniel asserts that as a society we must recognize and accept the aging process and all that goes with it as a reality, a natural part of the life cycle, and reverse our societal attitude of aging as an affliction. Daniel believes that instead of spending billions on walling off the aged, we should spend more to improve the quality of life of the aged.

Looking Ahead: Challenge Questions

Do most people see older persons as sexually inactive? Why?

Do Americans generally look upon old age as a desirable or an undesirable status? Why?

How do the attitudes of children toward older persons differ from those of adults toward their elders?

How are attitudes toward old age likely to change as older persons become a larger segment of the total population?

UNIT 3

On the Edge of Age Discrimination

Baby boomers are poised to attack an issue that is new only to them: the way employers treat workers they deem too old.

By Marianne Lavelle

LARUE SIMPSON MADE $196,000 A year, played golf and owned thoroughbred racehorses before his life derailed, he contends, on the prejudice that does not discriminate by race, sex or class. A jury agreed that Simpson lost his job as a partner in the Cincinnati office of the accounting giant Ernst & Young because, at the age of 47, he was deemed too old by his firm.

With Ernst & Young prepared to ask the United States Supreme Court to overturn the $3.7 million verdict the accountant won in 1994, Simpson's age-discrimination case may prove to be a watershed for baby-boom professionals. Ernst & Young is fighting for the right of big law, accounting and consulting firms to decide whom they hire and fire as they always have — in the decorum of partnership agreements and without resort to unseemly (and unpredictable) lawsuits. But for Simpson and all who came of age at the birth of the civil rights movement, no course of action could be more proper than to imbue one's personal struggle with universal significance by taking it to court. His suit and others like it signal that, with all the vigor they once summoned to fight the Vietnam War, environmental pollution and repression of any kind, baby boomers are poised to attack an issue that is new only to them: how employers treat workers with long careers.

One indication of the trend is the series of record age-discrimination settlements the United States Equal Employment Opportunity Commission racked up in the past year, like Monsanto and Chevron's agreement to pay $18.3 million to 43 laid-off sellers of Ortho lawn-care chemicals — some of them as young

Marianne Lavelle, a writer for The National Law Journal, is a co-author of "Toxic Deception," a book about how dangerous products stay on the market.

as 41. The E.E.O.C. has no statistics yet to prove it, but at a meeting last June on age discrimination, the agency's chairman, Gilbert Casellas, noted the profusion of high-profile claims by workers "at the younger end of this protected class." Even though, he might have added, those complaints require a person who should be in the peak years of a career to make an unabashed declaration of helplessness.

Simpson's case against Ernst & Young, for example, turns on a semantic issue: what is it to be a "partner" in a mammoth organization where you have no real decision-making power? And in a way, that question captures the loss of meaning, the slipping away of personal definition, that is the essence of age-discrimination cases. But Simpson was no weary Willy Loman. The 6-foot-5 former University of Kentucky basketball player struck a youthful pose in a local business journal in gym shorts three years before he was fired. And while Arthur Miller's tragic figure pleaded vainly to his boss, "Pay attention," as his work and life slipped from him, Simpson already has forced partnerships across the nation to take note. His case is a portent that the generation that glorified youth may revolutionize the value of age in the American workplace.

This year marks the 30th anniversary of the Age Discrimination in Employment Act, the Federal law protecting workers over 40 from not being hired or fired or from other work decisions based on age. Its passage was a little-noted flourish in the civil rights movement; racial and sexual equality attracted more attention on campuses then filled with students in the leading edge of the baby boom. The facts that one-half of the private-sector job openings at the time were advertised as closed to applicants over 55 and that one-quarter of those barred workers as young as 45 seemed far-off concerns.

Now that half of the labor force will be over 40 by the year 2005, there is no civil rights cause

more relevant to baby boomers. Nor is there one more universal. If, for lack of kinship, any white man on a conservative career track could not fully appreciate the struggle of minorities and women against prejudice, statistics indicate that he will. More than 86 percent of age-discrimination complaints in the mid-1980's were filed by men, 79 percent by white-collar workers and 57 percent by managers, according to E.E.O.C. and other studies.

Three decades after the law's passage, older job applicants will be discriminated against one in four times when competing with younger applicants with the same credentials. Research in 1994 by the Fair Employment Council of Greater Washington for the American Association of Retired Persons showed that discrimination against older workers was about the same as that against African-Americans and Hispanics of all ages. The researchers also learned that older applicants could boost their chances only by hiding their age or emphasizing their youthful qualities. The worst strategy for an older applicant is to emphasize experience, stability, loyalty and maturity — stereotypical qualities, positive though they may be, associated with age. More than one in three such résumés were rejected outright.

Age-discrimination complaints filed annually before the E.E.O.C. or state and local employment agencies, the first step in any civil rights action, climbed from 24,813 in fiscal 1990 to a high of 32,145 in 1992. The agency calculates that employers in fiscal 1996 paid more than ever before in per-worker precourt resolutions of age-discrimination cases: $40.9 million to settle 1,931 cases. In those cases that make it to court, headlines suggest that employers are agreeing to multimillion-dollar payments. Most notably, the defense giant Lockheed Martin consented last November to pay $13 million to 2,000 nonunion employees who lost jobs in the old Martin Marietta Astronautics Group from 1990 to 1994.

It's too bad our bodies fall apart a little bit.
It takes me longer to make up my face now.
Ruth Bernhard, 91
Photographer

I travel alone, I live alone, I cook my dinners and lunches and breakfasts. I browse in the neighborhood and have my hair and nails done. I can do the same things I always did. It makes me resentful when I go down the stairs and they want to hold my arm. For heaven's sake, I say. Leave me alone.

If I had an older woman's body to photograph, I would do what I could to make it as beautiful as possible. But I would not emphasize the age, because I don't like the way my body looks at the age of 91. I think it's too bad our bodies fall apart a little bit. The skin is not as beautiful. It takes me longer to make up my face now.

But I would never neglect myself and not be perfectly well dressed and perfectly combed when I leave my house. I see women of my age who no longer have the energy to take care of themselves and I resent that.

I always feel that when I am given something to do I must say yes to it. I haven't mastered the art of saying no yet. I find that to be needed and to be asked to give whatever I have is very stimulating. I don't think there is enough time left for me to say no.

Lockheed never admitted to bias, and many other managers argue that they are unfairly accused of age discrimination when decisions are purely economic. "Regrettably, when a company has to reduce the workforce, it often has to remove lots of qualified people," says Ann Elizabeth Reesman, general counsel of the Equal Employment Advisory Council, an association of private-sector employers. "That doesn't mean they are not any good or poor employees; it's just that the company doesn't have as many spaces. And that creates resentment for employees, especially long-term employees." Time and again, courts have ruled it legal for an employer to select workers with larger salaries for dismissal, even if they happen to be the older workers.

Kmart is defending itself against age-discrimination suits in part by arguing that dismissals of longtime store managers were legitimate business decisions. Kmart's managers, according to the argument, were once needed to keep inventory of clothing, toys, toaster ovens and other wares on store shelves. But the need for managers in whom to invest such trust evaporated with the introduction of scanners at checkout counters. Inventory decisions could be made by computer. Some of the ex-managers that now are charging the retailer with age discrimination are not yet in the over-50 population that as recently as the mid-1980's made up 82 percent of age-discrimination complainants.

Pamela Poff, a deputy general counsel at Paine Webber, says these cases are not "warm and fuzzy" as they once were, when employers were so ignorant of the law that they would simply tell workers they were too old. Today, she says, "there are instances where, technologically or organizationally, a worker rises to a level where he or she no longer fits within the budgetary constraints of the department."

As a result, age bias has a different edge than racial or sex bias. Its victims are wounded not because of the skin or sex they were born with, but because of what they have become. For LaRue Simpson, pursuing an age-discrimination case meant defending in public what Ernst & Young used to justify his firing — his personal loans with firm clients, his thwarted ambition to become an office managing partner, his choice of serving small entrepreneurial clients that generated little revenue growth. The accounting firm still maintains that Simpson's firing had nothing to do with age. "Ernst & Young is a firm that makes its hiring and retention decisions based on merit," says Kathryn A. Oberly, the firm's general counsel. "That policy was followed in this case." She would not discuss it further pending the Supreme Court petition.

BABY BOOMERS WILL LEARN, IF THEY haven't already, that the age-discrimination claim that begins with the grandest clarion call for civil rights devolves — sooner or later — into the tinny noise of a trial over someone's job performance. Courts often clash over the resolution of such cases. A manager's comment to a diesel mechanic that "at your age you cannot produce like you once could" was ruled a "neutral observation" by a judge in Alabama; the Federal appeals court in Atlanta in 1994 said the remark was "the very essence of age discrimination."

The Commonwealth Fund, a New York-based philanthropic group, financed research on whether worker performance declines with age for its "Americans Over 55 at Work" project — a program aimed at encouraging companies to attract, retrain and retain senior workers. A review of sociological literature showed that the only jobs for which performance appeared to decline with age were in manual labor, where many workers continue to be protected by union seniority rules. Researchers found no correlation between age and work quality for the group that lodges most age-discrimination complaints — supervisors and professionals. Skills actually appear to improve over the years for people in sales.

But skills that workers have perfected through experience may become less important with each passing year. The Commonwealth Fund noted that 48 percent of the executives surveyed see technology as important to the future of their business, but only 11 percent rated their older workers comfortable with new technology. Poff says that older workers may find themselves particularly vulnerable.

Jack Levin, a sociology professor at Northeastern University and the author of the 1980 book "Ageism," argues that while laying off older workers may appear justifiable on the surface, such decisions are based on prejudice, nevertheless. "Workers are told they lack certain qualities deemed absolutely essential," Levin says. "And I think you can summarize those qualities in one code word — versatility. The term is seen as a way of eliminating older workers based on a quality that they lack, as opposed to age. And I think many of those views are based on a stereotypical notion that you can't teach old workers new tricks."

The Commonwealth Fund concluded that not enough research has been done to gauge whether older workers are less trainable than younger employees. But researchers found that 90 percent of workers — young and old — will have to be retrained during their careers. And the payoff for training younger workers, who are more likely to hop to new jobs, may actually be less than for training older workers who stay put. However, employers have to craft training with care for older workers, who respond best to low-pressure training. Does a company's reluctance to invest in a program tailored to older workers constitute discrimination?

It will be a long time before the courts are asked to decide such a subtle issue. Most workers simply agree to cash settlements before volleys of charges and countercharges about their performance and trainability become public. The workers that make it to trial are those who find the paper trail, who hear the stray comment that suggests their cases, indeed, have something to do with youth and age. Exhibit A in the case of hundreds of Kmart store managers, expected to go to trial in Federal court in Atlanta later this year, is a videotaped news conference by Joseph Antonini, the former Kmart chief executive officer, at the unveiling of a new company logo in September 1990. "We are blessed with an officer group whose average age is slightly under 50 years," Antonini said. "Our middle management group … many of whom are here today, whose average age is 40, all are dedicated and committed to our strategies for the 90's."

For LaRue Simpson, the smoking gun was the agenda of Ernst & Young's management-committee meeting of Feb. 21, 1990, including the items "Resignations and retirements — where we stand in the process" and "Comparison of partner ages in 1990." Ernst & Young compiled lists of the names, ages and years of service for every partner over 51. There also was a list of partners who had recently quit and their ages. Jesse Miles, Ernst & Young's co-chairman, said that management merely was gauging what positions would be vacated soon through retirement. As for the detail in which ages were noted, even for younger departing partners, Miles said, "The only way I could describe it is, being accountants, we like to total things."

Simpson's lawyer, Janet Abaray of Cincinnati, had another explanation. When Simpson and 98 other partners over 40 were fired, the company promoted 112 accountants under 40 to partnership. The salary saving alone was $5.5 million per year.

"Ladies and gentlemen, this is not a downsizing — this is an age-sizing," Abaray said at trial. Under questioning by Abaray, Miles had said, "We have to have bright capable young people joining us . . . on an annual basis in order to keep the lifeblood of the organization growing and growing and growing."

A jury's 1994 decision to award Simpson $3.7 million was a signal that baby boomers will not permit organizations like Ernst & Young to hire and fire as they have in the past. Casellas, the E.E.O.C. chairman, says: "While those in or just past the baby-boom years may be the targets of age discrimination, they may also be its final arbiters. Would a trial with a jury most likely made up of the middle-aged peers of those let go from Chevron have proved too risky for the company?"

Levin, the sociologist, sees in such stories hope that the present generation of older workers, by sheer force of numbers, can erode corporate prejudice against senior employees. "The baby boomers have the cultural clout to significantly reduce age discrimination," he says. "What an opportunity for them to take some of the influence, authority and marketplace power that they have and benefit everyone, especially themselves."

Time and again, courts have ruled it legal for an employer to select workers with larger salaries for dismissal, even if they happen to be the older workers.

Children's perceptions and attitudes about aging and older adults are investigated using a version of Children's Views on Aging (CVoA), a four-part validated instrument designed to assess school-age children's views on older adults and aging. The instrument has been adapted to enable children to make value judgements about their responses to questions on the CVoA. The study reports children's perceptions and attitudes about aging are not as negative as adults conclude. Children are positively affected by interactions with older adults, they describe physical signs of aging without judgement, and respond negatively to some of the unpleasant conditions associated with aging.
Key Words: Older adult resources, Intergenerational interaction, Children's attitudes

Children's Views on Aging: Their Attitudes and Values[1]

Sally Newman, PhD,[2] Robert Faux, ABD,[3] and Barbara Larimer, MA MEd[4]

As more and more people live longer and healthier lives, and the number of older adults increases, it is incumbent upon society to reflect upon the nature and genesis of the attitudes and perceptions of its younger people toward older adults. With their numbers increasing, older adults are becoming actively involved in many aspects of community life (Newman, 1985). While their numbers may be large, older adults are often the focus of negative social attitudes, which makes them vulnerable to a form of prejudice known as ageism (Falchikov, 1990; Seefeldt, Jantz, Galper, & Serock, 1977). Laws (1995) argues that age should be studied as a component of a complex framework of social relations between individuals. Ageism can be defined as a set of social practices. Laws suggests that society has transformed biological and chronological age into social and cultural signs. Thus, perceived differences between young and old people are socially constructed, and are not necessarily reducible to biological causes. How a culture views age, therefore, is often based upon socially/culturally agreed upon standards. Researchers have been interpreting results from children using adult standards. The question is: is there a need to be more sensitive to children's socially/culturally derived standards in the context of interpreting their responses?

How are children's attitudes about and perceptions of older adults formed? The answer to this question is complex. Marks, Newman, and Onawola (1985) used the Children's Views on Aging (CVoA) questionnaire to demonstrate the complexity and diversity of children's attitudes toward older adults. They found that, although children's attitudes toward the aging process were often negative, their general attitudes about older adults were positive. Marks and colleagues concluded that children appear to recognize the positive and negative aspects of aging. Beyond making this distinction, the children displayed appropriate affective responses to each aspect of the aging process and to older people. Based upon their research, Marks et al. have suggested the need to look beyond children's attitudes and at the underlying components of those attitudes.

By the time children enter school they may have already developed negative attitudes toward some older adults. Research on the development of such attitudes may help in modifying them before they become well established (Isaacs & Bearison, 1986). Though older adults as a group may be perceived in a negative light, individual older adults within that aggregate may be perceived either positively or negatively. McTavish (1971) has found that negative perceptions can result in an overall rejection of older adults. McTavish argues that children fear growing old because of their misconception that aging is bad. Children's attitudes and stereotypes develop early and remain fairly constant, guiding their behavior toward others (Klausmeier & Ripple, 1971). As Aronson (1976) reminds us, attitudes are resistant to change, and people will go to great lengths to maintain them.

[1]The authors wish to thank Sandra Harris for her assistance in the preparation of this article, and Valerie Balavage for her assistance in the editing of the final review of the article.

[2]Address correspondence to Sally Newman, PhD, Director, Generations Together, University of Pittsburgh, Pittsburgh, PA 15260.

[3]Department of Psychology and Education, University of Pittsburgh, Pittsburgh, PA.

[4]Department of Administration and Policy, University of Pittsburgh, Pittsburgh, PA.

While much of the literature on this issue reports empirical support for the notion that children and young people hold negative stereotypes about older adults, there is a body of research that indicates no significant differences in attitudes between the young and the old, and some report positive perceptions of older adults (Puckett, Petty, Cacioppo, & Fisher, 1983). For example, Fillmer (1984) asked children to react to pictures of young and old people. When a semantic differential scale was used, children's attitudes tended to be more positive toward older adults than towards young people. However, using a Likert-scale, Fillmer found children's attitudes toward older adults to be more negative. While it is essential that we understand the nature and structure of children's beliefs about older adults, owing to the conflicting findings of past research, it is equally important to examine the methodologies employed. It is possible that the methodologies utilized and measurement instruments used influenced the results reported by researchers (Kite & Johnson, 1988). For example, Marks et al. (1985), in their study of children's views of aging, found diversity among children's attitudes toward older adults. From open-ended evaluations, negative perceptions about the aging process emerged; however, when a semantic differential scale was used, children's responses about older persons were relatively positive, suggesting that the children in this study have concerns about "growing old" rather than about older persons.

Kite and Johnson (1988), in their meta-analysis of the literature on the attitudes of children toward older and younger adults, found that attitudes are complex; they are composed of conceptually different domains and are multivariately determined. It is presumed that attitudes guide behavior; thus, one could predict behavior by understanding the attitudes that underlie it. Essential to the formation of attitudes are beliefs, for they serve as an "information base" (Fishbein & Ajzen, 1975, p. 14). Fishbein and Ajzen suggest that new beliefs are built upon prior beliefs through various inference processes.

The beliefs one has about a person or object underlie the formation of attitudes about the person or object. Thus, an individual's attitude toward a person or object is based on beliefs held about particular characteristics or attributes (Fishbein & Ajzen, 1975) of the person or object. For example, an eight-year-old girl may adopt a negative attitude toward older adults if her beliefs about older people are connected to negative attributes. According to Fishbein and Ajzen, beliefs and attitudes are not necessarily consistent. For example, this same eight-year-old may hold various beliefs about older adults and growing old, some favorable and some not, which will affect the way in which she interacts with older adults. Thus, attitudes can be characterized by their dualistic nature: thinking and emotional feeling. Attitudes and beliefs come together to form a complex framework that serves many functions for individuals. Therefore, it is possible for people to have a variety of beliefs about older adults. Kite and Johnson (1988) argue that research must be undertaken that will describe and explain the complexity of attitudes toward older adults, and how attitudes influence behavior.

Owing to the complexity and the multidimensional quality of attitudes, McTavish (1971) argued that the total context in which the young and the old interact must be taken into account. Seefeldt, Jantz, Galper, and Serock (1977) investigated three related components of children's attitudes toward aging and older adults. The components explored were cognition, affect, and behavior. Seefeldt et al. investigated children's knowledge of age, the various types of interaction and behaviors they displayed toward older adults, and their feelings about older adults and the aging process. To this end, Seefeldt and colleagues used a picture series and structured interviews. One hundred eighty children were selected in groups of twenty from each of two school levels (nursery school and grade school levels K through 6). Each of these children was shown four pictures of one man as he aged from 20 years to 80 years. The interviews were aimed at exploring children's ability to identify the oldest man in the pictures and the criteria used to make that identification. After being shown a picture of an 80-year-old man, the children were asked what it would be like to be old. The types of helping behaviors and interactions between young and old were also explored. Children were also asked which of the men they preferred spending time with. Seefeldt et al. also sought to explore children's concepts of age and whether they could arrange the pictures chronologically. Finally, children were asked to assign ages to the men in the pictures. This study indicated that 165 of the 180 (91.6%) children selected and interviewed understood the concept of being old. First graders were able to put the pictures in correct sequence, youngest to oldest. Observable physical characteristics of aging were found to be crucial factors that influenced children's choice of the oldest man.

In previous studies, children's perceptions of aging and older adults were interpreted by adult researchers. It is essential that research begin to assess the values and importance children themselves place upon older adults and aging. Falchikov (1990) analyzed children's drawings of young and old people to ascertain their ideas about aging and older adults. Employing various modes of data analyses, Falchikov found that boys' drawings of young women and girls' pictures of old men were stereotypical. The pictures of older adults were no more stereotyped than pictures of young people, but did contain more negative content, and pictures of older adults were significantly smaller than pictures of young people. While Falchikov acknowledges the simplicity of the methodology employed, it does provide some insights into the way in which children think about aging.

Falchikov (1990) was able to show the various ways that children conceptualize aging. To understand fully children's perceptions of the negative and positive characteristics of aging, it is important to allow children to express the value(s) they place upon their own aging, and the aging of others. It is equally important to understand the genesis of children's attitudes toward aging. For example, how do children learn about aging and older adults? Do they learn about aging and older adults through the media, including television and movies? Or is their knowledge based on personal experience with an older adult, a grandparent or other older adult? What is the nature of their interaction with older adults, and how is that reflected in their attitudes? The aim of this study is to allow children to express the perceptions they have of aging and older adults, and to better understand what value they place upon these perceptions.

Subjects

Seventy-one fourth- and fifth-grade students completed the Children's Views on Aging (CVOA) Questionnaire. These students were participants in a program that brought older adults into their classrooms on a weekly basis to serve as resource persons. Forty-eight females and 23 males responded on the pretest, and 46 females and 25 males responded on the post-test. These children are from predominately low socioeconomic backgrounds, and live in three economically depressed communities in southwestern Pennsylvania. These formerly thriving communities have experienced economic reversal with the sharp decline in the steel industry. The children are predominately African-American, reflecting the racial distribution of the communities in which they live. The elementary schools they attend are all located within thirty miles of Pittsburgh, Pennsylvania.

Method

The Children's Views of Aging (CVoA) is a validated instrument designed to yield information on the attitudes of children toward the aging process and older people, and to help determine the impact of intergenerational programs on these attitudes. The CVoA is designed to be administered on a pretest/post-test schedule. It contains four sections with a variety of open-ended questions. Section I asks the children to think about becoming an old person and to answer nine open-ended questions regarding their perceptions of aging (i.e., "how it feels to be old"). The children are then asked whether they judge their response "a good thing to happen," "a bad thing to happen" or "neither good nor bad." Section II asks for information regarding the frequency and nature of grandparent contact and the ages of grandparents. Section III asks the child questions related to having an older person in the classroom, what the child believes the older person might or could do with them in the classroom, and the child's perceptions of why older adults want to participate in the classroom. Section IV lists twelve

bipolar word pairs that describe characteristics of older adults in a semantic differential scale and asks the child to indicate what characteristics they ascribe to older people (i.e., good/bad, pleasant/unpleasant, mean/kind, etc.).

The CVoA was administered in classrooms by a graduate student from Generations Together. There were approximately 20 to 30 children in each classroom. Depending upon the reading ability of the children, questions would either be read aloud by the graduate student or children would read and answer each question individually. In two cases the CVOA was administered in the school cafeteria after school with children seated at lunch tables.

Results

The following summarizes the responses to a subset of items from Sections I and II of both the pretest and post-test questionnaires. The pre-test was administered before older adults became weekly volunteers in the classroom. The post-test was administered several months after older adults had been a consistent weekly presence in the classroom. These items were chosen because they provide examples of some recurring themes in children's attitudes about the aging process that were noted in their response on the CVoA. For example, when asked how they can tell when people are growing old, 80% of the children listed physical attributes such as graying hair and wrinkles, 5% identified loss of sight, hearing, and memory. Other responses related to observable physical disabilities and decreased activities (15%). A small number (6%) reported a change in personality, while most focused upon the physical changes that may occur with age: loss of hair, graying of hair, and so forth. When children were asked if they thought the changes were good, bad or neither good nor bad, 20% said it was "good," 30% said that it was "bad," and 50% said that it was "neither good nor bad." Children tend to perceive observable aspects of aging in the context of physical characteristics without placing a value on these characteristics.

When asked how they thought it felt to be an old person, children's responses ranged from thinking it would be fun and good (12%) to scary, weird, and lonely (35%). These responses mirror the responses children gave when asked how they will feel when they are old. The responses to this latter question ranged from good, happy, and fine to bad, lonely, and sad. However, there was an added condition related to some of the responses, such as worn out, in pain, sick, and helpless (30%). When asked whether they thought this was good, bad, or neither good nor bad, 19% said it was "good," 46% said it was "bad," and 33% said it was "neither good nor bad." Children seem to understand the complexity of the aging process and the feelings that accompany the unpleasant conditions associated with aging. It would appear that while the children did not view the aging process as negative, when asked to describe how it would feel to be old, almost half of them expressed negative impressions of some conditions they related to being old. The children's perceptions of physical and other manifestations of aging (i.e., wrinkles, use of canes, etc.) were not viewed as negative. However, perceptions of their own aging process reflects a negative view of some conditions associated with this process. In summation, while these children do not seem to view old people in a negative way, they anticipate some negative conditions as they become old. This distinction is essential to our understanding of children's overriding perceptions of this stage of life. Children's appreciation of the complexity of aging reflects a more realistic perception of this stage of life than adults may have expected.

Children responded that when a person gets old, they die or go to a nursing home (18%) or they get sick and weak and cannot do things (43%). Others said that old people become grandparents (6%). Some said that old people do fun and exciting things (11%). Asked what they will do when they are old, these children said they would sit around, watch TV, and play games (32%). A small number said that they would go to a nursing or retirement home or die (6%). Other responses provided by the children reflected a sense of maintaining a certain level of activity and involvement with others in the form of work (7%) and recreation (21%). When asked whether they thought this was good, bad, or neither good nor bad, 19% said it was "good," 47% said it was "bad," and 33% said it was "neither good nor bad." These responses are consistent with those of the previous question. It appears that the children have some negative perceptions about how it feels to be old and some of the conditions associated with being old. However, these feelings do not seem to transfer to their feelings *about* older people.

When asked where or from whom they learned most about old persons, most of the children said they learned about old people from their grandparents (62%). The next most frequent source of information was from parents (22%). Other sources of information included TV, movies, books, and friends (8%).

In Section II, 95% of the children reported having grandparents. Children reported a mean age of 66 years for grandfathers and 63 years for grandmothers. Most of the children (69%) said that their grandparents are the oldest people they know, and most reported seeing them daily or weekly (72%). The children reported engaging in indoor (30%) and outdoor (39%) activities with their grandparents when they are with them. Some of the children (21%) said they talk with their grandparents and have fun with them. It is interesting to note that children's relationship with their grandparents do not generalize to "all old people." Grandparents are typically seen as a "special persons" whose behaviors and characteristics are unique to the family constellation.

The children's responses are interesting in several

respects. It is notable that when asked how "old" people felt about being old and how they thought they would feel when they are old, the responses were very similar and ranged from negative — weird and sad, to positive — good and great. Also of interest are the responses to the question "How you can tell when someone is old?" Many of the responses focused on functional characteristics such as decreased activity and physical characteristics of aging such as gray hair or baldness. A few children reported that an individual's personality may change with age. The breadth of responses to the question "What happens when a person gets old?" is notable. There is a wide range of responses, including going to a nursing or retirement home or dying, to doing fun and exciting things. When asked what they will do when they are old, the children responded similarly, with some responses reflecting a desire to remain active and to be involved with other people. It would appear that children display a wide range of perceptions about aging and its consequences. They do not appear to view the physical changes as overwhelmingly negative. At the same time, they seem to have more negative expectations on how it will feel to actually be old and what will happen to them as a result of being old. They do not report viewing the aging of others as negative.

Section III of the CVoA focuses on the children's perception of the presence and roles of older adults in the classroom. A comparison of pre- and post-test responses on selected representative items from Section III of CVoA is reported in the following tables.

Item:

Why do you think an old person would visit your classroom? (see Table 1)

Item:

Would you like having an old person in your classroom as a helper? (see Table 2)

Table 1 Childrens' Attributions of Reasons Why Elders Visit Their Classrooms

Reason	Pre-test %			Post-test %		
	Yes	No	Don't Know	Yes	No	Don't Know
To teach children	83	3	14	81	4	15
To help children	88	3	9	89	3	8
Because they like children	67	8	25	72	4	24
To make them feel useful	55	19	26	42	24	34
They are lonely	44	27	29	48	19	33
They have nothing else to do	19	48	33	24	32	44

Pre- and post-participation responses did not show great differences. Perceptions that the older adults wanted to teach and help children remained very positive from pre-test to post-test. Slightly more children at the time of the post-test thought that the older adults came to their classroom because they liked children. After participation, fewer children thought that the older adults were there because they wanted to feel useful. On the post-

Table 2. Desirability of the Presence of an Older Adult Aide

Pre-test %			Post-test %		
Yes	No	Don't Know	Yes	No	Don't Know
84	8	8	89	4	7

test, slightly more children reported thinking that the older adults came to their classrooms because they were lonely, and that they had nothing interesting to do.

When asked if they wanted an older adult in their classroom as a helper, more children said 'yes' on the post-test questionnaire. This change reflects an increase of 6%, from 83% on the pre-test to 89% on the post-test, indicating a positive reaction of children to the interaction with the older adult volunteer.

Section IV of the CVoA addresses children's perceptions of older adults using selected bipolar word pairs of characteristics drawn from the Osgood semantic differential scale. The children identify along a 5-point Likert-type scale their rating of older people's characteristics. In general, there is a marked positive shift along a 5-point rating scale in perception of "old people" after older adults had been present weekly in the classrooms as school volunteers. Table 3 summarizes the percentage of positive change in student responses from pre-test to post-test for selected characteristics.

In general, ratings were more positive after interaction with the older adults. In addition, the data suggest that the descriptions tended toward "very" positive on the post-test. For most descriptors, the percentage of "very" positive change ranged from about 10–20%.

Some incremental increases in negative descriptions were also documented. However, the percentage of change as well as the strength of the descriptions was substantially less than for the positive results. For example, a small increase (7%) from pre-test to post-test is observed for the descriptor "boring." At the same time, a 15% increase is observed on the other end of the scale for "interesting." The small increases in negative descriptors were in all cases more than offset by change on the positive end of the scale. Other descriptors for which a small increase on the negative side was offset by the percentage of positive change were: slow, mean, and hated. It should be stressed that negative increases were incremental and tended to appear in the "a little" category. Observed changes were generally positive.

In addition to these findings, some other differences were noted. For example, when the percentage of students who responded "not sure" decreased from pre-test to post-test, the greatest corresponding increase was observed in the positive or very positive category. In other words, if the students were "not sure" whether they would "describe old people" as "good" at the time of the pre-test, the percentage who were "not sure" at the time of the post-test was

Table 3. Adjectives That Children Endorsed to Describe Older Adults

Adjective	Pre-test %		Post-test %	
	Very Much*	Very Little+	Very Much	Very Little
Good	60	4	80	0
Pleasant	47	10	64	4
Happy	59	12	68	8
Fast	5	20	7	16
Pretty	27	29	36	24
Interesting	58	14	72	4
Kind	55	12	68	4
Loved	52	8	64	8

Note: *,+Very Much and Very Little were used as the extreme values of a five-point rating scale. Not included in the table are counts for intermediate values; we merely wish to describe the shift. We cannot designate the ends of the scale as either positive or negative because we discovered that the children themselves do not perceive their own ratings in that way.

substantially lower and the positive attribution increased proportionately. Those who were uncertain tended to give more positive descriptions of older adults after they had participated in the school volunteer program.

Summary

The results of pre-test and post-test administration of the CVoA, including differences between pre-test and post-test, show a shift in childrens' feelings about their responses to a more positive value. Children who were previously unsure of the emotional quality of their responses have shifted from "not sure" in pre-test measures to "good" or better in post-test measures. The typical child in this study tends to have positive perceptions of older people, but negative feelings about his or her own aging. They have a realistic and consistent perception of why older adults work with them in the classroom. There is little change in their understanding of the reasons why older adults serve as classroom volunteers between the pre-test and post-test.

Children in this study identify physical changes due to aging, and do not have a negative perception of them. Previous reports of childrens' negative perceptions of the physical aging process may have been prompted more by the attributions and interpretations of the research than by concrete evidence gathered from the children themselves. They consistently identified positive affective characteristics associated with aging, which were clearly demonstrated in their responses to the semantic differential scale. The children accurately and consistently identified the reasons why older adults came to their classrooms, and that they and their classmates generally felt good about their presence. The children in this study tend to associate their negative feelings with some conditions accompanying the aging process, and they tend to attribute the same feelings about aging to the older adults as well.

Overall, these children had positive perceptions of and emotional responses to older people. This study is important because it provides adults with new insights into children's perceptions of aging through the child's own values. It demonstrates the value of interpreting a child's responses using the child's own values rather than interpreting children's responses using adult values.

This study, therefore, differs from earlier studies in which researchers assigned adult values to their interpresentation of children's responses without consulting the children on how they valued their responses.

Implications for Further Research

It appears from this study that children are positively affected by their interactions with older adults, have a realistic perception of the aging process, and can place a value on their perception. Intergenerational interaction is shown to further enhance positive perceptions of aging. This study suggests the importance of involving children in articulating their values. Professionals may be cautioned not to infer adult interpretations to the responses of children, but rather to gain insight on children's perceptions from the children themselves.

The complexities associated with children's multidimensional responses to aging and older persons requires that researchers provide more accurate interpretations of their findings through the use of children's and youth's values and interpretations of their own responses.

With the consistent increase nationally of intergenerational programs involving children, youth and older adults, it is essential that we understand the impact of these programs on our children and youth in the context of the cross-generational outcome behaviors and attitudes.

This study presents additional insights related to the anticipated outcomes of intergenerational programs, a social phenomenon whose intent is to positively impact the behaviors and attitudes of our country's young and old.

References

Aronson, E. (1976). *The social animal.* San Francisco: Freeman.
Falchikov, N. (1990). Youthful ideas about old age: An analysis of children's drawings. *International Journal of Aging and Human Development, 31*(2), 79–99.
Fillmer, H. (1984). Children's descriptions of and attitudes toward the elderly. *Educational Gerontology, 10,* 99-107.
Fishbein, M., & Ajzen, I. (1975). *Belief, attitude, intention, and behavior: An introduction to theory and research.* Reading, MA: Addison-Wesley.
Isaacs, L. W., & Bearison, D. J. (1986). The development of children's prejudice against the aged. *International Journal of Aging and Human Development, 23,* 175–194.
Kite, M. E., & Johnson, B. T. (1988). Attitudes toward older and younger adults: A meta-analysis. *Psychology and Aging, 3,* 233–244.
Klausmeier, J. J., & Ripple, R. (1971). *Learning and human abilities.* New York: Harper & Row.
Laws, G. (1995). Understanding ageism: Lessons from feminism and postmodernism. *The Gerontologist, 35,* 112–118.
Marks, R., Newman, S., & Onawola, R. (1985). Latency-aged children's views on aging. *Educational Gerontology, 11*(2–3), 89–99.
McTavish, D. G. (1971). Perceptions of old people: A review of research methodologies and findings. *The Gerontologist, 11,* 90–101.
Newman, S., & Marks, R. (1997). *Children's views on aging.* Pittsburgh, PA: Generations Together.
Newman, S. (1985, November). *A curriculum on aging on our schools: Its time has come.* Paper presented at the Bridging the Gap Conference, New York, NY.
Puckett, J. M., Petty, R. E., Cacioppo, J. T., & Fisher, D. L. (1983). The relative impact of age and attractiveness stereotypes on persuasion. *The Journals of Gerontology, 18,* 340–343.
Seefeldt, C., Jantz, R. K., Galper, A., & Serock, K. (1977). Using pictures to explore children's attitudes toward the elderly. *The Gerontologist, 17,* 506-512.

Received March 18, 1996
Accepted December 20, 1996

WHAT DOCTORS AND OTHERS NEED TO KNOW

Six Facts on Human Sexuality and Aging

Richard J. Cross, MD

Certified Specialist in Internal Medicine, Professor Emeritus at the Robert Wood Johnson Medical School, NJ

Most of us find that our definition of old age changes as we mature. To a child, anyone over forty seems ancient. Sixty-five and older is the common governmental definition of a senior citizen, and it is the definition that I will follow here, although the author (who is in his late 70s) long ago began to find it hard to accept. There is, of course, no specific turning point, but rather a series of gradual physical and emotional changes, some in response to societal rules about retirement and entitlement to particular benefits.

Demographically, the elderly are a rapidly growing segment of the population. In 1900, there were about three million older Americans; by the year 2000, there will be close to 31 million older Americans. Because of high male mortality rates, older women outnumber men 1.5 to 1, and since most are paired off, single women outnumber single men by about 4 to 1. By definition, the elderly were born in the pre-World War I era. Most were thoroughly indoctrinated in the restrictive attitudes toward sex that characterized these times.

In my opinion, the care of the elderly could be significantly improved if doctors and other health workers would remember the following six, simple facts.

Fact #1: All Older People Are Sexual

Older people are not all sexually active, as is also true of the young, but they all have sexual beliefs, values, memories, and feelings. To deny this sexuality is to exclude a significant part of the lives of older people. In recent decades, this simple truth has been repeatedly stated by almost every authority who has written about sexuality, but somehow the myth persists that the elderly have lost all competence, desire, and interest in sexuality, and that those who remain sexual, particularly if sexually active, are regarded as abnormal and, by some, even perverted. This myth would seem to have at least three components. First, it is a carryover of the Victorian belief that sex is dan-

gerous and evil, though necessary for reproduction, and that sex for recreational purposes is improper and disgusting. Second is what Mary S. Calderone, SIECUS co-founder, has called a tendency for society to castrate its dependent members: to deny the sexuality of the disabled, of prisoners, and of the elderly. This perhaps reflects a subconscious desire to dehumanize those whom we believe to be less fortunate than ourselves in order to assuage our guilt feelings. Third, Freud and many others have pointed out that most of us have a hard time thinking of our parents as being sexually active, and we tend to identify all older people with our parents and grandparents.

For whatever reason, it is unfortunate that young people so often deny the sexuality of those who are older. It is even more tragic when older people themselves believe the myth and then are tortured by guilt when they experience normal, healthy sexual feelings. Doctors and other health workers need to identify and alleviate such feelings of guilt.

How many people are sexually active? It is generally agreed upon by experts that the proportion of both males and females who are sexually active declines, decade by decade, ranging according to one study from 98% of married men in their 50s to 50% for unmarried women aged 70 and over.[1] At each decade, there are also some people who are inactive. It is important to accept abstinence as a valid lifestyle as well—at any age—as long as it is freely chosen.

Fact #2: Many Older People Have a Need for a Good Sexual Relationship

To a varying extent, the elderly experience and must adapt to gradual physical and mental changes. They may find themselves no longer easily able to do the enjoyable things they used to do; their future may seem fearful; retirement and an "empty nest" may leave many with reduced incomes and no clear goals in life; friends and/or a lifetime partner may move away, become ill, or die; and the threat of loneliness may be a major concern. Fortunately, many older people are not infirm, frustrated, fearful, bored, or lonely; nonetheless, some of these elements may be affecting their lives. An excellent antidote for all this is the

Reprinted with permission from the *SIECUS Report*, June/July 1993, pp. 7-9. © 1993 by the Sex Information and Education Council of the U.S., Inc., 130 West 42nd Street, Suite 350, New York, NY 10036.

Research Note

Andrew Greeley, priest, author, and sociologist at the University of Chicago analyzed national-poll data of 6,000 respondents and found that sexual activity is plentiful, even after the age of 60. He reported in 1992 that 37 percent of married people over 60 have sexual relations at least once a week—and one in six respondents had sexual relations more often. Greeley concluded that sexually active married men are happier with their spouses at 60 than 20-year-old single males who have many sexual partners. His report, "Sex After Sixty: A Report," based on surveys by the Gallup Organization and the National Opinion Research Center included the following results:

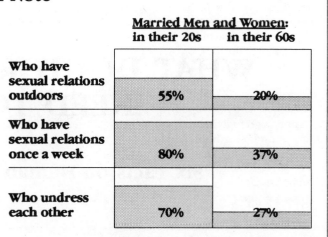

| | Married Men and Women: | |
	in their 20s	in their 60s
Who have sexual relations outdoors	55%	20%
Who have sexual relations once a week	80%	37%
Who undress each other	70%	27%

warmth, intimacy, and security of a good sexual relationship.

Fact #3: Sexual Physiology Changes with Age

In general, physiological changes are gradual and are easily compensated for, if one knows how. But when they sneak up on an unsuspecting, unknowledgeable individual, they can be disastrous. Health workers need to be familiar with these changes and with how they can help patients adapt to them.

Older men commonly find that their erections are less frequent, take longer to achieve, are less firm, and are more easily lost. Ejaculation takes longer, is less forceful, and produces a smaller amount of semen. The refractory period (the interval between ejaculation and another erection) is often prolonged to many hours or even days. The slowing down of the sexual response cycle can be compensated for simply by taking more time, a step usually gratifying to one's partner, especially if he or she is elderly. But in our society many men grow up believing that their manliness, their power, and their competence depend on their ability to "get it up, keep it up, and get it off." For such an individual, slowing of the cycle may induce performance anxiety, complete impotence, and panic. Good counseling about the many advantages of a leisurely approach can make a world of difference for such an individual.

The prolonged refractory period may prevent a man from having sexual relations as often as he formerly did, but only if he requires that the sexual act build up to his ejaculation. If he can learn that good, soul-satisfying sexual activity is possible without male ejaculation, then he can participate as often as he and his partner wish. Finally, men (and sometimes their partners) need to learn that wonderful sex is possible without an erect penis. Tongues, fingers, vibrators, and many other gadgets can make wonderful stimulators and can alleviate performance anxiety.

Some women find the arrival of menopause disturbing; others feel liberated. If one has grown up in a society that believes that the major role for women is bearing children, then the loss of that ability may make one feel no longer a "real woman." The most common sexual problem of older women, however, is vaginal dryness, which can make sexual intercourse painful, particularly if her partner is wearing an unlubricated condom. The obvious solution is to use one of the many water-soluble lubricants available in drug stores. Saliva is a fairly good lubricant and it does have four advantages over commercial products: 1) it is readily available where one may be; 2) it is free; 3) it is at the right temperature; and 4) its application is more intimate than something from a tube.

An alternative approach attacks the root of the problem. Vaginal drying results from a decrease in estrogen and can be reversed with estrogen replacement which also prevents other consequences of menopause like hot flashes and loss of calcium from the skeleton. But estrogen administration may increase the risk of uterine cancer; therefore, each woman and her doctor will need to balance out the risks and benefits in her particular situation.

Aging inevitably changes physical appearance and, in our youth-oriented culture, this can have a profound impact on sexuality. It is not easy to reverse the influence of many decades of advertisements for cosmetics and clothes, but doctors can at least try to avoid adding to the problem. Many medical procedures—particularly mastectomy, amputations, chemotherapy, and ostomies—have a profound impact on body image. It is of utmost importance to discuss this impact before surgery and to be fully aware of the patient's need to readjust during the post-operative period. When possible, involvement of the patient's sexual partner in these discussions can be very helpful.

Fact #4: Social Attitudes Are Often Frustrating

As indicated above, society tends to deny the sexuality of the aged, and in so doing creates complications in their already difficult lives. Laws and customs restrict the sexual behavior of older people in many ways. This is particularly true for women, since they have traditionally enjoyed less freedom and because, demographically, there are fewer potential partners for heterosexual, single women, and many of the few men that are available are pursuing women half their age.

Some professionals have suggested that women explore sexual behaviors with other women. However, we know that sexual orientation, although potentially fluid through-out a life-span, is more complicated than the suggestion implies. While some women discover lesbian sexuality at an older age, it is rarely the result of a decrease in the availability of male partners. When doctors see an older woman as a patient, they can, at least, inquire into sexual satisfaction. If sexual frustration is expressed, they can be understanding. Some women can be encouraged to try masturbating, and some will find a vibrator a delightful way to achieve orgasm.

Older people are living in a variety of retirement communities and nursing homes. This brings potential sexual partners together, but tends to exaggerate the gender imbalance. In retirement homes, single women often outnumber single men, eight or ten to one. Furthermore, rules, customs, and lack of privacy severely inhibit the establishment of intimate relationships at these sites. Administrators of such homes are often blamed for this phenomenon. Some are, indeed, unsympathetic, but we must also consider the attitudes of the trustees, the neighbors, and the legislators who oversee the operation, and particularly the attitudes of the family members. If two residents establish a sexual relationship, it is often followed by a son or daughter pounding the administrator's desk and angrily shouting, "That's not what I put Mom (Dad) here for!"

Fact #5: Use It Or Lose It
Sexual activity is not a commodity that can be stored and saved for a rainy day. Rather, it is a physiologic function that tends to deteriorate if not exercised, and it is particularly fragile in the elderly. If interrupted, it may be difficult (though not impossible) to reinvigorate. Doctors should work with the patient and partner on reestablishing the ability if desired.

Fact #6: Older Folks Do It Better
This may seem like an arrogant statement to some, but much depends on what is meant by "better." If the basis is how hard the penis is, how moist the vagina, how many strokes per minute, then the young will win out, but if the measure is satisfaction achieved, the elderly can enjoy several advantages. First, they have usually had considerable experience, not necessarily with many different partners. One can become very experienced with a single partner. Second, they often have more time, and a good sexual relationship takes a lot of time. The young are often pressured by studies, jobs, hobbies, etc., and squeeze their sexual activities into a very full schedule. Older folks can be more leisurely and relaxed. Finally, attitudes often improve with aging. The young are frequently insecure, playing games, and acting out traditional roles because they have not explored other options. Some older folks have mellowed and learned to roll with the punches. They no longer need to prove themselves and can settle down to relating with their partner and meeting his or her needs. Obviously one does not have to be old to gain experience, to set aside time, or to develop sound attitudes. Perhaps the next generation of Americans will discover how to learn these simple things without wasting thirty or forty years of their lives playing silly games. One hopes so.

Conclusion
In summary, older people are sexual, often urgently need sexual contact, and yet encounter many obstacles to enjoying its pleasures, some medical, most societal. Doctors and other healthcare providers need to be aware of these problems and need to help those who are aging cope with them.

Dr. Richard J. Cross originally wrote this article for the SIECUS Report in 1988.

Author's References
1 Brecher EM. *Love, Sex, and Aging.* New York: Little, Brown and Company, 1984.

AMAZING GREYS

Old images of aging are changing in an era when seniors are living longer, healthier, wealthier and more independently than they ever have before

Mary Nemeth

In his office across from Parliament Hill hang framed newspaper cartoons spoofing Mitchell Sharp at various points in his long career. Once a high-profile civil servant, a successful businessman and a cabinet minister, and now—for $1 a year—Prime Minister Jean Chrétien's special adviser, the 82-year-old Sharp remembers a time when society's entire focus was on youth. "People in their 70s and 80s," he says, "were considered incapable of having a reasonable opinion about current events." The fact that the Prime Minister has turned to Sharp for assistance—not *in spite* of his age but because of his seniority—is evidence of a dramatic shift in popular images of aging. "People pay more attention to what I say now than perhaps they should," laughs Sharp. "I think there is quite a significant change in attitude going on. Somehow, once again, experience counts."

North Americans, raised on evil old crones like the one in *Hansel and Gretel* and bombarded by Hollywood images of youthful beauty, have long ignored, even feared, old age. Blanket stereotypes afflicted anyone over 65: sickly, feebleminded, confined to nursing homes, a burden on their children, haggard and bitter—or, at best, cute and childlike. True, many seniors *are* very ill, some are impoverished, some are physically abused. And some who live with their grown children require more care than younger families can provide. But those troubled seniors are in a minority, often at the top end of an aging scale that can last into the 80s, 90s and beyond. "Old age is not all frailty," notes Neena Chappell, director of the University of Victoria's Centre on Aging. "Without minimizing the difficulties of those who are really suffering, in truth the majority of seniors are doing very well, thank you."

Canadian seniors, in fact, are living longer, healthier, wealthier and more independently than ever before. And old stereotypes are under assault. American author Betty Friedan, whose 1963 book, *The Feminine Mystique,* inspired modern feminism, has turned to the myths surrounding the elderly. In her latest book, *The Fountain of Age,* the 72-year-old Friedan refutes the "image of age as inevitable decline." She argues that gerontologists concentrate too much "on the victims of the most extreme ravages of senility, the sick, helpless old." That focus, she writes, may have blinded not only the profession but older people themselves to the possibilities of life after 60. But Friedan is only at the thin edge of a demographic wedge: the number of Canadians over 65 is expected to grow from 3.2 million now to 8.7 million within four decades. The first of the baby boomers—the group that used to distrust anyone over 30—will start turning 65 in the year 2011. That generation, through force of numbers, has dictated trends in everything from hairstyles to consumer spending, and is certain to demand an end to negative stereotypes of aging, as well.

Already, Hollywood seems to sense a shifting wind. Among a spate of recent movies featuring older characters, Billy Crystal was slathered with wrinkle and liver-spot makeup for his role as a fading comic in the 1992 *Mr. Saturday Night,* and an equally made-up Bette Midler played a past-her-prime siren in the 1991 *For the Boys.* But Robin Williams said that in his latest movie, *Mrs. Doubtfire*—after first making him up to look like a haggard old crone—film-makers settled on a more attractive older woman character.

And advertisers now poke fun at the aged only at their peril. In response to public outrage over a recent Doritos tortilla chip commercial—which showed a befuddled old woman getting steamrolled into wet cement—the contrite manufacturer delivered cases of free chips to a food bank. "I do think some sensitivity is developing," says Ethel Meade, 74, co-chairman of the Older Women's Network, a Toronto advocacy group. "Of course, lots of older women are busy and active. They are breaking stereotypes by showing what older women can do."

Senior men and women volunteer or work part time. They travel to exotic locations and take study vacations at home. A Kingston, Ont.-based group called

Elderhostel Canada offers courses in subjects ranging from cross-country skiing to watercolor painting. And the Raging Grannies, who caricature aging stereotypes by dressing up in floppy hats and frilly dresses, campaign against everything from nuclear arms to the GST. Another grandmother, 73-year-old Lenore Wedlake from Halifax, teaches a weekly class in t'ai chi, a Chinese martial art that focuses on relaxation and meditation. "I guess, because of my age, they thought I would be a good role model," says Wedlake, who maintains that "old" is a concept "perpetuated by younger people." She adds: "When you get to be older, you just don't feel that much older inside. I don't have quite as much energy as I once did. But generally, I've been blessed with good health."

Even as seniors swing into action, however, some people argue that the anti-ageism movement has missed its mark. Tracy Kidder, a Pulitzer Prize–winning author, just published *Old Friends,* based on patients in a Massachusetts nursing home. In a recent interview, he argued that the increasingly common images of seniors in tennis shoes implies that the only way to age "successfully" is to be in good health. That, he says, ignores the real problems of the disabled and the weak. "There are people who are very sick," says Kidder, "who manage against the odds to lead meaningful lives." Among them, he says, is an arthritic elderly man at the nursing home who insisted on dressing himself, even though it took him 1½ hours each morning. "When it takes 1½ hours," says Kidder, "the fact that you do it for your own dignity is a kind of routine heroism."

Of course, physical health does decline with age. According to the University of Victoria's Chappell, studies have shown that anywhere from 13 to 20 per cent of all seniors endure disabilities severe enough to hamper independent living–the inability to get dressed, go to the bathroom, get around the house–that can be caused by anything from arthritis to a stroke. But health may vary vastly depending on how old a senior is. According to Statistics Canada, 82 per cent of people aged 85 and over report some level of disability, compared with only 37 per cent of those aged 65 to 74. For most people, says Chappell, deteriorating health "tends to be gradual and things we can cope with."

Nils Hoas is among the golden oldies. A 66-year-old retired railway worker, he plays golf and slow-pitch baseball in the summer. And he was curling recently at the Peace Arch Curling Club in White Rock, B.C., at a bonspiel for those aged 60 and over. Hoas argues that inactivity can be demoralizing. When many of his co-workers retired, he says, "they just stopped, they didn't do anything–they just sort of vegetated and seemed to give up on life."

Elsie McKenzie skipped the masters bonspiel–she travelled about 100 km from Vancouver to Chilliwack for an over-80s tournament instead. McKenzie talks gleefully of the time when, as a 67-year-old, she and three friends won a bonspiel in Scotland–even beating a squad of fit young Canadian airmen visiting from a base in Germany. That was in 1969. Now 91, McKenzie still curls at least once a week. "I think I would have been dead years ago, she says, "If I hadn't been curling."

As it happens, there has been some debate over whether seniors, as a group, are healthier than ever. In the past century, the life expectancy of Canadians has approximately doubled to 73 years for men, 80 for women. But some researchers say that as average life span continues to grow, healthy life does not. Even as heart diseases decrease, the argument goes, some cancers are increasing. But Statistics Canada senior analyst Russell Wilkins found that in 1986 Canadians' average life span was 76.4 years, up 7.8 years from 1951. Wilkins calculated that 2.8 of those extra years were lived with some disability. But most of the increase–five of the extra eight years of life–was disability-free.

When life expectancy was shorter, the few people who did live into their senior years had likely lost their spouses. Only in this century, writes Andrew Greeley, 65, an American priest and sociologist, have large numbers of men and women "survived into the 'senior' category in good health and with sexual desire still very much alive." But attitudes lag behind. Greeley published a study last year to counter perceptions that passionate love is non-existent among seniors. He found that about 37 per cent of married men and women over 60 have sex at least once a week; 20 per cent of those in their 60s report making love outdoors. Such data, he writes, is ignored amid "the snide snicker of the prevailing culture."

Al Bennett, a retired Toronto accountant, knows firsthand about late-blooming love. A widower, he met his match through an introduction agency. "I was just looking for companionship," says Bennett, 66. "But then the lights went on and the whistles blew." He and Margaret, a 59-year-old widow, plan to marry next year. "There's a whole new world in front of us, he says, adding that their families–seven children and eight grandchildren between them–have been supportive. "But I think some children throw roadblocks," he says. "They think someone else will get the inheritance, or they think daddy or mommy shouldn't be doing these things."

As for sex, Bennett allows that some seniors may not require it. "But it shouldn't be taken for granted that because you're 65, you're dead from the waist down." While sex "may not be as frequent in many cases," he says, "it is far more satisfying. We are who we are, we're not trying to demonstrate that we are Michelle Pfeiffer or whoever."

Grey may not only be beautiful–it can be bountiful. According to Andrew Wister, associate professor of gerontology at Simon Fraser University in Burnaby, B.C., "wealth and health work together." Health-promotion programs, which push nutrition and more vigorous exercise, seem to reach higher-educated, and usually wealthier, people. The good news is that the overall financial picture for seniors is also improving. Unattached senior women are the poorest group. According to the National Advisory Council on Aging, 38 per cent of them were below the low-income cutoff, or poverty line, in 1990, but that was a marked improvement over 1980, when 60 per cent were below the poverty line. Only 26 per cent of unattached senior men were in that category in 1990, compared with 53 per cent in 1980. And among senior couples, only 4 per cent, down from 13 per cent, were that poor.

Improved financial circumstances have helped ever greater numbers of seniors live independently. StatsCan reports that even among seniors aged 75 and over, 59 per cent of women and 75 per cent of men were either living with a spouse or alone in 1991—an increase of more than 10 percentage points in the past two decades.

Independent seniors are making important contributions. A renowned trapper in the Yukon, 77-year-old Alex Van Bibber was awarded the Order of Canada last year for teaching younger generations about the wilderness. Among other skills, he now teaches other trappers about the proper care of fur and about the new quick-kill traps favored by animal-rights activists. At the same time, the Yukon's native elders—once a significant force in maintaining native culture—are getting more involved again in guiding their commu-

RETIREMENT: WHO PAYS?

Canada has been greying since Confederation. But with increasing longevity and lower fertility, the pace has accelerated since the 1970s. And when the baby boomers start to turn 65 just 17 years from now, the bulge in the senior population will be enormous. There is mounting alarm that the generation born after the mid-1960s will be unable—or unwilling—to bear the cost of social security for retiring baby boomers. But that potential crisis, experts say, can be contained—if only Canadians take steps now to prepare for the senior surge. "There has been a horrendous exaggeration of the magnitude of the problem," maintains Robert Brown, a professor of actuarial science at Ontario's University of Waterloo. "Yes, there are some concerns, but if we start to deal with them sooner, they will be manageable."

Most of those concerns surround the Canada Pension Plan, which now siphons off 5.2 per cent of earnings, split evenly between employees and employers. The CPP uses a pay-as-you-go system that will work only if future generations keep up their obligations—which are certain to grow. According to Sta-

tistics Canada, over the next four decades the number of seniors will increase 168 per cent to 8.7 million from 3.2 million. At the same time, the working-age population will grow by only 28 per cent. As a result, the CPP schedule calls for the rate of contributions to rise to as high as 13 per cent of earnings by the year 2030. "If the economy stays on line," says Jean Dumas, head of current demographic analysis at StatsCan, "the demographic burden will be heavy on the shoulders of wage earners. If the economy booms, there will be no problem."

The economy, of course, is notoriously unco-operative. But some experts say that, even without an economic turnaround, the government can help alleviate potential pension problems. It could marginally reduce CPP payments. Or it could follow the American example. In the year 2002, the United States will begin increasing the age of eligibility for pensions by an average of one month a year for 25 years, ultimately raising the age to 67 from 65. For Canada, says Brown, "the time to do something is now so we have a gradual transition, rather than walking to the edge of the cliff." According to the

Canadian Institute of Actuaries, based in Ottawa, the government could reduce future CPP contributions—to 10 per cent from 13 per cent—by raising the age of eligibility for retirement from 65 to 70.

Such measures would require major adjustments—including, perhaps, working longer. Seven provinces allow employers to impose mandatory retirement. The exceptions are Manitoba, Quebec and New Brunswick, plus the federal civil service. "Employers will have to stop saying, 'At 65, you're out,'" says Ellen Gee, a demographer at Simon Fraser University in Burnaby, B.C. "And employees will have to realize that they can't go fishing for the next 30 years." With baby boomers not getting any younger, the debate over how to finance future pensions is sure to heat up. But that debate, advises Ann Robertson, a University of Toronto social scientist, should focus on "who we are as a society, and not pit one generation against another. We don't have to buy the apocalyptic scenario that the elderly will bankrupt us."

SHARON DOYLE DRIEDGER

nities. "The elders can see what our young people have lost, there are so many problems with identity, self-esteem," says Pearl Keenan, 73, a Tlingit elder living in Whitehorse. "They are pulling us off our rocking chairs and crying for help." last fall, she says, elders representing each of the 14 Yukon First Nations held their second annual conference, passing recommendations on alcohol and drug abuse, gambling, education, language and culture.

Elsewhere, as well, seniors are doing good works. Blake Caldwell, a pastor at the Moncton Wesleyan Church in New Brunswick, argues that they have not only a right, but a responsibility, to grow spiritually. "It's not enough to get over the line, to say, 'I've become a Christian, I've arrived,'" says Caldwell, who runs the church's Golden Years Fellowship. As many as 100 seniors participate in the interdenominational program each week, doing Bible study, babysitting or visiting other seniors in nursing homes. "We're trying," adds Caldwell, "to defeat that rocking-chair mentality that it's time for me to sit back and let the younger people do things." Not that there is anything wrong with rocking chairs. But as a symbol of the lifestyles of all Canadians over the age of 65, they seem increasingly outdated.

With WARREN CARAGATA in Ottawa, CHRIS WOOD in Vancouver, JOHN DeMONT in Halifax and CHUCK TOBIN in Whitehorse

Learning to *Love* *(GULP!)* Growing *Old*

Fear of aging speeds the very decline we dread most. And it ultimately robs our life of any meaning. No wonder there's an attitude shift in the making.

Jere Daniel

Jere Daniel is a free-lance writer specializing in health and human behavior. His articles have appeared in publications as diverse as The New York Times Magazine, American Health, *and* Family Circle. *He has pioneered corporate communications on health and produced a newsletter for America's leading companies. He is also the author of numerous television and radio scripts. He resides in Brooklyn Heights, New York.*

Technically, they are all still baby boomers. But on the cusp of 50, much to their surprise, having come late into maturity, they can suddenly envision themselves becoming obsolete, just as their fathers, mothers, grandparents, uncles, and aunts did when they crossed the age-65 barrier, the moment society now defines as the border line between maturity and old age.

Although they may be unprepared psychologically, they are certainly fortified demographically to notice the problems their elders now face—isolation, loneliness, lack of respect, and above all, virtual disenfranchisement from the society they built. The number of people reaching the increasingly mythic retirement age of 65 has zoomed from about seven and a half million in the 1930s (when Social Security legislation decreed 65 as the age of obsolescence) to 34 million today. By the turn of the century, that figure will be 61.4 million.

If the boomers' luck holds out, they will be spared what amounts to the psychological torture of uselessness and burdensomeness that every graying generation this century has faced before them. For there is an attitude shift in the wind. In an irony that boomers will no doubt appreciate (as

rebellion is an act usually reserved for the young), a revolution in attitude about age is coming largely from a corner of the population that has traditionally been content to enjoy the status quo—a cultural elite whose median age is surely over 65.

A small but growing gaggle of experts (themselves mostly elders)—a diverse lot of gerontologists, physicians, psychologists, sociologists, anthropologists, philosophers, ethicists, cultural observers, and spiritual leaders—are the vanguard of a movement to change the way society looks at and deals with growing old. They seek to have us stop viewing old age as a problem—as an incurable disease, if you will—to be "solved" by spending billions of dollars on plastic surgery in an attempt to mask visible signs of aging, other billions on medical research to extend the life span itself,

"We pretend that old age can be turned into an endless middle age, thereby giving people a false road map to the future."

and billions more on nursing and retirement homes as a way to isolate those who fail at the quest to deny aging.

Separately and together, this cultural elite is exploring ways to move us and our social institutions toward a new concept of aging, one they call "conscious aging." They want us to be aware of and accept what aging actually is—a notice that life has not only a beginning and a middle but an end—and to eliminate the denial that now prevents us from anticipating, fruitfully using, and even appreciating what are lost to euphemism as "the golden years."

"Conscious aging is a new way of looking at and experiencing aging that moves beyond our cultural obsession with youth toward a respect and need for the wisdom of age," explains Stephan Rechtschaffen, M.D., a holistic physician who directs the Omega Institute, a kind of New Age think tank that is a driving force in this attitude shift. He would have us:

• Recognize and accept the aging process and all that goes with it as a reality, a natural part of the life cycle; it happens to us all. The goal is to change the prevailing view of aging as something to be feared and the aged as worthless.

• Reverse our societal attitude of aging as an affliction, and instead of spending billions on walling off the aging, spend more to improve the quality of life among the aged.

Our denial of aging has its costs. Rechtschaffen is adamant that it is not merely our elders who suffer. Quoting the late psychoanalyst Erik Erikson, he says, "Lacking a culturally viable ideal of old age, our civilization does not really harbor a concept of the whole of life."

We now live, and die, psychologically and spiritually incomplete. It may be a troubling sense of incompleteness that most stirs an appreciation for age among the baby boomers, so unfamiliar is any sense of incompleteness to the generation that invented the possibility of and has prided itself on "having it all."

Next month, a group of these thinkers will gather at an open-to-the-public conference under the auspices of the Omega

Institute. Participants range from Sherwin Nuland, M.D., surgeon-author of the surprise best-seller *How We Die*, to Betty Friedan, who has dissected American attitudes toward aging in her latest book, *Fountain of Youth*, to spiritualist Ram Dass, Columbia University gerontologist Renee Solomon, Ph.D., and Dean Ornish, M.D., director of the University of California's Preventive Medicine Research Institute.

Until now, the conventional wisdom has been that only the aged, or those approaching its border, worry about its consequences: rejection, isolation, loneliness, and mandated obsolescence. Only they care about how they can give purpose to this final stage of their lives.

Sherwin Nuland has clear new evidence to the contrary. His book, *How We Die*, paints a shimmeringly lucid and remarkably unsentimental picture of death—the process and its meaning to the dying and to those around them. The biggest group of readers of this best-seller? Not the elderly, as most observers, and even the author himself, had anticipated. It's the baby boomers. Curiosity about age and death is booming among the boomers.

"The baby boomers, who started out rejecting the wisdom and experience of anyone over 30, are buying my book in droves," Nuland told *Psychology Today*. "To young people, death is an abstract concept. But face-to-face with aging parents and illnesses like cancer and strokes among themselves, newly graying baby boomers stare into their own mortality totally unprepared. Now this best-educated of all our generations wants information and doesn't want to turn away from what it's been trying to escape—the effects of getting old."

We fear and deny aging, the Omega experts emphasize, because we fear and deny death. "In our denial of death and the aging of the body, we have rejected the wisdom of the aged, and in doing so have robbed old age of its meaning and youth of its direction," Rechtschaffen asserts. We pretend that old age can be turned into a kind of endless middle age, thereby

giving young people a false road map to the future, one that does not show them how to plan for their whole life, gain insight into themselves, or to develop spiritually.

The signs of denial and anxiety over aging permeate every aspect of our lives. We have no role models for growing old gracefully, only for postponing it. For example:

• The vast dependence on plastic surgery specifically to hide the visual signs of aging is arguably the sharpest index of our anxiety. In just two decades, from the 1960s to the 1980s, the number of rhytidectomies, wrinkle-removing face-lifts, rose from 60,000 to an estimated 2 million a year at an annual cost of $10 billion.

• The negative view of aging is disastrously reinforced by the media. Articles and advertising never show a mature model, even in displaying fashions designed for women over 50. A *Newsweek* cover of a sweating, gray-haired young man bears the cover line, "Oh God...I'm really turning 50." Nursing home ads ask: "What shall we do about Mother?" By some sleight of mind, we not only come to accept these images, we come to expect them as truths.

We denigrate aging, Friedan persuasively notes, by universally equating it with second childhood, "so negatively stereotyped that getting old has become something to dread and feel threatened by." A series of studies by psychologists Ellen Langer, Ph.D. of Harvard and University of Pennsylvania President Judith Rodin, Ph.D. (then at Yale) suggests how we grow to revile our aging selves.

Influenced by the fairy tales we hear as children, and what we see on television and hear in everyday life, we develop negative stereotypes about aging by the time we are six years old, the same age we develop negative stereotypes about race and sex. These stereotypes persist as we grow up, completely unaware that we even acquired them or granted them our unconditional acceptance. With our understanding of the subject forever frozen, we grow into old age assuming the stereotypes to be true. And we live down to them.

If there is a single myth about aging that most symbolizes our dread, it is the assumption that our memory will inevitably decline in old age. In a stunning new study, psychologist Langer has demonstrated that it is our own psychology—the near-universal expectation of memory loss—that actually brings that fate upon us. The lesson to be learned is an extraordinary one: Fear of aging is the single most powerful agent creating exactly what we fear.

The negative stereotypes acquired in childhood parade across the adult life span as expectations. As people age, Langer finds, low expectations lead to "decreased effort, less use of adaptive strategies, avoidance of challenging situations, and failure to seek medical attention for disease-related symptoms."

In her newest study, Langer and Harvard colleague Rebecca Levy, Ph.D., confirm the effect of these negative stereotypes on aging Americans. Using standard psychological measurements of memory, the researchers studied two populations of people who hold their elders in high esteem—elderly mainland Chinese and older, deaf Americans—and compared them to a group of elderly mainstream Americans. In addition, the researchers compared memory retention in the elderly with younger people in all three groups.

Not only did the mainland Chinese and American deaf far outperform the mainstream Americans on four psychological memory tests, but the oldest in these two groups, especially the Chinese, performed almost as well as the youngest. Their performance was so strong even the researchers were surprised. They conclude that the results can be explained entirely by the fact that the Chinese have the most positive, active, and "internal" image of aging across the three cultures studied.

What is particularly striking about the Langer–Levy study is that it meticulously tracks how our fears, which are so culturally constructed, become self-fulfilling prophecies. "The social, psychological component of memory retention may be even stronger than we believed."

Just as our fear of memory loss can create actual memory decline, the dread of aging may be taking its toll on many other body systems.

The current collective view of aging is so relentlessly negative that neither our social institutions nor the aging themselves believe what worldwide research points to—that those of us alive today may be aging better than our parents.

A landmark, 15-year longitudinal study of older people, begun in 1970 by Alvar Svanborg in the industrial city of Gothenburg, Sweden, showed no measur-able decline in many body functions until after age 70, and very little decline by 81. Cognitive abilities were intact to at least age 75, and still intact in almost all who had reached 81, although speed at rote memory declined. "The vitality of old people in Sweden today, among the longest-lived people in the world, seems to be greater than it was only five or 10 years ago," Svanborg asserts.

American studies of healthy people aging in their own communities, as opposed to those shunted off to institutions, failed to show evidence of decline in intelligence, cognitive skills, and even memory that had appeared in all previous cross-sectional studies of aging. The combined thrust of the studies of "normal aging" is inescapable. Physical and mental decline is not inevitable. Belief that it is accelerates whatever decline occurs.

Still, we continue to mythologize and denigrate aging because we devalue death itself. "We refuse even to admit that we die of old age," says Nuland, a retired Yale surgeon, whose book embodies the proposition that death is a normal stage in the life cycle. This refusal is perpetuated by the medical profession and the law. "I cannot write 'Old Age' on a death certificate even though people over 70 die because they're over 70," he says.

"An octogenarian who dies of myocardial infarction is not simply a weather-beaten senior citizen with heart disease—he is the victim of an insidious progression that involves all of him, and that progression is called aging," Nuland says. He deplores the prevailing view of aging as a disease that can be cured and the biomedical search for a fountain of youth.

"Though biomedical science has vastly increased mankind's average life expectancy (78.6 years for American women, 71.6 for men), the maximum (114 years) has not changed in verifiable recorded history. Even the home-cultured yogurt of the Caucasus cannot vanquish nature," Nuland says. "Trying to add a few more years to the human life span is meaningless and wasteful."

The promise of an extended life span simply adds unnecessary stress to the ability to accept aging. "An extended life span without extended awareness of the possibilities of a productive old age means we aren't sure we're living longer. Maybe we're just dying longer," says Rabbi Zalman Schachter-Shalomi, founder of a pioneering Spiritual Eldering Project at Philadelphia's B'nai Or Religious Fellowship. Schachter-Shalomi is the recipient of the first annual Conscious Aging Award by the Omega Institute. In place of fear of death we'd be better off with a belief in the possibilities of life, as long as it is lived.

"If age itself is defined as a 'problem,' then those over 65 who can no longer 'pass' as young are its carriers and must be quarantined lest they contaminate, in mind or body, the rest of society," Friedan asserts. So we banish the elderly from our midst and wall them off in nursing homes. We encourage them to isolate themselves in retirement homes and communities, in San Diego condos and Miami Beach hotels.

But isolating ourselves into ageist groups only sets the stage for a class warfare that is bound to get louder and more violent. Younger generations grow to resent the older, and vice versa. And so, says Nuland, the elderly grow demanding and greedy for health and custodial care while the rest of the population bemoans the financial drain the aged make on society, all the while feeling guilty for the situation.

With the old now successfully segregated out, Americans are in no position to exploit the benefits of age—or even to recognize or acknowledge that there are any. Which brings us to the special brand of intelligence called wisdom.

Sure, we have our "elder" statesmen, but the titles are honorary, often conferred with an underlying tinge of humor. They signify reverence for past accomplishments more than real respect for the wisdom that only elders have to contribute. Wisdom remains a very special commodity, a great natural resource that is undervalued—and almost totally untapped in doing what it's meant for: guiding the young. And there's only one way to get it.

It is not easy to talk about wisdom without lapsing into platitudes and vagueness, so a team of European researchers—no surprise there—has taken on the challenge to isolate the features of wisdom in clinical detail. From their ongoing studies of the aging mind, psychologists Paul B. Baltes and Ursula M. Staudinger, both of the Max Planck Institute for Human Development in Berlin, define wisdom:

• It's an expertise that wraps information in the human context of life and relates it to generational and historical flow.

• It is factual and procedural knowledge about the world and human affairs.

• It mingles insight and judgment involving complex and uncertain matters of the human condition; there is an appreciation for and understanding of the uncertainties of life.

• It involves a fine-tuned coordination of cognition, motivation, and emotion, knowledge about the self and other people and society.

• It carries knowledge about strategies to manage the peaks and valleys of life.

• It integrates past, present, and future.

A product of cultural and knowledge-based factors, rather than biologically based mechanics of the mind, wisdom accumulates with time—but only among those who remain open to new experiences. If we must insist on outwitting the constraints of biology, then wisdom—and not the scalpel—is our thing.

It may be that we ignore wisdom because, especially over the lifetime of the boomers, we have come to overvalue, say, rocket science. The technological advancement of modern society has bred in us an infatuation with the data we have accumulated. "We've traded information for wisdom," Rechtschaffen offers.

We have confounded the accumulation of data with its application, or even an understanding of it. Wisdom, on the other hand, always puts information back in the context of human life.

Sherwin Nuland is a man forced by the exigencies of his profession to look time squarely in the eye. Old age, he says, is a "time to become contemplative, to recognize our value to people younger than ourselves." Now in his sixties, Nuland stopped operating when "I realized I was no longer as nimble as a 45-year-old. But I expect to continue contributing my knowledge and experience as long as possible." Unfortunately, he says, "the younger generation doesn't always accept it, from me or others. They see their elders as crotchety and selfish, their maturity and wisdom of no use—outdated. Age warfare continues."

Perhaps we don't recognize the wisdom of aging because our anxiety about the future—of the world, of ourselves—has overwhelmed our respect for history. We live, Rechtschaffen says, with only a linear sense of time. We push inexorably toward the future; the past is nothing. In other eras, we lived by a more circular sense of time, which allowed for a father's, even a grandfather's, experience to guide us. There was an intuitive apprehension—wisdom, if you will—that the way to deal with the future rests in an understanding of the past. Even today, many indigenous tribal societies and Eastern cultures live by a circular sense of time.

The baby boomers have made it successfully, albeit noisily, through the first two-thirds of their lives, having rejected—indeed defying—the teachings of their elders. But the prospect of making it through the next third satisfied with their accomplishments and their selves requires they find inner meaning in their lives.

To give their lives purpose, they might turn from what Nuland calls "the hurly-burly of getting and spending" to a more contemplative life. And they might pay more attention to those who have already crossed the border into old age, to value their experience; to embrace their elders is to embrace their future selves. Perhaps, most of all, they might begin to think of their own death. After all, to be fully alive includes being fully aware of dying.

So long as we lock ourselves into an obsession with the youth culture, we can only develop age rage and dehumanize ourselves, says Betty Friedan. Those who give up their denial of age, who age consciously, "grow and become aware of new capacities they develop while aging....[They] become more authentically themselves."

Problems and Potentials of Aging

Viewed as part of the life cycle, aging might be considered a period of decline, poor health, increasing dependence, social isolation, and—ultimately—death. It often means retirement, decreased income, chronic health problems, and death of a spouse. In contrast, the first 50 years of life are seen as a period of growth and development.

For a young child, life centers around the home, and then the neighborhood. Later, the community and state become a part of the young person's environment. Finally, as an adult, the person is prepared to consider national and international issues—wars, alliances, changing economic cycles, and world problems.

During the later years, however, life space narrows. Retirement may distance the individual from national and international concerns, although he or she may remain actively involved in community affairs. Later, even community involvement may decrease, and the person may begin to stay close to home and the neighborhood. For some, the final years of life may once again focus on the confines of home, be it an apartment or a nursing home.

Many older Americans try to remain masters of their own destinies for as long as possible. They fear dependence and try to avoid it. Many are successful at maintaining independence and the right to make their own decisions. Others are less successful and must depend on their families for care and to make critical decisions.

Most older persons are able to overcome the difficulties of aging and to lead comfortable and enjoyable lives. According to the essay "American Maturity," the young elderly (65–74) and the old elderly (75 and older) are viewed as distinct groups with quite different problems and interests.

Brian Gratton and Carole Haber, in "Three Phases in the History of American Grandparents: Authority, Burden, and Companion," trace the changing generational relations between grandparents and grandchildren as the United States moved from being primarily an agricultural economy to the current industrial economy.

Mary Gordon, in "My Mother Is Speaking from the Desert," observes the anguish that she experiences as she watches her mother's steady deterioration during her final years while residing in a nursing home.

In the final unit article, "Understanding Elder Abuse and Neglect," Rosalie Wolf describes the four basic kinds of elder abuse—physical abuse, psychological abuse, financial abuse, and neglect. Wolf believes that labeling behavior as abusive depends on its duration, intensity, severity, and consequences.

Looking Ahead: Challenge Questions

Which aspects of life after 65 are desirable and should be anticipated with some degree of pleasure?

Which aspects of life after 65 are undesirable and should be a cause of concern to people of all ages?

What significant steps might be taken by both business and the local community to assist the elderly in overcoming the problems of aging?

How does drug abuse among young people differ from drug abuse among the elderly?

Three Phases in the History of American Grandparents:

AUTHORITY, BURDEN, COMPANION

BY BRIAN GRATTON AND CAROLE HABER

Two eighteenth-century portraits, "The Grandfather's Advice" and "The Grandmother's Present," vividly depicted that era's idealized relationship between grandparents and grandchildren: elderly people sat with adoring children on their knees, imparting wisdom and experience. The inscription gave the lesson: "Honor thy Father and thy Mother." Such adages fit the functional connections between generations in a society in which family exchange governed much of life. Two hundred years later, the bond between grandparents and grandchildren was rarely expressed in such terms. Mid-twentieth-century images of intergenerational relations idealized independence for the elderly and companionship between grandparents and grandchildren. These images represented a sharp reaction to an intervening period in which grandparents symbolized a threat to a proper family life. In the late nineteenth and early twentieth centuries, negative imagery about aging, and the

In each of these periods in the history of American grandparents, reality often conflicted with ideals— but such ideals have had a powerful influence on the experiences of the elderly and their families.

growing prospect of trigenerational households, led family experts, public welfare advocates, and the elderly themselves to criticize coresidence and dependence between generations. In each of these periods in the history of American grandparents, reality often conflicted with ideals—but such ideals have had a powerful influence

on the experiences of the elderly and their families.

FIGURES OF AUTHORITY

"Respect and honor," colonial ministers and magistrates commanded, revealing the power structure not just of civil but of personal generational relationships. Grandparents, particularly grandfathers, exerted considerable economic and social control in a society based on land ownership. Elderly male landholders generally retained their land and authority over their families until they died. High fertility and mortality rates, along with a late age of marriage, ensured that most old couples had relatively young, unmarried children still at home. Although married children almost always set up separate households, the older family members maintained roles of authority if the younger couple still depended on their parents' land or assets. The elders' authority diminished, however, if married children migrated or separated themselves financially. The life of Martha Ballard, a prominent midwife in a frontier Maine community in the late eighteenth and early nineteenth centuries, provides a good example of such changes across the life span. While her daughters were unmarried, Ballard enjoyed their assistance in her many tasks as seamstress, gardener, housewife, and medical caregiver. Once they married, she lost these services and found it much more difficult to carry out her work. Moreover, she could not subsequently call on her grandchildren for the same assistance because they lived too far away (Ulrich, 1991).

A small minority of the old lived with grandchildren, but these cases rarely signified a continuance of dignified position and power. In eighteenth-century Hingham, Massachusetts, for example, about 20 percent of the old resided in homes in which they were not listed as the head (Smith, 1978). For elderly men and married couples, this status was clearly the exception: It generally reflected ill health or increasing helplessness. For elderly women, however, this dependent residential status frequently resulted from the death of a spouse. Widows received the traditional "dowagers' third" or more detailed maintenance wills, often designed for coresidence. In 1715, for example, Timothy Richardson of Woburn, Massachusetts, was not granted his father's estate until he agreed to "give, sign and pass unto his mother, the widow of the deceased, good and sufficient security . . . during the widowhood" (Keyssar, 1974). Ministers lectured the young adults that, because their elders had cared for them as babies, they were obligated to support their elders when they became old and infirm (Premo, 1990).

Ministers' admonitions did not, however, induce children to endow elderly women with control. At age seventy, Martha Ballard was outraged when her son and daughter-in-law took possession of her house and relegated her to a single room. Her daughter-in-law, she noted, was "an inconsiderate or very imprudent

woman to treat me as she does." Such behavior led Ballard to remark bitterly that her children ought to "consider they may be old and receiv like Treatment [sic]" (Ulrich, 1991).

The status of widows in this period suggests how critical economic relationships were to the elderly and their kin. Although religious and cultural ideals extolled respect and deference to the old, the economic ties that made the young dependent on their elders constituted the primary source of elders' authority. But such dependence created tensions within the household that could not be denied. A seventeenth century marriage treatise stressed this lesson to its readers: "The mixing of governours in an household, or subordinating or uniting of two Masters, or two Dames under one roof, doth fall outmost times to be a matter of much unquietness to all parties" (Ulrich, 1991).

A BURDEN AND A THREAT

Although coresidence became more likely in the nineteenth century, it did not become a happier prospect. Industrialization undermined the authority of aged landholders, while demographic shifts raised the probability that trigenerational households might be formed. Unlike prior generations, late-nineteenth-century farmers rarely retained power through the possession of land. In Bucks County, Pennsylvania, for example, a significant evolution in inheritance patterns occurred in the course of two centuries. During the colonial period, 87 percent of all testators passed their farms or other businesses to their heirs; in the 1790s, the proportion had fallen to 71 percent. By 1890, only about a third bequeathed their property to their offspring (Shammas, Salmon, and Dahlin, 1987). The elderly no longer used inheritance provisions to maintain authority over their heirs. Instead, the old sold the property and created their own "nest egg" for retirement.

Industrialization and technological change also stripped away the authority once granted to experience. New

technology often made the talents of the old appear obsolete and the new economy offered an attractive alternative to young men and women who, in the past, might have chosen to stay on as dutiful workers in the family enterprise. Although older workers competed relatively well, and the overall economic well-being of the aged improved, the culture of the industrial era clearly indicated that the skills of the elderly were outdated and no longer essential to society (Achenbaum, 1978; Cole, 1993; Haber, 1983).

Demographic change accompanied these economic and ideological shifts. A larger proportion of people survived to old age, and earlier ages for marriage and childbearing increased the probability that three generations of family members would be alive simultaneously. By 1900, the proportion of trigenerational households had reached its peak in American history (Ruggles, 1987). Given the modest real wealth of the period, only middle class families tended to have the housing and resources necessary to shelter additional relatives (Smith, 1979; Smith, 1982b). Although older married couples and aging men had little risk of living under a child's roof, aging widows often had little choice but to reside in the same home as children and grandchildren. In 1900, 70 percent of all individuals age sixty and over lived as the head of the household or the spouse of the head; census data listed only about one-tenth of men but over one-third of aging women as "parent" of the household head (Haber and Gratton, 1994).

The increasing possibility of coresidence was accompanied by a rising sentiment against it. Within complex households, lines of authority often led to conflict and dissension (Bodnar, 1982). In Utica, New York, for example, Julia and Bildad Merrill, Jr., moved into his parents' household because of his father's growing disability. Trading independence for the support of the younger generation did not yield harmonious relations; the elderly couple found it difficult to relinquish

101

their authority to their offspring. Both mother and daughter-in-law claimed command over the servants and pre-eminence with the children. Ultimately, their dispute led to an outbreak of violence between the two women and an ignominious church trial. After public apologies and resolutions, they returned to share the same abode and many of the same generational tensions (Ryan, 1981).

In the smaller families of the industrial era, both the elderly and their offspring lost the privilege of choice (Gratton, 1986; Rubinow, [1930] 1972). The aged could not select the most congenial environment, nor could the children choose who among several siblings would take primary responsibility for aging parents. The rising risk of burden led to a cultural and political debate about the proper place and care of the elderly in American society. Many Americans honored the ideal of family interdependence, but its conflict with another goal, separation of household, moved bourgeois commentators to criticism. As Samuel Butler wrote in 1885,

> I believe that more unhappiness comes from this source than from any other—I mean from the attempt to prolong the family connection unduly and to make people hang together artificially who would never naturally do so. . . . And the old people do not really like it so much better than the young.

In the early 1930s, an anonymous female writer recalled the problems of three-generational households:

> When I was a child, I took it for granted that a grandmother or grandfather should live in the house of nearly every one of my playmates. Soon I came to take it for granted, also, that these houses should be full of friction. The association of grandparents with friction took such a hold in my mind that I called myself lucky because my own were dead! (Anon., 1931; Heaton and Hoppe, 1987)

In adulthood this author found herself compelled to take her aging mother into her household. The results were disastrous. "Harmony is gone. Rest has vanished." Her daily routine, her children's lives, and her

marriage, she asserted, had been reduced to sheer chaos. Friends and acquaintances reported similar consequences from coresidence with an aging parent. "The intrusion," she argued, "is probably a common cause of divorce, and most certainly of marital unhappiness and problems in children" (Anon., 1931).

A new legion of family experts agreed, arguing that grandparents in the home limited the happiness and

The desire of all generations for independent households explains the unique popularity of Social Security.

prosperity of young and old alike. Although advisors never attacked the central myth of family obligation, they counseled that such duties were best carried out across separate thresholds. This cultural transition, strongly rooted in the growing independence of adult children from their parents' assets and resources, was joined by a political movement that shared many of its sentiments. The need for separate residences for grandparents, in fact, became a cornerstone of the early-twentieth-century campaign for publicly funded old age pensions. "It seems a pity," wrote Abraham Epstein, a pension advocate, "to force any father or mother in this twentieth century to decide between supporting old parents and contenting themselves with a little less food, less room, less clothing, and the curtailment of their children's education, or sending their parents to the poorhouse." The solu-

tion was state funds that could guarantee separate residences for grandparents and "increase filial affection and respect." Epstein put the matter more bluntly, exposing the negative imagery that had come to be connected to grandparents. In 1928, he declared that "we all know among our acquaintances, some people whose young lives have been made pitiably wretched, and in some instances totally ruined, by the constant 'pestering' of an old father-in-law or mother-in-law" (Epstein, [1928] 1976).

Such arguments fit an emerging view of the aged as burdensome and nonproductive that was clearly visible in medical interpretations of aging as a disease, in pessimistic evaluations of older people's capacity as workers, and in criticisms of their value inside the family circle (Haber and Gratton, 1994). Even popular culture depicted declining abilities as the essence of growing old. In tunes such as "Denied a Home" (1895), "Don't Leave Your Mother When Her Hair Turns Grey" (1900), and "There's a Mother Old and Gray Who Needs Me Now" (1911), elderly individuals were portrayed as being physically weak and unable to provide for themselves. "Don't leave your old home now," advised Chas. Osborne and Ernest J. Symons in "Stick to Your Mother, Mary" (1913). "She's old and gray and wants you to stay. So don't take a year of her life away" (Cohen and Kruschwitz, 1990).

When possible, the middle class responded by limiting the household to the nuclear family (Ruggles, 1987). Between 1900 and 1940, the proportion of men age sixty-five and over who lived as dependents in children's homes declined from 16 percent to 11 percent; for women the percentage fell from 34 to 23 (Smith, 1982a). In more prosperous families, elderly individuals were able to amass sufficient wealth to live independently (Ruggles, 1987). Rising economic well-being brought the vision of permanently separate homes for all generations within reach. By the early twentieth century, the extended family no longer seemed a sanctuary of middle-class support and affection. Its value for grandchildren and grandparents had been seriously challenged. Experts advised that extended family arrangements symbolized impoverishment and failure. Only the poor, or those with foreign values—immigrants, for example—would live in this manner; all others would choose to reside independently.

A NEW IDEAL: COMPANIONSHIP

Within this context of increasing possibility of extension and increasing resistance to it that the impact of the Great Depression must be gauged. Before this calamity, middle-class sentiment had been moving away from the functional intrafamilial systems characteristic of previous eras. The authoritative role of grandparents, rooted in the family economy, had begun to vanish, but no affective, sentimental role yet held sway. In family advice literature, the portrait of the powerful, authoritative, and somewhat intimidating elder (Cole, 1992) had completely faded, replaced by a depiction of senescence that emphasized the inescapable weaknesses and infirmities of age. Indeed, the focus among family experts and pension advocates on the threat posed by dependent coresident older people added to the rising negative imagery surrounding the aged (Haber and Gratton, 1994).

The Depression gave this threat a new and visceral meaning. Economic collapse dashed the hopes of many middle-class elderly for an independent and secure old age. For their children and grandchildren, it meant facing new and often disagreeable household arrangements. Families that had been able to establish independent households found themselves "doubling up" to cut expenses. In a 1937 article reprinted in *Reader's Digest,* the anonymous author, a seventy-three year-old woman, wrote, "When declining health and declining finances left me no alternative but to live with my daughter, my first feeling was one of bitterness." The author

pledged to make herself as little of a burden as possible through numerous rules: "I must not be around when she was getting her work done, or when she had her friends in. I must ask no questions and give no unasked advice. I resolved to spend the greater part of each day alone in my room."

Social Security directly addressed these fears and met the widespread desire for financial and residential independence. Guaranteed monthly checks reduced anxiety over family failure and assured steady support in old age. The desire of *all* generations for independent households explains the unique popularity of Social Security. After 1950, its increasingly generous benefits, the spread of private pensions, and rising wealth among older persons had still more profound implications. In short, the threat of coresidence had been reduced substantially for most grandparents. Among white women age fifty-five to sixty-four in 1940, 8 percent lived as a dependent "parent" (of the household head). In 1950, when these women were sixty-five to seventy-four, their cohort had experienced a 19 percent increase in widowhood. This translated into only an 8 percent increase in their status as dependent parent but an 11 percent increase in their role as houehold head. Social Security and other resources allowed most white widows to maintain or create autonomous and separate households. For groups less likely to have such resources, a different picture emerges. Among Mexican-born women, for example, a 23 percent increase in widowhood led to an 18 percent increase in the status of parent and to a decline in the proportion who headed their own households (Gratton and Ito, 1995).

The rapid shift toward autonomy has been identified by a number of observers. In the 1950s, recipients of Social Security began to establish a clear pattern of separate residences (Schorr, 1958). Whereas in 1900 over 60 percent of the elderly had lived with children (as head or parent), by 1962 the proportion had dropped to

25 percent, and by 1975 to only 14 percent (Smith, 1982b). Although the trend has affected men, the most significant transformation occurred in the residence patterns of unmarried women. In 1940, 58 percent of elderly women who were not living with husbands resided with kin; by 1970, only 29 percent of these individuals shared homes with relatives (Kobrin, 1976; Mindel, 1979).

For the first time in history, even aged widows had the financial resources necessary to continue residing in their own dwellings. Such arrangements fit manifest desires, not just of adult children but of the elderly themselves. Current studies confirm that, when able, the elderly choose to maintain independent households. In one study, three-quarters of the black elderly and nine in ten of the white elderly opposed residing in a multigenerational household. Nearly all elderly individuals agreed that "it usually does not work out too well for older people to live with the children and grandchildren" (Kasschau, 1978; Rosenmayr and Kockeis, 1963, Shanas, 1979).

Such views fit the newly predominant cultural view of grandparents as independent individuals whose most important responsibility was to maintain their autonomy. Stressing the advantages of retirement, experts warned their readers of the need to be financially secure. No aged person, they argued, should depend on relatives for support. "Most elderly," wrote David A. Tombs, "want to be independent. They do not want to rely on their children for housing, care, or money" (Tombs, 1984; Silverstone and Hyman, 1989). Mid-twentieth-century advice books did not portray the elderly as powerful family members or as helpless and incipient burdens. Rather, they concurred that if the old were informed about their legal, economic, and social rights, they could control their separate fates (Kapp and Bigot, 1985).

Advisors to the old, therefore, attempted to provide readers with the means to guarantee autonomy and use leisure well. Their books, as one author explained, were intended "to offer the knowledge and tools necessary for elderly people to get what they want—in their medical treatment, their finances, and their right to maintain control over their lives" (Myers, 1989). Exploring such issues as Medicare, Medicaid, life insurance, pensions, and Social Security, the authors agreed that in matters of health, housing, or resources, elderly people who could chart and command their daily lives experienced satisfaction and contentment (Ader, 1975; Averyt, 1987; Baumhover and Jones, 1987; Smith, 1989; Tombs, 1984).

This sense of independence also shaped experts' counsel on intergenerational relations. Experts outlined strategies that would allow elderly individuals to dwell in their own households or enter alternate living arrangements that guaranteed continued control (Bellak, 1975; Silverstone and Hyman, 1989; Tombs, 1984). Contact with younger generations, although not devoid of support, was governed by symbols of equality rather than interdependence. Grandparents should strive for love and friendship with their grandchildren rather than demand respect and obedience. Grandparents coddled and cuddled rather than disciplined; they listened affectionately rather than spoke authoritatively.

Could the new ideal of this third phase be realized? For the financially secure and the healthy, yes. Other articles in this issue will show, however, that many have found it difficult, if not impossible, to achieve. Among African American women, for example, grandparenthood often brings coresidence with grandchildren, new economic and personal burdens, and new and demanding roles (Gratton, 1987). The proportion of grandparents living with grandchildren, although small, has risen, especially in populations with large numbers of young, unmarried mothers.

Moreover, the demands of caring for an increasingly long-lived parental generation have presented new challenges. Although adult children are less likely than their historical peers to remain in parents' households or take a needy parent into their home, they are much more likely to have an aging parent depend on them for some type of assistance. The aging of the population and the declining number of children per family mean that greater proportions of middle-aged people must provide some form of assistance to their elderly kin. Significant and often expensive obligations for the support of elderly family members fall primarily on the middle-aged, who are already responsible for children, spouses, and their own careers (Treas, 1977; Miller and Cafasso, 1992). For such families, an ideal of pure autonomy has surely not been achieved.

SUMMARY

Three distinct phases mark the history of American grandparents. Until the mid-nineteenth century, their vital economic and social role made them figures of authority. Relationships with their children and grandchildren reflected their critical importance in society and the interdependence of generations. By the early twentieth century, their status had precipitously declined, especially in the middle class. Physicians viewed old age as an illness, critics denigrated the capacities of older workers, and family experts opposed extended and complex households. Demographic pressures made grandparents a burden and a threat rather than a valued resource. The Great Depression raised anew the prospect of a physical proximity that most Americans had come to oppose. Social Security, private pension programs, and rising wealth provided an escape and created the third phase in the history of American grandparents. As autonomous, retired individuals, they had no important economic role in family life, but neither did they pose a threat. Their independence allowed them to become companions and friends to their grandchildren. Although it exists only for some, and new caregiving demands have emerged, the affectionate, autonomous role of grandparent remains the central image of modern American grandparenthood.

Brian Gratton, Ph.D., is professor, Department of History, Arizona State University, Tempe. Carole Haber, Ph.D., is professor and chair, Department of History, University of North Carolina-Charlotte.

REFERENCES

Achenbaum, W. A. 1978. *Old Age in the New Land.* Baltimore, Md.: Johns Hopkins University Press.

Ader, J. 1975. *The Retirement Book.* New York: William Morrow.

Anon. 1931. "Old Age Intestate." *Harper's Magazine* 162 (May): 715–18.

Averyt, A. C. 1987. *Successful Aging: A Source Book for Older People and Their Families.* New York: Ballentine Books.

Baumhover, L. A., and Jones, J. D., eds. 1987. *Handbook of American Aging Programs.* Westport, Conn.: Greenwood Press.

Bellak, L. 1975. *The Best Years of Your Life: A Guide to the Art and Science of Aging.* New York: Atheneum.

Bodnar, J. 1982. *Workers' World: Kinship, Community, and Protest in an Industrial Society, 1900–1940.* Baltimore, Md.: Johns Hopkins University Press.

Butler, S. Ca. 1885. *Note-Books.* Cited in Ruggles, S. 1987, *Prolonged Connections: The Rise of the Extended Family in Nineteenth-Century England and America.* Madison: University of Wisconsin Press.

Cohen, E. S., and Kruschwitz, A. L. 1990. "Old Age in America Represented in Nineteenth and Twentieth Century Popular Sheet Music." *Gerontologist* 30(3): 345–54.

Cole, T. 1992. Personal communication with authors.

Cole, T. 1993. *The Journey of Life.* New York: Cambridge University Press.

Epstein, A., [1928] 1976. *The Challenge of the Aged.* Reprint, New York: Arno Press.

Gratton, B. 1986. *Urban Elders: Family, Work and Welfare among Boston's Aged, 1890–1950.* Philadelphia: Temple University Press.

Gratton, B. 1987. "Familism Among the Black and Mexican-American Elderly: Myth or Reality?" *Journal of Aging Studies* 1(1): 19–32.

Gratton, B., and Ito, R., II. 1995. "Family Transitions: Changes in Mexican-American Household Structure Across the 1940s." Paper presented at the meeting of the Social Science History Association, Chicago, Ill.

Haber, C. 1983. *Beyond Sixty-Five.* New York: Cambridge University Press.

Haber, C., and Gratton, B. 1994. *Old Age and the Search for Security.* Bloomington: Indiana University Press.

Heaton, T. B., and Hoppe, C. 1987. "Widowed and Married: Comparative Change in Living Arrangements, 1900 and 1980." *Social Science History* 11(3): 261–80.

Kapp, M. B., and Bigot, A. 1985. *Geriatrics and the Law.* New York: Springer.

Kasschau, P. L. 1978. *Aging and Social Policy.* New York: Praeger.

Keyssar, A. 1974. "Widowhood in Eighteenth-Century Massachusetts: A Problem in the History of the Family." *Perspectives in American History* 8: 83–119.

Kobrin, F. E. 1976. "The Fall in Household Size and the Rise of the Primary Individual in the United States." *Demography* 13(1): 127–38.

Miller, B., and Cafasso, L. 1992. "Gender Differences in Caregiving: Fact or Artifact." *Gerontologist* 32(4): 498–507.

Mindel, C. H. 1979. "Multigenerational Family Households: Recent Trends and Implications for the Future." *Gerontologist* 19(5): 456–63.

Myers, T. S. 1989. *How to Keep Control of Your Life after Sixty.* Lexington, Mass.: D.C. Heath.

Premo, T. 1990. *Winter Friends: Women Growing Old in the New Republic, 1785–1835.*

Urbana: University of Illinois Press.

Reader's Digest. 1937. "I Am the Mother-in-Law in the Home" (Nov.): 11–14.

Rosenmayr, L., and Kockeis, E. 1963. "Propositions for a Sociological Theory of Ageing and the Family." *International Social Science Journal* 15(3): 410–26.

Rubinow, I. M., [1930] 1972. "The Care of the Aged." In D. J. Rothman, ed., *The Aged and the Depression.* New York: Arno Press.

Ruggles, S. 1987. *Prolonged Connections: The Rise of the Extended Family in Nineteenth-Century England and America.* Madison: University of Wisconsin Press.

Ryan, M. 1981. *Cradle of the Middle Class.* Cambridge: Cambridge University Press.

Schorr, A. L. 1958. *Filial Responsibility in the Modern American Family.* Washington, D.C.: Government Printing Office.

Shammas, C., Salmon, M., and Dahlin, M. 1987. *Inheritance in America: From Colonial Times to the Present.* New Brunswick, N.J.: Rutgers University Press.

Shanas, E. 1979. "Social Myth as Hypothesis: The Case of the Family Relations of Old People." *Gerontologist* 19(1): 3–9.

Silverstone, B., and Hyman, H. K. 1989.

You and Your Aging Parent. New York: Pantheon Books.

Smith, D. S. 1978. "Old Age and the 'Great Transformation.'" In S. F. Spicker, K. M. Woodward, and D. D. Van Tassel, eds., *Aging and the Elderly.* Atlantic Highland, N.J.: Humanities Press.

Smith, D. S. 1979. "Life Course, Norms, and the Family System of Older Americans in 1900." *Journal of Family History* 4(3): 285–98.

Smith, D. S. 1982a. "The Elderly in Economically Developed Countries." In P. N. Stearns, ed., *Old Age in Preindustrial Society.* New York: Holmes & Meier.

Smith, D. S. 1982b. "Historical Change in the Household Structure of the Elderly in Economically Developed Societies." In P. N. Stearns, ed., *Old Age in Preindustrial Society.* New York: Holmes & Meier.

Smith, W. J. 1989. *The Senior Citizens' Handbook.* Los Angeles: Price Stern Sloan.

Tombs, D. A. 1984. *Growing Old: A Handbook for You and Your Aging Parent.* New York: Viking Press.

Treas, J. 1977. "Family Support Systems for the Aged." *Gerontologist* 16(6): 486–91.

Ulrich, L. T. 1991. *A Midwife's Tale: The Life of Martha Ballard based on her Diary.* New York: Random House.

American Maturity

SUMMARY *Americans aged 65 and older are a fast-growing and formidable market. Some older people move to be closer to their family, and some move to a better climate, but most stay put. The "young" elderly, aged 65 to 74, are a relatively affluent and healthy group. The "older" elderly, aged 75 and older, are far more likely to be disabled. Elderly people with disabilities cluster in the fast-growing Southeast, while the Midwest has a slow-growing but healthy elderly population.*

Diane Crispell and William H. Frey

Diane Crispell is executive editor of American Demographics *and editorial director of* The Numbers News *and* American Demographics Books. *William H. Frey is research scientist and associate director for training at the Population Studies Center, University of Michigan, Ann Arbor.*

As your car speeds down Interstate 95, pine trees and scrub palms blur into a wash of green and brown. You could be anywhere in central Florida—until you reach The Watertower. A huge blue inverted waterdrop marks the entrance to "Palm Coast," America's newest population oasis. Stop the car at the edge of Palm Coast. Get out, and you can almost hear the town creaking under the weight of rapid growth and demographic change. This is Flagler County, the place with the fastest-growing elderly population in the country.

In the 1980s, an explosion of Americans aged 65 and older added a new dimension to demographic change. Because of increased longevity and the aging of larger generations, most U.S. counties saw their elderly populations grow rapidly. The 1990 census counted 31.2 million Americans aged 65 or older, a 22 percent increase since 1980. Elderly people are now 13 percent of the U.S. adult population, up from 11 percent in 1980.

Growth in the mature market presents a new set of opportunities for businesses. But to reach mature Americans effectively, businesses must understand this market's considerable diversity. One aspect of this diversity is geographic. America's elderly populations are growing in different places for different reasons.

CLOSER TO FAMILY

Willie Tomlinson, a 74-year-old retired teacher, lived in the same house in Falls Church, Virginia, for 47 years. Then she moved to Peachtree City, Georgia, a small but rapidly growing town in Fayette County. She moved to be closer to her son, a colonel stationed at nearby Fort McPherson.

Tomlinson's story is a common one among older residents of Peachtree City. Retirees move to the planned developments southwest of Atlanta because of their low crime rates, unhurried and friendly atmosphere, temperate climate, and other amenities. But the main reason, many willingly concede, is to be near their children and grandchildren.

At first glance, elderly people may seem isolated. The 1990 census found that fewer than two-thirds of the elderly live in family households, compared with 83 percent of adults aged 18 to 64. More than one in four people aged 65 or older lives alone, compared with 9 percent of younger adults. But at least one demographic trend keeps older people from getting too lonely. Life expectancy has risen for both men and

> **To reach mature Americans, businesses must understand this market's considerable diversity.**

women. Consequently, couples who don't divorce may live together well past the age of 65.

Today's elderly people are nearly as likely as younger adults to be married (in each group, about half are married). About 56 percent of people aged 65 or older either head a family or are married to a family householder. Their numbers have grown 25 percent since 1980, when the proportion stood at 55 percent.

Even so, women live an average of seven years longer than men. Moreover, most women marry older men. As a result, nearly half of elderly women are widowed, compared with just 14 percent of elderly men. The number of elderly people who live alone grew 27 percent during the 1980s, and the proportion who live alone rose from 28 percent to 30 percent. Nearly 80 percent of elderly Americans who live alone are women, and elderly people make up 40 percent of all single-person households, according to the census.

But living alone and being lonely are two different things. Other research shows that the share of elderly parents who live within 25 miles of adult children has hovered around 75 percent for the past 30 years. A 1992 *Modern Maturity/Roper Organization* study finds that 58 percent of grandparents see their grandchildren quite often. Grown children and their offspring often remain within drop-in distance of grandma and grandpa. And sometimes older people relocate to be near the kids and grandkids, especially if the kids have moved to a southern clime.

A BETTER CLIMATE

Migrants young and old accounted for virtually all of the growth in Flagler County during the 1980s. Thirty years ago, the Palm Coast region was a rural area known best for growing telephone poles. Then International Telephone and Telegraph (ITT) changed its focus from tree farming to city building. Flagler's population grew 163 percent during the 1980s, making it the fastest-growing county in the U.S. Its elderly population grew even faster, by 267 percent. But in seven of the years between 1967 and 1987, the number of deaths in Flagler exceeded the number of births.

Flagler County lies on the Atlantic coast midway between St. Augustine and Daytona Beach, at the eastern fringes of the Orlando and Jacksonville metropolitan areas. In this way, it is similar to many other counties that have fast-growing elderly populations. Magnets of elderly growth cluster in the coastal regions, the Southwest, and the Rocky Mountains. Some are large, economically prosperous areas. Others are rural counties where the climate and scenery attract younger and older people alike.

Four of the top-ten growth counties for the elderly are also among the fastest-growing counties for all ages. These are Flagler and Hernando in Florida; Fayette, Georgia; and Matanuska-Susitna Borough, Alaska. In contrast, a broad swath of counties in the nation's heartland—including the farmbelt, rustbelt, and oil-patch states—saw slow growth or

> **"The average retirement migrant household's overall impact on the local economy is $71,600 a year."**

even declines in both their younger and older populations during the 1980s. These places had struggling economies that could do little to attract or retain people.

As a result, places with fast-growing elderly populations are often better-off and healthier markets than those with slow-growing elderly populations. Many are retirement areas that attract long-distance migrants, both seasonal and permanent. Long-distance moves are espe-cially popular among "sixtysomething" couples who have both the financial resources and wanderlust to relocate during their early elderly years. Retirement migrants of the 1980s favored Hernando, St. Lucie, Collier, and Marion counties in Florida. They also chose newly popular retirement areas in South Atlantic coastal states (Beaufort County, South Carolina) and the Rocky Mountains (Summit County, Colorado).

Retirees may not be employed, but their presence creates jobs and consumer demand. "The average retirement migrant household's overall impact on the local economy is $71,600 a year," according to a 1992 analysis prepared for the Appalachian Regional Commission. Estimates of the number of jobs retirees create range from one-third to one full job for each new migrant.

The longer a retirement migrant stays put, the better for the magnet area. "Major durable expenditures are not so much a function of age as . . . the length of time a household resides in an area," says the commission report.

Retirement migrants like Willie Tomlinson are one reason for Fayette County's fast-growing elderly population, which ranked fourth in the U.S. during the 1980s. But the main reason is a phenomenon called "aging in place."

In the 1970s, thousands of people moved to rural Fayette County in search of roomy homes in tranquil subdivisions, good schools, and a quick commute to Atlanta. "It's not so much that a lot of older people have moved into the county, but that a lot of middle-aged people moved

> **Suburban areas are becoming havens for retirees who choose not to move.**

in a while ago. Now they have gotten old," says Bart Lewis of the Atlanta Regional Commission.

Most counties with fast-growing elderly populations have also experienced aging in place. Many of these are affluent suburbs or exurbs of small metropolitan areas. These areas have spent the past few decades building up a sizable working-age population, and now those migrants are getting older. Nevada, Alaska, Colorado, New Mexico, Utah, California, and Texas have many such communities.

Suburban areas all over the country are becoming havens for retirees who choose not to move. They include Fayette and Gwinnett counties in suburban Atlanta, Virginia's Fairfax and Prince William counties in suburban Washington, D.C., and Howard County in suburban Baltimore. Many other counties with fast-growing suburban elderly populations don't appear on the top-50 list: these include St. Charles County in suburban St. Louis, Anoka County in suburban Minneapolis-St. Paul, Macomb County in suburban Detroit, and Bucks County in suburban Philadelphia.

THE "YOUNG" ELDERLY

The scattering of counties with large shares of elderly people are tempting targets for businesses that market to mature Americans. But a focus on total elderly share can be misleading. Some counties with high elderly shares have fast-growing older populations, while in many others, elderly populations have declined.

A good way to understand elderly growth is to divide the elderly into two age groups: 65 to 74, and 75 and older. In 1990, the U.S. had 18 million 65-to-74-year-olds. Most people in this group live with a spouse, are in good health, and are financially comfortable. They are a prime target for leisure markets such as travel and recreation. But most of the 13 million Americans aged 75 or older are women. "Older" elderly people have poorer health, and they are more likely to live alone, with relatives, or in institutions. They are a different market than the "younger" elderly, and they also concentrate in different places.

Younger elderly are more likely than their older counterparts to move, and they are also the ones who age into "elderhood" by staying put. As a result, counties with high shares of young elderly are the best

places to find fast-growing elderly populations. Seven of the top-ten counties for share of 65-to-74-year-olds are also among the 50 fastest-growing elderly counties. All are in Florida: Hernando, Charlotte, Highlands, Citrus, Flagler, Indian River, and Martin. But only two of the top-ten counties for share of people aged 75 or older are also on the top-50 growth list (Highlands and Charlotte).

Many counties with large shares of very old people have lost younger people. As a result, the aged-in-place in these counties make up a bigger piece of a diminishing pie. They cluster in rural regions and in cities with sustained economic declines. The exceptions are older retirement communities that have seen their younger elderly age in place. Florida counties such as Sarasota, Pasco, and Pinellas have high concentrations of both younger old and older old people.

Despite its concentration of affluent older people, Fayette, Georgia, is not a true retirement county. Only 7 percent of its population is aged 65 or older, lower than the average for Atlanta or the U.S. But James Price, executive director of Fayette Senior Services, believes that most of the county's middle-aged residents will stay put. He wants to expand his operations by opening a new senior center. Peachtree City grew from about 2,000 residents in 1975 to 22,000 in 1990 and is planning for about 45,000 residents by 2000. The area should draw active retirees with its abundant parks, two golf courses and lakes, an amphitheater, and numerous pools and tennis courts.

Many independent elderly move to retirement communities while they are still physically and financially able to enjoy recreational and social activities. Retirement meccas like Peachtree City have sprouted up in many areas of the South and West. Not all of these meccas have the kind of family ties that Peachtree City residents commonly mention, but they make up for it in other ways. Retirement migrants value companionship with peers, and they insist on access to high-quality health services.

DISABLED IN THE SOUTHEAST

Even the healthiest elderly must face the future possibility of long-term disability. This is an especially crucial concern for those who don't have family nearby. The number of elderly people living in group quarters, mostly in nursing homes, grew 17 percent during the 1980s. The share of the population in group quarters remained stable, at about 6 percent.

Although the share of elderly in nursing homes is small at a given point in time, a person's risk of being institutionalized later in life is high. Almost half (43 percent) of people who turned 65 in 1990 may end up in a nursing home at some time in their lives, according to Peter Kemper and Christopher Murtaugh. Even vigorous states like Alaska, which had the smallest number and share of people in nursing homes in 1990, have a fast-growing older population at risk of becoming institutionalized. Three of the top-ten counties for growth of the elderly population in the 1980s were Alaskan boroughs.

Younger people take their good health for granted, but older people cannot. Chronic conditions begin to accumulate after age 45. Twenty-four percent of people aged 65 to 74 have hearing impairments, 38 percent have high blood pressure, and

> **Almost two-thirds of elderly Americans are free of serious chronic health problems.**

44 percent have arthritis, according to the National Center for Health Statistics' 1989 National Health Interview Survey. The share with cataracts rises from 11 percent of those aged 65 to 74 to 23 percent of those aged 75 or older. Reflexes also slow with age, and activities like shopping and driving become difficult and unsafe.

The 1990 census asked people about three kinds of limitations that affect their daily lives. In the census definition, people with disabilities have a physical or mental condition lasting six months or more. A work disability prevents them from working or limits the work they can do. People with "mobility limitations" have difficulty getting out of the house on their own, and those with "self-care limitations" have trouble doing things like dressing, bathing, and feeding themselves. Some people have all three types of limitations; others have just one or two.

All told, 62 percent of noninstitutionalized elderly Americans have no limitations that interfere with their daily lives. But 33 percent are unable to work as much as they want to, 16 percent have a mobility limitation, and 12 percent have a self-care limitation. Seven percent have both mobility and self-care limitations.

Elderly men are less likely than elderly women to have mobility or self-care limitations. One reason is that more elderly men are in the 65-to-74 age group, but this doesn't explain all of the difference. Even among 65-to-74-year-olds, 15 percent of women have trouble getting around or taking care of themselves, compared with 12 percent of men. Among those aged 75 or older, 34 percent of women have mobility or self-care limitations, compared with 24 percent of men. Women of all ages are more likely than men to suffer from chronic conditions such as arthritis, bursitis, and osteoporosis.

> **Elderly men are less likely than elderly women to have mobility or self-care limitations.**

SLOW-GROWING BUT HEALTHY

It could be that mountain air is good for elderly circulation systems. Perhaps only sturdy lungs can endure the high altitudes. Whatever the reason, six of the top-ten counties for elderly people who suffer from no mobility or self-care limitations are in the Mountain states of Colorado, Wyoming, and Utah. Most of the 50 best counties for physically fit elderly are scattered throughout the North and West, with five each in Colorado, Minnesota, and Wisconsin; four each in Idaho and Nebraska; three each in Washington and Alaska; two each in Montana, Kansas, North Dakota, Utah, and Wyoming; and one each in Oregon, South Dakota, Vermont, Nevada, Pennsylvania, Maine, New Hampshire, and California. But only two counties on this list are in the South, both in Florida. Altogether, there are 621 U.S. counties where at least 85 percent of the elderly population are free of mobility or self-care limitations.

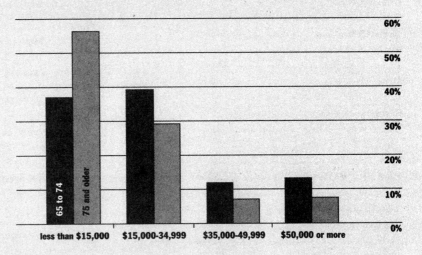

Mature Money

The majority of older elderly householders have low household incomes, while younger elderly fall in the low- to middle-income range.

(percent of households headed by people aged 65 to 74 and 75 and older by 1989 household income)

Source: 1990 census

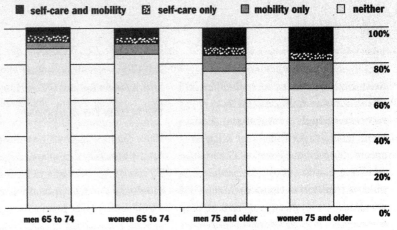

Reaching Limits

Even among older elderly women, two-thirds have no mobility or self-care limitations that interfere with their daily lives.

(percent of men and women aged 65 to 74 and 75 and older by type of limitation, 1990)

■ self-care and mobility   ▨ self-care only   ▨ mobility only   □ neither

Source: 1990 census

Younger Old

Nine of the top-ten counties with the highest share of population aged 65 to 74 are in Florida.

(counties ranked by percent aged 65 to 74, and number aged 65 to 74, 1990)

rank	county (metropolitan area)	number aged 65 to 74	percent aged 65 to 74
1	Hernando, FL (Tampa-St. Petersburg-Clearwater)	21,312	21.1%
2	Charlotte, FL	23,195	20.9
3	Highlands, FL	14,081	20.6
4	Citrus, FL	18,525	19.8
5	Llano, TX	2,273	19.5
6	Flagler, FL	5,496	19.2
7	Pasco, FL (Tampa-St. Petersburg-Clearwater)	53,270	19.0
8	Sarasota, FL (Sarasota)	49,857	18.0
9	Indian River, FL	15,444	17.1
10	Martin, FL (Fort Pierce)	16,828	16.7
11	Baxter, AR	5,137	16.5
12	Lake, FL	24,641	16.2
13	Roscommon, MI	3,189	16.1
14	Curry, OR	3,033	15.7
15	Manatee, FL (Bradenton)	33,028	15.6
16	Northumberland, VA	1,638	15.6
17	Sharp, AR	2,191	15.5
18	Lee, FL (Fort Myers-Cape Coral)	51,424	15.4
19	Yavapai, AZ	16,351	15.2
20	Van Buren, AR	2,112	15.1

U.S. average equals 7.3 percent.
Note: Includes only counties with 10,000 or more people. Metro areas defined before December 1992.

Source: 1990 census

Older Old

Just 5.3 percent of the U.S. population is aged 75 and older, but 15 percent are this old in Llano County, Texas.

(counties ranked by percent aged 75 and older, and number aged 75 and older, 1990)

rank	county (metropolitan area)	number aged 75 and older	percent aged 65 to 74
1	Llano, TX	1,692	14.6%
2	Sarasota, FL (Sarasota)	39,551	14.2
3	Cloud, KS	1,500	13.6
4	Pasco, FL (Tampa-St. Petersburg-Clearwater)	37,553	13.4
5	Highlands, FL	8,816	12.9
6	Charlotte, FL	14,294	12.9
7	Baxter, AR	3,970	12.7
8	Pinellas, FL (Tampa-St. Petersburg-Clearwater)	106,792	12.5
9	Manatee, FL (Bradenton)	26,380	12.5
10	Monona, IA	1,231	12.3
11	Marion, KS	1,578	12.2
12	Marshall, KS	1,425	12.2
13	Iron, MI	1,599	12.1
14	Bosque, TX	1,831	12.1
15	Comanche, TX	1,615	12.1
16	Kiowa, OK	1,363	12.0
17	Linn, MO	1,641	11.8
18	Cottonwood, MN	1,494	11.8
19	Sharp, AR	1,643	11.7
20	Montgomery, IA	1,405	11.6

U.S. average equals 5.3 percent.
Note: Includes only counties with 10,000 or more people. Metro areas defined before December 1992.

Source: 1990 census

Because physical condition deteriorates with age, it seems contradictory that regions with high concentrations of relatively fit elderly people are the same places that have high shares of people aged 75 or older. But if you insist on living in Minnesota at the age of 80, you should be able to shovel your driveway. Those who can't take the cold move south, whatever their age.

Elderly people who are plagued with arthritis and other disabling conditions are clustered in milder climates. They are also found in regions where the jobs are dangerous (such as coal mining) and poverty is common. Kentucky has six of the top-ten counties for share of elderly with mobility or self-care limitations: Knox, Breathitt, Lawrence, Leslie, Letcher, and Clay. All but one of the top-50 counties for

share of elderly with limitations are in the South—13 in Kentucky, 12 in Mississippi, 7 in Alabama, 4 each in West Virginia and Georgia, 2 each in Virginia and Oklahoma, and 1 each in Arkansas, Louisiana, South Carolina, Tennessee, and Florida. Apache County, Arizona, is the only nonsouthern county on the top-50 list, and it also happens to rank number 1 in its share of eld-

> **One of the biggest unknowns older people face is whether they will become disabled and how much it will cost.**

erly with mobility or self-care limitations.

Apache is the northeasternmost county in Arizona, bordering on both New Mexico and Utah. Thirty-eight percent of its elderly residents are restricted by mobility or self-care limitations. The county is rural and poor, and two-thirds of its residents live on the Navajo Reservation. Native Americans, particularly elders, are known to suffer from poor health. But the high limitation rate may be due to both the physical condition of older Indians and the lack of public transportation, according to Joe Weidman of the Northern Arizona Council of Governments. "The older people on the reservations have a hard time getting out of the house. They are quite isolated," says Weidman. On the other hand, there's no place they really have to go. "The young people often live and work off-reserva-

The Healthiest Elderly

*The most physically fit older bodies
are in nonmetro areas of the West and Midwest.*

(counties ranked by percent of population aged 65 and older with
no mobility or self-care limitations, and number aged 65 and older, 1990)

rank	county (metropolitan area)	number aged 65 and older	percent without limitations
1	Pitkin, CO	549	94.0%
2	Gunnison, CO	615	93.7
3	Union, SD	1,592	93.0
4	McLean, ND	1,869	92.9
5	Lincoln, WY	1,265	92.7
6	Summit, CO	283	92.2
7	Curry, OR	4,669	92.1
8	Summit, UT	892	91.9
9	Jefferson, WA	4,089	91.6
10	Routt, CO	772	91.6
11	Holt, NE	2,011	91.5
12	Whitman, WA	3,527	91.4
13	Gooding, ID	1,926	91.3
14	Blaine, ID	871	91.2
15	Lamoille, VT	2,018	91.1
16	Seward, KS	1,701	91.1
17	San Juan, WA	2,064	91.1
18	Douglas, NV	3,295	90.9
19	Swift, MN	2,365	90.8
20	Marshall, MN	1,921	90.6

U.S. average equals 79.9 percent.
Note: Includes only counties with 10,000 or more people. For definitions of limitations, see text.

Source: 1990 census

The Sickest Elderly

*Elderly people who have trouble getting around concentrate
in the poorer southern states.*

(counties ranked by percent of population aged 65 and older with mobility or
self-care limitations, and number aged 65 and older, 1990)

rank	county (metropolitan area)	number aged 65 and older	percent with limitations
1	Apache, AZ	3,863	38.2%
2	Lowndes, AL	1,605	37.4
3	Knox, KY	3,640	37.2
4	Breathitt, KY	1,609	37.2
5	Lawrence, KY	1,732	37.0
6	Leslie, KY	1,198	36.2
7	Clarke, AL	3,457	36.1
8	Montgomery, MS	1,964	36.1
9	Letcher, KY	3,080	36.0
10	Clay, KY	2,201	35.9
11	Dickenson, VA	2,085	35.8
12	Jefferson Davis, MS	1,950	35.7
13	Smith, MS	2,028	35.7
14	Greene, MS	1,145	35.6
15	Floyd, KY	4,923	35.5
16	Wayne, MS	2,238	35.4
17	George, MS	1,827	35.4
18	Noxubee, MS	1,668	35.4
19	Mingo, WV	3,394	35.3
20	Simpson, MS	2,931	35.1

U.S. average equals 20.1 percent.
Includes only counties with 10,000 or more people.

Source: 1990 census

tion," says Weidman. "But they come back on weekends to be with their families."

THE ECONOMICS OF OLD AGE

One of the biggest unknowns older people face is whether they will become disabled and how much it will cost. In the 1980s, Social Security payments kept up with the cost of living better than salaries did. Many of today's elderly also enjoy substantial pensions. Yet advancing age usually brings declining income and increasing health costs. Forty-five percent of households headed by someone aged 65 or older had a 1989 annual income below $15,000, according to the census. Many householders aged 75 or older are widowed women without substantial survivor or retirement benefits, and 56 percent of householders this old had 1989 household incomes below $15,000.

The share of affluent elderly households is not insignificant, however. Eleven percent of households headed by someone aged 65 or older had 1989 incomes of $50,000 or more, and 4 percent had incomes of $75,000 or more. These people often hoard considerable assets and savings. Except for health care, older people often spend less than younger adults do; their homes are paid off, and they are no longer supporting children.

The treasure troves guarded by elderly Americans may empty a bit in the future. Baby boomers got a late start buying homes and raising families, and growing shares of adults will have children and mortgages to support even after they reach "retirement age." If life expectancy continues to rise, more and more boomers will also have to support their own elderly

parents. But the news isn't all bad: many retired boomer couples will collect two Social Security and pension checks.

Things will be different for older people in the 21st century. Today's elderly Americans come from a different era. When they were younger, women were half as likely as men to have a college education,

> As boomers age, the educational equality and ethnic diversity of elderly people will increase.

and minorities were not as numerous or visible as they are today. As boomers age, the educational equality and ethnic diversity of elderly people will increase.

Maturing Rapidly

Florida is not the only state experiencing rapid growth among its elderly population. Counties in Nevada, Georgia, and even Alaska rank high on the top-50 list for elderly growth.

(counties ranked by percent increase in number aged 65 and older, 1980-90, and total aged 65 and older, 1990)

rank	county (metropolitan area)	number aged 65 and older	percent increase 1980-90
1	Flagler, FL	7,345	266.7%
2	Hernando, FL (Tampa-St. Petersburg-Clearwater)	31,048	186.1
3	Nye, NV	2,179	166.4
4	Fayette, GA (Atlanta)	4,468	159.5
5	Matanuska-Susitna, AK	1,866	155.6
6	Summit, CO	300	145.9
7	Kenai Peninsula, AK	2,015	143.7
8	Anchorage, AK (Anchorage)	8,258	134.6
9	Los Alamos, NM (Santa Fe)	1,668	131.0
10	Washington, UT	7,898	127.0
11	Mohave, AZ	19,273	125.5
12	Clark, NV (Las Vegas)	77,678	121.2
13	Douglas, NV	3,352	116.3
14	Douglas, CO (Denver PMSA)	2,524	115.7
15	St. Lucie, FL (Fort Pierce)	31,534	113.1
16	Collier, FL (Naples)	34,583	111.0
17	Okaloosa, FL (Fort Walton Beach)	13,319	109.0
18	Marion, FL (Ocala)	43,189	106.7
19	Indian River, FL	24,592	101.9
20	Beaufort, SC	10,664	101.1
21	Pitkin, CO	557	100.4
22	Fairbanks North Star, AK	2,540	99.1
23	Okeechobee, FL	4,807	96.1
24	Gwinnett, GA (Atlanta)	16,776	95.9
25	Virginia Beach city, VA Norfolk-Virginia Beach-Newport News)	23,214	94.9
26	Brunswick, NC	7,494	94.8
27	Fairfax, Fairfax,* Falls Church,* VA (Washington)	57,118	94.4%
28	Arapahoe, CO (Denver)	29,171	94.3
29	Horry, SC	18,229	94.0
30	Lyon, NV	3,019	93.7
31	Yavapai, AZ	25,613	92.0
32	Columbia, GA (Augusta)	3,872	91.5
33	Brevard, FL (Melbourne-Titusville-Palm Beach)	66,382	91.5
34	Chesterfield, Colonial Heights,* VA (Richmond-Petersburg)	15,305	91.1
35	Santa Rosa, FL (Pensacola)	7,759	90.6
36	Charlotte, FL	37,489	88.8
37	Howard, MD (Baltimore)	11,399	87.5
38	Sandoval, NM	6,385	86.6
39	Citrus, FL	29,283	84.5
40	St. Johns, FL (Jacksonville)	13,791	83.9
41	Hood, TX	4,668	83.1
42	Highlands, FL	22,897	82.8
43	Carson City, NV	6,041	82.3
44	Clay, FL (Jacksonville)	8,984	82.2
45	Lee, FL (Fort Myers-Cape Coral)	83,003	81.0
46	Nevada, CA	14,251	81.0
47	Davis, UT (Salt Lake City-Ogden)	11,567	77.8
48	Prince William, Manassas,* Manassas Park,* VA (Washington)	8,167	77.5
49	Juneau, AK	1,364	76.9
50	Martin, FL (Fort Pierce)	27,690	76.9

U.S. average equals 22.3 percent.
* Independent city.
Note: Includes only counties with 10,000 or more people in 1990. Metro areas defined before December 1992.

Source: 1990 and 1980 censuses

Some things may never change, however. Retired boomers of the 21st century may resemble Adele Carson, a spunky 84-year-old who maneuvers her golf cart around a 60-mile network of paved paths that winds through the forested neighborhoods, golf courses, and shopping centers of Peachtree City. Life is good for Mrs. Carson, despite her failing eyesight. "It's one reason I came here," she says. "I knew I could drive a golf cart."

But the biggest reason for Mrs. Carson's move had nothing to do with golf-cart paths. "Who are we kidding? Nobody would come from Montana or wherever just because we have a senior citizens' center," she says. "If it were a desert, we would live here—just to be near the family." *—Additional reporting by John Hoeffel and Ron Cossman Maps prepared by Linda Jacobsen*

MY MOTHER IS SPEAKING FROM THE DESERT

**They get old and their minds start to go.
They forget about their children.
But their children can't forget about them.**

BY MARY GORDON

MY MOTHER IS SPEAKING FROM THE DESERT. EVERYTHING she says now is spoken from the desert, a desert she has in part created. But only in part. Mostly, I suppose, the desert was created because she is 86 and something has hardened or broken or worn out. The part she made came about through a dark will and sense of worthlessness. Believing she deserves nothing, she surrounds herself with empty air. The sun gleams in her eyes. Her eyes can sometimes seem colorless, as if they were ruined by looking at the sun. Sometimes she looks blind. Her eyes are very beautiful. The rest of her face is gaunt now and so you must look at her eyes: you can't look at anything else.

When she hasn't combed her hair, when she has lost a tooth she won't have attended to, when she won't cut or file her nails, or change her clothes, she is distressing to look at. She used to be a very buoyant person, fleshy, with a wonderful skin that always made you think of the inner flesh of fruit: an apple or a peach. When she wore sleeveless dresses in summer, the cool, thick muscles of her upper arms made you want to rest your hot cheeks against them. The freshness and crispness of those dresses

was a miracle. Their colors were the colors of nature: sea green, sky blue. It was as if she were wearing the elements themselves—the limitless sky, the refreshing sea—instead of a dress made of material whose shade was only a reminder of sea or sky.

In winter she wore hats with feathers and tailored suits, made of men's fabric, with shoulder pads and serious straight skirts. She "went to business." She was a legal secretary. She worked for one lawyer from 1937 to 1970, when he died; then she became his partner's secretary. She was proud of her business clothes, different from the clothes of other mothers who had nothing at stake in what they wore; they could slop around the house wearing anything, and what would it matter? In her handbag she carried a gold compact, lipsticks that smelled like nothing else except themselves but I knew would taste delicious if I could only taste them. I wanted to taste everything: her skin, warmed or cooled by a light dusting of freckles, her light dresses, her lipstick, her perfume.

But underneath this freshness, this crispness, this robust, delightful not only health but healthfulness, there must always have been a secret devotion to rot. Perhaps it was connected to her polio, which she was stricken with at the age of 3 and which left her with one leg shorter than the other, barely able to walk. A love of rot buried beneath

Mary Gordon's latest book is "The Rest of Life," a collection of novellas. This article is from a memoir in progress.

her grief and shame about her body, and beneath the stoicism that concealed her grief and shame like a softening tuber underneath a field.

Now the healthfulness is gone; she has burrowed down to a deeper place, a darker place, perhaps one she feels to be more truthful. Or, perhaps, thought of another way, it is a place she goes to in the desert. The peace of carrion. She lies down beside it, she makes her home in it: there she is at peace.

I failed to keep her from this place because my attempt to keep her from it was not an act of love, but of terror and hatred. My mother's rotting body has taught me things I would otherwise never have known. About myself and the world. My mother's body rotting at the center of my history is the tight heart at the center of everything I know.

If I could understand how she changed from the fresh, lovely mother to the rotting one, what would I understand?

Everything. The darkness.

Or perhaps not. Perhaps I would only understand my mother.

Or perhaps not even that. Perhaps only something, but only one thing, having to do only with her.

SHE HAS LOST HER MEMORY. EACH SENTENCE SHE SPEAKS IS in the present tense. She is letting the past slip from her hand, a fish into the dark water. She is letting it drop through a scrim of tissue paper into the night air. She is allowing it to disappear in snow.

I believe she is doing this in part because of a great sorrow. A sorrow I can do nothing to help, a sorrow I probably helped bring about because of my hatred of her body. Because I abetted her in a project that would enact her hatred of her body. She yearned for its corruption because she believed, above all else, in its degradation. I sense that she thinks what she is doing now is nothing more than telling the truth.

She is in a nursing home now because of her desire to rot. There is no way around it—you cannot devote yourself to rot and have a place in the civilized world. Something must be done for you, to you. And I was the one to do it.

I was living in a small town along the Hudson River. In 1983, when my mother retired at the age of 75, I bought her a house two blocks from mine. I thought it was a perfect plan: she could stop working and be with her grandchildren. She was an enchanting grandmother when Anna, my first child, named for her, was little: inventive, doting, amusing and amused. She said it would be a privilege and a pleasure to see the children growing. She'd worked every day—except for six weeks off when I was born—since she was 18. I sensed that her competence was slipping, that they were getting impatient with her at the office. I wanted her to leave of her own accord: the idea that they should force her to retire would have been the worst possible disgrace for her.

But bringing her to the country was a disaster. She didn't want to do anything. Take courses at the college, I

suggested, Italian, opera—your father sang opera, and you could learn his language. Tutor children. Take in typing. Volunteer at the rectory. No, she said, I've worked long enough. She only wanted to be served. Five weeks after my son was born, she had a fall. Or something: it was some sort of grotesque physical mishap. She told me that her brace and shoes were off, and she wanted to go to the bathroom, so she simply crawled in. But she fell out of bed trying to get onto the floor. I knew that she'd been drinking. After that, she was confined to a wheelchair for six months and she never regained much mobility.

Six years later, when I moved to New York, I decided to leave her in the country. My husband would be there most of the week and we would be there on weekends. I hired a Taiwanese woman to live in. She'd been a nurse in Taiwan; she was getting a master's degree in psychology. She was a pretty, boyish, sharp-witted person, with an excellent sense of humor. After a month, she told me she wanted to quit; living with my mother was too depressing. I begged her to stay till Christmas. But around Halloween, when I took my mother to her regular semiannual physical, I discovered that she hadn't taken her shoes off since the end of the summer. She'd slept in her shoes—high, built-up, tightly laced boots—for three months. The doctor forbade her to take her shoes off in his office. He said he'd come to the house later. When she took off her shoes the room was filled with the stench of rotting flesh. He said if she'd waited much longer, gangrene would have set in.

I pulled every string to get my mother into a first-rate Catholic nursing home quite near where I lived. When I told her, she got blind drunk, cursed me and cried.

This made my decision: she'd have to go into a nursing home. An evaluating nurse, sent by the state, determined that my mother met the criteria to be in what was called a primary care facility. Most of the criteria had to do with urine and feces. The mind, the abilities of the imagination and the spirit, had almost no weight in these questions. I pulled every string to get my mother into a first-rate Catholic nursing home quite near where I lived. When I told her, she got blind drunk, cursed me and cried. Li, the Taiwanese nurse, wept. I stood firm. "You can go to Mass every day," I told my mother. "Soon I'll be dead," she said, "then I won't need to go to Mass."

IF I COME UPON MY MOTHER NOW AND SHE ISN'T EXPECTING ME, I find her sitting with her head buried in her hands. There is no need for her to do anything now but adopt this formal posture of grief. Yet I don't think she would like to die. She will not, I believe, die soon. She has, I have been told by many doctors, the heart and blood pressure of a teenager.

If I were an allegorist, if I decided to do something in the manner of Giotto—embodying the virtues in a living figure—I would paint my mother in her wheelchair, her head in her hands, wearing her magenta sweater (the only one she wears although there are a dozen in her cupboard). I would call it "The Death of Hope."

She hopes for nothing, and because I believe that nothing can be done for her, because I have given her up, I hope for nothing on her behalf. Now everything in her life points out the futility of hope. But if I had wanted to paint hope, the embodied virtue, I would have painted my young mother in her sea green or sky blue dress, her lovely arms, her white skin and her strong and useful, perhaps rather dangerous teeth. Because hope can be dangerous. In that it leads to the death of hope. But it does not lead in a straight path to death. There is the animal, with the animal's hope. This is not human, it is not our own. It is something, but it is not ours.

There is a link between hope and memory. Remembering nothing, one cannot hope for anything. And so time means nothing. It is a useless element. Living in time without memory or hope: a fish in air. A bird in water. Some unfortunate creature doomed to the wrong medium. Yet not, alas, to death.

I don't know what my mother does all day. She eats her meals. She sleeps. In the time that she's been in the home she's made three friends; one died, one is her roommate, whom she bullies and then when the roommate rebels, she refuses to speak to. She has one friend who is completely charming: intelligent, loving and aware. I don't know why she likes my mother; but she says my mother means the world to her, that if anything happened to my mother, she doesn't know what she'd do. I know it would be rude to ask the reasons for such a statement, but I'm genuinely puzzled. I want to tell my mother's friend: "But you're too good for her. You can do much better than my mother. Find somebody else." Then I cover my mother with kisses, atoning for my betrayal. She doesn't know why I'm doing it, and, wisely, she doesn't respond.

I know that she prays. But I don't know what she's doing when she prays. What is she saying? Where is she? Is she in a blank silence, the presence of God, where there is nothing without meaning and she knows she is where she has always belonged, perhaps where she has always been? Is she silent, or is she saying words to God? Her own words or the formal words of prayer? Or is she having simple conversations, too banal to repeat, yet placing her exactly at the true, safe center of the universe? She says she prays for me. She says she prays for me and my family all the time. I believe her. But I don't know

what she is thinking of when she prays. Or even who, since she sometimes forgets that she has grandchildren.

I think she must be happy, praying. Or at least not suffering, in a place beyond memory. With God, since both of them are outside time, memory is irrelevant. So I can think of her praying, be both admiring and calm. Praying, she is in the place where she belongs. A place where she is still what she often was: outstanding. I believe she sees the face of God. But who can see the face of God and live? Who can see the face of God and remember it? Perhaps that is the point. Perhaps it is the point most especially for my mother, for the way she must live now. The way she has no other choice but to live. Praying, she comes alive. Free of her body. Beautiful again: a spirit. Joyous. Not weighed down. Not even tragic. Partaking of greatness. Great.

I TAKE MY MOTHER TO A DOCTOR AT MOUNT SINAI TO SEE IF THERE is anything she can do that might reclaim her memory, return her zest for life. The doctor asks her questions.

She answers with words from the desert. "I don't have my memory any more. I don't think about things. They were all sad."

The doctor, who is beautiful and lively and wonderfully intelligent, says gently: "What about the happy things. Do you think about your mother? You had happy times with her."

She says: "That's sad too. Because everything is lost."

There's nothing I can say when my mother speaks like this, because everything she says is true.

The doctor begins to ask her the questions on what is a standard diagnostic test for depression. But we run out of time and the doctor suggests that perhaps I could ask her the questions and simply circle the answers on the form. Some of the questions are these:

Are you basically satisfied with your life?
Do you feel that your life is empty?
Are you hopeful about the future?
Are you bothered by thoughts you can't get out of your head?
Are you in good spirits most of the time?
Do you often feel helpless?
Do you frequently worry about the future?
Do you feel you have more problems with memory than most?
Do you think it's wonderful to be alive now?
Do you often feel downhearted and blue?
Do you feel pretty worthless the way you are now?
Do you worry a lot about the past?
Do you find life very exciting?

When I first ask my mother the questions she answers everything positively. She is satisfied with her life, she isn't bored, she's hopeful, she's in good spirits, she doesn't worry. I think I understand something. I ask her if she thinks that saying there's anything wrong with her life means that she's complaining, that she's ungrateful for what she has, that she's a weakling, a crybaby. Of course that's what I think, she says, looking at me from the desert.

I tell her that's not the way it is; they need to know how she really feels for their work. It's their business to get an accurate picture, I tell her. "You have to do it for them." I never tell her who "them" is and she never asks. "O.K., if it's their business," she says.

She answers the questions slowly. She isn't satisfied with her life, she isn't happy, she often feels helpless, she often feels downhearted and blue, she feels her situation is hopeless. She frequently feels like crying. On the other hand, she doesn't feel that her life is empty, she is hopeful about the future, she is not afraid that something bad is going to happen, she thinks it is wonderful to be alive. Her most heartfelt response is to the question: "Do you feel pretty worthless the way you are now?" "Oh, yes," she says, "completely worthless." She is speaking from the desert. She is looking at me with those eyes burned by the sun. There is no softening landscape. No hidden refreshing spring. The dry land. The harsh rock. The sky, unmediated. When I start to cry she says, "What are you crying about, how else would I be?" And I tell her all the wonderful things she's done, how much she's been treasured and beloved. "That was then," she says. "I thought you were talking about now."

WHEN I CALL THE DOCTOR AND READ HER THE RESULTS of the test, she says my mother is on the border of dysphoric and depressed. She thinks my mother might be helped with antidepressants, but because she may be suffering from senile dementia as well, the chances are slim. She'd like to have an M.R.I. done on my mother, because some of the neurological signs were a bit confusing.

I don't tell my mother that we're going for a test that is frightening, claustrophobia-inducing. I don't tell her till a day before that she's going to have a test at all. I try to describe the procedure to her. The put you into a kind of tube. You're a bit shut in, but if you relax it's quite bearable. I tell her I had one myself, and that I fell asleep during it, which was true. I decide to take her on the city bus, which lowers itself for people in wheelchairs, because the first time we went to the doctor, we waited for the ambulance for an hour and a half one way, two hours the next. "They've got you over a barrel, and they know it and they don't care," the woman at the nursing home tells me. I think how pleased I would be to firebomb the ambulance headquarters; the relief of seeing the place, and the people, go up in flames.

On the bus, I understand that not having a memory makes my mother ashamed. The shame of the bankrupt. She pretends she remembers things. "Oh, yes, I remember these people. I've seen them before. Their faces are familiar." On Madison Avenue in the 80's, where she has never been in my lifetime, she says, "I remember this was where we used to get off." I can't imagine she was ever on a Madison Avenue bus. When she was young, she came to the city to go the theater, or the rodeo at Madison Square Garden. She loved the rodeo; when it was in town

she went to it every night. She had some dates with rodeo cowboys, whose names remained dear to her. Turk Greeneau and Cecil Henley. Turk married Sally Rand, the fan dancer, who was famous for causing a stir at the 1933 World's Fair in Chicago. My mother always said, with real indignation at the loss to the rodeo world, "She broke his stride for good." If I laughed when she said that, she'd get angry.

She also regularly went to a retreat house on 29th Street. Or to St. Patrick's Cathedral. Everything I know of her history makes me sure that she was never on the Upper East Side. And I know she has never seen her fellow passengers. I have to fight my desire to tell her, "You're wrong, you've never been here before." I wonder if she thinks she's been on these streets and seen these people before because all people and places are the same to her. Memory enables a sense of difference. The present is different from the past. The remembered event is different from the current experience, the difference is recognizable and therefore the events can be differentiated.

Is everything for my mother in the present? Does she live like God?

No, she still experiences fear and loss.

How dreadful that these should be the last to go. One day, when I arrive at the nursing home, she's trembling. A bishop is going to say Mass for them on the next day. She's been selected to read the epistle. She's afraid she won't be able to do it. She's afraid she won't know when to come in. I find the num who's in charge: she assures my mother that she'll hand her the microphone when the time comes. I go over the reading with her. She's letter perfect. I say I'll come the next day to be with her for support.

She reads the epistle. She reads out Philippians 3:16-21 as Philippians, March 16, 1921. She doesn't know she's made a mistake. After Mass the Bishop is extravagantly warm, full of praise. She doesn't respond to him. She doesn't know what he's talking about. The 45 minutes of Mass is enough time to have erased the experience for her. But she was able to experience 36 hours of anticipatory anxiety and dread.

But she doesn't seem to dread the M.R.I. Perhaps because I've underrepresented its discomfort. The technician tells her to lie completely still, or the pictures will be useless. After a few minutes, I see her beginning to thrash. Through a microphone the technician tells her in an accusing voice that she is ruining everything. Instantly, I know what to do. I jump up, run over to the hole her legs are sticking out of, and thrust my head in. "We're going to say the Rosary," I tell her. And into the hole I shout, "The five Sorrowful Mysteries, the first mystery, the Agony in the Garden." Our Fathers. Hail Marys. The second mystery. The third. She settles down and lies quietly. The test is done.

I realize that for me, who claims to live by words, there are no words that could automatically take away my terror. No poetry, no passages from great novels could be shouted at me and cause me to lie still. She is, in this way, more fortunate than I.

When we get to the doctor's office, on the other side of the medical center, the doctor asks my mother if the test was difficult. What test? she asks. The doctor describes the M.R.I. I don't remember anything like that, she says.

Another piece of good fortune; without memory there is no re-living of terror. The past no longer haunts. It is finished, and for good.

BECAUSE OF MY MOTHER'S POLIO, MY EARLIEST VISION includes the vision of a damaged female body. For many years, the only adult female body I saw unclothed was, it must be said, grotesque, lopsided, with one dwarf leg and a foot and a belly with a huge scar, biting into and discoloring unfirm flesh. She'd point to it and say, "This is what happened when I had you."

For many years as a child, much longer than I should have, I imagined that all women had this slit belly and when I had children I would, too.

I should feel more loyalty to my mother's body. Because, if I hate my mother's body, what can I feel about my own?

But my body is not like hers. She is crippled, I am not. It shaped the way we lived: this difference between us. What was always in the front of both our minds was that the crucial thing was that she must not fall. We lived both our lives in terror of her falling. It was like living on a fault line or on the top of a volcano. The anxiety that the thoughtless move, the too-forceful move, the unexpected move would cause calamity. My mother's falling seemed like a natural disaster. The crash, the crying out. Then the immobility. I never remember her rising up after she fell. She had to be brought to bed. Where she would lie and weep with her eyes closed. Sometimes she would moan aloud. No sense of when she might get up again. Perhaps never.

Because she was a cripple she felt free to give up ordinary kinds of pride and to ask help without stopping to consider where the help might come from or what the helper's response might be. I think she felt that any able-bodied person was more adult than she.

She had, I suppose, the necessary lack of physical shame that helps cripples get by. She would do things that mortified me, like going down a too-steep flight of stairs on her behind. She would crawl up hills on her hands and knees. I would want to beg her not to, so deep was my mortification when she did something like this, even if no one could see us, but I knew that she was right: there was no alternative. It made me literally want to die, because there was too much to feel. It was easier to die than feel all of it. There was mortification of the spectacle, pity for her, shame at my own shame, pride in her, hatred for her, perhaps a vague sense of her sadism in insisting that all this be visible. It was too much for a child. It has never stopped being too much.

But the child of a cripple was never really a child, and so has never really passed satisfactorily through childhood. You are always resentful because *you* are always in charge. You are always more able. You envy people whose parents don't need to be watched or cared for with an envy that has the taste of hate. You want to say to the crippled parent: You have stolen my childhood, you have taken my youth. But how can you? Always, they have suffered more than you, a suffering from which there is no respite, no escape. They cannot but live with their damaged body.

Should you come at them with the face of your deprivation and its rage, leaving them diminished, shaken, unsteady, adding to what they know about themselves—that they are damaged, second-rate—you would still be able to walk away, able and intact. Leaving the wounded one now doubly wounded. Naming yourself a monster. In such a situation, therefore, rage is impossible. Or at least the expression of rage. It's like being angry at a starving man for depriving you of a profiterole, a cream puff, an éclair. You live always in a state of remorse for what you have not done for them and cannot do. And the fear that somehow you might weaken them, because they know what you are thinking.

And suppose one day they are thinking about your rage, and it takes away their hope. You know how much they need their hope. They need it because the effort of living is so great. Simple actions—if there are any, demand much more consideration from them. Planning, strategizing. This kind of attentiveness requires hope. And suppose they give up hope because of you. Because of you, the monster, the obscenely healthy brute. Standing above them in a wholeness that can only be called sadistic, insisting on something they could never have given. Only a monster could ever have thought of saying it. The monster you are. The monstrous, healthy animal. The monster child.

I learned quite early that it is my fate always to be the most able-bodied in any room. That is the way I have always lived, alert for the scar, the concealed false limb, the tremor, the flicker of anxiety at the prospect of uncertain terrain, the slurred speech, the hesitant, reluctant gesture. I always find it and I always know that because of this I am called upon, not only to act, but also to find a solution for the damage that must be accommodated, made up for, got around. I believe that I will always find a solution and that it will always be right. This is the source of my worst qualities: arrogance, self-righteousness, also intense self-pity, then resentment and contempt.

WHEN YOU ARE WITH MY MOTHER, IT IS BEST TO HAVE CONVERSATIONS that don't require a reference to the past. No interpretation. Narrative is second best, a far second after description. Plain description is what's called for.

Our best visits consist of my taking her to the garden in Riverside Park. I wheel her chair down the hill. I have to struggle to keep the momentum from hurtling her to disaster. I bend my legs and strain my body to keep her safe. The next day my back always hurts. But I keep my posture easily because of the horrifying vision of what would happen if I did not. My mother, hurtling forward. Her head gashed on the pavement. I see the bloody forehead, the wound with pebbles imbedded in it. Inattentiveness could bring about a tragedy: I must be hypervigilant about everything, every variation of the surface.

We wheel around the enclosed garden. We say the names of flowers or colors. Peony, we say, foxglove, lily, pansy, phlox. The words are beautiful in themselves. And we say the names of colors: red, yellow, purple, blue, deep rose. Sometimes we sing. She remembers the words to songs. Doing these things, we are both happy.

When we are doing these things, I wonder, "Is it possible I still have a mother?"

"Of course," I say, "how could it not?"

She kissed men right on the mouth; she would grab the microphone at public gatherings to sing. She loved foods she could crunch and chew.

But then, how can it be?

A mother without memory of the stories of the past means that I must accept the possibility that I have never been a child.

MY MOTHER IS SPEAKING FROM THE DESERT, WHERE SHE would like to disappear. But how can she disappear there, when there is no place to hide. Perhaps by the sheer force of something whose name I do not know. Perhaps it is her sorrow, creating a fog, in which she will disappear. Yet she is visible to me, partly because I have ineradicable memories of her vividness. She was, above all, a vivid creature. She raged so, people were careful not to cross her. She kissed men right on the mouth; she'd grab the microphone at public gatherings to sing. She laughed so loudly in the movies that people she knew would meet her in the lobby afterward and say they knew just where she had been sitting. She loved foods that she could crunch and chew, particularly nuts; she would indulge herself in an extravagant purchase of cashews and almonds every year at the end of Lent.

She was always admirable, attractive, enjoyable. Even when she was committed to a course of degradation, to her love of rot, the vivacious animal held sway.

She was the life of the party. Now she is barely alive.

For many years, she used alcohol to allow herself to fall into the pit of shame, of stupor, of oblivion. Now she can enter it without chemical aid. Age provides her with a stupor from which she has no desire to escape, even if she could. For years I have stood at the edge of the pit, trying to keep her back. The same muscles I use when I push her wheelchair down a hill, holding her back from hurtling forward. Now I realize that her desire for stupor is stronger than my ability to keep her lively. I give in to her need for darkness. I give her up. I turn my back on her.

FOR THREE WEEKS, AT ANY TIME DURING THE DAY WHEN MY MIND IS not taken up with the business of living: reading, writing, caring for children, shopping, cooking, speaking to friends, calling insurance companies or the super, what I am thinking about is my mother's fingernails.

She has given up attending to her nails, at the same time that the head nurse on her floor has taken three weeks' vacation. This woman oversees her charges with a benevolent general's intelligence and interest in the welfare of her troops. While she's away, things slip a bit. My mother's nails are not quite claws yet; they haven't begun to turn under. I know she's waiting for me to cut her nails. Everyone is waiting for me. The substitute nurse says they have no nail scissors, it's up to me to produce one. And do I? Three weeks in a row I forget. She refuses to file her nails, the nursing home says I must bring the clippers and I forget. All of us joined in an insistence that my mother will appear more animal than she needs to.

They care for her body with attention and dignity. But it is up to me to keep an eye on the details. She is a difficult patient for them because she refuses to take a shower. I tell them that she has never taken showers, because she has never been able to walk without her shoes. As I tell them that I realize what an extraordinary thing it is: my mother has never taken a shower. Very few people in the modern West can say such a thing. Occasionally, perhaps once a year when she was younger, she would, with great difficulty, requiring much assistance (my father's, her mother's, and then, after her mother's death, mine), take a bath. Would the nurses believe me if I told them that for most of her life she was exceptionally clean? That she reminded me of sheets hung out in the wind, of the white flesh of apples? Would they believe me, or would they say, quite properly, what does that have to do with now?

When I have to remind her to groom herself, or arrange an appointment with the hairdresser or dentist, I am covered over in rage and panic that literally takes my breath away. I can hardly speak. I want to cry. At the same time as I am her advocate, I want to scream at her and say, "How can you allow this to go on?" It makes me want to end her life. At the same time I want to sit in her lap and say, "Don't you understand that I'm your child and a child shouldn't have to do this?" And have a transformed mother, fragrant, buoyant, say what she was almost never able to say, "Don't worry about anything, I'll take care of everything."

What I miss most is the sense of rightness, of right choices that she represented, her crispness, her business acumen, the fact that up and down the street and all around the parish, people asked her advice about "letters from the government" or tax returns, or wills. She put her blue-framed glasses on and within minutes, solved their problems. Or she would get on the phone. She was brilliant on the phone. She prided herself on having "a good telephone voice." How irresistible she was on the telephone. Of course no one could resist her. And she was delightful around anything having to do with money: at the bank, where she was immediately given pride of place because her boss was the bank's attorney. (She never had to stand on line; she could get any check approved.) Or even in the butcher shop, the vegetable market. As long as she was touching coins or bills, or something representing them, she was at ease, and powerful, and most of all effective. Yet she didn't care about money, in the sense of accumulating it for herself. She only liked being involved in its movement.

I understood very well that my father's death had only enhanced her social position, therefore mine. She had been the unfortunate wife of an unfortunate husband: a failed writer who could not make a living. Now she was the noble widow and I the gallant orphan. There was no place where we went that this was not immediately legible. But never more so than when we entered our pew in the front of the church, always getting there early so my mother wouldn't be jostled by crowds and be thrown off balance. There was a terrible crush at Sunday Mass in those days. The whole congregation had an admiring eye on us. We were consistently admired.

And she would occasionally, though sparingly, use her status as a noble and competent cripple for my good. There was the memorable incident that occurred when I was 13, the only one in the class with a working mother. I invited some boys and girls over one afternoon to dance. It was a disaster. The boys stood on one side of the room and smoked. The girls danced with each other. One boy, trying to be cool and light his cigarette from the gas stove, set his hair on fire. One of our neighbors reported all this to the Rosary Society; it spread through the parish. The principal threatened me with not being allowed to graduate publicly. My mother went up to the school. She made a point of how difficult it was for her to walk down the long corridors, and that she had to take time off from work. She said to the principal: "What do you think those kids were doing. I don't think they were doing anything. It shows the difference in our minds." She never blamed me, which was unusual for her. I was tremendously proud of her—none of the other parents stood up to the nuns—but it made me feel unworthy. And I was aware I had been spared punishment because she was a cripple and a widow.

But that was only part of it. I was spared because she was daring and articulate. When she knew she was right,

she was fearless. Part of the pride she felt she had to give up as a cripple transformed itself into something morally positive: she didn't care what people thought about her. She took pride in appearing outrageous, vulgar even, in saying "hell," and "goddamn" freely and in all company. But it was this same lack of regard for public opinion that allowed her to stop grooming herself, to give in to her love of rot. Looked at in this way, a regard for the opinion of the world, a consciousness of and concern for how one is seen, seems infinitely precious and humanizing. But my mother's dashing lack of regard for public opinion gave her, when she was younger, a richer and fuller humanity, more fun, more scope for self-expression and satisfaction of her strong nature. And it was a great gift to me: I never had to endure what many girls did, the blunt hoof of propriety crushing my chest, the beast mother, with her blood red eyes, enforcing the implacable rules of the household gods. She was not afraid of being in the world, as the mothers of many of my friends were. She took me into it.

When we went to restaurants—only two of them, but they were important ones in the place we lived—she was always given the best table, and always waited on by someone she knew. After my father died, she made a little home for us in restaurants. No, not a little home. A vacation spot, A resort.

I understood that all the food I was eating on these occasions came to us because of my mother's relationship to money. She made it; she could spend it; she was willing to spend it on fun. I don't know if it was because of all this that all the food connected to my mother on these occasions seemed extraordinarily delicious. Bright colors, good textures, satisfying, clear, unclouded tastes. Many foods frightened me to the point of panic in those years. Mayonnaise, cocoa, fat and gristle on meat, the smallest spot on the skin of a tomato. I thought they would poison me or choke me; they would, in some way, be the cause of my death. My mother seemed magically able to avoid all these disturbing food elements on our outings together. She assured, by her assurance in ordering, that we would come near none of these things. She made it so that they didn't exist, a distant memory from a deprived past. Everything she suggested we eat was festive, modern, possibly unnourishing, but full of the electric joy of life.

In the local luncheonette, we were waited on by her friend Tess, an iron-haired, thin-lipped woman, who seemed to come to life around my mother. She always said, "God bless her," to me, always brought us our orders without having to ask for it. She knew what we wanted: "The regular." Grilled cheese sandwiches, chocolate milk for me, coffee for my mother. For my dessert the specialty of the house: lemon ice cream.

Every time I got a good report card (and I always did) she would drive to the next town to a bar and grill called the Brick Cafe. It was owned by a man named Charlie, an ex-prizefighter who had briefly been one of my mother's beaus. It is rather unusual that my mother, a cripple, though a beautiful one, had one beau who was a prizefighter and another who was a rodeo cowboy. These are the only two she ever spoke of, but I think they were the only ones. Except for John Gallagher, a widower, an undertaker. John wanted to marry her. The cowboy and the prizefighter, I think, did not. My father, a writer and Jewish convert, must have had the slightly illegal appeal that the prizefighter and the cowboy did, but he was sanctioned by the priests she worshiped. And he did, remarkably, want to marry her. People who knew them when they were courting say they were publicly, almost embarrassingly amorous. They kissed on the subway. And he wrote her poetry. He would buy her greeting cards, then cut or rip out the printed verse on the inside and substitute one of his own. In 1945, her birthday message included the words: "Never in all the annals of recorded time/existed such sweet pretext for a rhyme."

MY MOTHER'S 86TH BIRTHDAY. I HAVE BROUGHT HER WHAT IS PLEASANT to the senses: roses, flavored tea, a whipped cream cake. Every year before she went into the nursing home, every year that is, since my grandmother died when I was 12, I made her a peach shortcake for her birthday. She took a pride in not liking sweet things, in caring nothing for chocolate. The tartness of the peaches pleased her, the plainness of the underlying cake. This year I don't make her a shortcake, I buy it and it is not peach, but strawberry. At the Metropolitan Museum, I buy a postcard of a Byzantine icon and an expensive frame in which to place it. This is her birthday gift. I have collected people who are well disposed toward her. During the party she sits like a stone. One of her bottom teeth is rotting, in a way so that it is gradually turning into a splinter or a fang.

The temperature is nearly 100 degrees and, after I leave her, I can do nothing for the rest of the day but lie in my bed, paralyzed by what I can only call despair.

Her power over my life is enormous.

I WANT TO TAKE HER TO THE GARDEN THIS MORNING BECAUSE I STARTED the day having such terrible thoughts about her. I have to do something for or with her that has in it some semblance of pleasure, something that lifts me from the unbearable state of rage and responsibility and shame.

The social worker in charge of my mother's case has written to tell me that I must sign a D.N.R. form. Do Not Resuscitate. Do not use unusual means. Don't keep her alive. Let her die.

I sign a piece of paper that authorizes that someone will look on while my mother dies.

We walk down to the garden. Or, we don't walk, I push her. Making sure not to let her momentum drag us down. We get to the level part, where it is no longer difficult to walk. I point out day lilies, a pair of infant twins, a pigeon pecking at mulberries. I name colors. I insist that she look. I insist that she tell me which of the flowers is her favorite. "I like them all," she says. "No, you have to pick one." "The purple one," she says. "Hibiscus," I tell her.

I say that it's my favorite one too.

"I know that," she says. "That's why I said it."

I would like to believe that she is still capable of liking one color more than another, but it's probably too much to ask. Does she still remember that I like purple? Or is she faking again?

I believe that somehow, unfocused, but in a white light she sees all the time, there is her love for me. Which may be the only thing that she still knows.

She keeps telling me it's too hard for me to push her that far. She keeps telling me the time. It's 11:30. Lunch is at noon. She keeps saying we'd better get back, that if we're late to lunch they won't keep anything for her.

I can tell that she wants nothing more than to get back. I have no way of knowing whether it's a good thing to take her to the garden, if she's still capable of being pleased, if she would prefer, above all, not to be bothered, to be left alone. If I am taking her to the garden because I think it is pleasant for her, because I can tell people about it and they will think I'm doing something pleasant for her, think how good I am. *Such a good daughter. She takes her mother to the garden.* But perhaps my mother would prefer to be left alone.

I leave her in the dining room. She asks when she'll see me again. I tell her in a week. "What are you doing with yourself between now and then?" she asks, with a hint of her old bite.

"Gallivanting," I say.

"Just as I thought," she says, opening the cellophane that holds her plastic fork, and knife, and spoon.

I leave the dining room and, standing a little to one side of the doorway, watch my mother as she eats. She doesn't talk to her neighbors at the table. Her face shows no enjoyment in her food. She stares ahead of her, her glance vacant as a blind woman's, chewing as if it were a mildly difficult task she knows she must perform. She is staring ahead at an infinite present which holds no savor for her. I don't know what it holds.

MY MOTHER IS SPEAKING FROM THE DESERT.

"I think I'm very lucky, not to be in pain."

"I don't remember anything."

"If you knew how much I love you."

"These flowers are yellow. These are purple. Those are blue."

"I don't think of dying, but I'm not afraid to die."

UNDERSTANDING ELDER ABUSE AND NEGLECT

ROSALIE S. WOLF, PH.D.

Rosalie S. Wolf, Ph.D. is Executive Director of the Institute on Aging at The Medical Center of Central Massachusetts in Worcester. She is the organizer and president of the National Committee for the Prevention of Elder Abuse and co-editor of the *Journal of Elder Abuse and Neglect.*

In spite of the headway that has been made in explaining how and why elder abuse occurs, it still remains a poorly understood problem. No simple definition can encompass its many aspects. Elder mistreatment may be an act of commission (abuse) or omission (neglect). It may be an intentional act, that is, a conscious attempt to inflict suffering, or it may be unintentional because of inadequate knowledge, infirmity, or laziness on the part of the person responsible. The manifestations of elder mistreatment are numerous but are generally grouped under four headings:

Physical abuse, the infliction of physical pain or injury, e.g., slapping, bruising, sexually molesting, restraining;

Psychological abuse, the infliction of mental anguish, e.g., humiliating, intimidating, threatening;

Financial abuse, the illegal or improper exploitation and/or use of funds; and

Neglect, refusal or failure to fulfill a caretaking obligation, e.g., abandonment, denial of food or health related services.

Whether behavior is labelled as abusive or neglectful may depend on how frequently the mistreatment occurs, its duration, intensity, severity, and consequences. Adding to the complexity of identification and reporting of cases is the fact that each state operates under its own set of definitions. An act may be considered abuse in one state but not another. Some states do not even use the word "abuse." Neglect may refer either to the condition of the victim or the intent of the person responsible. Inconsistent definitions have hindered efforts to obtain prevalence and incidence data and have prevented useful comparisons among research findings. Without an agreed upon meaning, the criteria and principles needed for clinical practice or policymaking cannot be standardized. Most recently, some researchers have ques-

tioned the legal and professional definitions of elder mistreatment, suggesting that the older person's perception of a particular behavior may be the salient factor in identification and intervention.

Variations in definitions have not been the only barrier to progress in the field. When elder abuse first received national attention, there was an over-reliance on the child abuse model in dealing with the problem. Victims were viewed by agency staff and researchers as very dependent older women mistreated by well-meaning, but overburdened, adult daughters. Within a relatively short time, most states had passed mandatory reporting legislation patterned after child abuse statutes. But many situations did not fit that model. Later findings suggested that spouse abuse might offer a more useful framework for study and intervention since the individuals involved were legally independent adults. To some health researchers, however, the family violence paradigm was also not suitable in the majority of cases. They recommended that

elder abuse be considered from the perspective of "inadequate care," since it is easier to measure unmet needs than inappropriate behavior. It is now very clear that no one interpretation can cover all aspects of the problem. Agreement on clear principles to guide collection of data and clinical practice is further complicated by other sets of issues relating to institutional abuse and self-neglect, two problems which are not covered in this discussion.

RISK FACTORS AND CHARACTERISTICS

A multitude of risk factors for elder abuse has been proposed from "violence as a way of life in America" to "ageism in society." Based on the limited research on abuse and neglect, the explanations that seem to be the most likely at this time are the unhealthy dependency of the perpetrator on the victim and vice versa, the disturbed psychological state of the perpetrator, the frailty, disability or impairment of the victim, and the social isolation of the family. According to the studies so far, stress factors, such as

From *Aging*, No. 367, 1996, pp. 4-13. Reprinted by permission of *Aging*, a publication of the Administration on Aging, U.S. Department of Health and Human Services.

of the victims seemed to be relatively unimportant. However, the victims were generally unmarried and had few social contacts. Rather than interpersonal pathology or victim dependency, the risk factors appeared to be financial needs or "greed" of the perpetrator and loneliness of the victim.

While a specific case may not exactly conform to a profile, knowledge of these distinctive patterns have been helpful in identifying risk factors and in designing intervention strategies.

A comparison of parent abuse cases (abuse perpetrated by adult children on their parents) and spouse abuse showed that older mistreated spouses were more likely to be physically abused, to be in poorer emotional health, and to be more dependent on their abusers for companionship. Adult children were more likely to neglect their elderly parents or to abuse them psychologically. These children tended to have money problems, to be financially dependent on their elderly parents, and to have a history of mental illness and alcoholism. The abusing spouses were more apt to have medical complaints and to have experienced a recent decline in physical health. For some couples, the stresses of later life, particularly physical illness, exacerbate an already tension-filled and unhappy marriage.

The impact of gender and racial differences on elder abuse is still unclear. In cases drawn from a number of adult protection programs, the abusive daughters, compared to

poverty, job status, loss of family support, etc. do not seem to be important. The cycle of violence theory, which predicts that victims become perpetrators, and is closely associated with child and spouse abuse, has not been substantiated in elder abuse cases. One constant, however, is that as with other forms of domestic violence, alcohol is present in a large proportion of elder abuse cases.

The need to understand how familial and individual circumstances relate to elder abuse has led researchers to compare cases by type of mistreatment, victim-perpetrator relationship, gender, and most recently, race. When 328

physical, psychological, and financial abuse and neglect cases, reported to elder abuse projects in three states, were analyzed, three distinct profiles emerged. In the case of *physical and psychological abuse*, the perpetrators were more likely to have a history of psychopathology and to be dependent on the victim for financial resources. The elderly victims were apt to be in poor emotional health but relatively independent in their activities of daily living. Since this type of abuse involved family members who were most intimately related and emotionally connected (perpetrators were spouses and adult children), the violence may be attributed to unhealthy

interpersonal relationships that become more highly charged because of illness or financial need.

In *neglect* cases, the victim was more likely to be widowed, very old, cognitively and physically impaired, with few social contacts. In sharp contrast to the cases of physical/psychological abuse, those involving neglect appeared to be very much related to the frailty and disability and dependency needs of the victim. Neither psychological problems nor financial dependency were significant factors in the lives of the persons responsible. For them, the victim was a source of stress.

In cases of *financial abuse*, the physical and mental state

the abusive sons, were more likely to be perpetrators of neglect and to be caring for parents who were more impaired or who had more severe health problems. The limited research on elder mistreatment among ethnic populations suggests that their perceptions of elder abuse and neglect may differ from the community standards. For instance, a research team found that one Native American tribe viewed physical abuse as a health problem related to the dysfunction of the community rather than the shortcomings of the abuser. Another team reported that when Korean-American, African-American, and Caucasian-American elderly women were asked to comment on vignettes describing abusive and neglectful behavior, the Korean-American women were far less likely to perceive a given situation as abusive. Indeed, for them, family harmony was more important than individual well-being.

Another factor being studied is whether elder abuse is more likely when family members are caring for a person with Alzheimer's disease or another form of dementia. The relatively high proportion of abusive behavior in these families, caregiver to patient and patient to caregiver, is a cause for concern. Clearly, to understand the etiology of abuse and neglect, it is important to discriminate between abusive behavior resulting from a disease and abuse arising from long-standing personality traits and intrafamily conflict.

PREVALENCE AND INCIDENCE

Although estimates of the prevalence of elder abuse in the United States have ranged from about 4 to 10 percent of the population 65 years and older, there has been only one community-based study. Using a methodology that was validated previously in two national family violence surveys, a research team surveyed over 2,000 non-institutionalized elders living in the metropolitan Boston area and found that 3.2 percent had experienced physical abuse, verbal aggression, and/or neglect since they had reached 65 years of age. Spouse abuse (58 percent) was more prevalent than abuse by adult children (24 percent), the proportion of victims was roughly equally divided between males and females, and economic status and age were not related to the risk of abuse.

This survey, to which the category of financial abuse was added, was repeated in Canada with a nationally representative sample. Four percent of Canadian elders able to respond on the telephone were found to have recently experienced one or more forms of mistreatment. Again, the rates for men and women were about equal, but financial abuse was more prevalent than physical abuse, verbal aggression, or neglect. Two other studies have been reported in the literature. One used written questionnaires and clinical evaluations to determine the rate of abuse and neglect in a small semi-industrialized town in Finland. The results indi-

cated a 2.5 percent elder mistreatment prevalence rate for men and 7.0 percent for women, or 5.4 percent for both sexes.

The second study, conducted in Britain, added several questions from the Boston and Canadian forms to a national representative survey. It found that 5 percent of individuals aged 65 years and over reported having been recently verbally abused by a close family member or relative, 2 percent, physically abused, and 2 percent financially abused. Since all these surveys are based on self-reporting, it is safe to say that the percentages represent an underestimate of the problem rather than an exaggeration.

Knowing whether cases are on the increase or not cannot be determined without good national prevalence data collected over a span of years. However, state reports of abuse and neglect cases have shown a steady rise since first summarized in 1987, from an estimated 117,000 nationwide to 227,000 in 1991. It appears that a substantial part of this increase is due in great part to heightened awareness of elder abuse by the public and professionals and more highly developed systems for reporting. Of the estimated 227,000 reports, slightly more than half were substantiated cases, and were about equally divided among abuse, neglect, and exploitation by others, and self-neglect. However, cases that come to the attention of adult protective services are believed to represent only a small fraction of the

estimated one and one-half million to two million cases of elder abuse and neglect in the elderly living in the community.

SERVICE DELIVERY

All of the 50 states have some form of legislation (e.g., elder abuse, adult protective services, domestic violence laws, mental health commitment laws) that authorizes the state to protect and provide services to vulnerable, incapacitated, or disabled adults. In more than three-quarters of the states, the services are provided through the state social service department (adult protective services); in the remaining states, the State Units on Aging have the major responsibility. Calls are received on special phone lines (in some states operating 24 hours a day, 7 days a week) and are screened for potential seriousness. If mistreatment is suspected, an investigation is conducted. If the case is deemed an emergency, the investigation must be completed within a few hours of the receipt of the call. On the basis of a comprehensive assessment, a care plan is developed which might involve, for example, obtaining emergency shelter for the victim, admitting the victim to the hospital, arranging for home care, calling the police, or referring the case to the state prosecuting attorney. In most states, once the immediate situation has been addressed, the case is turned over to other community agencies for ongoing case management and service delivery.

When elder abuse was thought to be mainly a result of caregiving stress, helping the caregiver was the treatment of choice: bringing into the home skilled nursing, homemaker assistance, personal care, meals-on-wheels, chore services, and respite care, or placing the victim in adult day care, or enhancing the ability of the caregiver to cope through counseling, training, and skill building. Although these services are still very much a part of care plans, the strong association between dependency of the abuser (adult children) and physical abuse has suggested another approach: overcoming the financial and emotional dependency of the perpetrator through vocational counseling, job placement, housing assistance, alcohol and drug treatment, mental health services, and financial support, and providing counseling for the victim. Because physical abuse as well as financial abuse often involves criminal or civil offenses, law enforcement personnel and officials of the criminal justice system are increasingly being called upon to assist. Many communities have found multidisciplinary teams with representation from various professions to be extremely useful in dealing with these very complicated cases.

CONCLUSION

Significant progress has been made during the past decade in understanding the nature and scope of elder mistreatment, developing methods of intervention, and disseminating information and materials. Yet, the increasing number of reported cases and the specter of even greater numbers in the future necessitate that a more aggressive approach be taken. New research on the problem is sorely needed to provide a more solid knowledge base for policy, planning, and practice purposes.

If we are serious about reducing the risk of abuse and neglect among the older population, we must give more attention to primary prevention, beginning with informing citizens and training professionals about elder abuse, how to recognize the risk factors, and where to turn for help. A closer partnership between the mental health system, substance abuse programs, and elder abuse services is vital given the high proportion of emotional problems and alcoholism in abusive families. Support groups and training for elders that emphasize elder rights and advocacy, outreach efforts to inform minority communities, financial management programs, and instructional sessions in behavior management for caregivers of Alzheimer's patients are other ways of reducing the potential for abuse and neglect.

Above all, we need to emphasize the fact that older persons need not tolerate situations that threaten their physical and mental well-being. In all communities, there are people and organizations that can help. Convincing older people of this fact remains one of the greatest challenges facing the elder abuse system.

Warning Signs
ELDER ABUSE
and NEGLECT

These are some of the common warning signs of adult abuse or neglect. Not all of these, by themselves, indicate that mistreatment or self-neglect is occurring. However, if several are seen in combination, there may be cause to suspect something is wrong. Report your suspicions by calling Adult Protective Services in your county. If the number is not listed in the phone book, call the nearest county or city Office on Aging or the police department to find out the number.

Indications of Physical Abuse

Multiple injuries in various stages of healing

Bruises from hitting, shoving, slapping, pinching, or kicking

Discoloration causing bilateral stripes on upper arms or clustered on other body parts

Burns caused by cigarettes, caustics, hot objects

Friction from ropes, chains or other physical restraints

Fractures, sprains, lacerations and abrasions

Injuries caused by biting, cutting, poking, punching, whipping or twisting of limbs

Disorientation, stupor or other effects of deliberate overmedication

Behavioral Indications of Physical/Sexual Abuse (Victim)

Easily frightened or fearful

Exhibiting denial

Agitated or trembling

Hesitant to talk openly

Implausible stories

Extreme upset when assisted with bathing or other physical caregiving

Depression or poor self-esteem

Eating disturbances (Overeating or undereating)

Fears, phobias

Compulsive behavior

Sleep disorders (nightmares, fear of sleep, excessive sleeping)

Indicators of Neglect

Neglected bedsores

Skin disorders or rashes

Untreated injuries or medical problems

Poor hygiene

Hunger, malnutrition, dehydration

Pallor, sunken eyes or cheeks

Inadequate supply of food

Absence of, or failure to provide, prescribed medication

Lack of clean bedding or clothing

Inadequate heating

Unsanitary or unsafe living conditions

Lack of required dentures, hearing aids or eyeglasses

Frequent trips to the emergency room with undefined illnesses or complaints

Indicators from Caregivers

Verbal berating, harassment, or intimidation

Threats of punishment or depriving of essential needs

Isolating a person from friends and other family members

Treating the individual like an infant

Leaving a person alone for long periods of time

Withholding affection to gain compliance

Unwillingness to comply with service providers in planning for care

Obvious absence of assistance, attitude of indifference or anger toward the victim

Giving a person no privacy

Denying a person the right to make decisions

Forcing a person to leave home or to go into a care facility

Suspicious Explanations
Common explanations in physical abuse cases:

"The injury was an accident."

"The victim fell."

"There was no abuse—she/he bruises easily."

Common explanations for financial abuse cases:

"It was a gift."

"She owed me the money."

"He gave me permission to have, use, borrow it."

"I was going to give it back."

Common explanations in neglect cases:

"She refuses to eat anything."

"He refuses services."

(Based on information taken from "Innovative Training Package for Detecting and Aiding Victims of Domestic Elder Abuse," developed by the Police Executive Research Forum for the Department of Justice, and on "Guidelines for Investigation of Elder and Dependent Adult Abuse" by the Office of the Attorney General of the State of California, Mary Joy Quinn and Susan Tomita. *Elder Abuse: Causes, Diagnosis and Treatment,* New York: Springer, 1986. Some indicators also drawn from material prepared by the Nebraska Domestic Violence Sexual Assault Coalition, May 1993).

Retirement: American Dream or Dilemma?

Since 1900 the number of persons in America who are aged 65 and over has been increasing steadily, but a decreasing proportion of that age group remains in the workforce. In 1900 nearly two-thirds of those over 65 worked outside the home. By 1947 this figure had declined to about 48 percent (less than half), and in 1975 about 22 percent of men 65 and older were still in the workforce. The long-range trend indicates that fewer and fewer persons are being employed beyond the age of 65. Some people choose to retire at age 65 or earlier; for others, retirement is mandatory. A recent change in the law, however, allows individuals to work to age 70 before retiring.

Gordon Strieb and Clement Schneider (*Retirement in American Society*, 1971) observed that for retirement to become an institutionalized social pattern in any society, certain conditions must be present. A large group of people must live long enough to retire; the economy must be productive enough to support people who are not in the workforce; and there must be pensions or insurance programs to support retirees.

Retirement is a rite of passage. People can consider it as either the culmination of the American Dream or as a serious problem. Those who have ample incomes, interesting things to do, and friends to associate with often find the freedom of time and choice that retirement offers very rewarding. For others, however, retirement brings problems and personal losses. Often, these individuals find their incomes decreased, and they miss the status, privilege, and power associated with holding a position in the occupational hierarchy. They may feel socially isolated if they do not find new activities to replace their previous work-related ones. Additionally, they might have to cope with the death of a spouse and/or their own failing health.

The articles in this section provide a clearer picture of the factors in the retirement decision. In "The Busy Ethic: Moral Continuity between Work and Retirement," David Ekerdt maintains that the "busy ethic" justifies the leisure of retirement, defends retired people against negative judgments by significant others, and gives definition to the retirement role. Then, the authors of "Does Retirement Hurt Well-Being? Factors Influencing Self-Esteem and Depression among Retirees and Workers" compare retired persons with those still working. Their research indicates that the retirees scored higher on measures of self-esteem and lower on measures of depression. Next, Paula Mergenhagen, in "Rethinking Retirement," examines the different reasons that workers choose to retire early.

Finally, *The Economist*'s survey essay, "The Economics of Ageing," examines the economic impact of an ever-growing and longer-living elderly population for both wealthy and poor countries. Even in the wealthy countries, the financing of health care and pensions for older persons is seen as a forthcoming dilemma.

Looking Ahead: Challenge Questions

If given the choice of retiring or continuing to work, some people would choose to continue working. What would be some of the reasons to decide not to retire?

Why do you believe many older persons decide to retire early? What factors are crucial to this decision?

In your opinion, what are the major advantages of retirement? What are its major disadvantages?

From an economic point of view, should people be encouraged to retire earlier or later? Why?

UNIT 5

This paper suggests that retirement is legitimated on a day-to-day basis in part by an ethic that esteems leisure that is earnest, active, and occupied. This busy ethic, named for the emphasis people place on keeping busy in retirement, endorses conduct that is consistent with the abstract ideals of the work ethic. The busy ethic justifies the leisure of retirement, defends retired people against judgments of senescence, and gives definition to the retirement role. In all, it helps individuals adapt to retirement, and it in turn adapts retirement to prevailing societal values.

Key Words: Leisure, Norms, Socialization, Transitions, Values

The Busy Ethic: Moral Continuity Between Work and Retirement[1]

David J. Ekerdt, PhD[2]

There is a way that people talk about retirement that emphasizes the importance of being busy. Just as there is a work ethic that holds industriousness and self-reliance as virtues so, too, there is a "busy ethic" for retirement that honors an active life. It represents people's attempts to justify retirement in terms of their long-standing beliefs and values.

The modern institution of retirement has required that our society make many provisions for it. Foremost among these are the economic arrangements and mechanisms that support Social Security, private pensions, and other devices for retirement financing. Political understandings have also been reached about the claim of younger workers on employment and the claim of older people on a measure of income security. At the same time, our cultural map of the life course has now been altered to include a separate stage of life called retirement, much as the life course once came to include the new stage of "adolescence" (Keniston, 1974).

Among other provisions, we should also expect that some moral arrangements may have emerged to validate and defend the lifestyle of retirement. After all, a society that traditionally identifies work and productivity as a wellspring of virtue would seem to need some justification for a life of pensioned leisure. How do retirees and observers alike come to feel comfortable with a "retired" life? In this paper I will suggest that retirement is morally managed and legitimated on a day-to-day basis in part by an ethic that esteems leisure that is earnest, occupied, and filled with activity — a "busy ethic." The ideas in this paper developed out of research on the retirement process at the Normative Aging Study, a prospective study of aging in community-dwelling men (Bosse et al., 1984).

The Work Ethic in Use

Before discussing how the busy ethic functions, it is important to note a few aspects about its parent work ethic. The work ethic, like any ethic, is a set of beliefs and values that identifies what is good and affirms ideals of conduct. It provides criteria for the evaluation of behavior and action. The work ethic historically has identified work with virtue and has held up for esteem a conflation of such traits and habits as diligence, initiative, temperance, industriousness, competitiveness, self-reliance, and the capacity for deferred gratification. The work ethic, however, has never had a single consistent expression nor has it enjoyed universal assent within Western cultures.

Another important point is that the work ethic historically has torn away from its context, become more abstract and therefore more widely useful (Rodgers, 1978). When the work ethic was Calvinist and held out hope of heavenly rewards, believers toiled for the glory of God. When 19th century moralists shifted the promise toward earthly rewards, the work ethic motivated the middle class to toil because it was useful to oneself and the common weal. The coming of the modern factory system, however, with its painful labor conditions and de-emphasis on the self-sufficient worker, created a moral uncertainty about the essential nobility and instrumentality of work that made individuals want to take refuge in the old phrases and homilies all the more. As work ideals became increasingly abstract, they grew more available. Rodgers (1978) pointed out that workingmen now could invoke the work ethic as a weapon in the battle for status and self-respect, and so defend the dignity of labor and wrap themselves in a rhetoric of pride. Politicians of all persuasions could appeal to the work ethic and cast policy issues as morality plays about industry and laziness. Thus, despite the failed spiritual and instrumental validity of the work ethic, it persisted in powerful abstraction. And it is an abstract work ethic that persists today lacking, as do

[1]Supported in part by the Medical Research Service of the Veterans Administration and by grants from the Administration on Aging (90-A-1194) and the National Institute on Aging (AG02287). The author thanks Raymond Bosse, Thomas Cole, and Linda Evans for helpful comments.

[2]Normative Aging Study, Veterans Administration Outpatient Clinic, 17 Court St., Boston, MA 02108.

From *The Gerontologist*, June 1986, pp. 239-244. © 1986 by The Gerontological Society of America. Reprinted by permission.

many other of our moral precepts, those contexts from which their original significance derived (MacIntyre, 1981). While there is constant concern about the health of the work ethic (Lewis, 1982; Yankelovich & Immerwhar, 1984), belief in the goodness of work continues as a piece of civic rhetoric that is important out of all proportion to its behavioral manifestations or utilitarian rewards.

Among persons approaching retirement, surveys show no fall-off in work commitment and subscription to values about work (Hanlon, 1983). Thus, assuming that a positive value orientation toward work is carried up to the threshold of retirement, the question becomes: What do people do with a work ethic when they no longer work?

Continuity of Beliefs and Values

The emergence of a busy ethic is no coincidence. It is, rather, a logical part of people's attempts to manage a smooth transition from work to retirement. Theorists of the life course have identified several conditions that ease an individual's transitions from one status to another. For example, transitions are easier to the extent that the new position has a well-defined role, or provides opportunities for attaining valued social goals, or when it entails a formal program of socialization (Burr, 1973; Rosow, 1974). Transitions are also easier when beliefs are continuous between two positions, that is, when action in the new position is built upon or integrated with the existing values of the person. Moral continuity is a benefit for the individual who is in transition, and for the wider social community as well.

In the abstract, retirement ought to entail the unlearning of values and attitudes — in particular, the work ethic — so that these should be no obstacle to adaptation. Upon withdrawal from work, emotional investment in, and commitment to, the work ethic should by rights be extinguished in favor of accepting leisure as a morally desirable lifestyle. Along these lines, there is a common recommendation that older workers, beginning in their 50s, should be "educated for leisure" in preparation for retirement. For example, the 1971 White House Conference on Aging recommended that "Society should adopt a policy of preparation for retirement, leisure, and education for life off the job . . . to prepare persons to understand and benefit from the changes produced by retirement" (p. 53).

But the work ethic is not unlearned in some resocialization process. Rather, it is transformed. There are two devices of this transformation that allow a moral continuity between work and retired life. One — the busy ethic — defends the daily conduct of retired life. The other — an ideology of pensions — legitimates retirees' claim to income without the obligation to work. As to the latter, a special restitutive rhetoric has evolved that characterizes pensions as entitlements for former productivity. Unlike others, such as welfare recipients, who stand outside the productive process, whose idleness incurs moral censure, and who are very grudgingly tendered financial support (Beck, 1967), the inoccupation of retirees is considered to have been *earned* by virtue of having *formerly* been productive. This veteranship status (Nelson, 1982) justifies the receipt of income without work, preserves the self-respect of retirees, and keeps retirement consistent with the dominant societal prestige system, which rewards members primarily to the extent that they are economically productive.

The Busy Ethic: Functions and Participants

Along with an ideology that defends the receipt of income without the obligation to work, there is an ethic that defends life without work. This "busy ethic" is at once a statement of value as well as an expectation of retired people — shared by retirees and nonretirees alike — that their lives should be active and earnest. (Retirees' actual levels of activity are, as shall be explained, another matter altogether; the emphasis here is on shared values about the conduct of life.) The busy ethic is named after the common question put to people of retireable age, "What will you do (or are you doing) to keep yourself busy?", and their equally common reports that "I have a lot to keep me busy" and "I'm as busy as ever." Expressions of the busy ethic also have their pejorative opposites, for example, "I'd rot if I just sat around." In naming the busy ethic, the connotation of busyness is more one of involvement and engagement than of mere bustle and hubbub.

The busy ethic serves several purposes: it legitimates the leisure of retirement, it defends retired people against judgments of obsolescence, it gives definition to retirement role, and it "domesticates" retirement by adapting retired life to prevailing societal norms. Before discussing these functions of the busy ethic, it is important to emphasize that any normative feature of social life entails endorsement and management by multiple parties. There are three parties to the busy ethic.

First, of course, are the subjects of the busy ethic — older workers and retirees — who are parties to it by virtue of their status. They participate in the busy ethic to the degree that they subscribe to the desirability of an active, engaged lifestyle. When called upon to account for their lives as retirees, subjects of the busy ethic should profess to be "doing things" in retirement or, if still working, be planning to "do things." Retirees can testify to their level of involvement in blanket terms, asserting: I've got plenty to do, I'm busier than when I was working. Or they can maintain in reserve a descriptive, mental list of activities (perhaps exaggerated or even fictitious) that can be offered to illustrate a sufficient level of engagement. These engagements run heavily to maintenance activities (e.g., tasks around the house, shopping) and involvement with children and grandchildren. Obviously, part-time jobs, volunteering, or major life projects ("I've always wanted to learn how to play the piano") can be offered as evidence of an active lifestyle. Less serious leisure pursuits (hobbies, pastimes, socializing) can also contribute to a picture of the busy life as long as such pursuits are characterized as involving and time consuming. In honoring the busy ethic, exactly what one does to keep busy is secondary to the fact that one purportedly *is* busy.

A second group of parties to the busy ethic comprises the other participants — friends, relatives, coworkers — who talk to older workers and retirees about the conduct of retired life. Their role is primarily one of keeping conversation about retirement continually focused on the topic of activity, without necessarily upholding ideals of busyness. Conversation with retirees also serves to assure these others that there is life after work. Indeed, apart from money matters, conversation about retired life *per se* is chiefly conversation about what one does with it, how time is filled. Inquiries about the retiree's lifestyle ("So what are you doing with yourself?") may come from sincere interest or may only be polite conversation. Inquiries, too, can be mean-spirited, condescending, or envious. Whatever the source or course of discussion, it nonetheless frequently comes to assurances that, yes, it is good to keep busy.

The third group can be called institutional conservators of the busy ethic, and their role is more clearly normative. These parties hold up implicit and explicit models of what retired life should be like, models that evince an importance placed on being active and engaged. Prominent institutional conservators of the busy ethic are the marketers of products and services to seniors, the gerontology profession, and the popular media. More shall be said about these later.

Returning to the purposes that the busy ethic serves, its primary function is to legitimate the leisure of retirement. Leisure without the eventual obligation of working is an anomalous feature of adulthood. Excepting the idle rich and those incapable of holding a job, few adults escape the obligation to work. Retirement and pension policies, however, are devised to exclude older adults from the labor force. In addition, age bias operates to foreclose opportunities for their further employment. How can our value system defend this situation — retirement — when it is elsewhere engaged in conferring honor on people who work and work hard? The answer lies in an ethic that endorses leisure that is analogous to work. As noted above, leisure pursuits can range from the serious to the self-indulgent. What legitimates these as an authentic adult lifestyle is their correspondence with the *form* of working life, which is to be occupied by activities that are regarded as serious and engaging. The busy ethic rescues retirement from the stigma of retreat and aimlessness and defines it as a succession to new or renewed foci of engagement. It reconciles for retirees and their social others the adult obligation to work with a life of leisure. This is the nature of continuity in self-respect between the job and retirement (Atchley, 1971).

In an essay that anticipates some of the present

argument, Miller (1965) took a stricter view about what justifies retirement leisure. Mere activity is not meaningful enough; it must have the added rationale of being infused with aspects of work that are culturally esteemed. Activity legitimates retirement if it is, for example, economically instrumental (profitable hobbies), or contributes to the general good (community service), or is potentially productive (education or skill development). Whether people in fact recognize a hierarchy of desirable, work-correlative activities at which retirees can be busy remains to be determined. What Miller's essay and the present argument have in common, nonetheless, is the view that what validates retirement, in part, is activity that is analogous to work.

The busy ethic serves a second purpose for its subjects, which is to symbolically defend retirees against aging. Based on the belief that vigor preserves well-being, subscription to the norm of busyness can recast retirement as "middle-age like." Adherence to the busy ethic can be a defense — even to oneself — against possible judgments of obsolescence or senescence. To accentuate the contrast between the vital and senescent elder, there is an entire vocabulary of pejorative references to rocking chairs and sitting and idleness. As an illustration, a recent piece in my local newspaper about a job placement service for seniors quoted one of the program's participants, who said: "I am not working for income. I am working for therapy, to keep busy. There is nothing that will hurt an elderly person as much as just sitting alone all day long, doing nothing, thinking about nothing." It is appropriate to note here that, in scope, the busy ethic does not apply to all retirees. The busy life is more likely to be an expectation on the conduct of the "young-old" retiree, or at least the retiree who has not been made frail by chronic illness.

A third purpose of the busy ethic is that it places a boundary on the retirement role and thus permits some true leisure. Just as working adults cycle between time at work and time off, retirees too can have "time off." Because the busy ethic justifies *some* of one's time, the balance of one's time needs no justification. For example, if the morning was spent running errands or caring for grandchildren, one can feel comfortable with napping or a stretch of TV viewing in the afternoon. The existence of fulfillable expectations allows one to balance being active with taking it easy — one can slip out of the retirement role, one is allowed time offstage. Being busy, like working, "pays" for one's rest and relaxation.

The busy ethic serves a fourth function, and this for the wider society by "domesticating" retirement to mainstream societal values. It could be otherwise. Why not an ethic of hedonism, nonconformity, and carefree self-indulgence as a logical response to societal policies that define older workers as obsolescent and expendable? Free of adult workaday constraints, retirees could become true dropouts thumbing their noses at convention. Or why not an ethic of repose, with retirees resolutely unembarrassed about slowing down to enjoy leisure in very individual ways? Retirees do often describe retirement as a time for sheer gratification. In response to open-ended questions on Normative Aging Study surveys about the primary advantages of retirement, men overwhelmingly emphasize: freedom to do as I wish, no more schedules, now I can do what I want, just relax, enjoy life. Such sentiments, however, do not tend to serve drop-out or contemplative models of retired life because retirees will go on to indicate that their leisure is nonetheless responsibly busy. The busy ethic tames the potentially unfettered pleasures of retirement to prevailing values about engagement that apply to adulthood. For nonretirees, this renders retirement as something intelligible and consistent with other stages of life. Additionally, the busy ethic, in holding that retirees can and should be participating in the world, probably salves some concern about their having been unfairly put on the shelf.

The active domestication of retirement is the province of the institutional conservators of the busy ethic. The popular media are strenuous conservators. An article in my local newspaper last year bore the headline, "They've retired but still keep busy," which was reprised only a few months later in another headline, "He keeps busy in his retirement." Both articles assured the reader that these seniors were happily compensating for their withdrawal from work. It is common for "senior set" features to depict older people in an upbeat fashion, though in all fairness the genre of newspapers' lifestyle sections generally portrays everybody as occupied by varied and wonderful activities regardless of age. The popular media are also staunch promoters of aged exemplars of activity and achievement — Grandma Moses, Pablo Casals, George Burns, and so on through such lists (Wallechinsky et al., 1977). A current National Public Radio series on aging and creativity bears the preceptive title: "I'm Too Busy to Talk Now: Conversations with American Artists over Seventy."

Marketers, with the golf club as their chief prop, have been instrumental in fostering the busy image. A recent analysis of advertising in magazines designed specifically for older people found that the highest percentage of ads in these magazines concerned travel and more often than not portrayed older people in an active setting such as golfing, bicycling, or swimming (Kvasnicka et al., 1982). Calhoun (1978) credited the ads and brochures of the retirement home industry, in particular, with promoting an energetic image of older Americans. This industry built houses and, more importantly, built a market for those houses, which consisted of the dynamic retiree. While few retirees ever live in retirement communities, the model of such communities has been most influential in the creation of an active, if shallowly commercial, image of the elderly. One writer (Fitzgerald, 1983), visiting Sun City Center in Florida ("The town too busy to retire"), reflected:

Possibly some people still imagine retirement communities as boarding houses with rocking chairs, but, thanks to Del Webb and a few other pioneer developers, the notion of 'active' retirement has become entirely familiar; indeed, since the sixties it has been the guiding principle of retirement-home builders across the country. Almost all developers now advertise recreational facilities and print glossy brochures with photos of gray-haired people playing golf, tennis, and shuffleboard. (p. 74)

The visitor noted that residents talked a great deal about their schedules and activities. The visitor also noted how their emphasis on activities was an attempt to legitimate retirement and knit it to long-standing beliefs and values:

Sun Citians' insistence on busyness — and the slightly defensive tone of their town boosterism — came, I began to imagine, from the fact that their philosophies, and, presumably, the [conservative, work ethic] beliefs they had grown up with, did not really support them in this enterprise of retirement. (p. 91)

The gerontological community has been an important conservator of aspects of the busy ethic. Cumming and Henry (1961) early on pointed out the nonscientific presuppositions of mainstream gerontology's "implicit theory" of aging, which include the projection of middle-aged standards of instrumentality, activity, and usefulness into later life. This implicit, so-called "activity theory" of aging entailed the unabashed value judgment that "the older person who ages optimally is the person who stays active and manages to resist the shrinkage of his social world" (Havighurst et al., 1968, p. 161). Gubrium (1973) has noted the Calvinistic aura of this perspective: "Successful aging, as the activity theorists portray it, is a life style that is visibly 'busy' " (p. 7). Continuing this orientation over the last decade, gerontology's campaign against ageism has, according to Cole (1983), promoted an alternative image of older people as healthy, sexually active, engaged, productive, and self-reliant.

Institutional conservators of the busy ethic are by no means monolithic in their efforts to uphold ideals of busyness. Rather, in pursuing their diverse objectives they find it useful to highlight particular images of retirement and later life that coalesce around the desirability of engagement.

Sources of Authority

The busy ethic is useful, therefore, because it legitimates leisure, it wards off disturbing thoughts about aging, it permits retirees some rest and relaxation, and it adapts retirement to prevailing societal norms. These benefits to the participants of the busy ethic are functional only in an analytic sense. No one in daily life approves of busy retirements because such approval is "functional." It is useful at this point to ask why people ultimately assent to the notion that it is good to be busy.

The busy ethic has moral force because it participates in two great strong value complexes — ethics themselves — that axiomatize it. One, of course, is the work ethic, which holds that it is ennobling to be exerting oneself in the world. The other basis for the busy ethic's authority is the profound importance placed on good health and the stimulating, wholesome manner of living that is believed to ensure its maintenance. The maintenance of health is an ideal with a deep tradition that has long carried moral as well as medical significance. Haley (1978), for example, has pointed out how Victorian thinkers promoted the tonic qualities of a robust and energetic lifestyle. The preservation of health was seen to be a duty because the well-knit body reflected a well-formed mind, and the harmony of mind and body signified spiritual health and the reach for higher human excellence. Ill, unkempt, and indolent conditions, by contrast, indicated probable moral failure. Times change, but current fashions in health maintenance still imply that a fit and strenuous life will have medical benefits and testify as well to the quality of one's will and character. Thus, admonitions to older people that they "keep busy" and "keep going" are authoritative because they advocate an accepted therapy for body and soul.

Correspondence with Behavior

One crucial issue is the correspondence between the busy ethic and actual behavior. It is important to mention that not all self-reports about busy retirements are conscious presentations of conformity to a busy ethic. There are retirees who by any reckoning are very active. But in the more general case, if people believe it is important to keep busy, should they not therefore *be* busy by some standard or another?

This paper's argument in favor of the busy ethic has implied that belief is not necessarily behavior. On one hand, the busy ethic may — as any ethic should — motivate retirees to use their time in constructive or involving pursuits. It may get them out of the unhealthful rocking chair or away from the can-of-beer-in-front-of-the-TV. On the other hand, the busy ethic can motivate people to *interpret* their style of life as conforming to ideals about activity. An individual can take a disparate, even limited, set of activities and spin them together into a representation of a very busy life. It would be difficult to contradict such a manner of thinking on empirical grounds; "engagement" is a subjective quality of time use that simple counts of activities or classifications of their relative seriousness or instrumentality are not likely to measure. Indeed, gerontologists should be wary about the extent to which the busy ethic may shape people's responses on surveys about their leisure, frequency of activities, and experience in retirement.

In posing the question, "How busy do retirees have to be under such a set of values?", the answer is they don't objectively have to be very busy at all. Just as with the work ethic, which has been an abstract set of ideals for some time (Rodgers, 1978), it is not the actual pace of activity but the preoccupation with activity and the affirmation of its desirability that matters. After all, all of us are not always honest, but we would all agree that honesty is the best policy. The busy ethic, like the work ethic and other commonplace values, should be evaluated less for its implied link with actual behavior than for its ability to badger or comfort the conscience. The busy ethic, at bottom, is self-validating: because it is important to be busy, people will say they are busy.

Conclusion

The busy ethic is an idea that people have about the appropriate quality of a retired lifestyle. It solves the problem of moral continuity: how to integrate existing beliefs and values about work into a new status that constitutes a withdrawal from work. The postulation of a busy ethic is an attempt to examine sociologically people's judgments of value and obligation regarding the conduct of daily life — their expectations of each other and of themselves.

To be sure, there are other superseding expectations on the conduct of retirees. Writing about the duties of a possible retirement role, Atchley (1976) has noted that a stability of behavior is expected, as well as self-reliance and independence in managing one's affairs. Such normative preferences are fairly vague and open-ended. Rosow (1974) surveyed the prospects for socialization to later life, in which the retirement role is nested, and found that behavioral prescriptions for older people are open and flexible, and norms are limited, weak, and ambiguous. Even admonitions to be active carry virtually no guidance about the preferred content of such activity. Perhaps this is just as well. Streib and Schneider (1971), summarizing findings from the Cornell Study of Occupational Retirement, pointed out that the vagueness of retirees' role expectations may protect retirees from demands that they might be disinclined to fulfill or from standards that diminished health and financial resources might not allow them to meet.

The busy ethic, too, comprises vague expectations on behavior. It is a modest sort of prescription — less a spur to conformity and more a way to comfortably knit a new circumstance to long-held values. Social disapproval is its only sanction. Not all retirees assent to this image of retirement, nor do they need to. Judging by the ubiquity of the idea, however, subscribers to the busy ethic are probably in the majority; one cannot talk to retirees for very long without hearing the rhetoric of busyness. The busy ethic also legitimates the daily conduct of retired life in a lower key than has been claimed by some gerontologists, who propose that work substitutes and instrumental activity are essential to indemnify retirement. While some retirees do need to work at retirement to psychologically recoup the social utility that working supplied (Hooker & Ventis, 1984), for most it is enough to participate in a rather abstract esteem for an active lifestyle and to represent their own retirement as busy in some way.

To conclude, the busy ethic, as an idealization and expectation of retired life, illustrates how retirement is socially managed, not just politically and economically, but also morally — by means of everyday talk and conversation as well as by more formal institutions. Drawing its authority from the work ethic and from a traditional faith in the therapeutic value of activity, the busy ethic counsels a habit of engagement that is continuous with general cultural prescriptions for adulthood. It legitimates the leisure of retirement, it defends retired people against judgments of senescence, and it gives definition to the retirement role. In all, the busy ethic helps individuals adapt to retirement, and it in turn adapts retirement to prevailing societal norms.

References

Atchley, R. C. (1971). Retirement and leisure participation: Continuity or crisis? *The Gerontologist, 11,* 13–17.

Atchley, R. C. (1976). *The sociology of retirement.* New York: Halsted Press.

Bosse, R., Ekerdt, D. J., & Silbert, J. E. (1984). The Veterans Administration Normative Aging Study. In S. A. Mednick, M. Harway, & K. M. Finello (Eds.), *Handbook of longitudinal research. Vol. 2, Teenage and adult cohorts.* New York: Praeger.

Beck, B. (1967). Welfare as a moral category. *Social Problems, 14,* 258–277.

Burr, W. R. (1973). *Theory construction and the sociology of the family.* New York: John Wiley.

Calhoun, R. B. (1978). *In search of the new old: Redefining old age in America, 1945–1970.* New York: Elsevier.

Cole, T. R. (1983). The 'enlightened' view of aging: Victorian morality in a new key. *Hastings Center Report, 13,* 34–40.

Cumming, E., & Henry, W. H. (1961). *Growing old: The process of disengagement.* New York: Basic Books.

Fitzgerald, F. (1983, April 25). Interlude (Sun City Center). *New Yorker,* pp. 54–109.

Gubrium, J. F. (1973). *The myth of the golden years: A socio-environmental theory of aging.* Springfield, IL: Charles C Thomas.

Haley, B. (1978). *The healthy body and Victorian culture.* Cambridge, MA: Harvard University Press.

Hanlon, M. D. (1983). Age and the commitment to work. Flushing, NY: Queens College, City University of New York, Department of Urban Studies (ERIC Document Reproduction Service # ED 243 003).

Havighurst, R. J., Neugarten, B. L., & Tobin, S. S. (1968). Disengagement and patterns of aging. In B. L. Neugarten (Ed.), *Middle age and aging: A reader in social psychology.* Chicago: University of Chicago Press.

Hooker, K., & Ventis, D. G. (1984). Work ethic, daily activities, and retirement satisfaction. *Journal of Gerontology, 39,* 478–484.

Keniston, K. (1974). Youth and its ideology. In S. Arieti (Ed.), *American handbook of psychiatry. Vol. 1, The foundations of psychiatry.* 2nd ed. New York: Basic Books.

Kvasnicka, B., Beymer, B., & Perloff, R. M. (1982). Portrayals of the elderly in magazine advertisements. *Journalism Quarterly, 59,* 656–658.

Lewis, L. S. (1982). Working at leisure. *Society, 19* (July/August), 27–32.

MacIntyre, A. (1981). *After virtue: A study in moral theory.* Notre Dame, IN: University of Notre Dame Press.

Miller, S. J. (1965). The social dilemma of the aging leisure participant. In A. M. Rose & W. Peterson (Eds.), *Older people and their social worlds.* Philadelphia: F. A. Davis.

Nelson, D. W. (1982). Alternate images of old age as the bases for policy. In B. L. Neugarten (Ed.), *Age or need? Public policies for older people.* Beverly Hills, CA: Sage.

Rodgers, D. T. (1978). *The work ethic in industrial America: 1850–1920.* Chicago: University of Chicago Press.

Rosow, I. (1974). *Socialization to old age.* Berkeley, CA: University of California Press.

Streib, G. F., & Schneider, C. J. (1971). *Retirement in American society: Impact and process.* Ithaca, NY: Cornell University Press.

Wallechinsky, D., Wallace, I., & Wallace, A. (1977). *The People's Almanac presents the book of lists.* New York: William Morrow.

White House Conference on Aging. (1971). *Toward a national policy on aging: Proceedings of the 1971 White House conference on Aging, Vol. II.* Washington, DC: U.S. Government Printing Office.

Yankelovich D., & Immerwhar, J. (1984). Putting the work ethic to work. *Society, 21* (January/February), 58–76.

A set of older workers from the Raleigh-Durham-Chapel Hill metropolitan area were followed for two years in order to explore the social psychological consequences of retirement. Three findings are of particular interest. First, when we separated workers who retired from those who continued to work and compared their self-esteem and depression scores over the two-year interval, we found that self-esteem scores did not change for either group, but that depression scores declined for workers who retired. Turning to differences between retirees and those who continued to work, regression analyses revealed that retirement had a positive influence on self-esteem and a negative influence on depression. In addition, earlier worker identity meanings had a stronger negative effect on the depression scores of respondents who continued to work than on those who retired.
Key Words: Retirement, Well-being, Self-esteem, Depression

Does Retirement Hurt Well-Being? Factors Influencing Self-Esteem and Depression Among Retirees and Workers[1]

Donald C. Reitzes, PhD,[2] Elizabeth J. Mutran, PhD,[3] and Maria E. Fernandez, PhD[3]

One of the important demographic trends in the United States since the end of World War II has been the increase in the number of retired men and women and the increasing length of time that men and women spend in retirement as life expectancy increases and age at retirement decreases (U. S. Bureau of the Census, 1992). Not surprisingly, there has also been an increased research interest in retirement and the multifaceted implications of the retirement process (Ekerdt & DeViney, 1993; Hanks, 1990; Hardy & Quadagno, 1995; Knesek, 1992; Richardson & Kilty, 1991). Yet, our understanding of the social psychological consequences of retirement and factors that increase (or decrease) the well-being of retired men and women remains modest. The simple questions, "Does retirement improve well-being?" or "Are retired people better off?" are not so simple to answer because retirement is not a single, monolithic process that is similarly experienced by all (Atchley, 1982).

Not surprisingly, both methodological and theoretical issues hinder a clearer understanding of the social psychological consequences of retirement. First, there may be more than one outcome of retirement (George, Fillenbaum, & Palmore, 1984). Thus, measures of happiness, self-esteem, depression, or well-being not only are theoretically different, but may be influenced by retirement in different ways. Second, analyses of the consequences of retirement (Palmore, Fillenbaum, & George, 1984; Richardson & Kilty, 1991) suggest at least two comparisons — (a) a comparison of the same set of individuals as they move from preretirement into postretirement; and (b) a comparison between men and women who have retired with comparably-aged men and women who have continued their full-time employment. Finally, in addition to probing the impact of objective factors (e.g., health, financial resources) on the adjustment to retirement, subjective factors, such as the strength of worker identity and commitment to the role of worker may be just as important in understanding the retirement experience (Erdner & Guy, 1990; Matthews & Brown, 1987; Maxwell, 1985).

In this study, we investigate changes in self-esteem and depression as older workers either move into retirement or continue their full-time employment. We are interested in whether the transition into retirement has had social psychological effects on men and women and whether there are differences in self-esteem and depression scores between retired workers and those who continued to work full-time. Additionally, we are interested in exploring the implication of commitment to the role of worker and identities as competent, sociable, and confident workers during preretirement on later self-esteem and depression. In other words, will a positive investment in the worker role and identity meanings help or hinder well-being in either retirement and/or as men and women continue their work careers?

[1]This research was supported in part by a grant from the National Institute on Aging (R01 AG-07410).

[2]Address correspondence to Donald C. Reitzes, PhD, Georgia State University, Department of Sociology, College of Arts and Sciences, University Plaza, Atlanta, GA 30303-3083.

[3]University of North Carolina at Chapel Hill.

Research Expectations

Retirement as an ongoing process provides an opportunity to explore how previously established roles and identity meanings can continue to influence the ways that individuals evaluate and assess themselves. It provides an opportunity to explicitly link symbolic interaction-inspired identity theory (Rosenberg, 1981; Stryker, 1980) with the empirical investigation of the transition into retirement. Symbolic interactionists have long held (Stone, 1962; Turner, 1956) that individuals do not passively internalize roles, but actively negotiate role boundaries and outcomes. Thus, role learning entails not only "identification of," the process of learning the shared meanings of a role, but also "identification with," the process of infusing a role with self-meanings. Indeed, individuals are motivated to construct self-meanings that support and maintain their well-being.

Two outcomes of "identification with" will be considered in this study. First, identity refers to self-meanings in a role. Burke (1980) argued that identity meanings are typically multidimensional and used evaluation, potency, and activity to measure the meanings of gender roles. More recently, Mutran and Burke (1979) applied a similar procedure to distinguish the old-aged from middle-aged and young adult identities, and Reitzes and Burke (1983) found that college student identity meanings influenced self-esteem. Second, commitment refers to a person's belonging or attachment to a role and focuses on the tie that connects a person to a role. While worker commitment has long been understood to influence performance on the job (Jans, 1982; Morrow, 1983), this study considers whether commitment to their preretirement worker role continues to serve as a foundation for self-esteem and to reduce depression for both retired and working men and women.

In a series of works that spans more than two decades, Atchley (1971, 1976, 1984, 1993) has been developing and refining "continuity theory" to better understand the process of retirement. Among Atchley's insights into retirement, three are especially important for this research. First, retirement entails more than just the loss of the worker role. Retirement also means culturally transmitted rights, such as the rights of a retired person to economic support and the right to autonomy concerning the management of one's time as well as duties, such as assuming responsibility for the management of one's own life (Atchley, 1976). Second, retirement covers a temporal span that begins in preretirement and continues into postretirement. Atchley's (1976) seven stages clearly present retirement as a process that links a set of roles before and after the actual end of the full-time employment and/or the beginning of a pension. Third, retirement is variable in form and consequences. Atchley (1982) argues that the retirement outcomes are influenced in part by social background characteristics, such as a person's health and the adequacy of

retirement income, as well as the circumstances surrounding the retirement event, such as whether retirement was voluntary and expected.

We are interested in investigating the social psychological consequences of retirement. Self-esteem and depression reflect theoretically and empirically distinct dimensions of well-being. Self-esteem captures the cognitive and evaluative assessment of self-concept, and therefore may be sensitive to changes in social status and social background as individuals make the transition into retirement. Depression focuses on the affective, emotional components of personality, and so captures feelings of disorientation or anxiety as individuals face retirement. Thus, self-esteem and depression may be influenced by retirement in different ways.

We begin by exploring changes in self-esteem and depression as workers move into retirement. Miller (1965) proposed that retirement would create an "identity crisis." His argument was that, given the prominence of the role of worker, retirement would be a negative, if not degrading experience. Furthermore, leisure roles could not replace the work role as a source of self-respect. Atchley (1971) countered with "continuity theory" and the prediction that retirement typically would not negatively impact well-being. He argued that individuals occupy multiple roles and proceeded to imply that the continuity of family, friendship, and religious roles into retirement would typically prevent an overall negative consequence of retirement. Thus, our first research expectation is that well-being will not be negatively affected by retirement. In other words, we do not expect that self-esteem scores in retirement will be lower or depression scores higher than they were in preretirement.

A second reference for interpreting the consequences of retirement is to compare the well-being of retired men and women with those who continued to work full-time. "Crisis theory" suggests that men and women who remain working have retained the social status associated with their work roles and have been spared the disruption that may accompany retirement. On the other hand, retirement may offer relief from job pressures and performance expectations that may actually improve well-being. "Continuity theory" suggests that retirement may not necessarily have negative consequences for well-being. Atchley (1971, 1976, 1993) has argued that for most people the work role may not necessarily be their most central or salient role. Indeed, there is evidence that for both older working men and women family roles are more important (ranked higher) than the work role (Reitzes, Mutran, & Fernandez, 1994). Further, retirement may offer the opportunity to spend more time in the valued roles of friend and family member. Thus, our second research expectation is that the well-being of retired men and women will not be lower than the well-being of workers. So, retirees' self-esteem scores will not be lower and their depression scores will not be higher than those of men and women who continue to work.

Third, we are interested in exploring the impact of earlier and preretirement commitment to the role of worker and worker identity meanings on the later self-esteem and depression scores of both retirees and workers. Atchley (1971, 1976, 1993) argued that an important source of continuity during retirement is that individuals continue to hold an occupational identity even after they retire. Ebaugh (1988) described the lingering effects of a former role as a "hangover identity," and noted that in adult roles a new identity is often influenced by former identities. So, retired workers may continue to use their ex-identity as a foundation or framework for assessing self-worth. An implication of this process is that social background and worker-identity factors should have a similar pattern of effects on well-being. The research expectation, therefore, would be that social background and worker identity variables have a linear and additive effect on self-esteem and depression, while retirement status would exert either a positive effect or no effect on well-being. In other words, there should not be significant retirement status interaction effects that influence self-esteem or depression.

Another possibility, also in line with symbolic interaction theory, is that retirement may be more difficult for men and women who have greater commitment to the worker role (Stryker & Serpe, 1994). Men and women who were committed to the worker role and held positive worker identity meanings will have lost a key anchoring identity. They will be more likely to feel uneasy, anomic, or depreciated until they have gone through the process of readjusting or reforming their role hierarchies. The research implication would be that while worker commitment and identity meanings will exert positive effects on well-being for men and women who continue to work, the effects may be negative for retirees. A less extreme version is that preretirement worker commitment and worker-identity meanings will exert positive effects on later self-esteem and negative effects on depression, but the strength of the effects will be weaker than they will be for men and women who continue to work full-time. Thus, in either version, the research expectation is that there will be significant interaction effects between worker identity and retirement status that influence self-esteem or depression.

Method

Data

The two waves of data were collected in 1992 and 1994 as part of our ongoing study of the transition into retirement (Carolina Health and Transitions Study [CHATS]). Beginning with the earlier data set, the sampling procedures were designed to identify approximately 400 men and 400 women aged 58 to 64 years old who are working at least 35 hours a week and residing in the Raleigh-Durham-Chapel Hill, North Carolina metropolitan area. In order to gather a representative sample of middle-aged working men and women, we began by obtaining the driver history files maintained by the North Carolina Department of Motor Vehicles. The file is estimated to include over 80% of the entire population in the age group. From the list, which records age, address, and gender but not the telephone number or work status of applicants, we randomly selected names in proportion to the size of the three counties included in the study area. Following Dillman (1978) we sent out two introductory letters and screening postcards (three weeks apart) and follow-up telephone calls (up to 9 tries) to verify telephone numbers and identify full-time working subjects living in the area. Of the people identified by our screening procedures as eligible, 62% (826) consented and participated in our two 20-minute telephone interviews (60% of the men, 64% of the women; see Reitzes et al., 1994 for more details of the sampling and data collection).

Each of the 826 workers were tracked at six-month intervals over the next two years. By July 1994, 758 of the respondents had either retired or remained working full-time. The attrition rate of 8.2% reflects the loss of 68 cases (14 died and 54 dropped out). An additional 21 people provided incomplete information and were dropped from the investigation. Of the 757 respondents who provided usable follow-up interviews, 438 were still employed full-time and 299 had retired. Overall, the sample contains a diverse set of workers and retirees with a variety of social background characteristics, including 73% married, 83% white, and 52% female. It will allow us to proceed with the primary goals of testing hypotheses and exploring changes in self-esteem and depression as older workers either move into retirement or continue with their work careers.

Variables

Three sets of variables are used in the data analysis. Beginning with the dependent variables, self-esteem is measured at two points in time (self-esteem '92, $\alpha = .89$, and self-esteem '94, $\alpha = .88$). The measures are both derived from Rosenberg's (1965) self-esteem scale, which has proven to be a durable and useful measure of a person's summary or global assessment of self. The scales include ten items, such as, "I feel that I'm a person of worth, at least on an equal basis with others," "I am able to do things as well as most other people," and "I wish I could have more respect for myself" (recoded). Responses ranged from "strongly agree" (4) to "strongly disagree" (1). Depression is also measured at two points in time (depression '92, $\alpha = .89$, and depression '94, $\alpha = .85$) using Radloff's (1977) 20-item Center for Epidemiological Studies Depression Scale (CES-D). Sample items include: "I felt that I was just as good as other people" (recoded), "I had trouble keeping my mind on what I was doing," and "My sleep was restless." The four response categories are, "rarely or none of the time" (0), "a little of the time" (1), "a moderate amount of the time" (2), and "most of the time'' (3). As expected, the two sets of well-being measures are negatively correlated (for *self-esteem '92* and *depression '92*, $r = -.39$ and for *self-esteem '94* and *depression '94*, $r = -.45$).

The second set of variables includes the retirement and social background measures. *Retire* is a dummy variable (1 = retired, 0 = working). *Poor health* is a measure of functional limitation in 1992 and is based on a 7-item scale of difficulties in activities such as walking, using stairs, standing, or sitting for long periods of time, bending, lifting weights up to 10 pounds, and reaching above your head with responses of ''never,'' ''sometimes,'' or ''often'' (α = .79). *Age* reflects age in 1992 and is measured in years. Less than 1% of the sample self-identified as Asian or as neither white nor black, so racial diversity is limited to blacks and whites. *White* is a dummy variable. Marital status, *married*, is measured in 1994 with a dummy variable coded in the direction of being married, and *female* is a gender dummy variable. *Income* comes from a question that asks for the total 1994 household income, with 10 response categories ranging from ''$7,500 or less'' (1), ''$35,001 to $50,000'' (5), and ''$200,001 and over'' (10). *Education* is based on the highest grade completed in school and coded in years. *Occupation* refers to 1992 occupation, and is measured by a 100-point occupational prestige scale using 1980 U.S. Census occupational classifications and 1989 National Opinion Research Center prestige scores. Scores range from ''86'' for physicians and ''75'' for lawyers to ''09'' for shoe shiners and ''19'' for news vendors (National Opinion Research Center, 1991; U.S. Bureau of the Census, 1982).

The third set of variables contains the 1992 commitment to the work role and worker identity measures. *Worker commitment* is composed of a scale containing 6 items: (1) ''I feel I'm truly at home when I'm at work''; (2) ''I'm very committed to my work''; (3) ''It is important to me that I succeed in my work''; (4) ''I would feel a deep sense of personal loss if I failed in my work''; (5) ''I wish I were not in this line of work'' (recoded); and (6) ''If I could, I would give up being a worker'' (recoded) with four response categories ranging from strongly agree (4) to strongly disagree (1) (α = .71).

Identity meanings refer to shared meanings a person attributes to him/herself in a role. Mortimer, Finch, and Kumka (1982) suggest a multidimensional identity measure, which we adapted to identities in the worker role. After the leading phrase, ''As a worker, I am . . .'' adjective pairs were organized in a semantic differential 5-point format (Osgood, Succi, & Tannenbaum, 1957). Worker identity dimensions include: *competent* — active-inactive, successful-unsuccessful, and competent-not competent (α = .63); *confident* — relaxed-tense, happy-sad, confident-anxious (α = .58); *sociable* — interested in others-interested in self, warm-cold, open-closed, and social-solitary (α = .64). We found only modest correlations between worker commitment and each of the three worker-identity meanings (ranging from $r = .19$ to $r = .26$). Further, as expected, there are moderate correlations between the three worker identity items (ranging from $r = .40$ to $r = .45$). The findings confirm the related but distinct character of the measures of worker commitment and the three worker-identity meanings.

Results

Descriptive Overview

The data analysis begins with Table 1. Our interest is in investigating the social psychological consequences of retirement. We are interested in two sets of comparisons. The first probes whether there are differences in well-being as workers begin the passage from preretirement into retirement or continue to work. The results presented in the upper panel suggest that the move into retirement does not negatively impact their well-being. There is not a statistically significant change in self-esteem as workers retire, and retired workers actually are less depressed than when they were still working. The pres-

Table 1. Means and Standard Deviations

	Time 1 (1992)			Time 2 (1994)		
	Mean	SD	n	Mean	SD	n
Self-Esteem: Retired	34.075	4.010	295	34.380	3.972	295
Self-Esteem: Continue Working	34.208	4.039	432	34.542	4.025	432
Depression: Retired	6.240***	6.677	291	4.673***	5.557	291
Depression: Continue Working	5.705	6.576	427	5.358	6.622	427

	Retired			Continue Working		
	Mean	SD	n	Mean	SD	n
Self-Esteem '94	34.380	3.972	295	34.542	4.025	432
Depression '94	4.673	5.557	291	5.358	6.622	427
Self-Esteem '92	34.075	4.010	295	34.208	4.039	432
Depression '92	6.240	6.677	291	5.705	6.576	427

Note: t-tests and Chi-squares indicate whether differences by self-esteem and depression scores are statistically significant.
*$p < .05$; **$p < .01$; ***$p < .001$.

sures of work and/or the uncertainty or fear of impending retirement may have a more negative effect on mental health than the reality of retirement. Not surprisingly, the second and fourth rows reveal that there are not statistically significant changes in the well-being of workers who continue with their work careers.

The lower panel provides information on the comparison between the well-being of retirees and workers. The first two rows reveal that retirees have similar mean self-esteem and depression scores as workers who continue to work. Further, rows 3 and 4 indicate that there were no differences in the 1992 self-esteem and depression scores between workers who would retire two years later and those who would continue to work.

Factors Influencing Self-Esteem and Depression

The regression analyses presented in Tables 2 and 3 allow us to continue our investigation of the impact of retirement on self-esteem and depression. The zero-order comparison suggested that there were not statistically significant differences between the

mean self-esteem and depression scores of retirees and workers. The regression analyses allow us to probe further into whether retirement has effects even when controlling for social background and past worker-identity meanings. Equation 1 in Tables 2 and 3 reveals that retirement does influence well-being. Being retired has a positive effect on self-esteem independent of social background characteristics, past worker-identity meanings, and past self-esteem or depression. Similarly, men and women who retired were less depressed in 1994 than those who continued to work full-time. Thus, rather than having a negative effect on the well-being, retirement seems to have a positive effect on the well-being of older workers.

We proceed now to the separate analyses of self-esteem and depression. Our interest is in exploring whether social background characteristics, past worker-identity meanings, and past self-esteem or depression influence self-esteem or depression in similar or different ways for retirees and those who continue to work. Chow (1960) proposed a test of the equality between sets of coefficients in two linear equations. His test compares the residual sum of

Table 2. Regression Analysis: Self-Esteem '94

Independent Variables	Entire Sample (1)	Retired (2)	Continue Working (3)
Retire	.068*	—	—
	(.551)		
Poor Health	−.055	−.044	−.080*
	(−.082)	(−.060)	(−.131)
Age	−.063*	−.048	−.066
	(−.137)	(−.109)	(−.145)
White	.022	.012	.025
	(.236)	(.116)	(.282)
Married	−.035	−.028	−.048
	(−.312)	(−.255)	(−.435)
Female	.034	.043	.019
	(.268)	(.349)	(.150)
Income	.097*	.120*	.076
	(.207)	(.287)	(.169)
Education	.090**	.162**a	.041a
	(.116)	(.214)	(.052)
Occupation	.050	.047	.043
	(.015)	(.014)	(.014)
Worker Commitment	.028	.036	.016
	(.044)	(.055)	(.025)
Worker Competent	.062	.025	.075
	(.171)	(.069)	(.206)
Worker Confident	.080*	.083	.082
	(.149)	(.153)	(.156)
Worker Sociable	.039	.064	.024
	(.057)	(.095)	(.035)
Self–Esteem '92	.467***	.428***a	.492***a
	(.464)	(.428)	(.489)
R^2	.38	.37	.38
N	737	299	438

Note: Standardized coefficients are presented with unstandardized coefficients in parentheses.

aDifference between coefficients significant at the .05 level.

*p < .05; **p < .01; ***p < .001.

Table 3. Regression Analysis: Depression '94

Independent Variables	Entire Sample (1)	Retired (2)	Continue Working (3)
Retire	−.132***	—	—
	(−1.655)		
Poor Health	.111***	.138**	.083
	(.255)	(.258)	(.221)
Age	−.015	.040	−.034
	(−.050)	(.126)	(−.121)
White	−.064	−.058	−.043
	(−1.065)	(−.797)	(−.797)
Married	.011	−.049	.032
	(.152)	(−.615)	(.478)
Female	.030	.011	.058
	(.373)	(.123)	(.765)
Income	−.120**	−.077	−.112*
	(−.393)	(−.255)	(−.406)
Education	.059**	.151**	.009
	(.117)	(.275)	(.018)
Occupation	−.074	−.164*	−.022
	(−.035)	(−.068)	(−.012)
Worker Commitment	−.039	−.060	−.021
	(−.094)	(−.127)	(−.055)
Worker Competent	−.072*	−.072a	−.095*a
	(−.306)	(−.272)	(−.424)
Worker Confident	−.161***	−.037a	−.234***a
	(−.465)	(−.095)	(−.724)
Worker Sociable	−.039	.062a	−.082a
	(−.090)	(.128)	(−.198)
Depression '92	.261***	.380***	.192***
	(.245)	(.317)	(.193)
R^2	.24	.28	.24
N	737	299	438

Note: Standardized coefficients are presented with unstandardized coefficients in parentheses.

aDifference between coefficients significant at the .05 level.

*p < .05; **p < .01; ***p < .001.

squares from the pooled sample with the sum of the two residual sums of squares from the separate analyses of retirees and workers. We found that the separate equations for retirees and workers are not significantly different from an equation which pool retirees and workers ($F = .83$, $df = 13, 711$). In other words, there are not overall differences in the way that the set of social background, past worker-identity meanings, and past self-esteem influence self-esteem for retirees and workers. Equation 1 finds that increased age lowers self-esteem; while higher income, better education, earlier worker-identity meanings as confident, and higher earlier self-esteem improve self-esteem for the entire sample.

However, to explore whether individual variables may exert different effects on the self-esteem of retirees and workers, we created an interaction term (retire × independent variable) for each of the independent variables and separately included them in 13 regression analyses. Only two of the interaction terms were statistically significant. Education, for retirees, had a stronger positive effect on self-esteem than it did for those who continued to work, and earlier self-esteem (1992) had a stronger positive effect on continuing workers than it did on retirees. So, contrary to the expectation that positive worker-identity meanings may hinder adjusting to retirement, we found no differences between retirees and workers in the way that the earlier worker-identity meanings influence self-esteem.

Turning to depression, we found that there were statistically significant differences ($p < .05$) between the regression equations for retirees and workers and a pooled equation of both retirees and workers ($F = 3.03$, $df = 13, 711$), so we proceeded with the separate analyses. For workers who retired, depression was fairly stable. Depression '92 has a modest effect on depression '94 ($\beta = .380$). In addition, retirees who were more educated than others and those in poor health experienced an increase in depression, while those who retired from more prestigious occupations were less likely than others to experience increased depression. Among workers who continued to work, there was a great deal of change in depression as witnessed by the low stability coefficient between depression '92 and depression '94 ($\beta = .192$). The change in depression was associated with income and identity meanings. Workers with higher incomes and earlier worker-identity meanings as competent and confident experienced a decrease in depression.

With the inclusion of interaction terms, there were statistically significant differences between retirees and workers with regard to the impact of the three worker-identity meanings on depression. Each of the three worker-identity meanings had a stronger negative effect on depression for workers than for retirees. So, for those who continued to work full time, earlier worker-identity meanings tended to lower depression scores, while for retirees, preretirement worker-identity meanings did not alleviate depression.

Discussion

Taken as a whole, the data tend to support Atchley's "continuity theory." Retirement can have positive social psychological consequences, and there is continuity between preretirement and postretirement as well as between earlier and later periods in the work career. We interpret the data to suggest that retirement entails more than the negative experience of losing the worker role, and that earlier self-esteem and depression continue to influence current well-being.

Beginning with our interest in comparing well-being over time and between retirees and workers, the zero-order difference of mean tests presented in Table 1 provided a helpful overview. We found evidence of continuity in the absence of differences between preretirement and postretirement self-esteem scores, and evidence of retirement adjustment by the decrease in depression scores as workers moved into retirement. Further, there was no evidence of a negative retirement effect when we compared workers and retirees. There were no differences in their 1994 self-esteem and depression scores. Similarly, there were no differences in earlier (1992) self-esteem and depression scores between workers who would retire in the next two years and those who would continue working full time. Thus, it does not appear to be the case that workers enter retirement with well-being scores any different than those of workers who continue to work.

The regression analyses allow us to continue our comparison of retirees and workers and to probe the impact of preretirement worker-identity meanings on the later well-being of retirees and workers. Simultaneously controlling for social background characteristics, identity measures, and earlier self-esteem or depression, we found that retirement had a positive effect on self-esteem and a negative effect on depression. Wheaton (1990) proposed that role transitions in and of themselves may not be negative. To the extent that individuals experience the work role as stressful or fear the anticipated consequences of role loss, exiting the role and dealing with the reality, as opposed to the fear of retirement, may in fact improve well-being.

In the analysis of self-esteem, we found that a single additive model fit the data for both retirees and workers. The finding supports the expectation derived from "continuity theory" that retirement is part of an ongoing process, as opposed to reflecting a radical departure from the past or a sharp difference with the experiences of workers who continue their work careers. Furthermore, continuity is also suggested by the finding that earlier self-esteem influences later self-esteem, although the effect is stronger for those who continue to work.

The findings also suggest that workers with greater commitment to their earlier worker roles and who perceive themselves as competent, confident, or sociable workers were not negatively affected in their later self-esteem. The expectation that workers who have more positive worker-identity meanings would experience an identity crisis and lower their self-esteem in retirement did not occur.

The process is different when we investigate depression. Here we did find statistically significant differences in the way that retirees and workers were affected by social background characteristics, worker identity measures, and past depression. We found that for retirees, preretirement worker-identity meanings did not influence postretirement depression, while for those who continued to work, earlier worker-identity meanings lowered later depression scores. The findings suggest that we did not find evidence of an "identity hangover," a lingering effect of the former work role for retirees. Instead, worker-identity meanings are becoming less relevant to individuals as they move into retirement. However, for those who continue to work a positive set of earlier worker-identity meanings helps to resist or lower depression.

In conclusion, this investigation advances the study of the social psychological consequences of retirement in four ways. First, the longitudinal data allow us to control for past self-esteem and depression as we probe retirement effects. Without the 1992 self-esteem and depression measures, the positive effects of retirement could be mistakenly interpreted as reflecting a self-selection process — that is, workers with higher self-esteem and lower depression are opting for retirement. With the earlier measures included in the analysis, however, the findings suggest more strongly that the effects are due to retirement-related processes. Second, the comparison of workers who continued to work with workers who retired provides us with a reference group to interpret the results. The comparison was especially helpful in the analysis of depression, where we found that there were differences in the way that retirees and workers were affected by social background characteristics, worker identity measures, and past depression variables. Third, the recognition that well-being is multidimensional suggests the need for multiple measures of well-being. Indeed, the same set of variables may exert different effects on self-esteem than on depression. Finally, the inclusion of commitment to the worker role and the three worker-identity meanings suggests an important new direction for research. We found that earlier worker-role meanings influenced later depression scores for workers who continued to work.

We also must recognize at least four limitations of this investigation. First, retirement is not a single or a monolithic process. Variations in work and retirement experiences may influence the impact of retirement on well-being and the extent to which preretirement worker-identity variables may influence self-esteem and depression in retirement. Thus, the conditions and circumstances that surround retirement, such as whether retirement was voluntary, anticipated, and "on time" may influence the impact of retirement on well-being. In addition, work history factors such as whether the person is retiring from his/her main occupation and job, as well as the extent of past periods of unemployment may also modify the impact of retirement on well-being. Second, there is the problem of random measurement error, which increases when using multiplicative terms to test for interaction effects. The reliability of the cross-product will be lower than the least reliable of the component measures. A third limitation of the study is that it only covers a two-year period, and so only captures an initial wave of retirees. Over the next four to five years, most of the respondents who are still working will also retire. It would be interesting to explore whether there are differences between those who retired in the first two years and those who retired four or five years after the 1992 interviews.

Finally, the next step is to include spouse and parent identity measures that bridge the transition into retirement. We expect that spouse and parent identity meanings may help to foster well-being as individuals make the transition from full-time work into retirement. As a process, we expect that in the early stages of retirement, individuals tend to rely on past roles and identity meanings to provide a sense of well-being. However, as individuals begin to adjust to retirement, we expect that they will rely less on past roles and more on ongoing and new identities. Thus, retirement may entail the gradual process of realigning existing roles and infusing them with greater meaning and importance.

References

Atchley, R. C. (1971). Retirement and leisure participation: Continuity or crisis? *The Gerontologist, 11,* 13–17.
Atchley, R. C. (1976). *The sociology of retirement.* New York: John Wiley.
Atchley, R. C. (1982). Retirement: Leaving the world of work. *Annals of the American Academy of Political and Social Science, 464,* 120–131.
Atchley, R. C. (1989). A continuity theory of normal aging. *The Gerontologist, 29,* 183–190.
Atchley, R. C. (1993). Continuity theory and the evolution of activity in later life. In J. R. Kelly (Ed.), *Activity and aging: Staying involved in later life.* Newbury Park, CA: Sage.
Burke, P. J. (1980). The self: Measurement implications from a symbolic interactionist perspective. *Social Psychology Quarterly, 43,* 18–29.
Chow, G. C. (1960). Tests of equality between sets of coefficients in two linear regressions. *Econometrica, 28,* 591–605.
Dillman, D. A. (1978). *Mail and telephone surveys: The total design method.* New York: Wiley.
Ebaugh, H. R. F. (1988). *Becoming an ex: The process of role exit.* Chicago: University of Chicago Press.
Ekerdt, D. J., & DeViney, S. (1993). Evidence for a preretirement process among older male workers. *Journal of Gerontology: Social Sciences, 48,* S35–S43.
Erdner, R. A., & Guy, R. F. (1990). Career identification and women's attitudes toward retirement. *International Journal of Aging and Human Development, 30,* 129–139.
George, L. K., Fillenbaum, G. G., & Palmore, E. (1984). Sex differences in the antecedents and consequences of retirement. *Journal of Gerontology, 39,* 364–371.
Hanks, R. S. (1990). The impact of early retirement incentives on retirees and their families. *Journal of Family Issues, 11,* 424–437.
Hardy, M., & Quadagno, J. (1995). Satisfaction with early retirement: Making choices in the auto industry. *Journal of Gerontology, 50B: Social Sciences,* S217–S228.
Jans, N. A. (1982). The nature and measurement of work involvement. *Journal of Occupational Psychology, 55,* 57–67.
Knesek, G. E. (1992). Early versus regular retirement: differences in measures of life satisfaction. *Journal of Gerontological Social Work, 19*(1), 3–34.
Matthews, A. M., & Brown, K. H. (1987). Retirement as a critical life event. *Research On Aging, 9,* 548–571.
Maxwell, N. L. (1985). The retirement experience: Psychological and financial linkages to the labor market. *Social Science Quarterly, 66,* 22–33.

Miller, S. J. (1965). The social dilemma of the aging leisure participant. In A. Rose and W. Petersen (Eds.), *Older people and their social world.* Philadelphia: Davis.

Morrow, P. C. (1983). Concept redundancy in organizational research: The case of work commitment. *Academy of Management Review, 8,* 486–498.

Mortimer, J. T., Finch, M. D., & Kumka, D. (1982). Persistence and change in development: The multidimensional self-concept. *Life-Span Development and Behavior, 4,* 263–313.

Mutran, E., & Burke. P. J. (1979). Personalism as a component of old age identity. *Research On Aging, 1,* 37–64.

National Opinion Research Center. (1991). *General social surveys. 1972–1991: Cumulative codebook.* Chicago, IL: NORC.

Osgood, C. E., Succi, G. J., & Tannenbaum, P. H. (1957). *The Measurement of meaning.* Urbana, IL: University of Illinois Press.

Palmore, E., Fillenbaum, G. G., & George, L. (1984). Consequences of retirement. *Journal of Gerontology, 39,* 109–116.

Radloff, L. S. (1977). The CES-D scale: A self-report depression scale for research in the population. *Applied Psychological Measurement, 1,* 385–401.

Reitzes, D. C., & Burke, P. J. (1983). The processes and consequences of role identification among college students. *Research in Sociology of Education and Socialization, 4,* 129–154.

Reitzes, D. C., Mutran, E. J., & Fernandez, M. E. (1994). Middle-aged working men and women: Similar and different paths to self-esteem. *Research On Aging, 16,* 355–374.

Richardson, V., & Kilty, K. M. (1991). Adjustment to retirement: Continuity vs. discontinuity. *International Journal of Aging and Human Development, 33,* 151–169.

Rosenberg, M. (1965). *Society and the adolescent self-image.* Princeton, NJ: Princeton University Press.

Rosenberg, M. (1981). The self-concept: Social product and social force. In M. Rosenberg & R. Turner (Eds.), *Social psychology: Sociological Perspectives.* New York: Basic.

Stone, G. P. (1962). Appearance and the self. In A. M. Rose (Ed.), *Human behavior and social processes.* Boston, MA: Houghton Mifflin.

Stryker, S. (1980). *Symbolic interaction: A social structural version.* Menlo Park, CA: Benjamin/Cummings.

Stryker, S., & Serpe, R. T. (1994). Identity salience and psychological centrality: Equivalent, overlapping, or complementary concepts? *Social Psychology Quarterly, 57,* 16–35.

Turner, R. H. (1956). Role-taking, role standpoint, and reference-group behavior. *American Journal of Sociology, 61,* 316–328.

U.S. Bureau of the Census. (1982). *1980 census of population: alphabetical index of industries and occupations.* Washington DC: U.S. Government Printing Office.

U.S. Bureau of the Census. (1992). *Statistical abstract of the United States: 1992.* Washington, DC: U.S. Government Printing Office.

Wheaton, B. (1990). Life transitions, role histories, and mental health. *American Sociological Review, 55,* 209–223.

Received August 31, 1995
Accepted January 11, 1996

Rethinking Retirement

SUMMARY Since 1950, the average retirement age has declined from 67 to 63. Baby boomers want to retire even sooner, but can they afford it? One-third of retirees now return to work within a year. Retirement decisions depend on many factors, including pensions, savings, disability, job satisfaction, and social attitudes. All these and more will affect the boomers' ultimate quitting time.

Paula Mergenhagen

Paula Mergenhagen is a sociologist and researcher in Nashville, Tennessee. This article is adapted from her book, Targeting Transitions: Marketing to Consumers During Life Changes *(American Demographics Books, 1994).*

Before he retired in 1985, Gleason Pebley searched the Southeast for the perfect spot. At age 55, after 30 years in management positions with AT&T, Pebley and his wife left Basking Ridge, New Jersey, for Cookeville, Tennessee, population 24,000 in 1992.

Pebley isn't like most retirees for two reasons: 83 percent of 55-year-olds are still in the labor force, and only a small proportion of adults relocate when they retire. But he represents the well-established trends of early retirement and affluence in the mature market. Between the periods 1950-55 and 1985-90, the median retirement age dropped from 67 to 63.

Can baby boomers continue these trends? Although the majority of boomers say they would like to retire by age 60, many of them won't be able to afford it. Others will rejoin the labor force after they find that retirement isn't as enjoyable or as inexpensive as they had imagined.

At the turn of the century, the average American's life expectancy wasn't quite 50 years. As a result, most people never retired. Now, retirement can last 20 years or more, and a number of factors influence a person's decision to leave work. The most important are economic factors, such as the availability of pensions and Social Security benefits. Yet health, occupation, and social conventions also play important roles.

Men have traditionally been the breadwinners, so the husband's resources have steered most retirement decisions. But women will be a greater factor in the future, because many baby-boom women will enjoy full-fledged pensions of their own.

Trends in retirement age are important for several reasons. Retirees are a prime market for many products and services, including travel, health care, and new homes. People on the verge of retirement also buy services that can help prepare them financially and emotionally for this important transition. As baby boomers decide to retire, they will create huge markets for financial planners and retirement counselors.

ONE-THIRD RETURN

About 14 million men and 22 million women aged 55 and older are not in the labor force, according to 1993 data from the Bureau of Labor Statistics (BLS). Among those under age 60, 22 percent of men and 43 percent of women are not in the labor force. At ages 60 to 64, the shares increase to 49 percent of men and 63 percent of women. And among those

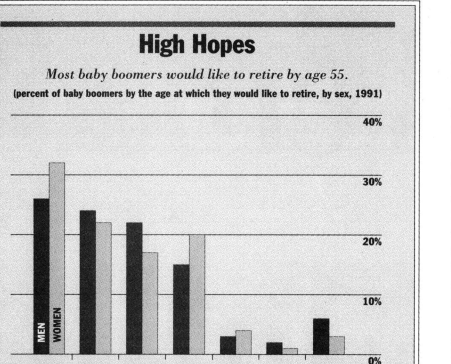

High Hopes

Most baby boomers would like to retire by age 55.

(percent of baby boomers by the age at which they would like to retire, by sex, 1991)

MEN WOMEN

under 50   51 to 55   56 to 60   61 to 65   66 to 70   71 and older   Never

Source: The Gallup Poll Monthly, *April 1991*

income receive some of their income from a company, union, or government pension, according to the 1992 Current Population Survey. So do 13 percent of men and 5 percent of women aged 45 to 64.

Starting in the 1970s, employers began providing incentives for early retirement by making pensions and other benefits available before age 65. In 1974, about one-half of individuals participating in employer pension plans could receive some benefits prior to age 65. By 1989, this proportion had reached three-fifths, according to the BLS. One analysis suggests that men who are eligible for full pension benefits before age 65 are nearly twice as likely as other men to retire early.

The retirement-buyout trend became pervasive during the recent recession. In 1992, 38 percent of early retirements from large companies were the result of early-retirement incentive offers. This proportion was 26 percent only two years earlier, according to a survey of primarily

aged 65 to 69, 75 percent of men and 84 percent of women aren't part of the labor force. At age 70 and older, the share reaches 90 percent of men and 95 percent of women.

> **Retirees are a prime market for many products and services, including travel, health care, and new homes.**

These labor force participation rates are not a perfect measure of permanent withdrawal from the labor force. Many older adults who don't work will eventually return to other full- or part-time jobs. Some find that their retirement benefits do not sustain their lifestyle. Others miss the structure and social interaction that a job provides.

Mark Hayward, a sociologist at Pennsylvania State University, and his colleagues tracked a group of retired men over 17 years. They found that almost one-

third of the men returned to work at some point, and most returnees came back in the first year after retirement. Professionals, salesworkers, farm laborers, and self-employed individuals were most likely to return to work, as were younger retirees. Over two-thirds of returnees took full-time jobs.

If retirement is defined as permanent withdrawal from the labor force, then an average of 1.3 million individuals retired each year between 1985 and 1990, according to Georgetown University senior research scholar Jacob Siegel. Today, the median age of retirement is about 63 for both men and women, according to research by Siegel and colleague Murray Gendell. During the early 1950s, the retirement age was about 67 for men and 68 for women.

"A person's readiness to retire is prompted by the receipt of a private pension," says Siegel. Such pensions have become more widespread over the years. About 49 percent of men and 22 percent of women aged 65 and older who have

> **Advances in pensions and Social Security account for about half of the decrease in retirement age.**

large employers by Charles D. Spencer and Associates of Chicago. Corporations seeking to cut their payrolls are pushing early retirement as a more humane alternative to mass layoffs. So far, workers seem eager to accept.

Almost 6 percent of retirement-age employees receive special early-retirement "window" offers, and 36 percent accept them, according to a 1992 random survey of retirement-age adults analyzed by University of Michigan economist Charles Brown. Employees who receive such offers are most likely to be managers and to work for large firms in high-wage industries. "Age 51 is clearly not 'too young' to get such an offer," writes Brown, "and 61 is not near enough to normal retirement to discourage special efforts by employers."

Early retirement got another boost when Social Security benefits were substantially increased in the 1970s. Moreover, these benefits were protected from inflation because future increases were automatically linked to the Consumer Price Index. "Older workers who had planned retirement based on real benefits prevailing during the 1960s must have been surprised by their new wealth. Given their nearness to retirement, the realization that substantially higher benefits awaited them than they had counted on may have influenced many to retire early," writes Richard Ippolito, chief economist with Pensions Benefit Guaranty Corporation in Washington, D.C.

Over 90 percent of the labor force is covered by the Social Security retirement system, with partial benefits available at age 62 and full benefits at age 65. In 1993, 14 million men and 20 million women aged 62 and older were receiving Social Security benefits.

Lower Expectations

The decline in retirement age has leveled off in recent years, but some demographers expect to see further declines after the turn of the century.

(median age of retirement by sex, for 5-year periods, 1950-90, and projections to 2005)

Source: *Bureau of Labor Statistics, Monthly Labor Review, July 1992*

PENSIONS AND SAVINGS

Advances in pensions and Social Security account for about half of the decrease in retirement age between 1970 and the mid-1980s, according to Ippolito. But the trend toward earlier retirement is leveling off. Between the periods 1980-85 and 1990-95, the median age of retirement is expected to hover around 63. Based on BLS employment projections, Gendell and Siegel say that retirement age will then resume its decline and dip below 62 between 2000 and 2005.

Not all researchers agree with them. "The retirement age is constant now. If anything, it will go up a bit because there has been a major change in government policy," says Syracuse University economist Richard Burkhauser. The age at which Social Security recipients can receive full benefits will increase to 67 in a phased-in process that will start after 2000. Some of the financial penalties that recipients face by continuing to work are being removed as well. And in many work-

places, mandatory retirement ages have been eliminated.

The burden of retirement planning is shifting from the employer to the employee. As a result, how well employees plan for their retirement will have a major impact on the age at which they retire. Few individuals stay with one employer for their entire careers. And the employees most likely to have pension

> **Professionals, managers, and salesworkers are least likely to retire early; blue-collar workers are most likely.**

plans—unionized workers in goods-producing industries—are a declining presence in the labor force. In 1945, 36 percent of employees were unionized. In 1992, 16 percent were. In 1920, goods-producing industries accounted for half of all U.S.

jobs. By 1990, the share was one in four.

In the old days, employer-provided pensions almost always guaranteed specific benefits to employees upon retirement, and it was up to the employer to invest pension money wisely. But today, about one-quarter of those with employer-provided coverage are enrolled in defined contribution plans. Employees make contributions to these plans and control how their money is invested. They also assume the risk for bad investments. "To the extent that employees don't accept this responsibility and don't save or invest in an effective way, we will have a large segment of our population that can't afford to retire," says Susan Velleman, managing director of William M. Mercer, Inc., a benefits consultant in Boston.

Enrollment in the most popular type of defined contribution plan—the 401(k)—tripled between 1984 and 1991. About 19 percent of all U.S. workers—more than 17 million people—are enrolled in 401(k) plans, according to the Census Bureau's

1991 Survey of Income and Program Participation (SIPP). Participants' median monthly earnings that year were $2,495. The 401(k) plan is usually a big-company benefit; 69 percent of enrolled workers are employed by companies with 1,000 or more employees, and just 3 percent work for employers with fewer than 25 employees.

ATTITUDES AND DISABILITY

Financial considerations are only part of the retirement decision, according to economist Charles Brown. Social conventions also guide many decisions to retire. When workers see their peers retiring, they may feel that it may be time for them to leave also. "The retirement spikes at 62 and 64 are partly incentive and partly convention," he says.

Disability is an important contributor to early retirement. In a study of people who retired at least six months before becoming eligible for Social Security, the Social Security Administration found 35 percent of men who left their last job before age 55 said health was the primary reason. That compared with 30 percent of those who left between ages 55 and 61½, 26 percent between age 61½ and 62, and 21 percent after age 62. As the health of older adults improves, they will probably decide to stay in the labor force longer.

Professionals, managers, and sales-workers are least likely to retire early; blue-collar workers are most likely, according to sociologist Mark Hayward and his colleagues. "If the nature of work remains attractive and the demand for their labor continues, workers may be more likely to delay retirement," they write. Blue-collar workers are a declining share of the work force, while professionals and managers are an increasing share. These trends should work against early retirement.

The emerging influence of women on retirement is still a wild card, as few researchers have considered its effects. Some studies suggest that single women are affected by the same factors that men are when considering retirement. Married women may be different, however.

"The retirement decision of [married] women seems to be closely tied to the retirement decision of their husbands, but not vice-versa," says Syracuse's Burkhauser. "You find a correlation between when he retires and when she retires."

Many women reaching retirement age today did not participate in the labor force, or did so only sporadically. In 1992, 39 percent of women Social Security recipients aged 62 and older were receiving benefits based on their husbands' employment, not their own. This proportion is decreasing—it was 43 percent in 1980 and 57 percent in 1960—and it will continue to decline in the future.

The career histories and earnings of baby-boom women more closely resemble those of men. In 1960, just 40 percent of women aged 25 to 44 were in the labor force, compared with 98 percent of men. In 1993, 75 percent were working, compared with 94 percent of men.

Employed women are now almost as likely as employed men to be covered by pension plans; 67 percent of women wage-and-salary workers aged 25 and older are covered by pension plans, compared with 69 percent of men, according to the 1991 SIPP. Yet men are still slightly ahead of women when it comes to pension benefits. Just 44 percent of women workers are vested in pension plans and will receive full benefits, compared with 50 percent of men.

Changes in Social Security and pensions have been important factors in dropping the retirement age of men. They have only begun to enter into the retirement decision for women.

QUITTING TIME

Some workers who don't want to retire in their mid- or late-50s may do so because of corporate downsizings and early-retirement packages. Some of these reluctant retirees are ill-equipped to handle such a sudden and unexpected change. This has created a market niche for outplacement companies that advise organizations on how to implement layoffs and then offer assistance to laid-off employees.

Right Associates, an outplacement firm headquartered in Philadelphia, began an enhanced retirement counseling program in 1993. "I see a big market for it," says Graham Smith, the Right consultant in Canada who developed the program. Most of Smith's clients for retirement outplacement services are in their early 60s. "But the age is dropping," he says.

Some companies even provide retirement preparation for employees who aren't being pushed out the door. In fact, **more than seven in ten benefits managers** offer employees some type of retirement preparation, according to a 1993 Merrill Lynch survey. Small businesses are just as likely as large employers to offer this kind of service. And the eligible employees in companies offering these services do take advantage of them, according to benefits managers. Seventy-six percent of eligible employees read retirement brochures, 67 percent participate in seminars, 53 percent use multimedia resources like video- or audio-tapes, and 49 percent take part in counseling.

Kirk Brenner and Chris Brooke, financial consultants at Merrill Lynch's Indianapolis office, spend the majority of their time producing seminars for a wide variety of companies—from hospitals to factories. Some of their seminars are totally focused on retirement issues; others offer retirement planning as a major component. Speakers include financial experts, gerontologists, nurses, and attorneys. Estate planning is one of the most popular topics, says Brenner. The consultants do not make sales pitches during the presentations, but the Merrill Lynch name receives favorable exposure—and many participants ultimately become clients.

Many people who are on the verge of retirement want help and don't want to wait for their company to provide it. They go to see financial planners on their own. Eight in ten certified financial planners offer a specialty in retirement planning, according to a 1993 survey by the College for Financial Planning in Denver. "People will come to me with a retirement account or a 401(k) plan and say, 'I'm 55 and I want to retire at 65. Tell me how I need to invest my money,'" says

Jane King, president of Fairfield Financial Advisors in Wellesley, Massachusetts.

As baby boomers edge closer to retirement age, they will be more likely to want this type of help. About 64 percent of women and 50 percent of men aged 25 to 44 say they could use some help from a financial advisor or planner, according to the Merrill Lynch survey. "[Baby boomers] are concerned about getting guidance about taking [investment] risks," says King. "They know they have to take risks because no one else is going to take care of them."

Retirement is one of the most difficult transitions in life, according to a 1993 survey from Roper Starch Worldwide in New York City. Forty-one percent of people who have retired say the adjustment was difficult. In contrast, adjustment is seen as difficult by only 12 percent of newlyweds and 23 percent of new parents. The younger the retiree, the

> **As baby boomers edge closer to retirement age, they will be more likely to want help with financial planning.**

harder the transition: 36 percent of retirees aged 60 and older say the transition is difficult, compared with 45 percent of those aged 45 to 59.

Today, baby boomers are fearful that they'll make the wrong retirement decisions. A 1991 Gallup Poll found that 61 percent of boomers would like to retire by age 60. But a 1993 Gallup Poll found that 59 percent of 30-to-49-year-olds are afraid they won't be able to afford retirement at a reasonable age. Soothing those fears will create loyal, affluent customers for financial-services firms.

TAKING IT FURTHER

Labor force participation data are available from the Bureau of Labor Statistics, Division of Labor Force Statistics; telephone (202) 606-6378. The Current Population Survey (CPS) and the Survey of Income and Program Participation (SIPP) are conducted by the Census Bureau and contain information on receipt of pensions, pension coverage, and participation in 401(k) plans. More information can be obtained by contacting the bureau's Housing and Household Economic Statistics Division; telephone (301) 763-8576.

The *Annual Statistical Supplement* to the *Social Security Bulletin* contains information on numbers of Social Security beneficiaries, types of benefits, and levels of awards. It can be ordered from the U.S. Government Printing Office at (202) 783-3238 and costs $18. The cost of a yearly subscription to the *Social Security Bulletin*, including four quarterly issues and the *Annual Statistical Supplement*, is $13.

THE ECONOMICS OF AGEING

The luxury of longer life

IN THE world's rich countries, when you retire at 65 you can expect to live, on average, for another 15 or 20 years. A hundred years ago you would, on average, have been already dead. The late 20th century has brought to many the ultimate gift: the luxury of ageing. But like any luxury, ageing is expensive. Governments are fretting about the cost already; but they also know that far worse is to come. Over the next 30 or 40 years, the demographic changes of longer lives and fewer births will force most countries to rethink in fundamental ways their arrangements for paying for and looking after older people.

In 1990 18% of people in OECD countries were aged over 60. By 2030 that figure will have risen to over 30%. The share of the "oldest old" (those over 80), now around 3%, is set to double. The vast majority of these older people will be consumers, not producers. Thanks to state transfers, being old in developed countries mostly no longer means being poor. The old people will expect decent pensions to live on; they will make heavy demands on medical services; and some will need expensive nursing care. Yet while their numbers are expanding fast, numbers of people at work—who will have to foot the bill—will stay much the same, so each worker will have to carry a much heavier burden.

Mass survival to a ripe old age will not be confined to rich countries. Most developing countries, whose populations are now much younger than the developed world's, are starting to age fast. In Latin America and most of Asia, the share of over-60s is set to double between now and 2030, to 14%. In China, it will increase from less than 10% now to around 22% in 2030, thanks partly to the government's stringent population-control measures. Only Africa is likely to remain exuberantly young right through to the middle of the next century, though AIDS may reduce population growth in some countries.

Already the numbers of old people in poor countries are beginning to dwarf those in the rich world. By 2000, there will be 400m people over 60 in developing countries, twice as many as in the developed. In many places, the ageing process is being compressed from the four or five generations that it took in rich countries to just one or two.

A new twist to getting old

This will produce a historical first: countries with big old populations that are also poor. All the other permutations are familiar: old and rich (most of the industrial world), young and poor (most of the developing world for now) and, less common, young and rich (Australia, New Zealand, Ireland; up to a point, America, though not for much longer). Eastern Europe is something of an odd case out, being old but, thanks to its communist past, not as rich as it should be; and in Russia life expectancy for men, against the trend elsewhere, is falling rather than rising.

The new combination of age and poverty in several countries in Latin America and Asia will create many problems that are already familiar to industrial countries, but with far fewer resources to tackle them. Ethical dilemmas over the use of scarce resources will be magnified. Financing of health care and pensions could be a nightmare.

In very poor countries, old people usually work on until frailty or ill health force them to stop. Most of them have no means of support or care other than, with luck, their families. But as countries become richer, more people are covered by formal retirement schemes. Worldwide, about 40% of the labour force are members of formal schemes of any kind, whereas in high-income countries nearly all workers and their dependants are included.

This survey will concentrate on the rich countries, which have been aware of their looming demographic problems for at least 20 years, and should by now have developed solutions that the poor countries might adapt for their own use. Yet solutions even in the better-off parts of the world are still in short supply.

When demographers first started drawing attention to the coming age bulge, the discovery was hailed as that rare thing in the affairs of nations, a foreseeable problem. Forewarned would, surely, mean forearmed. Even the tag invented for it, "the demographic time-bomb", seemed to imply that the bomb could be defused. The demographic facts were inescapable because the people concerned had already been born. The same baby boomers who crowded the nurseries after 1945 would be packing the nursing homes of the 2030s. Yet so far there has been more talk than action. And as the original baby boomers are only just beginning to turn 50 this year, there is still a tempting margin for more talk before the bomb explodes.

Some of the talk has revolved around boosting future working populations, and spreading the cost of looking after the old, by raising fertility rates and

The world is growing older. Time to face up to it, says Barbara Beck

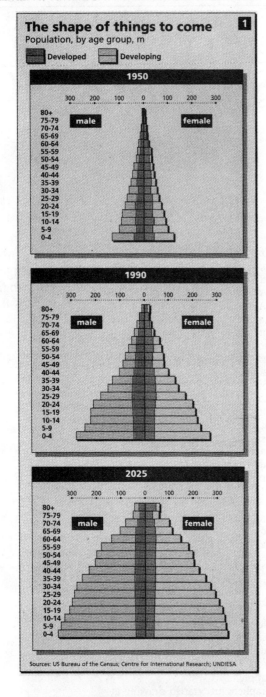

The shape of things to come 1
Population, by age group, m

■ Developed ▢ Developing

1950

300 200 100 0 100 200 300

80+
75-79
70-74
65-69
60-64
55-59
50-54
45-49
40-44
35-39
30-34
25-29
20-24
15-19
10-14
5-9
0-4

male   female

1990

300 200 100 0 100 200 300

80+
75-79
70-74
65-69
60-64
55-59
50-54
45-49
40-44
35-39
30-34
25-29
20-24
15-19
10-14
5-9
0-4

male   female

2025

300 200 100 0 100 200 300

80+
75-79
70-74
65-69
60-64
55-59
50-54
45-49
40-44
35-39
30-34
25-29
20-24
15-19
10-14
5-9
0-4

male   female

Sources: US Bureau of the Census; Centre for International Research; UNDIESA

subject. Allowing in enough immigrants to make a significant difference would be politically impossible. The OECD has calculated that if Japan, Germany and Italy wanted to compensate for the expected fall in their working-age populations between 2000 and 2050, they would have to import 13m-15m new workers apiece. And in due course the immigrants themselves would grow old.

Perhaps the most effective way of boosting the labour supply would be to raise the retirement age, which elegantly combines an increase in revenue from taxes and social-security contributions with a reduction in pension spending. But would-be pensioners would hate to wait for their benefits, and labour markets remain hostile to older workers, particularly at times of high unemployment.

That leaves only the most obvious methods of containing costs: raising contributions from the young, or cutting benefits, or a combination of the two. In health care, reforms have already been introduced in some countries, and in some cases have been quite successful at containing expenditure. But that spending still varies far more between countries than seems justified by the results. It is hard to believe that the Americans, who spend 14% of their GDP on health care, get twice as much out of it as the Japanese, who spend 7%. Yet reform in this area is a political minefield, as Bill Clinton found to his cost.

Progress on reforming pensions has been slow, partly because the prospective peak in spending is still several decades off. But several countries—eg, Britain, Germany and Japan—have made a start. Reform ideas are now getting enmeshed in a debate about the respective roles of public and private pensions. The World Bank has recently argued that most of the problems ahead could be averted by reducing state pension provision to a bare minimum, and introducing mandatory private-sector schemes in which each generation would pay for its own benefits. But most countries still believe that the state must go on playing a large role.

Long-term care for old and frail people has only recently emerged as a big issue, but it will become much more important as the numbers of very old people rise steeply. Several countries are concentrating their efforts on finding ways to look after people in their own homes rather than in expensive nursing homes. Some have introduced insurance schemes for long-term care. But most have yet to grasp this particular nettle.

Grey muscle

The trouble has been that the demographic problems ahead, however predictable, are still not imminent enough to create any real sense of urgency. Modern democracies with electoral cycles of four or five years are not designed to solve problems that impose short-term costs to reap long-term benefits.

In many countries, older people are still too small in number, and for the most part too politically passive, to act as an effective pressure group for long-term policies to further their own interests (perhaps to the detriment of other groups). But that is changing as their numbers increase, and they learn to flex their political muscles. By 2030, it would be a bold politician who neglected one voter in three—especially as older people in general turn

allowing more immigration. At present, few rich countries produce enough young even to keep their population stable, let alone increase it. If women could be persuaded to have more children, the argument goes, that would improve the ratio of working to retired people (though it would also temporarily put more pressure on the generation in the middle, which would have to pay for both young and old). An encouraging trend is emerging in rich Sweden, the "oldest" country in the world, where the birth rate has recently crept up to around replacement level. Among the bigger countries of the developed world, only America is similarly fertile. But will others follow?

As for fanciful talk about immigration as another way of rejuvenating the labour force, in rich countries immigration remains a highly touchy

out to vote in much bigger numbers than others.

Turn to America for a foretaste of things to come. Its American Association of Retired Persons (AARP), set up in 1958, is a highly effective lobbying organisation employing some 1,700 people, including 15 full-time lobbyists in Washington. With 33m members, it can afford to offer a lot for its $8-a-year subscription: insurance services, credit cards, discounts, low-price prescription medicines, motoring plans, advice of all kinds, even a training programme to help hard-up over-55s find jobs. Other, smaller organisations—such as the Seniors Coalition—are competing for the grey market. In America, at least, the politics of ageing is alive and well.

In other rich countries they are not as lively— yet. In Japan, older men are too busy working on beyond retirement age to spend time politicking. In Europe most people retire early, but still show little interest in joining pressure groups. Organisations such as Age Concern in Britain have more of a charitable image, providing help and information for older people, although they do campaign on issues such as old-age poverty. Germany has a few grey panthers stalking the land, but to little effect. Only in Holland have pensioners made much of a political mark: they set up two new parties in protest against a spending freeze, and caused much alarm by winning seven seats in the 1994 elections.

According to a Europe-wide poll, over three-quarters of the European Union's pensioners think their governments do not do enough for older people; 22% feel so strongly that they would join a political party formed to further their interests. Prominent among these interests are pensions, health

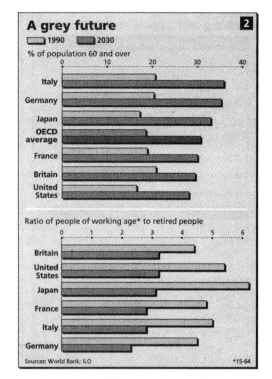

A grey future

care, long-term care and (for those who are still working, or would like to be) jobs. This survey will look at these in turn, starting with jobs. These matter to politicians too: if more people worked on for longer, the financial problems of ageing populations would be greatly eased.

A gradual goodbye

If people are living longer, they will have to work longer too

ONLY a generation ago, retirement in rich countries went by the book. The book generally said that men were entitled to a pension at age 65, women sometimes earlier. Until then, most people diligently worked on. In 1970, in most OECD countries 70-80% of men aged 60-64 were still at work.

Twenty years later that proportion had halved. The other half had quietly taken early retirement, often at their employers' suggestion. The arrangement suited both sides. Employers may have wanted to rejuvenate or reduce their workforce, or perhaps even had to close down. Offering older employees an attractive way out minimised the fuss and upheaval. And employees for the most part accepted eagerly, thinking of their neglected spouses, gardens or golf handicaps. Those who were not so eager did not have much choice. Governments, desperate to keep the unemployment figures down, colluded by easing the rules for early retirement and disability pensions. And trade unions often accepted the logic of paying off older workers to make room for younger ones, provided the pill could be suitably sweetened.

Today's workers have got into the way of thinking that it will be their turn next. In France, for example, new rules introduced in the 1970s allowed many people to retire at 60. In 1982 the pension age itself was reduced to 60. "Solidarity contracts" in the 1980s allowed many to go at 55. The railway workers, who recently went on strike against the French government's welfare reform plans, bow out as early as 50. In Europe and America an early-retirement culture has taken root.

Yet over the past few years many governments have had to rethink. If people even at the official retirement age can now typically expect to live another 15 or 20 years, an early exit might award them half an adult lifetime of economic inactivity. Since their numbers are growing fast, this will soon become unaffordable. So some countries are now raising their official retirement age, though they are treading softly. America, for example, is increasing the age at which it pays a full social security pension from 65 to 67, but in such tiny steps that it will take until 2022. Britain is bringing women's retirement age up to 65, in line with men's, but will not get there until 2020. Other countries, including Ger-

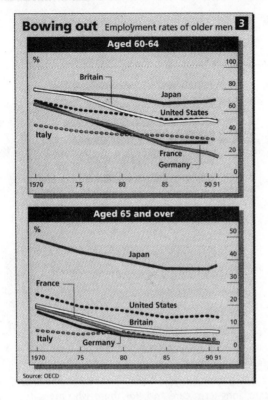

Bowing out Employment rates of older men **3**

Aged 60-64

Aged 65 and over

Source: OECD

many, Italy and Japan, are moving the same way.

On the face of it, raising the retirement age seems an ideal way of dealing with a bulge of old people. If people are living longer, they should also be fit for work for longer, and so can contribute to the cost of their own good fortune. However, paying pensions later will not necessarily keep people in work. The old are often the first to be made redundant. Once out of a job, they often find it hard to get another one. One future source of jobs for older people—provided they are fit enough—might be the care of the "oldest old", clearly a growth industry; but the pickings elsewhere will be slim.

Prejudice against older people at work is universal. In an opinion poll taken throughout the European Union, 80% of respondents—of all ages—believed that older workers were discriminated against in job recruitment. "Older" can mean as young as 40. Employers may be behaving quite rationally in discriminating. It often costs more to employ older workers than younger ones. Pay may be linked to seniority rather than to performance, and some occupational pension schemes require larger employers' contributions for older employees. Health insurance can also cost more.

But the main reason that employers steer clear of older workers is that they suspect them of not being up to the job. Again there may be a grain of truth in this. A World Health Organisation (WHO) study of older people's working capacity recently gathered together the biological facts and concluded that "the definition of an ageing worker could be considered to apply from 45 years." Physical performance, at a peak in the early 20s, declines gradually thereafter. Eyesight deteriorates and hearing gets worse. This may matter less as fewer jobs rely on physical strength, but depressingly the WHO also found that "the speed at which information is processed usually slows down substantially in older in-

dividuals." On the other hand, "while older managers take more time to reach decisions, they . . . appear to be as competent as younger managers in overall decision-making."

In praise of older workers

According to many employers, older workers—say those over 50—are more reliable, conscientious and loyal than younger ones. They tend to be good at dealing with people and happy to work in teams, though less likely to turn in a sparkling, rather than merely competent, performance. They are also considered less adaptable than younger workers, slower to grasp new ideas and, most damagingly, less likely to be able to use new technology such as computers. That is not surprising: older employees everywhere are last in the queue for training of any kind. Most employers do not bother to offer it, and employees are afraid to ask.

To some extent, older workers can compensate for their slower reactions by experience. In one much-quoted American study of typists aged between 19 and 72, the older women managed to work as fast as the younger ones, despite slower responses, simply by processing longer chunks of text in one go. In any case, differences in performance within each age group are far larger than those between age groups. Since older workers are not a homogeneous group, age is not much use for predicting how someone will perform in a job.

Some employers are taking the hint. In Britain, B&Q, a do-it-yourself chain, has tried staffing some of its stores with over-50s, who are more experienced and better at dealing with customers than younger workers. Sainsbury and Tesco, two large supermarket chains, have recently been recruiting staff up to 69, partly in response to labour shortages. In France, Aérospatiale has introduced incentives for its experienced staff to stay on until 60, and at Société Générale Sucrière employees between 55 and 60 in part-time retirement come to work during the beet harvest. In America, the Travelers Insurance Group offers pensioners the opportunity to come back part-time. There are other examples, but not many: the same names crop up over and over.

Legislation seems unlikely to help spread this good practice. America is the only country with a comprehensive law against discrimination in recruitment, training, promotion or dismissal on the basis of age. Its Age Discrimination in Employment Act, introduced in 1967, originally applied only to people aged between 40 and 65 but was later extended without limit, doing away with mandatory retirement on age grounds altogether. Yet in reviewing the legislation, the American Congress concluded that age discrimination remains an obstacle to employment for older workers, and that "statutory provisions . . . remain incomplete and somewhat ineffective." Opinion surveys show that 80% of Americans—the same proportion as in Europe—believe that most employers discriminate against older workers. Legislation may merely have made employers more careful to hide their prejudices.

Other countries have the odd law here and there, but nothing as comprehensive as America. The only country that has incorporated specific protection against age discrimination is Spain. In

France, a legal ban on age limits in job advertisements has been in place for some years, but is widely acknowledged to be ineffective. Something may be done at European Union level when the Maastricht treaty is revised later this year, perhaps in the form of a general article that would prohibit discrimination on a number of grounds including age. The hope is that this will help to create a climate of opinion against ageism.

Gently does it

Changing entrenched attitudes will take time. "The age of retirement will have to go up," says Winfried Schmähl, an expert on work for older people at Bremen University. "People understand what needs to be done—they are just not doing it yet." Another German academic, Gerd Naegele of the Institute of Gerontology at Dortmund University, agrees that the lead time must be long: "It takes 10-15 years for the business culture to adjust." But he also accepts that there are real problems employing older workers: "Many jobs have become psychologically more stressful, even if they are physically easier, and older people often find it difficult to handle that stress."

With retirement ages going up, many more older people are likely to run out of formal, conventional employment some time before they are able to draw their pensions. They will need "bridge" jobs, which are likely to be less prestigious, less well-paid and less skilled than the jobs they had in their main careers. They can also be hard to find. One way out, used widely in Japan and the United States, is for older workers to turn self-employed, usually in the same broad area that they worked in before. This can offer a dignified, flexible way to keep going.

The idea of making retirement less categorical and more gradual is catching on. In Britain, the Carnegie Inquiry into the Third Age, reporting in 1993, recommended flexible arrangements for older workers, including partial retirement, outplacements and secondments. In a recent report Geneviève Reday-Mulvey, of the International Association for the Study of Insurance Economics, and Lei Delsen of Nijmegen University argue strongly against what they call "guillotine retirement". Instead, they advocate a flexible transition period between a full-time career and full retirement, typically lasting about five years, which can both spread the pensions burden and give individuals more choice. The spread of part-time employment in a number of countries may offer opportunities along these lines.

Within Europe, such a policy has been successfully practised in Sweden for 20 years, and kept more older people at work than elsewhere in Europe, even through a severe recession. Sweden suffers less from age discrimination than other European countries, and is more used to flexible working, to part-time jobs and to state labour-market subsidies. But the scheme proved too good to last: faced with mounting budget deficits, the Swedish government is phasing out the financial incentives by 2000. Perhaps by then the Swedes will take gradual retirement for granted.

Of all the rich countries, Japan keeps its people (or at least its men) at work longest. Although at present the mandatory pension age is only 60, more than a third of Japanese men over 65 are still at work. Since life expectancies in Japan are now the highest in the world—76 at birth for a man, 82 for a woman—that may be a good thing. In a country which by 2030 will have some 32m over-65s, well over a quarter of the population, it would be unwise to encourage expectations of early retirement. To reinforce the message, Japan has reformed its pension system so that by early next century the basic state pension starts at 65, and early retirement will become less attractive. The government also offers various subsidies for firms employing people over 60.

Making this work has required flexibility all round. For example, the regular pay rises that in Japan go with increasing seniority now mostly stop at 50. Workers who retire at the mandatory retirement age of 60 are often re-employed either by their firms or by a subsidiary, but this always involves a big cut in pay and sometimes a move to part-time work. Many retirees become self-employed. In a survey of Japanese employees, some 60% said they wanted to go on working even after 65, possibly part-time—not so much for financial reasons, but because they thought it would help them maintain good health and remain active in society. Perhaps these long-lived people know something the West does not. But perhaps the size of their prospective pension has something to do with it after all.

Penury or plenty?

*It all depends on
your pension
scheme*

BLAME Bismarck. Until 1889, when Prussia's Iron Chancellor introduced the world's first national contributory pension scheme, governments were untroubled by any responsibility to provide for their citizens' declining years. If people grew too old to work—and not many survived that long—it was up to their families to look after them. Failing that, there was always the poorhouse.

These days, governments in the OECD countries spend an average of 9% of their gross domestic product on pensions; already a bit more than their average spending on health, and set to rise far faster. Some are more generous than others: in Austria, state pensions absorb nearly 15% of GDP, in America only 6.5%. But whatever the level of provision, the state everywhere remains in principle committed to supporting the old. Even in America, where the quest for a balanced budget has caused many assumptions to be re-examined, conversations about social security (the programme that pays for state pensions) always seem to lead up to the phrase: "It's like the third rail: touch it, and you're dead."

Yet in both America and Europe, people have

become more aware of the demographic problems that loom ahead, and most expect to get a worse pension than they have been promised. In a survey in 1994, 80% of Americans of working age felt "not too confident" or "not at all confident" that social security would provide them with the same benefits as today's pensioners. Not that they were doing much about it: almost the same percentage said that in order to live comfortably in retirement, they should be saving more than they were.

In most rich countries, retired people are on average much better off in relation to the rest of the

Some richer, some poorer 4
Median income of people over 65 as % of national median income*
- All elderly households
- Elderly married couples
- Elderly women living alone

Source: Luxembourg Income Study   *Latest available year †Western

population than they used to be (see chart 4). They get their income from a variety of sources: a state pension, sometimes an occupational pension, savings and investments, possibly a job. The relative importance of these sources depends on the country and the individual, but for most people in most countries the state pension is the biggest element, often making up half of total income.

Since pensioners have usually finished paying off their mortgages and bringing up their children, their expenses tend to be lower than those of younger households. As a group, therefore, they seem fairly comfortable. Many pensioners themselves are happy with their lot: in a survey in the European Union, a little over half said their pensions were "completely adequate" or "just about adequate". That, of course, leaves nearly half who said they were "somewhat inadequate" or "very inadequate", but most of those were concentrated in countries where pensioners get a poor deal. In Greece, over 80% said their pensions were inadequate; conversely, in Germany nearly 80% said theirs were adequate.

Pensioners' relative affluence is beginning to excite the imagination of marketing men, after a period of relative neglect. Older people spend differently from the young: they already have a lot of possessions, and wear them out less quickly than the young do. But they may be in the market for retirement property, and make a tempting target for many other items, including financial services, travel, leisure activities, health care and telecoms.

As a group, pensioners are also asset-rich, even if their cash-flow is lower than it was during their working lives. They have had a lifetime to acquire houses or financial assets, and some of them (eg, property owners in Japan) have seen their investments grow to many times their original values.

Some countries are now toying with reverse-mortgage schemes that allow home-owners to release that cash, but so far these have not caught on widely, except in France.

In America, people over 50 are said to own two-thirds of the nation's capital stock. But in America, too, over 10m of them have incomes at or below the official poverty threshold. The worst-off everywhere are older women, who live longer than men but, having often stayed out of the labour market, tend to fall through cracks in support systems.

In most rich countries, though, those support systems are reasonably effective. Since they are provided mainly by the state, the dramatic rise in the number of pensioners due in 30 years or so raises the question whether governments can go on providing the bulk of most people's retirement income. All state pension schemes, however they may be dressed up, work on the pay-as-you-go principle, which means that contributions collected from today's workers are recycled to today's pensioners. Some analysts argue that funded systems are cheaper and less risky, but the difficulty of getting from one to the other, placing a double burden on an unfortunate generation or two, has proved an effective deterrent.

The current ratio in most developed countries is around four or five people of working age for every person over 65. But by 2025 that ratio will be down to about three to one in America and around two-and-a-half to one in most European countries. Add in dependent children and young people, and workers look seriously overstretched.

Unmanageable

If nothing is done, not only will workers have to pay too much but public finances in some rich countries will take a spectacular turn for the worse. The OECD recently calculated that pension spending as a percentage of GDP, now in single figures in most countries (see chart 5), will rise to 14-20% in Japan, Germany, France and Italy in the first few decades of the next century. In America, Britain and Canada the share will remain more manageable at 5-8%, thanks to modest pensions and a relatively smaller number of elderly people. But the level of public debt is bound to rise sharply everywhere except in Britain. America's net debt is forecast to leap from about 40% of GDP now to around 100% by 2030, mainly because of burgeoning health-care costs. In France and Germany, bigger pension commitments are expected to push net debt to twice its current levels, and in Italy the prospects look even worse. In Japan, where the population is ageing more rapidly than anywhere else, net debt of just 13% of GDP now is forecast to rise to around 300% by 2030.

Can this possibly be allowed to happen? "None of the national programmes for the ageing in the main developed countries is sustainable," says Bill Lewis, head of the McKinsey Global Institute, a think-tank for the management consultancy of the same name. In a recent study on worldwide prospects for capital markets (which did not take in some of the most recent reforms), the institute came to similarly gloomy conclusions on future debt levels as the OECD, except for a more optimistic forecast for Japan. But McKinsey also thought that in

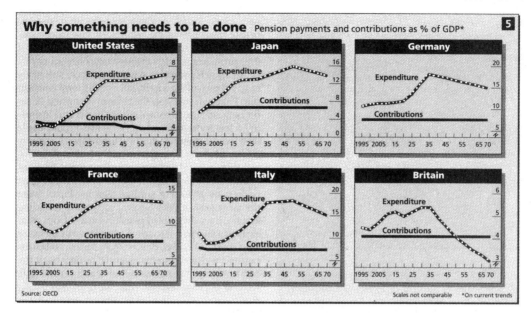

Why something needs to be done Pension payments and contributions as % of GDP* 5

United States — Japan — Germany — France — Italy — Britain

Source: OECD   Scales not comparable   *On current trends

the real world the debt ratios would never be allowed to rise to such levels, because any figure much above 150% of GDP would land the country concerned in a debt trap. Instead, says McKinsey, the countries with the worst prospects will have to cut spending, increase taxes or raise the retirement age—or a combination of all of these. If they fail to act, "they will face some form of crisis."

In the pensions debate, the word "crisis" crops up a lot. The World Bank caused a stir about a year ago with a weighty study entitled "Averting the Old Age Crisis", in which it argues that the present strong reliance on mandatory pay-as-you-go state pensions is doomed by demography. Public pensions' share in total retirement income, it says, should be reduced to around 20%, and their main role confined to "reducing poverty among the old". The main pension plank for the future should be mandatory, privately managed savings schemes that would be genuinely funded rather than pay-as-you-go. This would separate out the insurance function of pensions (a job for the state) from the savings function (a job for the private sector).

The sort of thing the Bank has in mind is the system that Chile introduced in 1981 to replace its unsatisfactory public pay-as-you-go scheme. The Chilean system requires all wage and salary earners to contribute 10% of their pay (up to a ceiling) to one of a number of private-sector pension funds that invest the money on their behalf. If a worker is not happy with his pension fund's performance, he can switch to another, a possibility that keeps the fund managers on their competitive toes. At retirement, the money in the fund provides each worker with an indexed annuity, or a pension based on his contribution. Neither employer nor state gets involved, nor is there any redistribution between the generations. What you put in, plus what the investment produces, is what you get out.

So far, so good for Chile. In the scheme's first 12 years, a time of rapid economic growth, the pension funds' average real rate of return was a whopping 14.7% a year. But what if growth had been slower or returns poorer? And what if Chile's public finances had not happened to be in surplus

when the scheme was introduced, enabling the government to pick up most of the considerable cost of switching from an unfunded (pay-as-you-go) to a funded system?

Saving grace

Critics of the World Bank report say that a system along Chilean lines is suitable only for developing countries with a poorly developed infrastructure. But the idea of giving the private sector a larger share of the pensions business is gaining ground in rich countries too. One advantage claimed for it is that it encourages saving. Savings ratios in most rich countries have been declining for several decades. By historical standards, they are currently low everywhere except in Japan. As populations age, both government and private savings are likely to come down further. Private pension schemes seem to make fewer inroads into other private saving than compulsory state schemes. One study in America showed that, for every dollar invested in funded occupational pension plans, other house-

No two alike

Main features of state pensions in OECD countries

	Normal retirement age women/men	Covered years required for full pension	Payroll tax for pensions, workers/employers combined	Indexation of pensions tied to:	Benefit type*
Australia	60/65	0	–	Prices	MT
Austria	60/65	15	22.9	Wages	CR
Britain	60/65	40	18.8	Prices	CR
Canada	65/65	1	4.6	Prices	UF-MT-CR
France	60/60	37.5	19.8	Wages	CR
Germany	65/65	5	17.8	Net wages	CR
Ireland	65/65	3	17.7	na	CR-MT
Italy	55/60	15	26.2	Prices and wages	CR
Japan	65/65	25	16.9	Prices	CR
Holland	65/65	49	15.2	Wages	CR
Spain	65/65	15	16.7	Prices and wages	CR
Sweden	65/65	3	21.0	Prices	CR-UF
United States	65/65	10	12.4	Prices	CR

Source: OECD   *Contribution-related/means-tested/universal flat

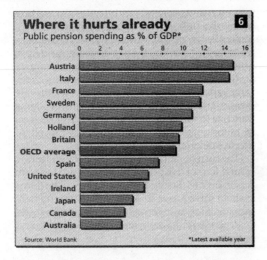

Where it hurts already
Public pension spending as % of GDP*

Source: World Bank   *Latest available year

thousands of pensioners would have been left penniless. Also in Britain, but in a different corner of the pensions jungle, a sudden burst of government enthusiasm for private portable pensions (not tied to a particular employer) enabled eager salesmen to talk large numbers of people into switching from perfectly good occupational pensions to overpriced and unsuitable private policies. The insurance companies have since been ordered to pay compensation. Such incidents suggest that governments must play a big regulatory role in occupational and private pension schemes—particularly if they provide a subsidy through tax concessions.

In all rich countries, governments are still likely to go on providing a hefty slice of the total pension pie. That will not stop them from trimming benefits here, adding to contributions there, and squeezing a few more years of working life out of people who would rather be tending their roses. Germany reformed its pension system in 1992, after discovering that if it carried on regardless, pension contributions would amount to well over a third of pay packets by 2030. For similar reasons, Japan went the same way in 1994. Several countries, including Britain, have decoupled pension growth from gross earnings and tied it to some less generous measure (see table). "Old" Sweden, with its luxurious but expensive welfare system, recently reined back the cost not only of pensions but of health care as well. As their populations age, will others follow?

hold savings declined by only 65 cents, leaving an appreciable net gain in total savings.

However, private pension schemes have their flaws. In Britain, where occupational pensions account for a large slice of total retirement income, the risks caught the limelight when Robert Maxwell, the head of a large company, was posthumously found to have used the company's pension fund money for a series of speculative ventures, and lost much of it. Without a huge rescue operation,

Downhill slide, uphill struggle

*Paying for a
mountain of
health-care bills*

A S PEOPLE everywhere are living longer, the hope is that they will also stay in good shape until a correspondingly later age. If they do, the medical costs of ageing populations should be containable; if they do not, the bills will mount fearfully. The evidence is patchy, and not particularly encouraging. For example, in a study in England and Wales, some 60% of the extra life expectancy gained in the past 20 years was found to be free of disability. That leaves 40% of the extra time spent in poor health.

What is clear is that the age at which people in rich countries are considered "old" has been creeping up. Old age used to start at the official retirement age of 65, if not earlier. In a pop song of the 1960s, the Beatles wondered:

When I get older, losing my hair,
Many years from now,
Will you still be sending me a Valentine,
Birthday greetings, bottle of wine ...
When I'm 64.

At the beginning of this century, those who made it to retirement age at all were in a small minority. At birth, a man born in America in 1900 could expect to live to 48, a woman—the longer-lived sex almost everywhere, despite the perils of childbirth—51. Yet Americans born in 1990 can expect to live to 72 and 79 respectively, thanks to healthier living conditions, better medical care, a lower risk of acute and infectious diseases, and less physical grind at work. So in less than a century their expected lifespan has

increased by around half, and still continues to rise.

There is little evidence, however, that the normal life span of human beings has been extended. Instead, many more people are reaching the age they were designed for, because they have fewer mishaps on the way. They no longer die "before their time" of some bug or accident, but succumb to some degenerative disease such as heart trouble or cancer. Indeed, even these can be curbed by healthier lifestyles. In Japan, for example, deaths from strokes have dropped dramatically over the past 25 years, simply because of a less salty diet and a higher consumption of fresh fruit and vegetables.

All this has meant that living to the magical age of 100 is no longer such a rare feat. In Britain, centenarians still get a telegram of congratulation from the queen, but her workload may soon become unsustainable. In America the 1990 census counted 38,000 people over 100. In the end, though, no matter how sensible the lifestyle and how good the medical care, human bodies still wear out. The oldest person in the world with documents to prove it, France's Jeanne Calment, is 120. For the moment, that seems to be about the limit—unless recent advances in gene therapy produce a breakthrough.

Governments and international organisations are now trying to measure "healthy life expectancy" for older people, which does not necessarily mean freedom from any kind of disease but freedom from crippling disability. Perhaps predictably, the figures that have emerged show wide variations, both between countries and between men and women. Although women on average live longer, men at advanced ages seem to suffer from fewer disabilities. The tentative conclusion so far is that while more people are surviving into old age, most will have some degree of handicap, perhaps because improved diagnosis and care are making chronic disease less often fatal.

Diminishing returns

That tallies with the evidence that in many countries it is the group of the "oldest old" (the least likely to be in rude health) that is growing fastest. In 1900 America had only 374,000 over-80s; by 1990, the figure had gone up to more than 7m. By 2020, the number of over-80s in all OECD countries will have at least doubled.

This suggests that health spending in future will be concentrated even more than it is now on the last third of life, and particularly on the last few years. Already in America the over-65s account for a third of total health spending, even though they make up only 13% of the population. Some treatments for mainly age-related problems, such as cataract operations and hip replacements, have become so widespread that older people in rich countries consider them routine. Hospital stays for over-65s are invariably longer than for younger people, and therefore more costly. Further medical advances are constantly adding new treatments, some of which are very expensive.

Where health care is being paid for from public funds—which means in most OECD countries— governments are making heroic efforts to ensure that the service is provided at the lowest possible cost: by better management, by more effective use of technology, and often tacitly by rationing. This is unlikely to work in older people's favour. Although medical ethics prescribe that the age of a patient should make no difference to the treatment proposed, the decision is bound to be affected by calculations of remaining lifespans.

In a recent study by two Swedish professors at the Stockholm School of Economics, Magnus Johannesson and Per-Olov Johansson, a random sample of Swedes were asked about their preferences for allocating scarce medical resources. To save the life of one 30-year-old, they were willing, on average, to trade the lives of five 50-year-olds or 35 70-year-olds. All age groups responded in much the same way. The professors also asked another sample of Swedes how much they would be willing to pay for a hypothetical programme to extend their life by one year beyond 75. On average, the respondents said they would pay no more than SKr10,000 (about $1,520). In a country where provision for old people is particularly generous, that response gives pause for thought.

Growing numbers of people are making "living wills", setting out in advance at what point they want medical intervention to stop in the event of terminal illness. In America, a majority of older people seems to approve of the idea that an individual should be able to choose when treatment stops. But whereas failure to keep someone alive in these circumstances is legally permissible, voluntary euthanasia requiring active intervention is illegal everywhere, although in Holland it is tolerated in some circumstances.

For most older people, and their families, the course of events after retirement will be more mundane. Initially, and often for a long time, they may be in good health and enjoy an active life. But as the decades slip by, they become more likely to suffer from any of a number of diseases that can cause chronic disability: heart trouble, stroke, osteoporosis, multiple sclerosis, Alzheimer's. Eventually they may find it difficult to get about and do simple everyday things such as housekeeping, eating, washing, dressing. At that point they will need help.

Whether they get it, and in what form, will be more a matter of good luck than good management. It depends, among other things, on the country they live in, their family circumstances, their cash-flow, and what is available in their particular locality (see box on next page). Traditionally, dependent old people have been cared for by their families. A large family was an insurance policy against indigent and lonely old age. But with families becoming smaller and more mobile, divorce much more common, and a great many more women working outside the home, this tradition is being eroded fast.

For a mixture of cultural and economic reasons, the practice has been most carefully preserved in Japan, where four out of five old people are still looked after in a family setting. But enthusiasm even there is waning, and Japanese women—who bear most of the burden of caring for the older generation—are becoming restive. Still, there is no suggestion of reviving the practice in Edo Japan's poor peasant families of *uba sute* (literally, throw old mother away): carrying old women off to the mountainside once their spouses had died, to save the cost of feeding them.

Given a choice, most old people in western countries would prefer to live on their own, just as their children would prefer not to have the older generation under the same roof. The proportion living alone has been rising steeply over the past few decades, and now averages 30-40%. In Denmark it has reached over half. This does not necessarily mean the older people are not on friendly terms with their families; they may live quite close and see a lot of each other. They just prefer to keep out of each other's hair. A study in Florida found that three-quarters of elderly parents lived within 25 miles of their children, and the vast majority saw them at least once a week.

But in real life people do not live happily ever after. As they get older, they may become frail or disabled and can no longer manage on their own. In the absence of a family carer, the last-ditch solution used to be to send them to a nursing home. But as pressures on public finances are rising, many countries are now shifting the emphasis away from residential care. The best policy, runs the new wisdom, is to enable the elderly to "age in place" by providing them with help in their own homes as and when they need it. Again, that also happens to be what most old people would prefer.

Decline with dignity

Much can be done by adapting fixtures and fittings, installing alarm buttons, providing home helps and offering day-care centres. But as an old person needs increasing amounts of care, an institution may become the most economical way to provide it. Much the biggest chunk of the money spent on long-term care still goes into institutions, despite the policy shift towards "ageing in place". Such institutions are, and always will be, expensive to run. The typical cost of keeping an old person in a nursing home in a rich country exceeds gross average earnings; and the typical length of stay is about three years. That adds up to serious money.

As more and more people survive to the age when they need nursing care, governments face a dilemma. Should they provide such care for everyone who needs it, and clobber the taxpayer with the bill? Or should they ask individuals to pay for themselves, coming to the (means-tested) rescue only when the money finally runs out—which seems to discriminate against those who have saved up during their working lives? A way out might be to encourage people to insure themselves privately against the possibility of long-term care. Such policies are on offer in several countries, but they can

be prohibitively expensive. The annual premium for a good long-term care policy in America is around $2,200 for a 65-year-old and about $7,700 for a 79-year-old. Insurance experts are concerned about adverse selection (meaning that such schemes attract the worst risks) and moral hazard (meaning that, knowing they are insured, people behave differently). It makes them wonder whether long-term care is an insurable risk at all.

If private insurance is impractical, and means-tested public provision not acceptable, what else can be done? A radical solution recently adopted in Germany (and now being seriously considered by Japan) is to have a mandatory insurance scheme covering the whole population. In Germany, since the beginning of last year all employers and employees have been contributing a joint 1% of payroll to a new mandatory long-term care scheme. Opposition from employers was overcome by abolishing one of Germany's many religious holidays, which shifted most of the cost to employees. Those in need

A place to call home

YO HATAKEYAMA, manager of the Fukueikai Home for Older People in Tokyo's Shinagawa ward, clearly takes his job seriously. Printed on the back of his visiting card is a handy summary of ten commandments to avoid becoming bedridden. "Don't stay in bed," says the first rule. The carer, too, is enjoined to foster independence: "Don't take too much care." Mr Hatakeyama explains: "If people are nursing an old person at home, they sometimes find it easier to do everything for him. But it would be better if the old person did more for himself."

Many of the residents of the Fukueikai Home for Older People are so frail that they cannot do much for themselves, but they are certainly encouraged to try. The modern seven-storey building houses 80 bedridden and 50 less disabled residents with an average age of 81. The place is spotlessly clean, as are the residents. The traditional Japanese bath on the premises is specially adapted for the wheelchair-bound. Recreation is of the sedentary kind: a little gardening in flower pots, a lot of snoozing and plenty of TV. Accommodation is mostly in four-bed rooms: again gleaming, but with little space for personal possessions.

The Fukueikai Home's 140 residents can consider themselves fortunate in several ways: their home is rated as "above average", and the local authority that owns it provides help for those who cannot afford the charges of ¥340,000 (about $3,200) a month. But their biggest stroke of luck is to be there

at all. Because of Tokyo's vertiginous land prices, nursing homes in the capital are in desperately short supply. Although only those without any family qualify, the waiting lists stretch to 10,000. So what do these people do while they wait? "Half of them are in hospital," says Mr Hatakeyama. In Japan, that is where old people in need of nursing care have traditionally ended up. Their average hospital stays are about ten times as long as in America, though they are now being cut short by increasingly cost-conscious managements. That tradition of hospital care may have inspired the Fukueikai Home's design: at a pinch, it could pass for a hospital itself.

The Miami Jewish Home & Hospital for the Aged at Douglas Gardens is, literally and figuratively, a world away from the Fukueikai Home. From small beginnings 50 years ago, Douglas Gardens now occupies a 20-acre campus in the middle of Miami's Haitian quarter that houses a 462-bed nursing home, a 32-bed geriatric hospital, a 68-bed short-term rehabilitation centre and 102 sheltered flats for older people. The average age of its residents—mainly, but not exclusively Jewish—is 87. It also provides outpatient services and day-care programmes for around 8,000 local people.

"This is the best thing that ever happened to me," says Edee, a resident in one of the flats. At 77 she is a comparative youngster, and still does part-time work in the home's office. She has no family, but the home, she says, provides

"tender loving care". Lilian, dressed in a neat white T-shirt and shorts exposing an artificial leg, has just finished taking a keep-fit class. At 80, she remains mentally as well as physically active. Her dearest wish is to see capitalism abolished, but political discussions do not go down well with co-residents.

Permanent summer and palm trees dotted around the courtyards help the relaxed atmosphere. Indoors, a lot of thought has gone into the design to make it more like a home and less like an institution—including such details as using only large-patterned wallpapers that old people can see.

But it takes more than the right wallpaper to become south-east Florida's largest centre for geriatric care. Among other things, it takes money. Douglas Gardens has been highly successful at persuading wealthy sponsors to pay for ever more capital investment, helped by its contacts among well-off members of the Jewish community and supported by a fund-raising staff of eight. One of the more recent additions is a series of 20 expensively furnished luxury suites in which seriously rich frail old people can be looked after in comfort. The charges of $7,000 a month are clearly no deterrent: the suites are always full. Such facilities, says the home, help to cross-subsidise its standard nursing-home beds, three-quarters of which are eligible for Medicaid, the federal/state programme for the poor.

It goes without saying that Douglas Gardens has not just one, but several waiting lists. Like the Fukueikai Home, it is rated as superior quality. And as in Tokyo, you need to be lucky to get in. Try sponsoring a new wing?

were immediately able to claim generous help with caring for old people at home, including cash allowances. Next July, when the contributions go up to 1.7% of payroll, the scheme will also cover most of the cost of nursing-home care.

For a country already groaning under a huge welfare burden, and still busy digesting the cost of unification, that seemed a rash move. But the debate had been going on for decades. Previously the state would pay for nursing care only if the individual had no money left, and had no close relatives who could be asked to help. Yet ordinary Germans with a full contributions record resented having to go to the state cap in hand. "People felt it was undignified," explains Klaus Achenbach at the labour ministry in Bonn.

The cost of nursing care, however heavy, may look like a problem for just a small minority: in rich countries, on average only about 5% of over-65s live in some kind of nursing home. But the average is misleading, because one in four very old people eventually ends up in a home. As populations age, demand will grow. For a glimpse of the future, go to Florida, where tomorrow's demographics are already in place.

The perfect sunset

In Florida, the future has already arrived

IF THERE is one place on earth that epitomises the modern retirement dream, it is Florida. In one of the richer states in the world's richest country, 3.2m over-60s are seeking golden years of leisured, happy maturity. Over the past 15 years the number of older people has risen by nearly half, and still they come (although a little more slowly now), bringing their savings and entitlements with them. Only a third of the state's 13.7m people are native Floridians. The over-60s account for nearly a quarter of the population, a proportion the rest of America does not expect to reach until well into the next century. Florida has got there double-quick.

What is the draw? One wealthy resident recalls that after the second world war Americans used to save up for a couple of weeks' holiday on Florida's sunny, palm-fringed beaches. By the 1960s they found they were able to buy apartments and houses there for quite modest sums, allowing them to come back over and over again—and eventually to retire there. So they bought, and Florida built, starting on the coast and gradually working away from it through the mangrove swamps, sometimes up to five or ten miles inland.

It was a cut-price paradise: no heating costs, no need to buy thick clothes or eat large meals to keep warm. Those savings proved handy when rapid inflation in the 1970s wrought havoc with occupational pensions, most of which were not index-linked. Some of the previously comfortable pensioners had to go back to work—say, bag-packing at the local supermarket—to make ends meet.

But that is only one side of Florida. There are also large numbers of rich pensioners living in considerable luxury, and any number of gradations in-between. The needs and interests of this diverse group of older people vary as much as those of any age group. "People look at the over-60s the way they look at homogenised milk", says a disapproving Bentley Lipscomb, secretary of Florida's Department of Elder Affairs (see box on terminology, next page). But unlike homogenised milk, the different groups rarely mix. Tell a Floridian where you live, and he will be able to take an educated guess not only at the state of your bank balance but also your political persuasion, home state and former occupation. But trailer park or grand mansion, Florida's sun shines on them all.

That, in essence, is what the pensioners have come for, and what gives the extra edge to the state's man-made attractions, which are numerous. Take Century Village at Pembroke Pines, mid-way between Miami and Fort Lauderdale, miles inland but criss-crossed with artificial lakes dug out to drain the swampy site. New houses and flats for 12,000 people are spread out over 700 acres of carefully planted and manicured greenery, including a golf course (on which players may not walk during main business hours: electric carts only). A $10m clubhouse with a surfeit of squashy seats, plastic potted plants, a vast theatre and a pool room offers a choice of activities including bridge, keep-fit sessions, classes in "creative clay" and plenty more. The key word is lifestyle. Having reached a certain age, the epicurean residents are absolutely determined to enjoy themselves today; for who knows what tomorrow holds?

They are also determined to have peace in every sense. Century Village is marketed as an "adult community", officially for people over 18, but in reality for the over-60s—often well over. Children and pets are banned, "except fully grown giraffes and elephants kept in your apartment", explains a salesman, allowing himself an end-of-day joke. Perhaps even more important is the peace of mind that comes with the sturdy fence around the whole community, the 24-hour guard on the entry gate and the regular security patrols throughout the village. Florida is a state with a reputation for violent crime. The sales brochure comes straight to the point: "You can take walks after dark or take off for a month or more, knowing that [only approved people] will be allowed access to the enclosed private community." The cheapest one-bedroom flats cost $60,000, and buyers also need to allow for charges and taxes starting at $300 a month. But plenty seem able to afford it: this is Century Village's fourth venture in Florida.

To be sure, the prospect of living in a vibrant community exclusively made up of senior citizens does not appeal to everybody. About 5% of those who come to settle in Florida eventually leave again, often when they get older and frailer and want to be near their families. And some get plain bored. One affluent couple who spend the summer in England and the winter in Florida (a species known as "snowbirds") are thinking of selling their luxurious house at Boca Raton. "There is not much to talk about. The main topic of conversation is money: the interest rate people are getting, how their investments are doing. And the men brag about their game of golf. After a while it gets monotonous."

But that is a minority view. On the whole, Florida makes it its business to deliver what the majority expects of it. "Older people are an industry here", says Harold Sheppard, a professor at the department of gerontology at Tampa University. That is why they have their own ministry, with a budget running to $200m in 1995-96. The department was set up in 1992 "to maximise opportunities for self-sufficiency and personal independence of Florida's elders and to plan, advocate and administer programmes and policies that assure accessible, responsive and comprehensive services and long-term care." A few other states with large old populations have similar departments, but Florida's is the only one with a seat at the state cabinet table. It even publishes a monthly newspaper, *Elder Update*, which carries a mass of useful information—from telephone numbers of "Elder Helplines" to advice on nutrition, health, claiming benefits and surviving hurricanes.

Some say Florida is paying too much attention to its old and not enough to its young. In a new book, Susan MacManus, another professor at Tampa University, points to intergenerational conflicts of interest that are already emerging in Flor-

ida and are likely to spread to the rest of America (and to other countries) as populations age. The most obvious example is a financial battle between education and law and order.

Slowly going mad

Another focus for Florida's older-people industry is health care, and making the most of Medicare and Medicaid, the two government programmes for older people that are now threatened by budget cuts. The energetic 65-year-olds who moved in 20 years ago are now less active and have become much heavier consumers of medical services and nursing care. Over the past 15 years the number of over-85s in Florida has more than doubled, to 266,000. At some point or other, around a quarter of them become residents of one of Florida's 600 nursing homes, where charges are typically around $38,000 a year. They pay for themselves until they run out of money, which on average happens after an all-too-brief two months. Then it is Medicaid's turn. No wonder the search is on for ways of looking after people at home instead of in nursing homes, at around a tenth of the cost. Fearing that once the beds are there, they will be used, Florida has become deliberately sticky about allowing new nursing homes to be built. Already Medicaid nursing-home spending in Florida has risen from $200m in 1980 to over $1.6 billion last year. If current trends continue, say forecasters, that figure could rise to $9 billion by 2010.

One trend that has helped to keep the nursing homes occupied has been a growing number of patients suffering from Alzheimer's disease (a form of senile dementia). Nobody really knows whether

You are old, Father William

FOR all its impending ubiquity, old age remains resolutely unfashionable. People want to look youthful. They pay money to have their hair tinted, face lifted, tummy tucked. They lie about their age. Marketing efforts aimed at older people invariably show beaming couples in peak condition, never old ladies in wheelchairs. Employers ostracise anyone with a hint of a wrinkle. Even geriatric medicine turns out to be an unpopular speciality.

American academics have combed the work of the great poets for role models for older people, and dismissed them as negative and unhelpful. The Bard himself is one of the worst. Everyone knows his unforgivable lines from "As You Like It" about the seven ages of man, ending with "Second childishness, and mere oblivion, sans teeth, sans eyes, sans taste, sans everything". Wordsworth does better with "An old age, serene and bright, and lovely as a Lapland night, shall lead thee to thy grave", but the poem turns out to be ad-

dressed to a young lady. Swift shows a flash of insight ahead of his time with "Every man desires to live long; but no man would be old."

Calling others old has become politically incorrect. In olden days, when few people lived to their dotage, being ancient was something to be proud of. But now that three score and ten is the norm for everyone, even the terminology needs a facelift.

So what might be a suitable late-20th-century alternative to the o-word? Clearly not "wrinklies"; that was invented by rude children in the 1980s to offend their parents. Not "dumpies", a disagreeable abbreviation for "destitute unprepared mature people". Not "golden oldies" either: that got the thumbs-down in a European Union poll aiming to discover what over-60s wanted to be called.

The same European poll also uncovered little enthusiasm for "the elderly". The Americans seem to agree. The state of Florida used to have a min-

istry called the "Department of Elderly Affairs", which suddenly resurfaced as the "Department of Elder Affairs". Similarly, what started off as the UN "year of the elderly" in 1999 was rebadged as the "year of older persons".

"Retired" is not quite the ticket either, if only because some of the people concerned are still working. Although the word appears in the title of the American Association of Retired Persons, nobody ever calls the organisation anything but the AARP. The AARP's magazine gets round the problem by calling itself *Modern Maturity*.

The two monikers that the Europeans liked best were, in ascending order, "older people" and "senior citizens". This last sounds like a winner. "Senior" oozes authority and experience, and "citizen" has a powerful resonance to it: citizens have rights and votes. Unfortunately the term has suffered from overuse in combinations such as "senior citizens' bus pass" and "senior citizens' coffee morning". Time, perhaps, to try something new, fresh and positive from America: "the chronologically advantaged".

this is becoming more widespread, or merely better diagnosed, but the figures are stark: 350,000 sufferers in Florida now, forecast to rise to around half a million by the end of the decade. The American Medical Association reckons that nearly one in two over-85s suffers from some stage of Alzheimer's, and no breakthrough cure is in sight. Since the disease attacks the mind rather than the body, it drags on: patients on average live for eight more years after diagnosis, often needing round-the-clock care. Even in Florida's sunshine, the old-people industry has its gloomy side.

No alternative

The contract between the generations needs renegotiating, not ditching

This survey has benefited from conversations with many individuals around the world, all of whom have been remarkably generous with their time and expertise. The survey has also drawn on a number of written sources, both published and unpublished. The OECD has produced an excellent range of comparative studies on various aspects of this subject. Other useful recent books referred to in the text include:
"Averting the Old Age Crisis", World Bank. Oxford University Press, 1994.
"Gradual Retirement in the OECD Countries", edited by Lei Delsen and Geneviève Reday-Mulvey. Dartmouth Publishing Company, 1996.
"Young v Old", by Susan A. MacManus. Westview Press, 1996.

WILL it all end in tears? The doomsters fear it must, unless something drastic is done now. Otherwise, they say, by around 2030, when in some developed countries each pensioner will be supported by only two workers, the young and the old will be at daggers drawn; and public finances will be in a fine old mess.

Such gloomy predictions have their uses. In this instance, they have prepared the ground for politically painful cuts in pensions and other spending on the elderly that will make it easier to adjust to ageing populations. Since the predicted calamity is still some way off, reactions have been slow, but some countries have made a start, notably by increasing the retirement age. That makes sense when people in rich countries now live 20-30 years longer than they did a century ago; it also needs to be announced a long way ahead to give them time to plan their lives. The other obvious remedies—raising contributions and limiting benefits in various ways—are also being pursued, though so far at a desultory pace.

Such specific measures apart, the most helpful thing that governments can do is to create the best possible environment for economic growth. The bigger the cake available for sharing out, the less vicious the fight over the crumbs is likely to be. Economists are now suggesting that quite modest growth rates, if sustained, could make life in 2030 look a lot more cheerful than it has been painted. "There has been a tendency to look at worst-case scenarios, because times have been bad recently," says Elizabeth Duskin, senior economist in the OECD's labour and social affairs directorate. The OECD is taking another look at all its recent studies on ageing to see what member countries should actually be doing to ward off the problems.

But even if a future with many more old people turns out less gloomy than advertised, it will be different from the past in important ways, because older people are different from younger people. In 1790 the median age in America was 16. In 1990 it was 33. By the middle of the next century it will be well over 40, maybe even 50. The trend in other developed countries is much the same. It is inconceivable that such a shift in a country's centre of gravity will make no difference to its habits and priorities.

If being middle-aged or older becomes the norm rather than the exception, the definition of "old" will have to be revisited. Already the present retirement age of 65 has stopped being considered a watershed for declining health and energy. The widespread silent assumption that "old" also means "decrepit" will have to be abandoned, or at least moved up the age scale by a couple of decades. Affluent older consumers will become an irresistible market for everything from cars to credit cards, all customised to suit their target group's tastes. The rise in the number of "oldest old", too, will open up new business opportunities, even if they are not to everybody's taste: nursing homes are already flourishing, and funeral parlours will get busier when the baby boomers start dying.

Intergenerational hostilities

Older voters, wielding ever-greater political power, will lend their support to policies that serve the interests of their age group: higher spending on health, social services and law and order. Spending on education may take a back seat. That could spell trouble between the generations. Already in America the young are complaining about "being screwed" by a well-organised and articulate older generation, many of whose members are more affluent than the younger people who have to contribute to their support. Perhaps neither of the two groups knows what makes the other tick: surveys suggest that most people think the young do not understand the elderly, and vice versa.

But a moment's reflection suggests that this divergence of interests should stop well short of intergenerational warfare. First, most older people have children who provide them with a window on the next generation or two, and may cause them to pursue their own interests less selfishly. Second, many younger people have surviving parents, whom they would rather see adequately supported by society than have to look after them personally. Third, younger people know full well that they themselves will get older, and tacitly assume that the next generation, collectively, will look after them in turn. By paying up today, they are accumulating a credit which they expect society to repay when they themselves get old. In short, they are investing in their own tomorrows.

The Experience of Dying

Modern science has allowed individuals to have some control over the conception of their children and has provided people with the ability to prolong life. But life and death still defy scientific explanation or reason. The world can be divided into two categories: sacred and secular. The sacred (that which is usually embodied in the religion of a culture) is used to explain all the forces of nature and the environment that can neither be understood nor controlled. On the other hand, the secular (defined as "of or relating to the world") is used to explain all the aspects of the world that *can* be understood or controlled. Through scientific invention, more and more of the natural world can be controlled. It still seems highly doubtful, however, that science will ever be able to provide an acceptable explanation of the meaning of death. In this domain, religion may always prevail.

Death is universally feared. Sometimes it is more bearable for those who believe in a life after death. Here, religion offers a solution to this dilemma. In the words of anthropologist Bronislaw Malinowski (1884–1942):

> Religion steps in, selecting the positive creed, the comforting view, the culturally valuable belief in immortality, in the spirit of the body, and in the continuance of life after death. (Bronislaw Malinowski, *Magic, Science and Religion and Other Essays*, Glencoe, Illinois: Free Press, 1948)

The fear of death leads people to develop defense mechanisms in order to insulate themselves psychologically from the reality of their own death. The individual knows that someday he/she must die, but this event is nearly always thought to be likely to occur in the far distant future. The individual does not think of himself or herself as dying tomorrow or the next day, but rather years from now. In this way people are able to control their anxiety about death.

Losing a close friend or relative brings people dangerously close to the reality of death. Individuals come face to face with the fact that there is always an end to life. Latent fears surface. During times of mourning, people grieve not only for the dead, but for themselves, and for the finiteness of life.

The readings in this section address bereavement, grief, arguments for and against euthanasia, and adjustments to the stages of dying. In "Euthanasia's Home: What the Death Experience Can Teach Americans about Assisted Suicide," the results of a nation's policy that has allowed physicians to assist the patient in dying as long as specified guidelines are followed are examined. Both the positive and negative results of legalized euthanasia are reviewed in "Euthanasia in the Netherlands," where the International Anti-Euthanasia Task Force points out the dangers of a nation that allows euthanasia. The group believes that the practice of euthanasia in the Netherlands has resulted in physicians and not patients making critical life or death decisions. Susan Brink, in "The American Way of Dying," observes that technologies available to doctors make it difficult for them to accept that there is nothing left to be done for the patient; thus living wills and other directives are often ignored in the hospital setting.

In the report "Going Home to Die," Karen Orloff Kaplan observes that more patients are choosing to die at home rather than in the hospital. Kaplan points out a number of advantages of dying at home for the dying person and to family members. Eleanor Weinel, in "Ashes to Ashes, Dust to Dust: Is There Any Future for Cemeteries?" points out that more people are opting for cremation. Many cemeteries, therefore, are now building columbariums (a structure of vaults for urns).

Looking Ahead: Challenge Questions

Is the fear of dying really universal? Do all people share it equally?

What are the techniques by which people alleviate their anxieties about dying?

Should dying patients be told the truth about their impending deaths, or should this information be withheld? Why?

Are the elderly more afraid of death than the young? Defend your answer.

UNIT 6

Euthanasia's home

What the Dutch experience can teach Americans about assisted suicide

Dr. Herbert Cohen was crossing the line. The elderly woman held out her arm and waited for an injection from the syringe in his hands. In the Netherlands, where Cohen is a physician, euthanasia is widely accepted. But this was 1976, when the practice was just gaining favor, and it was his first time. The woman closed her eyes. Her husband sat at her bedside. Twice, the doctor's needle missed her cramped veins. Then, a barbiturate and a muscle relaxant brought her sleep and death.

Cohen went on to perform euthanasia between 50 and 100 times (he won't give a precise number) until he gave up

Jack Kevorkian, the zealous Michigan suicide doctor, came. So did Timothy Quill, a physician who believes in the right to die and is a plaintiff in one of the cases before the Supreme Court. They found a compassionate system where patients can speak honestly about dying to supportive doctors like Cohen. Critics have also come, like psychiatrist Herbert Hendin. In his new book, *Seduced By Death,* he describes a system in which involuntary killing goes unpunished by the Dutch and courts grant dubious exceptions about who can be helped to die.

To all his American visitors, Cohen imparts the same message about copy-

year, usually because they moved. "That's not boasting," he says. "That's just the average." In general, a patient who gets help in dying has known the doctor an average of eight years: He is usually a *huisart.*

The bond between doctor and patient makes it easier for them to talk about death. Every midnight, Cohen visited the home of the woman who became his first euthanasia case. He gave her two injections, a painkiller and a diuretic to help her sleep. "This is a very particular night," she told the doctor on one call. "This is the 100th time you have come, and I think it's enough. I want it to stop." She had been reading about euthanasia and asked for Cohen's help. He stalled, hoping that her death would come naturally, but in the end gave in to her pleas.

In the American health care system, people switch doctors often. Some 150 million Americans, or 66 percent of the insured, are now in managed-care plans. Most of these provide good care, but there are growing clashes when doctors deny necessary care because of financial pressures to hold down costs.

A consensus society. On the books, euthanasia remains illegal in the Netherlands. Since the early 1970s, however, there has been an informal understanding between physicians and the government: Doctors who follow guidelines about euthanasia drawn up by doctors and endorsed by the government are rarely prosecuted. A patient must be mentally competent, request death voluntarily and repeatedly, and be suffering without prospect of relief. The doctor must consult with another physician. Under those circumstances, the courts ratify the consensus between doctors and prosecutors.

The Dutch pride themselves on civil discussion of the most difficult issues, without the kind of shouting from ex-

> DR. HERBERT COHEN SAYS DUTCH DOCTORS OFTEN DIVIDE THEIR LIVES INTO TWO ERAS—ONE BEFORE THEIR FIRST ASSISTED KILLING AND THE OTHER AFTER IT. HE'S ASSISTED IN DOZENS OF DEATHS.

his family practice a few years ago. Sometimes, he brought flowers. Sometimes, his patient gave him a bottle of wine and they toasted death together. Often, a minister present read the 23rd Psalm. Yet each time, Cohen says about helping a patient die, "it is a mountain you have to climb."

In the past generation, many Dutch doctors have made that ascent. The Netherlands has become the only country in the world that openly allows euthanasia. Both sides of the debate in the United States over physician-assisted suicide see the Netherlands as a model. The 24-year-old Dutch practice is extensively researched and unflinchingly considered. And Americans inevitably make their way to Cohen.

ing the Dutch system: "For goodness sakes, don't do it. You'll be in trouble." Other Dutch advocates of physician-assisted death repeat that warning. Euthanasia, says Gerrit van der Wal, a leading researcher of end-of-life care, "is not an export article." Conditions that make the practice of euthanasia acceptable in the Netherlands are absent in America. They are rooted in culture, politics and the provision of health care.

Doctor-patient relationship. The *huisart* (house doctor) is central to Dutch medicine. He is the gatekeeper who knows his patients well and refers them to specialists. An entire family may go to the same *huisart* for most of their lives. In Cohen's four decades of practice, only two or three patients left each

tremes that often marks American debate. Size helps explain why: Consensus is easier to achieve in a small country with a relatively homogenous population of only 15 million. So does national character: Individual choice is highly valued in a tolerant, secular country that has liberal attitudes about prostitution and marijuana use as well.

Dutch law is also based on consensus. Ethicist Evert Van Leeuwen thinks that a right to die like the one under review by the U.S. Supreme Court would undermine the trust among patients, doctors, and enforcers of the law that is central to the Dutch practice of euthanasia. In the Netherlands, patients cannot demand euthanasia. Patients and

dening their spouses and families: In a study in Washington State, that reason was cited by 75 percent of those who asked physicians to help them die. No wonder. In the United States, hospitalization and nursing home costs can impoverish. The Dutch face virtually no out-of-pocket expenses at the end of life.

A year ago, Pieter Bol, 71, suffered a stroke. Eight years ago, Francine van der Velden, 54, was paralyzed by a cerebral hemorrhage. They lie at the Rosendael Nursing Home and see euthanasia as a choice, not something that will be forced on them to avoid costly care. "From an ethical basis, you can only do euthanasia if you provide all other care as well," says their doctor, Johannes van

doctor) and 400 assisted suicides (by pills that the patient took himself). In 19,000 more cases—19 percent of all deaths that year—doctors ended treatment or administered potentially life-shortening dosages of pain control medicine. U.S. doctors do the same, but the Dutch are more candid about expecting the result of death.

The Dutch say their acceptance of euthanasia reflects respect for individual autonomy. After Elizabeth Pop's disabled granddaughter died, the elderly Dutch woman lost some of the identity she took from caring for the young woman. A year later, when Pop was diagnosed with leukemia, she sought euthanasia. Manda Kapil-Vissers is Pop's daughter. She says her mother was clearheaded, a "strong personality who hated being dependent." At 82, Pop set the date for her death, resolved issues with estranged family members, and planned details of her dying ceremony down to the color of the candles.

ELIZABETH POP METICULOUSLY PLANNED HER OWN DYING CEREMONY. DAUGHTER MANDA KAPIL-VISSERS NOW HAS A 'PASSPORT' AUTHORIZING HER OWN EUTHANASIA.

doctors talk about it as partners, and doctors make the final decision. "We do not talk in terms of rights," he says.

Surprisingly, only 37 percent of the patients who request help in dying actually get it, notes a government survey. Unlike what might be expected in America, however, the other 63 percent do not respond by going to court. In general, Dutch malpractice suits are rate. The cost of malpractice insurance for Cohen is about $100 a year. For the average American family physician, it is about $10,000 annually. In the concordant Netherlands, miscreant doctors often face tougher sanctions from their own medical society than from the courts.

Universal coverage. Ninety-nine percent of the Dutch have health insurance, which provides access to comprehensive care, including nursing homes. In the United States, by contrast, 40 million, about 15 percent of the population, have no insurance at all. In the Netherlands, then, "euthanasia is not a way out of social misery," Cohen says. "You don't have to request euthanasia because you can't get any medical attention."

Most Dutch patients—56 percent—seek euthanasia to avoid "useless suffering." On the other hand, Americans say they are motivated by the fear of bur-

Delden. "Otherwise, what's the point of offering a choice if there's really no choice?"

In the Netherlands as well, the rich and poor get comparable medical care. Unlike in the United States, family doctors are considered public servants and barely compete for the highest paying patients. When a widower with bone cancer asked for euthanasia, Dr. Gerrit Kimsma realized the man was lonely and lacked support from his family. The doctor called a meeting of the man's children and friends and arranged for someone to spend time with the dying man daily. Kimsma also visited, sometimes three times a day. He charged nothing for his visits. "Some activities," the doctor says, "have no price tag." In the United States, bottom-line pressures leave doctors with little time for personal care.

The practice of euthanasia is growing in the Netherlands. Requests for euthanasia jumped nearly 40 percent between 1990 and 1995. Most requests came from people with cancer who are 35 to 70 years old. The practice is particularly common for people with AIDS. One fifth to one third of deaths from the disease result from euthanasia. In 1995, there were 3,200 reported cases of euthanasia (by lethal injection from a

Still the requirement to notify prosecutors of euthanasia makes many doctors uncomfortable. As a result, and contrary to law, some three fifths of all Dutch cases of euthanasia go unreported. Some doctors say they want to spare themselves or their families the strain of scrutiny. Since 1981, in fact, only 20 doctors have been prosecuted for violating the Dutch guidelines and only six have received prison sentences—all suspended. But 1 in 5 of the unreported cases involved the most vexing kind of euthanasia, death without a patient's request.

There were 900 such cases in 1995. The Dutch do not even count them as euthanasia. In 79 percent of them, the patient was in a coma or unable to express a wish. And 52 percent of the time, the doctor claimed to know about the dying person's wish from talking with the patient. To critics, all 900 cases demonstrate that once a doctor has authority to end life, even under carefully regulated conditions, he will find it easy to do so in ambiguous situations.

Carlos Gomez, an American physician, interviewed Dutch doctors and discovered euthanasia cases that seemed to defy attempts to regulate the practice. One doctor told Gomez he had killed a newborn with Down's syndrome after the parents refused life-saving surgery. Another said he had ended the life of a man in a coma following an accident, to spare the grieving family any hard decisions about treatment.

Critics are also alarmed by what courts have expressly allowed. In 1990, a doctor provided suicide drugs to a 25-year-old woman treated unsuccessfully

niew Zylicz runs the three-year-old Rozenheuvel Hospice, where the symptoms of dying are eased. While Dutch hospitals have developed good pain-control techniques, the Polish-born doctor argues, the availability of euthanasia has

enough to say we can prevent all euthanasia," says Zylicz. "But there is a Christian duty to limit it as much as possible."

"Passports." Some opponents, like members of the Dutch Patients' Association, fear involuntary euthanasia. They carry anti-euthanasia "passports" to tell health care workers that they wish to live in case of emergency. But many thousands carry pro-euthanasia passports issued to them by the Dutch Voluntary Euthanasia Society, which advocates liberalizing euthanasia laws. Dutch faith in euthanasia remains strong. Polls consistently show that about 80 percent favor it, up from 44 percent during the early 1970s.

DR. ZBIGNIEW ZYLICZ HAS HELPED INTRODUCE HOSPICE CARE TO THE NETHERLANDS TO AID IN PREVENTING MORE SUICIDES.

for anorexia for 16 years. A jury acquitted the doctor after viewing a video of the woman explaining her decision. In 1994, the Dutch Supreme Court ruled that emotional suffering, not just physical suffering, was a basis for euthanasia. In that case, psychiatrist Boudewijin Chabot treated a woman grieving over the deaths of her two sons. When the woman did not respond after two months of therapy, Chabot gave in to her requests for a lethal prescription. Eugene Sutorious defended the doctors in both cases. To him they set the boundaries for what is acceptable in extraordinary circumstances.

One strategy of Dutch opponents has been to push for hospice care. Dr. Zbig-

kept hospice a rare option. Ineka Verlook is a Rozenheuval patient. Initially, she made an appointment with her doctor to request euthanasia because she had never heard about hospice. For a solution to the 65-year-old Verloop's cancer pain that could not be controlled by other doctors, Zylicz turned to the Internet. A doctor in South Korea proposed an effective strategy. "Here, they take away your fear and they put you at peace," says Verloop from the sunporch of the hospice. "They give you a sense that you are a person, not a patient." The Dutch Health Ministry has pledged to fund new initiatives in hospice care. Last month, Dutch Queen Beatrix visited four hospice programs. "I'm not arrogant

However, 17 times as many people die each year in the United States. Using that as a multiplier, there would be some 61,200 deaths per year by physician-assisted suicide—about the same number of fatalities by motor vehicle accidents and homicides combined. If the Netherlands and the United States were the same in every way but size, those high numbers alone suggest that the problems the Dutch have faced with assisted death would be magnified in America. Because they are not—because this is a country where access to health care is uncertain, doctors are viewed with distrust, and societal consensus is elusive—the problems likely would be even worse.

BY JOSEPH P. SHAPIRO
IN THE NETHERLANDS

Euthanasia in the Netherlands

Right-to-die advocates often point to Holland as the model for how well physician-assisted, voluntary euthanasia for terminally-ill, competent patients can work without abuse. But the facts indicate otherwise.

BACKGROUND INFORMATION

Dutch Penal Code Articles 293 and 294 make both euthanasia and assisted suicide illegal, even today. However, as the result of various court cases, doctors who directly kill patients or help patients kill themselves will not be prosecuted as long as they follow certain guidelines. In addition to the current requirements that physicians report every euthanasia/assisted-suicide death to the local prosecutor and that the patient's death request must be enduring (carefully considered and requested on more than one occasion), the Rotterdam court in 1981 established the following guidelines:

1. The patient must be experiencing unbearable pain.
2. The patient must be conscious.
3. The death request must be voluntary.
4. The patient must have been given alternatives to euthanasia and time to consider these alternatives.
5. There must be no other reasonable solutions to the problem.
6. The patient's death cannot inflict unnecessary suffering on others.
7. There must be more than one person involved in the euthanasia decision.
8. Only a doctor can euthanize a patient.
9. Great care must be taken in actually making the death decision. (1)

Since 1981, these guidelines have been interpreted by the Dutch courts and Royal Dutch Medical Association (KNMG) in ever-broadening terms. One example is the interpretation of the "unbearable pain" requirement reflected in the Hague Court of Appeal's 1986 decision. The court ruled that the pain guideline was not limited to physical pain, and that "psychic suffering" or "the potential disfigurement of personality" could also be grounds for euthanasia. (2)

The main argument *in favor* of euthanasia in Holland has always been the need for more patient autonomy—that patients have the right to make their own end-of-life decisions. Yet, over the past 20 years, Dutch euthanasia practice has ultimately given doctors, *not patients,* more and more power. The question of whether a patient should live or die is often decided exclusively by a doctor or a team of physicians. (3)

The Dutch define "euthanasia" in a very limited way: "Euthanasia is understood [as] an action which aims at taking the life of another *at the latter's expressed request.* It concerns an action of which death is the purpose and the result." (4) (Emphasis added.) This definition applies only to *voluntary* euthanasia and excludes what the rest of the world refers to as *non-voluntary* or *involuntary* euthanasia, the killing of a patient without the patient's knowledge or consent. The Dutch call this "life-terminating treatment."

Some physicians use this distinction between "euthanasia" and "life-terminating treatment" to avoid having a patient's death classified as "euthanasia," thus freeing doctors from following the established euthanasia guidelines and reporting the death to local authorities. One such example was discussed during the December 1990 Institute for Bioethics conference in Maastricht, Holland. A physician from The Netherlands Cancer Institute told of approximately 30 cases a year where doctors ended patients' lives after the patients intentionally had been put into a coma by means of a morphine injection. The Cancer Institute physician then stated that these deaths were not considered "euthanasia" because they were *not voluntary,* and that to have discussed the plan to end these patients' lives with the patients would have been "rude" since they all knew they had incurable conditions. (5)

For the sake of clarity in this fact sheet, the direct and intentional termination of a patient's life, performed *without* the patient's consent, will be termed "involuntary euthanasia."

THE FACTS

The Remmelink Report—On September 10, 1991, the results of the first, official government study of the practice of Dutch euthanasia were released. The two volume report (6)—popularly referred to as the Remmelink Report (after Professor J. Remmelink, M.J., attorney general of the High Council of the Netherlands, who headed the study committee)—documents the prevalence of *involuntary* euthanasia in Holland, as well as the fact that, to a large degree, doctors have taken over end-of-life decision making regarding euthanasia. The data indicate that, despite long-standing, court-approved euthanasia guidelines developed to protect patients, abuse has become an accepted norm. According to the Remmelink Report, in 1990:

- 2,300 people died as the result of doctors killing them upon request (active, voluntary euthanasia). (7)
- 400 people died as a result of doctors providing them with the means to kill themselves (physician-assisted suicide). (8)
- 1,040 people (an average of 3 per day) died from involuntary euthanasia, meaning that doctors actively killed these patients *without the patients' knowledge or consent.* (9)
- 14% of these patients were filly competent. (10)
- 72% had never given any indication that they would want their lives terminated. (11)
- In 8% of the cases, doctors performed involuntary euthanasia despite the fact that they believed alternative options were still possible. (12)
- In addition, 8,100 patients died as a result of doctors deliberately giving them overdoses of pain medication, not for the primary purpose of controlling pain, but to hasten the patient's death. (13) In 61% of these cases (4,941 patients), the intentional overdose was given *without the patient's consent.* (14)
- According to the Remmelink Report, Dutch physicians deliberately and intentionally ended the lives of 11,840 people by lethal overdoses or injections—a figure which accounts for 9.1% of the annual overall death rate of 130,000 per year. The majority of all euthanasia deaths in Holland are *involuntary deaths.*
- The Remmelink Report figures cited here do not include thousands of other cases, also reported in the study, in which life-sustaining treatment was withheld or withdrawn without the patient's consent and with the intention of causing the patient's death. (15) Nor do the figures include cases of involuntary euthanasia performed on disabled newborns, children with life-threatening conditions, or psychiatric patients. (16)

- The most frequently cited reasons given for ending the lives of patients *without* their knowledge or consent were: "low quality of life," "no prospect for improvement," and "the family couldn't take it anymore. "(17)
- In 45% of cases involving hospitalized patients who were *involuntarily* euthanized, the patients' families had no knowledge that their loved ones' lives were deliberately terminated by doctors. (18)
- According to the 1990 census, the population of Holland is approximately 15 million. That is only half the population of California. To get some idea of how the Remmelink Report statistics would apply to the U.S., those figures would have to be multiplied 16.6 times (based on the 1990 U.S. census population of approximately 250 million).

Falsified Death Certificates—In the overwhelming majority of Dutch euthanasia cases, doctors—in order to avoid additional paperwork and scrutiny from local authorities—deliberately falsify patients' death certificates, stating that the deaths occurred from natural causes. (19) In reference to Dutch euthanasia guidelines and the requirement that physicians report all euthanasia and assisted-suicide deaths to local prosecutors, a government health inspector recently told the New York Times: "In the end the system depends on the integrity of the physician, of what and how he reports. If the family doctor does not report a case of voluntary euthanasia or an assisted suicide, there is nothing to control." (20)

Inadequate Pain Control and Comfort Care—In 1988, the British Medical Association released the findings of a study on Dutch euthanasia conducted at the request of British right-to-die advocates. The study found that, in spite of the fact that medical care is provided to everyone in Holland, palliative care (comfort care) programs, with adequate pain control techniques and knowledge, were poorly developed. (21) Where euthanasia is an accepted medical solution to patients' pain and suffering, there is little incentive to develop programs which provide modern, available, and effective pain control for patients. As of mid-1990, only two hospice programs were in operation in all of Holland, and the services they provided were very limited. (22)

Broadening Interpretations of Euthanasia Guidelines

- In July 1992, the Dutch Pediatric Association announced that it was issuing formal guidelines for killing severely handicapped newborns. Dr. Zier Versluys, chairman of the association's Working Group on Neonatal Ethics, said that "Both for the parents and the children, an early death is better than life." Dr. Versluys also indicated that euthanasia is an integral part of good medical practice in relation to newborn babies. (23) Doctors would judge if a baby's "quality of life" is such that the baby should be killed.

- A 2/15/93 statement released by the Dutch Justice Ministry proposed extending the court-approved, euthanasia guidelines to formally include "active medical intervention to cut short life *without an express request.*" (Emphasis added.) Liesbeth Rensman, a spokesperson for the Ministry, said that this would be the first step toward the official sanctioning of euthanasia for those who cannot ask for it, particularly psychiatric patients and handicapped newborns. (24)
- A 4/21/93 landmark Dutch court decision affirmed euthanasia for psychiatric reasons. The court found that psychiatrist Dr. Boudewijn Chabot was medically justified and followed established euthanasia guidelines in helping his physically healthy, but depressed, patient commit suicide. The patient, 50-year-old Hilly Bosscher, said she wanted to die after the deaths of her two children and the subsequent breakup of her marriage. (25)

Euthanasia "Fallout"—The effects of euthanasia policy and practice have been felt in all segments of Dutch society:

- Some Dutch doctors provide "self-help programs" for adolescents to end their lives. (26)
- General practitioners wishing to admit elderly patients to hospitals have sometimes been advised to give the patients lethal injections instead. (27)
- Cost containment is one of the main aims of Dutch health care policy. (28)
- Euthanasia training has been part of both medical and nursing school curricula. (29)
- Euthanasia has been administered to people with diabetes, rheumatism, multiple sclerosis, AIDS, bronchitis, and accident victims. (30)
- In 1990, the Dutch Patients' Association, a disability rights organization, developed wallet-size cards which state that if the signer is admitted to a hospital "no treatment be administered with the intention to terminate life." Many in Holland see the card as a necessity to help prevent involuntary euthanasia being performed on those who do not want their lives ended, especially those whose lives are considered low in quality. (31)
- In 1993, the Dutch senior citizens' group, the Protestant Christian Elderly Society, surveyed 2,066 seniors on general health care issues. The Survey did **not** address the euthanasia issue in any way, yet ten percent of the elderly respondents clearly indicated that, because of the Dutch euthanasia policy, they are afraid that their lives could be terminated without their request. According to the Elderly Society director, Hans Homans, "They are afraid that at a certain moment, on the basis of age, a treatment will be considered no longer economically viable, and an early end to their lives will be made." (32)

The Irony of History—During World War II, Holland was the only occupied country whose doctors refused to participate in the German euthanasia program. Dutch physicians openly defied an order to treat only those patients who had a good chance of full recovery. They recognized that to comply with the order would have been the first step away from their duty to care for all patients. The German officer who gave that order was later executed for war crimes. Remarkably, during the entire German occupation of Holland, Dutch doctors never recommended nor participated in one euthanasia death. (33) Commenting on this fact in his essay "The Humane Holocaust," highly respected British journalist Malcolm Muggeridge wrote that it took only a few decades "to transform a war crime into an act of compassion." (34)

Implications of the Dutch Euthanasia Experience

- Right-to-die advocates often argue that euthanasia and assisted suicide are "choice issues." The Dutch experience clearly indicates that, where voluntary euthanasia and assisted suicide are accepted practice, a significant number of patients end up having no choice at all.
- Euthanasia does not remain a "right" only for the terminally-ill, competent adult who requests it, no matter how many safeguards are established. As a "right," it inevitably is applied to those who are chronically ill, disabled, elderly, mentally ill, mentally retarded, and depressed—the rationale being that such individuals should have the same "right" to end their suffering as anyone else, even if they do not or cannot voluntarily request death.
- Euthanasia, *by its very nature,* is an abuse and the ultimate abandonment of patients.
- In actual practice, euthanasia only gives doctors greater power and a license to kill.
- Once the power to kill is bestowed on physicians, the inherent nature of the doctor/patient relationship is adversely affected. A patient can no longer be sure what role the doctor will play—healer or killer.
- Unlike Holland, where medical care is automatically provided for everyone, in the U.S. millions of people cannot afford medical treatment. If euthanasia and assisted-suicide were to become accepted in the U.S., death would be the only "medical option" many could afford.

• Even with health care reform in the U.S., many people would still not have long-standing relationships with their doctors. Large numbers of Americans would belong to health maintenance organizations (HMOs) and managed care programs, and they often would not even know the physicians who end up treating them. Given those circumstances, doctors would be ill-equipped to recognize if a patient's euthanasia request was the result of depression or the sometimes subtle pressures placed on the patient to "get out of the way." Also, given the current push for health care cost containment in the U.S., medical groups and facilities many be tempted to view patients in terms of their treatment costs instead of their innate value as human beings. For some, the "bottom line" would be, "Dead patients cost less than live ones."

• Giving doctors the legal power to kill their patients is dangerous public policy.

Sources:

1. Carlos Gomez, *Regulating Death* (New York: Free Press, 1991), p. 32. Hereafter cited as *Regulating Death.*
2. Ibid., p. 39.
3. H. Jochemsen, trans., "Report of the Royal Dutch Society of Medicine on 'Life-Terminating Actions with Incompetent Patients, Part 1: Severely Handicapped Newborns.'" *Issues in Law & Medicine,* vol. 7, no. 3 (1991), p. 366.
4. From KNMG Euthanasia Guidelines as quoted in *Regulating Death,* p. 40.
5. Alexander Morgan Capron, "Euthanasia in the Netherlands—American Observations," *Hastings Center Report* (March, April 1992), p. 31.
6. *Medical Decisions About the End of Life, I. Report of the Committee to Study the Medical Practice Concerning Euthanasia. II. The Study for the Committee on Medical Practice Concerning Euthanasia* (2 vols.), The Hague, September 19, 1991. Hereafter cited as *Report I* and *Report II,* respectively.
7. *Report I,* p. 13.

8. Ibid.
9. Ibid., p. 15.
10. *Report II* p. 49, table 6.4.
11. Ibid., p. 50, table 6.6.
12. Ibid., table 6.5.
13. Ibid., p. 58, table 7.2.
14. Ibid., p. 72.
15. Ibid.
16. *Report I,* pp. 17–18.
17. *Report II,* p. 52, table 6.7.
18. Ibid., table 6.8.
19. I. J. Keown, "The Law and Practice of Euthanasia in The Netherlands," *The Law Quarterly Review* (January 1992), pp. 67–68.
20. Marlise Simons, "Dutch Move to Enact Law Making Euthanasia Easier," *New York Times,* 2/9/93, p. A1.
21. *Euthanasia: Report of the Working Party to Review the British Medical Association's Guidance on Euthanasia,* British Medical Association, May 5, 1988, p. 49, no. 195.
22. Rita L. Marker, *Deadly Compassion—The Death of Ann Humphry and the Truth About Euthanasia* (New York; William Morrow and Company, 1993), p. 157. Hereafter cited as *Deadly Compassion.*
23. Abner Katzman, "Dutch debate mercy killing of babies," *Contra Costa Times,* 7/30/92, p. 3B.
24. "Critics fear euthanasia soon needn't be requested," *Vancouver Sun,* 2/17/93, p. A10. Also, "Dutch may broaden rules to permit involuntary euthanasia," *Contra Costa Times,* 2/17/93, p. 4B.
25. *New York Times,* 4/5/93, p. A3, and *Washington Times,* 4/22/93, p. A2.
26. "It's Almost Over—More Letters on Debbie," Letter to the editor by G. B. Humphrey, M.D., Ph.D., University Hospital, Groningen, The Netherlands, *Journal of the American Medical Association,* vol. 260, no. 6 (8/12/88), p. 788.
27. "Involuntary Euthanasia in Holland," *Wall Street Journal,* 9/29/87, p. 3.
28. "Restructuring Health Care," *The Lancet* (1/28/89), p. 209.
29. "The Member's Aid Service of the Dutch Association for Voluntary Euthanasia," *Euthanasia Review,* vol. 1, no. 3 (Fall 1986), p. 153.
30. "Suicide on Prescription," *Sunday Observer* (London, England), 4/30/89, p. 22.
31. *Deadly Compassion,* p. 156.
32. "Elderly Dutch afraid of euthanasia policy," *Canberra Times* (Australia), 6/11/93.
33. Leo Alexander, "Medical Science Under Dictatorship," *New England Journal of Medicine,* vol. 241 (July 14, 1949), p. 45.
34. Nancy Gibbs, "Love and Let Die," *Time* Magazine (March 19, 1990), p. 67.

Going Home To Die

"... The decision to care for a dying loved one at home can ensure that the patient is well cared for and can die with dignity, in a manner that reflects the way he or she lived."

Karen Orloff Kaplan

Ms. Kaplan is executive director, Choice in Dying, Inc., New York.

THE ACT of completing an advance directive (the general term for living wills and durable powers of attorney for health care) raises thoughts about where and how one wants to die. Many people who opt to refuse life support also rather would refuse the entire experience of dying in an alien, depersonalized medical facility.

Going home to die may be a growing trend, at least for patients who are conscious and interactive. As sociologist Andrea Sankar notes in *Dying at Home: A Family Guide for Caregiving,* interest in home care has been spurred by five factors: patients' and families' desire to retain control over care; the spread of the hospice movement; a growing awareness of the limitations of medicine's abilities; advances in home-based care and technology; and reduced Medicare payments for hospital care when dying patients are not receiving active (*i.e.,* life-prolonging) treatment.

Caring for people at home can make them feel loved and allow them to stay connected to the things that enrich their lives. They may continue working, see loved ones, and enjoy social events. They can take leave of the world at their own pace.

According to William Lamers, a leader in the hospice movement, "the experience may also be invaluable to family and other survivors. Caring for a dying person can be an expression of love and a final gift to the person. Involvement in the dying process often helps the survivors cope better with their grief."

Home care of a dying patient is managed by a home health agency or a hospice program. In either case, family members or other loved ones act as the primary caregivers.

Broadly speaking, the two types of agencies differ in their philosophies and client groups. Hospice care is exclusively for dying people. It therefore brings expertise to helping patients and their families face issues specific to death and dying. To qualify for most hospice programs, patients must have a diagnosis of six months or less to live and must agree to forgo life-prolonging treatments.

Home health agencies, in contrast, accept a wider range of patients, not all of whom are dying, and generally offer a wider range of treatments, including life support. Like hospice programs, though, home health agencies tailor their care plans to the patient's wishes. "The key to successful care at home is the patient's involvement in the care plan," explains Robin Brenner, general manager of Protocare, a high-tech home care agency in New York State. Thus, a dying person still may refuse life support with a home health agency.

At heart, what these agencies have in common may be more important than how they differ. Both approach the provision of care holistically. "In contrast to the hospital, where death is seen as a medical event, hospice defines death socially," indicates Sankar. It "is concerned with the dying person as a whole person—with social, emotional and psychological needs— meaningfully connected to other people." This vision also can be found among home health providers.

In addition, both types of agencies consider the entire family as the unit of care and attend to the family's social, emotional, and psychological needs as well as the patient's. They offer an interdisciplinary team of health professionals, counselors, aids, and volunteers to meet the spectrum of the family's practical and psychological needs. Apart from other considerations, family caregivers need support so they can continue devoting their energies to the patient.

Successful home care

A successful home care plan requires three resources: a willing patient, preferably with a loved one to be the primary caregiver; a professional care agency to assist in managing the case, train and educate family caregiver(s), and provide skilled care and backup; and an insurance plan or other means of payment that covers enough of the care to make it affordable.

In addition, notes Brenner, "the physician is a key player. He needs to be supportive. He also needs to be available to the patient at home." If the patient's regular doctor is not supportive of the choice of home care, the patient may want to consider finding a new physician.

The doctor or a hospital discharge planner can help to locate appropriate care agencies, which work with the patient and family caregivers to help them identify helpful resources and explore what items will be needed in the residence to provide for a home death. The agency then works with the patient and the family, explains Brenner. "We look at the diagnosis and clinical needs, including the environment the patient is going to. We anticipate the diagnosis on its continuum, and look at insurance." An appropriate plan of care then is created.

Even when family members support the patient's wish to die at home, they may wonder whether this is legal. Ann Fade, associate executive director for legal services, Choice In Dying, points out that, "as death approaches, loved ones may fear that by keeping the patient at home they are illegally depriving him or her of medical treatment. But the law clearly states that a competent adult can refuse any medical care, even if that care is life-sustaining. This includes the right to refuse hospitalization. Therefore, as long as the patient, while competent, clearly expressed the desire to die at home, there can be no legal liability for abiding by that wish."

Perhaps the greatest concern surrounds the question of whether an emergency medical service (EMS) must be called when the patient nears death or dies. The answer is that there is no legal requirement to do so. In most instances, EMS should *not* be called. Emergency medical technicians in most states must attempt resuscitation, even if the patient is terminally ill and has a living will. Calling an ambulance, therefore, may force the patient to endure unwanted and ultimately futile medical treatment.

There are certain cases wherein the family *may* need to request emergency help. If the patient wants to go to the hospital, that wish should be honored by calling an ambulance. Additionally, if the patient experiences increased pain or difficulty in breathing, keeping him or her comfortable may necessitate obtaining oxygen or pain medication from EMS, even though he or she should not be resuscitated. To avoid further, unwanted treatment in such cases, the dying patient should consider using a nonhospital DNR (Do Not Resuscitate) order, if such orders are recognized by their state law.

"A nonhospital DNR order is a new way for patients to refuse unwanted emergency resuscitation, so that they can die peacefully at home," Fade explains. "However, nonhospital DNRs are unlike living wills in that they are *not* for everyone. Only those who are near the end of life should complete one. Many of the states that have enacted nonhospital DNR laws require a physician's signature on the document." Currently, 17 states have statutes that authorize nonhospital DNR orders.

"Another area of frequent concern arises when a patient can not eat or drink. Family members may fear that the law requires them to make sure the patient receives artificial nutrition and hydration. This is not the case. In fact, in its 1990 *Cruzan* opinion, the U.S. Supreme Court concluded that artificial nutrition and fluid is a medical treatment. Therefore, as with any treatment, a patient may refuse artificial nutrition and hydration."

There are a few steps that can be taken to make absolutely certain that no legal questions arise. Most importantly, the patient should complete both a living will and a durable power of attorney for health care, and use them to state his or her wish to die at home. A living will is a legal document that expresses an individual's wishes about treatment decisions at the end of life. A durable power of attorney for health care allows people to appoint someone else whom they trust to make medical decisions on their behalf. Some form of advance directive is recognized by all 50 states and the District of Columbia. Since the laws governing advance directives vary, it is important to get the forms that are authorized by your state. Individuals and their caregivers can get free, state-specific advance directives and advice about completing them from Choice In Dying (1-800-989-WILL).

"Completing an advance directive will accomplish two things: it will document the patient's desire to be at home, in case he or she becomes incompetent, and it will protect the family in the extremely unlikely event that someone suggests they are abusing or neglecting the patient," Fade indicates.

In addition, the patient's physician should write a letter setting forth the diagnosis and prognosis, and clearly state that the person is expected to die at home. This letter can be important because unexplained deaths must be referred to the coroner's office for investigation, which may include an autopsy.

The legal issues surrounding dying at home become more complicated if the patient is incompetent and has not left clear instructions concerning his or her wishes. Families in such circumstances should contact Choice In Dying or an attorney familiar with their state's health laws.

Financial considerations

When a family member, relative, or close partner makes the decision to care for the needs of the dying patient at home, they have transformed their role into that of a family caregiver. However, family caregivers may find that they cannot handle all of the responsibilities involved in caring for the patient. Professional caregivers, such as home health aides, can help to provide ancillary, supportive services. Regardless of what services are needed, family caregivers can be faced with significant decisions about how to pay for the comfort care they provide for the dying patient.

There is no question that providing care for the dying patient can be costly. Family caregivers may discover some free or "pay-what-you-can" services, but most should not bank on such good fortune. Insurance policies mainly cover skilled care, and have fewer provisions for the types of care that dying at home involves, such as a home health aide. Yet, the services of an aide often are what is needed most to ensure a successful, peaceful death. The home health aide sits with the dying person and handles the simple tasks of daily life, such as changing linen, cleaning up, and washing and feeding the patient. The family caregiver may choose to provide all these services, but, as the illness becomes more acute, most people find that more than one family caregiver is required. Family and friends are often extremely valuable in providing this supplemental help, but sometimes they must miss work and lose money in order to do so.

Changes in insurance reimbursement, including the prospective payment system instituted in 1984 by Medicare, support home death by providing some reimbursement. This system places financial constraints on hospital stays for patients who are not receiving active treatment. Except for a few hospitals that have in-patient hospices, a person defined as terminally ill must be receiving treatment, at least for pain or symptom relief, to remain in the hospital. An exception is a regulation that permits a home-based hospice to admit a dying person under its care to a hospital for a few days each month. The hospice benefit in Medicare and private insurance often does not cover *all* of the necessary

> *"After careful exploration of the pros and cons, the decision to care for a dying loved one at home can ensure that the patient is well cared for and can die with dignity, in a manner that reflects the way he or she lived."*

care for dying at home, though. Area Agencies on Aging (1-800-658-8898) and Medigap insurance companies can provide information about costs and reimbursement policies.

Sharing a home with a dying patient will introduce many changes in the caregiver's household, both positive and negative. "Caring for a dying person at home can be an enriching experience for all concerned. For dying patients, it can mean feeling secure, surrounded by people they love and among their own personal possessions; being able to allow others to take care of them in the privacy of their own home; and preparing for death and for the future of loved ones in the circle of family members and friends. For caregivers, the arrangement can be a way to preserve a loved one's last wishes and share selfless care with another person," maintains Sia Arnason, Brookdale Center on Aging, New York. However, caregiving also introduces stress, especially if the patient is demented, is faced with a progressively deteriorating condition, or requires hourly care and attention. The arrangement works well for some people, if major adjustments are expected and weathered, and if the caregiver has periodic respite from his or her duties.

According to Arnason, "the decision to care for the dying patient should not be made hastily. Thoughtful pre-planning will save the caregiver later guilt or resentment. Family caregivers must carefully weigh the pros and cons for themselves, the patient, and other members of the household for whom the caregiver is responsible. Caregivers should also seek advice on resources to enrich the patient's and family's life, such as home care services, hospice programs, counseling for the patient and family, and respite programs. Knowledge of

health care entitlement programs and what they cover is also crucial, so that the patient and family can make maximum use of the public and private resources available to them. Private geriatric care managers, hospital social workers and discharge planners, specific disease-related organizations, elder law attorneys, and Area Agencies on Aging all can help in the planning process, enabling the caregiver and other members of the household to decide whether caring for the patient at home is the right option."

Sankar writes that patients and family caregivers must confront their own fear of death and the fear of dying at home. Describing the death of a friend's father, she sums up her loss this way: "I've never been stretched emotionally to the extent that I was as I watched myself lose someone I cared so much about. I mean, I knew what the end was going to be. I knew he was never going to get up from that bed. I think you protect yourself in two ways: either you stay away or you involve yourself. I involved myself

because, as long as he was there, he wasn't dead. That to me was the most important thing.

"It isn't for everybody. I don't think it is the kind of responsibility that all children owe to their parents or spouses owe to each other, and it takes a Herculean amount of strength. It was only afterwards that I was aware of how drained I was. But, I couldn't have refused and I don't regret it for a moment."

The at-home death movement, while gaining increased support from the health care professional community, patients themselves, and family caregivers, still has hurdles to overcome. The choice of an at-home death must be made jointly by the patient and family caregivers for the right reasons. After careful exploration of the pros and cons, the decision to care for a dying loved one at home can ensure that the patient is well cared for and can die with dignity, in a manner that reflects the way he or she lived.

Ashes to Ashes, Dust to Dust:
IS THERE ANY FUTURE FOR
Cemeteries?

Changes in the economy, urban patterns, and favorable attitudes toward cremation may be dooming a centuries-old institution.

Eleanor Weinel

Dr. Weinel is associate professor of architecture, University of Oklahoma, Norman.

EVERY ANTHROPOLOGIST knows that burial customs are a rich source of information about past cultures, just as archaeologists mine the ruins of cities for physical evidence of distant civilizations. The cities of the dead and the cities of the living hold up a mirror to society's attitudes and desires.

The cemetery, like the city, originally was imported to America from Western Europe, more specifically from England, and brought with it the values of the founding community. There essentially were two cultures represented: the Puritan in the northern colonies; the Anglican and aristocratic in the southern colonies. The Puritan strictures against ornament worked with the traditional methods of building employed to create a similarity of house form that reflects the subordination of individuality. Generally linear in their arrangement, towns were organized around the meetinghouse, the civic and religious center of the community, and the burying ground grew up around that building in keeping with the ethic of the community—the emphasis on collective salvation over individual freedom.

That salvation was a matter of the spirit, rather than the flesh, so the physical location of the body was of less importance than the moral lesson of the churchyard itself. Tombstones represented not only the growing community of the faithful, but also spelled out individual virtues and recounted exemplary lives. The cemetery stood as mute testament to the moral fiber of the community and the inevitable conclusion to individual existence. While the Puritan ethic may have begun to dissipate over the course of the 18th century, the virtue of simplicity and conformity continued in both city and cemetery.

In the South, the influences were different, though no less traditional. Topography and culture favored

Photo courtesy of Eleanor Weinel

Mary Baker Eddy Memorial, Mt. Auburn Cemetery, Cambridge, Mass. This mausoleum, designed to house the remains of the founder of the Christian Science Church, [was] possible [because] of unoccupied land in American cemeteries during the early years of the 20th century.

From *USA Today Magazine*, January 1996, pp. 48-50. © 1996 by the Society for the Advancement of Education. Reprinted by permission.

county over town government, and the plantation was the structure of everyday life. Churches were less central and more isolated and followed the model of English parish churches, gathering their dead around them. Bruton Parish Church in Williamsburg, Va., is a prime example. Williamsburg saw itself as an important town, actually and potentially, and accorded this importance to its citizens. In this churchyard are found more individuality and singularity as well as recognition and status. Tombs, such as that of Edward Nott, governor of the colony, follow the tradition of burial in English cathedrals of the aristocracy and notable citizens. If, in America, the idea of aristocracy is diminished, the description of the person's life, accomplishments, and particular virtues is expanded.

The southern plantation tradition also indicated a transfer of burial from the churchyard to the family cemetery. The cemetery at Ayr Mount, an early-19th-century plantation in North Carolina, is typical—a fenced plot within the cleared "park" of the house. A more famous example is Thomas Jefferson's at Monticello, in Charlottesville, VA., but its cemetery does not differ fundamentally from Ayr Mount or from humbler roadside versions still in use today. The expediency of timely burial and transportation removed interment from the remote church to the plantation and from the religious to the secular realm.

This shift to secular and familial responsibility seems to have been equally important in the expanding nation, where new towns were established rapidly based on commercial, rather than religious, interests. Death was an ever-present reality in boom towns, where it was bound to precede settlement and civilizing institutions of church and state. Indeed, the cemetery is virtually all that exists of Sherman, Wyo., a railroad town that never grew up. The distinction between the religious and the secular is increasingly clear in places like San Diego, Calif., which developed because of the mission, but established its own burial ground, the Campo Santo, to accommodate increasingly diverse religious views.

Utopian visions like Robert Owen's industrially based Harmony, Ind., often included distinctive urban form. Although most never were realized physically, remnants of the ideology endure, as in the Amana communities in Iowa. The cemetery at High Amana evokes Owen's community design with a clearly defined perimeter and collective interior, reminiscent of medieval city form. While the repetitive headstones and simple white fence of the cemetery lack the monumentality of the utopian design, they serve the same purpose—the careful distinction between inside and outside, between life and death, between being part of the community and being an outsider.

The 19th century was a period of great change in both the city and the cemetery. The causes were essentially the same: transportation in the form of horsecar, cable car, and railroad, coupled with a proliferation of anti-urban philosophies that proclaimed the benefits of a closer proximity to nature, ranging from a simple physical and mental well-being to a more complex relationship with the deity. Llewellen Park, N.J., an early suburb founded on such a philosophy, was designed so roads and paths curve to follow the topography of their site while allowing for reasonable subdivision into building lots and maintain areas of common recreation and dramatic views. Entry to the community was defined clearly by an appropriately styled gatehouse. Individual lots tended to follow similar design premises, and houses ran to the picturesque, even the fanciful.

The same design principles applied to the rural cemeteries, established beginning in the 1830s. Like the suburbs, they included the favoring of the rural over the urban, emotion over reason, and individual initiative over authoritarian control. This latter idea is especially important as it frees the cemetery from the institution of the church *per se* and enables it to stand as the collective memory of the community, which, in the U.S., was an increasingly diverse gathering of individual expression. This supported perhaps the most important change in the cemetery—from a moral to an emotional intention.

The rural cemetery was laid out on picturesque principles of winding drives, even where topography did not dictate, and in marked contrast to the rational grid being extended across the country around the same time. Entry gates were usual, ranging from Egyptian Revival to Italianate to Gothic Revival. Paths and drives beckon to vistas, valleys, and picturesque groupings of tombstones.

Within the general layout of the cemetery, individual plots take on the aura and outline of the suburban residence. The family mausoleum was the most obvious example, often giving in the "heavenly mansion" a status not so clearly achieved in life. Fenced, hedged, and bordered plots are nearly universal, along with less common alignments of stones to form rectangles or the circles of stones at Pittsburgh's Allegheny Cemetery. Thus, boundaries are marked in various ways as a means of gathering the family in at last, as the final unit of stability in an increasingly complex urban environment of shifting and overlapping social institutions. In the same way, the move to the suburbs allowed for a more clearly defined statement of social and economic status than seemed possible in the more homogeneous, anonymous city.

In the period following the Civil War, the attitude of rugged individualism that produced the financiers and captains of industry wrought similar changes in both cemetery and city. Personal identity is monumentalized, and the mausoleum as well as the office building enter the realm of the architect. Richard Morris Hunt, architect to the Vanderbilts, designed for them office buildings

(New York City's Tribune tower), residences (Biltmore in North Carolina and the Breakers at Newport, R.I.), and the family mausoleum on Staten Island, N.Y. The variety of these buildings exhibited his own and the era's stylistic flexibility.

In the Midwest, Louis Sullivan designed both the Ryerson Building in Chicago and Martin Ryerson's tomb in Graceland Cemetery, as well as the Wainwright Building and tomb in St. Louis. Sullivan's newly devised system of ornament enhances his tomb designs with more subtlety than was often the case in design of the period. Increasingly, sculpture appears as a part of structures and as individual grave markers.

From simple portrait busts and chaste angels to complex floral motifs, elaborate figural statues, and narrative groupings, the art of the cemetery and its park-like setting were great attractions. They were visited not only by relatives of those interred, but by tourists and others noting a local landmark or seeking an elevating experience. The intent of the individual works was to produce emotion specific to the circumstances of the person: grief, heroism, magnanimity, even guilt. The effect of the whole was to invest the experience with memory, a recollection of human identity. The point seems neither moral nor religious, but social, a reminder of people's connectedness through common emotions.

While artistic diversity might be attractive in the cemetery, it drew a somewhat different response in the city. The facility with existing architectural styles and experimentation in the creation of new styles contained not only the germ of modern architecture (in Sullivan's phrase), but the seeds of its own destruction. The laissez-faire capitalism of the city promoted not only remarkable works of architecture, but unconscionable working and living conditions and inspired a generation of social critics. The cemetery was no less criticized for overemotionalism, overenthusiasm (or bad taste), and overcrowding. The high individualized design that speaks eloquently in isolation seems discordant, even cacophonous, in close company.

In trying to negotiate the expanded city, the focus on the monument also was important as a visual device and a key ingredient of formal planning. In the proposals devised by beautification groups in practically every American city, civic institutions—such as libraries, city halls, auditoriums, squares, and memorials—became organizing devices to give urban areas a center, an identity, and a sense of place, while re-ordering transportation routes, sewers, and gas and electric lines, noting that these private services now were under the control of the city.

The cemetery follows a similar pattern. Advocates for the "burial park" stressed ease of maintenance and serenity of atmosphere—uncluttered, unheroic, and uniform. Single elements take over the emotional content of individual monuments. This is represented by

Forest Lawn Cemetery in Los Angeles, begun around 1917. While the use of the terrain is meant to be reminiscent of the rural cemetery, the general attitude reflects the control of central planning, evocative of the suburban housing development that would spring up following World War II. Just as those developments signaled a constantly moving population, the modern memorial park suggests the shifting of care for the physical reality of the departed from the family to impersonal authority.

These are not places of visitation, of ties to memory. The monuments of the cemetery become the focus for the last big event—the funeral, the farewell to communality. They are icons familiar from history, art, or religion and sit rather uncomfortably in their surroundings: scaled-up for drive-by sightings until they are finally decultured markers on unpeopled plains that are maintained easily.

Having detached ourselves from the importance of corporeal reality in death and the related rituals of maintenance, we also have relinquished our conceptual link to the final resting place as a site of individual and collective memory. Our means of memory are too many and too real to require the aid of monuments and the emotions they elicit. Video tape, with its illusion of reality, supplants recollection in the private as well as the public sphere.

The simultaneous abandonment of cities and cemeteries has the same result in decay and destruction. The vandalism of cemeteries no longer seems to be the daring to assert life in the conquest of the city of the dead, but the undirected acting out of the need to establish power through the ability to destroy, easily accomplished in a deserted space. We are being warned that, like the city, the cemetery is not a safe place. The cemetery also loses its daily life as burials decrease in number. The land is filled up, and development as it were, is complete. The response has been a change in attitude toward interment just as changed economic and urban patterns have altered attitudes toward ownership and living space. Cremation is a more frequently selected option, and cemeteries use remaining space for the construction of columbariums—vaults for urns—just as cities convert existing buildings to condominiums.

The columbarium allows people to acknowledge the fact of individual existence while returning to collective identity, a fact, perhaps, that recently has led churches to reclaim some of their exterior space as "memorial gardens"—miniature churchyards. The early-20th-century architect, Ralph Adams Cram, who was noted for his Gothic churches, believed in a cyclical, rather than progressive, time line. Perhaps he was right and we have cycled city and cemetery back to the authority of institutions that alleviate us of the individual responsibility for the maintenance of meaning.

The American way of dying

Hospital culture is at war with patients' wishes about how they're treated in their final days

Most people hold in their hearts a special dread of a hospitalized, medicalized death. Yet about half of all Americans die in hospitals, in a tangle of tubes, surrounded by anxiety-producing technology. They suffer alone in the glare of a comfortless ward, their last hours guided by the training and instincts of highly specialized strangers. No one seems to know when to finally give in to death's certainty, and relentless procedures rob people of a death with comfort and dignity.

Many of those who dread that kind of death think they're doing something about it by signing living wills or otherwise making their wishes very explicit. But a large-scale study of terminal patients by the *Journal of the American Medical Association* showed last week just how futile those efforts are. While patients say they want peace, comfort, the sanctity of home and freedom from pain in their last hours, shockingly few of them actually had their wishes honored even at the five top medical centers that were featured in the JAMA study. Even more distressing, the study's authors found that when they tried to take steps using specially trained nurses to encourage communication between patients, their families and doctors, none of the interventions mattered.

JAMA's grim conclusions: The culture of major hospitals is at war with dying patients' desires. The culture emphasizes technological attacks on diseases and keeping lives going. Doctors don't listen to what patients want; they aren't honest with bad news; they manage pain poorly, and their decisions leave an alarming number of families broke or near broke. Some experts are cynical that things will ever change. "Doctors are the last to accept [with dying patients] that there is nothing left that medicine has to offer," says medical ethicist George Annas of Boston University. "If you want control over your death, you have to stay out of the hospital." To understand that argument and the pain embodied in the *JAMA* findings, *U.S. News* sought out stories that illustrate *JAMA*'s basic points:

■ **Patients' desires don't get attention.** Perry Elfmont hovers in an unknowable place that is not yet death but bears little resemblance to the life he knew. A recent autumn day is like every other since a day 18 months ago when, his wife, Sabina, believes, he was kept from his appointment with death. Elfmont, 90, lies in bed, stares at the ceiling and works a spoonful of strawberry Jell-O around his mouth. Sabina has put on a jolly demeanor, leaving her rage and her tears at the dining room table when she enters their bedroom. She tells him what a lovely day it is, playfully squeezing his toes through a plaid blanket.

He has not responded significantly for months, and her smile melts to searing sadness as she turns away from him to leave the room. He cannot communicate, but she says everything in his life before May 5, 1994, indicates that he would not want to live like this—unable to speak, understand or enjoy. On that day, his wife says, doctors at Mount Sinai Medical Center in Manhattan ignored the instructions he had recorded in a living will that he wanted no cardiac resuscitation, nor any life-sustaining treatment, including feeding tubes and respirators. "It was so important to him to have that living will filed. At his 85th birthday, he said, 'Whatever happens, I am protected,' " recalled Sabina.

But he was not. In the spring of his 88th year, suspecting a stroke, Sabina brought him to Mount Sinai. They spent a grueling 12 hours in the emergency room before he was admitted. Sabina, 78 at the time, gave in to her exhaustion and went home, but only, she says, after hearing assurances that her husband's wishes were known and would be respected. "It was midnight. I said, 'Do you have the living will?' They told me everything was under control. They told me not to worry, to go home," she says.

When she returned, she found her husband on oxygen and receiving intravenous antibiotics—two interventions she contends were against his written and expressed wishes. She found him in restraints because of his attempts to pull out the tubes. She says a resident told her that her husband was gone, and they brought him back. The hospital denies there was a cardiac resuscitation but will not discuss its other interventions, citing patient confidentiality. Following Elfmont's complaints, Mount Sinai initiated an educational program for staff members on advance directives, according to a hospital statement.

Perry Elfmont lives on with irreversible brain damage. Once, he was a family physician, a man fluent in five languages who loved Russian art and literature. He spent 25 years practicing family medicine in Long Island, N.Y., and another 23 years working for the Greater New York Blood Bank. He knew what a slow, agonizing death could do and tried to protect himself and his wife from the ordeal.

But now, Sabina Elfmont cannot grieve and cannot move on. She pretends cheer for his unknown feelings. She refuses to clear the clutter from his unused desk, fearing it would insult him to see his work put away forever. His reading glasses gather dust.

■ **Doctors shy away from grim news.** Marie Fifer never heard beforehand the hard reality of what her mother's life would be like after a feeding tube was inserted. Her mother had made her wishes known in a living will written 15 years before she suffered a stroke last May. But the wishes were seen by doctors as ambiguous. She wrote, "I direct that I be allowed to die and not be kept alive by medications, artificial means or heroic measures." There was no mention of feeding tubes. Still, her daughter knew that she would not have wanted one. "I'm her only child. I understood her desires. We had discussed it talking to each other across the table, but never in detail," said Fifer.

So following the stroke, when Fifer's mother could no longer swallow, her doctor wrote up an order for a surgically implanted permanent feeding tube. "He never really talked to me about it. He never talked to my mother either. I know because I was there for all his visits," she claims. When Fifer voiced an initial objection to the feeding tube, based on what she knew to be her mother's wishes, she felt the doctor implied that she was asking him to kill her mother. "And a nurse said, 'You don't want her to starve to death, do you?' " recalls Fifer. "It was too much for me to deal with. It was a weak moment, and I agreed."

Without thorough discussions in advance of urgent care, such weak moments commonly lead to care that is unwanted or poorly understood. The *JAMA* study found that about 60 percent of patients or their family members did not discuss their preferences about heroic resuscitation, or the likely consequences of such treatment, with a physician. Alfred Connors, head of critical-care medicine at Cleveland MetroHealth Medical Center and a principal investigator in the study, does not know Fifer or her mother. But his work often means hooking people up to high-technology care. "I work in an ICU. We don't put people on machines unless we feel we can get them off," he says. "We focus on a disease, not a person." Connors acknowledges that the full picture of a human life ebbing can be overlooked. "When death becomes imminent," he says, "we have trouble deciding to stop using technology."

Fifer's mother, whose name her daughter does not want published, will live the rest of her life in a nursing home, unable to swallow or speak, to tell aides if she's comfortable, or whether she needs her pink sweater. She's 86, and likely to survive for a long time. Fifer visits daily and watches her mother weep. "I think when she had the stroke, she wanted to die. Sometimes when I visit her, I can only stay for half an hour, and then I break down and I have to go home. It's not because she's in a nursing home. It's because she's hooked up to this thing," says Fifer. Had she had a more realistic picture of her mother's misery—and the duration of her joyless life—she says she would have stood firm and rejected a feeding tube.

■ **Too many patients suffer in pain.** Laurie Pross watched as her mother, Irene Pross, screamed and cried for two hours while doctors went about the business of keeping her alive. On hemodialysis because of kidney failure, the elder Pross had a shunt implanted in her body to accommodate the flow of her blood to and from the life-saving artificial-kidney machine. But clots would clog the shunt and needed to be cleaned out. The procedure normally required sedation, but eventually the elder Pross, who had a complex series of bad interactions between the many drugs she needed, could no longer tolerate any anesthesia, and the clots were cleared while she was fully awake.

Her daughter, Laurie, who was making decisions for her mother, reluctantly agreed to the agonizing procedures, just as she had sweated over dozens of similar decisions during her mother's two-year course of heart and renal failure, confusion and depression. The pain she witnessed as doctors cleared the shunt was the final straw. "That's when I said, no more," said Pross.

Without dialysis, Irene Pross's death was inevitable. Her daughter took her back to a nursing home and camped there. The toxins gathering in her mother's body provided a kind of sedation, and death, a week later, was peaceful.

The *JAMA* study's authors are the first to concede that pain is a complicated issue. They know that enduring pain is sometimes an essential price for a patient to pay for beneficial treatments. But they are convinced that hospital culture is weighted heavily toward focusing on treatments even if they are excruciating. The Pross case is typical in that respect. There was no medical way out of

---

THE FINAL STEPS

Having your wishes honored

While most people shy away from talking about death, it's very clear that engaging the issues directly can be an enduring comfort to people left behind. Listen to Marie Bassett: "When I read his words, it all came down to me what it meant."

When her husband, Chet, was diagnosed with cancer in 1990, he wrote that if he were permanently ill, with no chance of survival, he did not want his family to prolong the process. His wife, Marie, was with him when he talked about his wishes and put them into a living will, but during his struggle against disease, she had forgotten. So a nurse named Susan Kronenwetter who was working with the family found the document in his medical records and brought it before them two years later when family members convened in a hospital waiting room.

Indecision: Kronenwetter had seen the family agonizing in indecision— wanting so much for their husband and father to live to see the youngest of his four children, Christie, graduate from high school in six months. But they were torn by his deteriorating condition and knew a decision on whether to resuscitate him, if necessary, was imminent. In that waiting room, Kronenwetter recalls: "The family was stymied. They were all at different points." To help them, she brought out the living will so they could reread Chet Bassett's own wishes.

"These were their father's words and you could just see the impact," the nurse remembers. "As it went around, each person nodded agreement. They knew that it was finally

time to let him go." In January 1993, Bassett, 55, died surrounded by his family, each one having said goodbye.

Many families face this conflict. About 75 percent of people surveyed thought it was a good idea to have a living will or advance directives to set down wishes regarding medical treatment. But fewer than a third of people actually have one, according to a survey by the American Medical Association. To help people think through and write down their wishes, the American Association of Retired Persons and the American Bar Association have a free publication, *Shaping Your Health Care Future with Health Care Advance Directives*. Write to AARP Fulfillment (EE0940), 601 E Street, N.W., Washington, DC 20049.

But writing the words down is just the first step, says Karen Orloff Kaplan, executive director of Choice in Dying (phone: 800-989-9455), which helps families with personal and legal advice. She says it's important not only to talk about wishes with doctors and family members but to give each interested party a written copy. Designate one person—someone in tune with your desires—to carry out your wishes if you are no longer able to. Update your documents every few years.

Experts also suggest choosing a doctor who will stay involved, even if your care is transferred to a specialist. "Ask your doctor specifically if he'll honor your wishes," says Kaplan, "and if he'll continue to be your advocate even if another doctor will be treating you."

the pain, and technological procedures were paramount. Still, her doctor, Elizabeth Cobbs, was acutely aware of her suffering. "We never were successful in making her symptom-free in any of the procedures," says Cobbs, director of the Division for Aging Studies and Services at George Washington University Medical Center in Washington, D.C.

But other times, patients are stoic, reluctant to complain of pain, perhaps for fear of angering or insulting doctors. And sometimes doctors and nurses simply do not ask about pain. Dr. Humberto Vidaillet, a cardiologist in Marshfield, Wis., and an investigator in the study, said he knew cancer patients suffered, but was surprised that so many cardiac patients were among those experiencing pain in their final days.

■ **The cost of dying can crush survivors.** In the parlance of the hospital, "no code" or "DNR" means do not resuscitate. It means if a heart fails, if a life flickers, let it go. Edward Winter had a DNR order in his medical file at St. Francis–St. George Hospital in Cincinnati, according to a lawsuit filed by Winter's daughters against the hospital. "I saw the 'no code' in my father's chart. That's the only way he would consent to stay in the hospital," says Lynn Kroger, one of his three daughters. After seeing his wife die a slow, confused death, Winter was adamant about not wanting heroic efforts to save his life.

That was in 1988. His heart did indeed fail during that hospitalization, but Kroger and her sisters contend that hospital personnel ignored Winter's wishes and his primary physician's orders. A nurse used defibrillators to restore a steady heartbeat. Two days later, Winter suffered a paralyzing stroke. He lived about two more years, scarcely able to speak, incontinent, unable to walk or even roll over in bed. "It was his worst nightmare. He was enraged and depressed," says Kroger.

The extended life he did not want depleted his life's savings. About $100,000 that he had hoped to leave to his children went instead for nursing-home care. His daughters are suing the hospital for medical expenses and damages for pain and suffering. The case is likely to be heard by the Ohio Supreme Court next year. Hospital officials declined comment.

The suit is not about money, says Kroger. It's about following through on her father's wishes. The day after he was resuscitated against his will, he asked for an attorney and began the process of suing the hospital. He died in 1990, but his children fight on for him. "It's difficult to watch a parent's dreams for his children dissipate in that way," says Kroger. "But the most important thing was the amount of suffering he endured. Every day that he would wake up, he would cry — he would cry *because* he woke up." A handful of similar lawsuits are being litigated, but *JAMA* reports that most families simply foot the bills and watch their savings evaporate.

Epilogue. Surgeon Sherwin Nuland, who spent his career overseeing countless last-ditch efforts to rescue fading lives, is not surprised by the study results. The author of the bestselling book *How We Die*, Nuland argues, "We forget that death is something that belongs to the dying person."

The doctors and nurses most intimately involved in the study are more optimistic, and they are eloquent in speaking of what they've learned. "I believe in my heart of hearts that, at least anecdotally, communication was improved during the course of the study," says William Fulkerson Jr., director of the medical intensive care unit at Duke University Medical Center in Durham, N.C., and one of the study's principal investigators. He knows that learning to talk directly about dying will take a long time. But he believes that at his hospital, the effort has begun.

Others involved in the study look for meaning in the disappointing results. A geriatrics physician says he is now teaching the medical students he trains to start discussions of death planning when elderly patients are still vigorous and healthy. A nurse talks about the difficulty of giving patients bad news without destroying hope and suggests changing the focus from hope for a longer life to hope for a peaceful death. An ICU director says that since reviewing the study results, the first thing he does upon walking into the unit is ask if the patient is hurting. All of them hope the lessons learned from the study grow into a chorus of open talk about how to grant dying people their dignity.

BY SUSAN BRINK

Living Environments
in Later Life

Unit 4 noted that old age is often a period of shrinking life space. This concept is crucial to an understanding of the living environments of older Americans. When older people retire, they may find that they travel less frequently and over shorter distances because they no longer work and most neighborhoods have stores, gas stations, and churches in close proximity. As the retirement years roll by, older people may feel less in control of their environments due to a decline in their hearing and vision as well as other health problems. As the aging process continues, the elderly are likely to restrict their mobility to the areas where they feel most secure. This usually means that an increasing amount of time is spent at home. It has been estimated that individuals 65 and over spend 80 to 90

percent of their lives in their home environments. Of all the other age groups, only small children are as house- and neighborhood-bound.

The house, neighborhood, and community environments are, therefore, more crucial to the elderly than to any other adult age group. The interaction with others that they experience within their homes and neighborhoods can be either stimulating or foreboding, pleasant or threatening. Across the country, older Americans find themselves living in a variety of circumstances, ranging from desirable to undesirable.

Approximately 70 percent of the elderly live in a family setting, usually a husband-wife household; 20 percent live alone or with nonrelatives; and the remaining number live in institutions such as nursing homes. Although only about 5 percent of the elderly will be living in nursing homes at any one time, a total of 25 percent of persons 65 and over will spend some time in a nursing home setting. The longer one lives, the more likely he or she is to end up in a total care institution. Since most older Americans would prefer to live independently in their own homes for as long as possible, their relocation—to other houses, apartments, or nursing homes—is often accompanied by a considerable amount of trauma and unrest. The fact that the aged tend to be less mobile and more neighborhood-bound than any other age group makes their living environment most crucial to their sense of well-being.

Articles in this section focus on some of the alternatives available to the aged: institutionalization, the provision of adequate health care, and the dynamics of family care. The experiences of a 91-year-old woman after she was moved to a nursing home are presented in the essay "The Story of a Nursing Home Refugee." The advantages and disadvantages of nursing home living are examined.

Traditionally the family was the main support for elderly relatives, but the family's capacity to provide care has been eroded by economic pressures. Christopher Johnson, in the article "A Proposal for Minimum Standards for 'Low-Stimulus Alzheimer's Wings' in Nursing Facilities," addresses what can be done to make the living arrangements of Alzheimer's patients in the nursing home more predictable and less threatening to them.

In "Final Indignities: The Care of Elders with Dementia," Jennifer Foote observes that measures designed to improve the quality of care for dementia patients have largely failed, leaving the most vulnerable patients with the poorest care. Many of the dementia patients, she believes, are transferred to mental hospitals where they are more open to attack by stronger patients.

"Retirement Migration and Economic Development in High-Amenity Nonmetropolitan Areas," by D. Gordon Bennett, investigates the impact of retirement migration on the economy of seven high-amenity, rapidly growing, nonmetropolitan coastal counties in the Southeast. Potential economic development for these areas is suggested.

Finally, in "Caring for Aged Loved Ones," Jackie Fitzpatrick examines all the possibilities of different types of elderly care, including living with children, nursing homes, assisted living communities, and adult day care centers.

Looking Ahead: Challenge Questions

As medical technology increases the life expectancy of the average American, will it be more or less likely that individuals will spend some of their later years living in a nursing home setting? What are some positive and negative aspects of nursing home life?

As both the number and percentage of older Americans in the total population increases, will neighborhoods become more age-segregated? Why or why not?

What new kinds of living arrangements will become more common for older Americans in the future?

Since relocating sick or feeble older persons may be a threat to their health and survival, what alternatives would you suggest?

The story of a nursing home refugee

KATHARINE M. BUTTERWORTH
WHOLE EARTH REVIEW

Taking care of the elderly is not something we do very well in our society. Most older people prefer to live out their last years on their own or with loved ones rather than in a nursing home, so the burden of caring for them falls squarely on their family and friends. But because there is little public support—either in financial help or in tangible services—for those caretakers, sometimes that burden becomes too great and a nursing home becomes the only option. That's what happened to 91-year-old Katharine Butterworth, and this is her spirited account of that time. Dollars & Sense *magazine describes the mixed-up financial picture of aging policy in the United States and reminds us that with our rapidly growing population, the problem is only going to get worse.*

Young families who have the responsibility of caring for old people find it hard to tuck them in the chimney corner, mainly because there is no longer a chimney corner in which to tuck them.

A bulletin from my college proudly lists 10 graduates who lived to be 100, but every one of them is in a nursing home. A nursing home used to be a halfway house between hospital and going home. Now too often it is the permanent home, the last resort for a family desperate to handle an elderly invalid. Nursing homes are expensive and to receive any financial aid from the government, such as Medicaid, one must be destitute, but that is another story.

I know about three nursing homes, two for my husband, one for myself. My husband and I had had a good and healthy life when in our mid-80s he became ill, a bladder operation leaving him in need of a permanent catheter, the infection sometimes affecting his mind. I became ill and had to enter a hospital myself, so our children insisted he go into a nursing home.

When I recovered and returned home, I visited him. He had been given a small room opposite a noisy laundry room, and a woman patient next door was moaning all night. He said he was going to jump out the window, and I told him he was on the ground floor and could walk out. I sat with him in the dining room with three men who didn't talk; they had Alzheimer's disease. The trays were metal, and noisy when handed out. He was served a huge sausage, the kind he particularly disliked, no knife, and a little dish of stewed fruit with a limp piece of cake on top. No fruit juice or water, liquids he was supposed to have plenty of. In addition he was tied in a wheelchair, making it difficult for him to reach the table. It depressed both of us.

At a meeting with the head nurses and an accountant, in which I was asked to sign many papers to make my husband's acceptance in the nursing home permanent, plus pay a $3,000 deposit in case we got behind in our payments, I burst out, "He's coming home." The nursing home had started out as a solution to a problem but it had turned into a nightmare. We would both be home in our apartment, would manage some way and die together.

Our help at home was erratic and our children again insisted my husband be placed in a nursing home. He needed more care and often wandered at night, waking me up. Once he fell out of bed at 2 a.m., which entailed my calling the police because I could not lift him or help him to climb back in.

This second "home" was much more elegant, with Georgian-style architecture, trees, garden, the room itself large and pleasant, but help here was short and he was often left in bed most of the morning. The dining room had none of the clatter of metal trays and the varied food was attractively served, each person seated at an individual table or in a wheelchair with a tray. It seemed quietly civilized until one patient shoved his tray with everything from soup to dessert and it shot with a crash across the floor, requiring that some poor soul clean up the mess. The patients looked normal but, one could guess, often were not.

Then we found Sandy and a nursing home was no longer necessary. Sandy was with us part time for over a year until my husband died. She was going to college, wanted to earn extra money, and we paid her above the minimum wage. Never have I known a more dedicated, hard-working, cheerful, intelligent young girl. She likes old people, and plans to run her own nursing home some day. May her dream come true. She was ideal for us, permitting my husband to stay home where he was happiest. She was strong enough to give him a tub bath, for example, and because she was cheerfully persuasive there was little friction, and I began to relax. He died at home, which in itself was a comforting end.

Six months after my husband died I came down with pneumonia, and my son and daughter-in-law took me to the emergency room in the nearby hospital. Slowly I recovered physically. There were many complications, X-rays, medicines, a speech therapist and psychologist (which confused me, but apparently I had had a slight stroke that I didn't realize until later). The best medicine was my roommate, Ruth, a rollicking, cheerful woman who was seriously ill, but made everyone who came to our room—cleaning woman, nurse, or doctor—smile.

Eventually a physical therapist got me out of bed and walking, leaning on a walker. I was shocked at how wobbly I had become. I had been in the hospital two weeks and it was time for me to move out. My son, ever helpful and concerned, phoned, "Be ready, Ma, at nine, packed and dressed. The nursing home has a room for you." We decided that this was necessary because my son and daughter-in-law were away all day, and I could never manage alone.

This home was brand new, elegant and very expensive. The girl at the entrance desk was attractively dressed and gave the impression that we were being welcomed to some country estate although the two checks my son made out, one for a large deposit, the other for a week's stay in a double room, provided hard reality.

My first impression was that a great deal had been spent on decor—charming wallpaper, heavy pink bedspread, modern lamp at the bedside table, and a modern picture on the wall. All I wanted was to get undressed and into bed, and I promptly went to sleep.

Looking back I can see why I have been critical of my elegant surroundings. One loss was not having a telephone. In the hospital I could lie in bed and gossip with all my friends. My son usually called every day. Eventually I could use the nurses' phone down the hall, but I had to have the phone handed to me across the desk, stand up, and naturally the call had to be short.

I shared a room with Rose, a woman who had been there for some time and who was a favorite with all the nurses. Her dressing often needed changing at 2 a.m., a process that involved a great deal of nurse chatter, lights, and curtain noisily pulled for "privacy." That I was awoken was unimportant to everyone but me.

Rose had a telephone that her son had had installed. I asked Rose if I could use hers and would

pay her and she agreed. I used her phone just once, when she was taken for some test and I thought my conversation would not bother her. With my address book in hand I went to her bedside table to make the call. As I was dialing, a tall head nurse stalked in, accused me of using Rose's property when she was out, and snatched my address book, saying that I must have taken it from Rose's drawer. I was startled by this false accusation and angry that this woman could think I would use the phone without Rose's permission. Later I made a scene with a superintendent but nothing came of it. Rose laughed when she returned, and all that really happened was I couldn't sleep that night and was given a sleeping pill. It was a good example of the old and the weak versus the young and the strong.

Was I doomed to spend the rest of my life in this nursing home? For one thing I felt it was too expensive. How long would my money last, spent in this ridiculously extravagant fashion? It was up to me to get up and return to normal life. Weak, I got dressed and with my walker managed to make it to a big living room, where I had breakfast off a tray. There I found a dozen other more active people doing the same. The next day I carried in the portable radio my son had brought me and I came back to the world and listened to the news and my favorite classical music station. At lunch, again with my walker, I went to the dining room despite the 20 minutes it took me to travel the short distance down the hall. I began to feel that with determination I could grow strong.

The staff of this particular home worked hard to make things easy and pleasant for the patients—one could say they ought to for the price. There was an exercise class every morning, and I joined this. We sat in a big circle, some in wheelchairs, others in regular chairs. A young, peppy woman led us. She brought a huge lightweight ball that she would roll to each in turn and we would kick it back with right then left foot. Many of us were weak but one could see an improvement. There were exercises with arms, "pick the apple out of the tree, then put it down in the basket"; silly, but it got one's muscles moving.

The staff organized movies and an ice-cream party for those of us who could walk or get someone to push our wheelchairs to the parlor. I began to walk the corridors for exercise, and to explore different areas. There was one much more expensive-looking area that had a living room arranged with couches and easy chairs as in a private home. Here the public library had installed a wide choice of books in large print and this attracted me. Just by signing my name and room number I could help myself. I realized for the first time that my illness had been severe enough for me to give up reading. I took out a novel that looked lightweight and easy to follow, and this room became my favorite.

In my own area there was a music room that was not used much, and I would take my book here, pretending there were no hospital beds around the corner. This room had an expensive grand piano made in China. Here on Sunday afternoon there was a concert for piano and harp. A young lady brought in her harp, an undertaking that took more time than the concert itself. Unfortunately there were barely more than a dozen people who attended.

As I walked around more I became acquainted with more patients. There was one pleasant woman with one arm paralyzed, who was always in a wheelchair. She explained to me that when she and her husband found they had physical problems they could not solve, they sold their house and both entered this nursing home with the idea of ending their lives here. They had enough money to pay for the most expensive suite, brought their own furniture, and often had special meals ordered. I never met her husband, but she was such a cheerful realist she was a pleasure to talk to.

There was another alert old gentleman whose son visited him every Sunday, and he was eager to talk. He knew the area, had been in business all his life, and would have preferred to stay home. His wife had died, and he needed too much care for his daughter-in-law to handle. Again there was enough money for him not to worry.

Many of these old people grumbled and complained and were dull to talk to. The patients whose minds were affected I found depressing. One attractive woman beautifully dressed in different outfits was like a flitting bird. She explained that her children had left her here, and she wanted to escape but she didn't know how to get out. Then she would jump up and run down the hall. There was one man with Parkinson's disease who would walk endlessly up and down the hall never meeting one's eye, looking vaguely for someone, something, perhaps his own identity.

There was a dumpy little woman with Alzheimer's disease, and she too was a wanderer with fluttering hands. She liked my room and once tried to get into my bed, to my horror. Another time

Who cares for our elders?

"Why should a woman in her 60s feel she must use up her life savings—even sell her home—to keep her mother in a nursing home for less than two years?" asked American Association of Retired Persons vice president Robert Maxwell. "Why should a couple married for 30 years be forced to get a divorce in order to protect the wife's income and assets, while the husband impoverishes himself to qualify for Medicaid-funded nursing home care?"

They shouldn't, of course. These are consequences of government inaction on an issue that affects nearly all people at some time in their lives. Mention long-term care of older citizens to most Americans, and the first image that comes to mind is the nursing home. While nursing homes constitute a thriving industry in the United States, they are not where most care for elders takes place.

For elders who can no longer fully care for themselves, most care is provided at home by family members and friends. An estimated seven million older Americans require some sort of assistance—from once-a-week shopping help, to once-a-day meal preparation, to round-the-clock nursing care.

For incapacitated elders and their families, the choices are hard. Nursing home care is costly and of poor quality. Home care services are virtually non-existent in many states, and where they are available they are expensive. For most who quit their jobs to care for their parents, there is little income support. The lack of long-term care is indeed a national crisis.

Though most surveys of elders indicate they would rather not be institutionalized in nursing homes, institutionalization is precisely what our present system of long-term elderly care encourages.

Given the demographics of the United States, nursing homes are a growth industry. Roughly 1.6 million nursing home beds were in use in 1986. Because the number of elders in the U.S. population is projected to rise through the year 2030, the demand for nursing home beds is expected to increase to over two million in 2000, and to nearly three million by 2030.

Nursing homes are now a $38 billion industry with more than 19,000 homes. Once dominated by "mom-and-pop" operators and charitable organizations, the industry is increasingly composed of large, for-profit chains.

For nursing home residents, absentee ownership brings negative consequences. The Massachusetts Department of Public Health, charged with monitoring nursing home care, reports that absentee-owned homes have significantly more code violations than locally owned and non-profit homes.

For the patient or the patient's family, nursing home care is extremely costly. Average costs per day run as high as $100. Annual costs range from $25,000 to $40,000. Unless residents are extremely poor—or until they reach that point—most of the cost of nursing home care is borne by elders and their families. Medicare will pay only up to 100 days of acute medical and rehabilitative services in a nursing home, leaving people needing long-term care completely uncovered. Medicare pays only 2 percent of the nation's nursing home bill.

she stole a book I had carelessly left on my bed. I had a nurse search her room, but we never found it, and I wrote the public library apologizing, hoping someone would return it.

Unlike the pleasant woman and her husband who planned to make this their permanent home, my attitude from the beginning had been to get strong and to leave the nursing home as soon as possible. I was lucky that I had no debilitating disease, that I could walk, and that my mind was normal. My finances were not great enough to pay for this "hotel" (for a bed and meals were what it amounted to, with little mental stimulation). In a little over three weeks I persuaded my son and daughter-in-law to take me in.

When I got to their rather cold house (the nursing home had been overheated), and had to get my own breakfast and lunch, and be alone all day, I realized I had been too impatient. I was not as tough as I had thought I was. I often would crawl

back in bed and sleep an uneasy sleep, but soon I would force myself, warmly dressed, to walk around the back yard or go out for the mail. There was plenty to read, too much, but the most endearing feature was the family cat, Brandy. She too was lonely during the day, and she and I would lie down together on my bed, or she'd sit in my lap, and we'd talk and purr and were close company. Evenings and weekends were wonderful, with the stimulating company of my son and daughter-in-law, and delicious meals where all I did was set the table. The nursing home seemed far away. The next jump was to my own apartment, but this was cushioned by the arrival of my daughter, who cooked for me and spoiled me. Without the help of my children could I have recovered so quickly?

Now, two years later, at 91, I live alone. How long can I hope to keep moving about with family and friends, to take walks around the pond in the neighboring park? Can I hope to escape the permanent nursing home?

Medicaid, known as the long-term care insurance policy that requires impoverishment for a premium, is the major public payer for long-term care services. For the poor and those older Americans impoverished by the high costs of long-term care, Medicaid covers nearly all nursing home expenses. Medicaid pays nearly half the nation's nursing home bill, making it—by default rather than by design—the country's long-term care insurance policy.

Once on Medicaid, older people needing care are hardly free of worry. Medicaid sets a fixed payment rate for nursing home care that is on the average 15 to 20 percent lower than the rates charged private payers. This gives nursing home operators a strong incentive to discriminate against those on public assistance. Medicaid-supported elders seeking nursing home care typically wait four times as long for a bed in a nursing home as privately paying elders.

With all of the problems associated with nursing home care, it is perhaps not surprising that older people overwhelmingly prefer to be cared for in their own homes. Yet government spending for long-term care is heavily biased in favor of nursing homes. Neither Medicare nor Medicaid covers any significant part of home care services. As a result, 85 percent of home care is provided by friends and family members without institutional support. Of the 15 percent who receive care from paid providers, **60 percent pay the entire bill themselves. High turnover among home care workers, who are overworked and underpaid, further hampers the availability of adequate home care.**

Not surprisingly, most of the caregivers—paid and unpaid—are women. Women frequently care for their infirm husbands, whom they outlive by six years on average. The burden of care also falls on adult children, usually daughters and daughters-in-law, who give up paid work to care for frail family members. The vast majority of paid home care workers are also women.

Ironically, although home care tends to be much cheaper than nursing home care, cost containment is one of the major reasons for the government's bias toward institutional care. Public officials, recognizing that the number of elders currently going without publicly supported services far exceeds the number receiving support, fear a surge in demand for home care if the government were to provide it.

According to a recent survey commissioned by senior advocates, the U.S. public is greatly concerned about the inadequacy of long-term care. Sixty percent of respondents said they had direct experience with family members or friends needing long-term care, and more than 80 percent said nursing home costs would be a major hardship on their families. Most significant, over 70 percent said they wanted a government program providing universal long-term care and would be willing to pay higher taxes to support it.

—Dollars & Sense

Excerpted with permission from Dollars & Sense *(Jan./Feb. 1988). Subscriptions: $19.50/yr. (10 issues) from Economic Affairs Bureau, 1 Summer St., Somerville, MA 02143. Back issues: $3 from same address.*

A PROPOSAL FOR MINIMUM STANDARDS FOR "LOW-STIMULUS ALZHEIMER'S WINGS" IN NURSING FACILITIES

Christopher Jay Johnson, Ph.D.

Institute of Gerontology and Alzheimer's Research Center
Northeast Louisiana State University
Monroe, Louisiana

The concept of "low-stimulus Alzheimer's wings" has been advanced and developed over the past several years (Calkins, 1987–88; Hall et al. 1986; Hiatt, 1984; Johnson, 1989, 1990; Lawton, 1983). As a result, there has been a proliferation of both well-designed and "instant" Alzheimer's wings in nursing centers around the United States. However, there are no minimum standards for these facilities. The "instant" wings lack professional guidance in development or staff training, and rarely are designed in accordance with specifications recommended in the gerontological literature. Based on the author's clinical experience in developing low-stimulus Alzheimer's wings for nursing facilities, this article proposes minimum standards for such units.

A low-stimulus Alzheimer's wing is designed to provide both staff training and a safe environment for residents with dementia in nursing facilities (Johnson, 1989). These units provide quality care for such residents, promoting optimal physical, mental, social, and spiritual functioning according to a social model. The wing employs an enabling social milieu of activities, special design, colors, texture, furniture, cuing or wayfinding devices, activity areas, dining areas, unique feeding procedures with special diets, and noise control. Equal amounts of attention are given to special practice policies and staff training, which govern unit operation. Policies are needed to outline preadmission and discharge procedures and family visitation. These policies should be incorporated in the unit mission statement, along with goals and objectives. Well-developed daily care procedures provide guidelines for staff training and ensure optimum continuity of care and accountability.

BEHAVIORAL OBJECTIVES FOR THE ALZHEIMER'S RESIDENT

The mission statement of the facility should clearly state its commitment to restraint-free rehabilitative care (social model) rather than custodial care (medical model). First, the social model emphasizes the need for staff and families (caregivers) to be trained in social interaction techniques with residents with dementia. The following are key interactive objectives for staff and/or families to communicate to residents with dementia:

1. Convey clear expectations of appropriate actions to the resident.
2. Use classical conditioning actions (e.g., praise, hugs, etc.) to elicit positive feelings in AD persons.
3. Enhance residents' pleasure (through encouraging client recall of time and place by using life histories, reminiscence therapy and modified reality orientations).
4. Offer appropriate activities that focus on residents' remaining abilities through a minimum of two hours of consistently scheduled activities a day, administered by a certified activity director.
5. Foster residents' emotional health by facilitating special interpersonal relationships with family and staff. In-house family support groups should be de-

From *Illness, Crises & Loss*, Summer 1992, pp. 7-12. © 1992 by The Charles Press, Publishers, Inc. Reprinted by permission.

veloped and referrals made to local Alzheimer's support groups.

6. Use a modified reality orientation as opposed to a total reality orientation (e.g., do not correct faulty beliefs, go along with them).
7. Provide regular exercise and therapeutic activities as alternatives to polypharmacy.
8. Control behaviors through modified, high caloric and complex carbohydrate diets with no red food dyes, sugar or caffeine; in addition, high fiber and water consumption is encouraged for regularity of body functions, which enhances mood control.

The task of promoting healthy caregiver behavior is management's most important goal. Moore (1991) points out that modifications of interactions between AD persons and caregivers can be translated symbolically into positive actions for the Alzheimer's resident. Therefore, family members are encouraged to deal with their grief by either support groups or therapy. Numerous studies have indicated three keys to successful interaction and enabling of AD persons (Brody et al., 1973; Eisendoofer et al., 1981; Hellebrandt, 1978; Lawton, 1981):

1. Positively reinforce everything the staff do and say to the AD person to build trust and a sense of mastery in the resident.
2. Identify and promote the remaining capacity of the AD person.
3. Always seek the meaning and purpose of the behavior of the AD person.

For persons with AD, all behaviors are symbolic and packed with meaning and purpose, but it may be a challenge for the caregiver to interpret their actions. Persons with AD tend to rely on feelings rather than beliefs to interpret their world, and act accordingly. This is why a symbolically enabling environment helps the person with dementia deal more efficiently with the social world.

ENVIRONMENTAL OBJECTIVES FOR THE ALZHEIMER'S RESIDENT

The physical environment of an Alzheimer's wing in a nursing facility should enable the resident to carry out activities of daily living (ADLs) with optimum capacity and dignity. The daily offering of relationships and activities that are individualized for the differing cognitive capacities of each resident is the hallmark of a social model of care.

The following are some steps recommended for environmental modification of AD wings:

1. Remove overstimulation from noxious noise by eliminating paging systems, television, and loud radios. (Note: playing soft radio or taped songs in slow tempo is useful.)

2. Reduce sensory overload through specially designed dining rooms to maximize the probability of AD persons maintaining weight.
3. Reduce overstimulating glare from windows and reduce shadows through increased lighting in egg crate style fixtures.
4. Provide solid color, low gloss, and tile floors or thin stain-resistant carpet to reduce glare, noise and fatigue from wandering.
5. Stimulate a sense of touch and a need to clutch. A sense of touch is stimulated by providing residents with different textured wall hangings, carpet sample flip-charts, dolls, stuffed animals, pet therapy and plant/garden therapy (cf., Coons, 1985; Hall, et al., 1986; Johnson, 1989).
6. Reduce aimless wandering and increase safety by installing locked doors in the AD wing, allowing residents to wander as they please within the confined areas (including an outdoor wandering area with benches or sitting areas).
7. Use object cues or markers to direct residents to their rooms or territory.[1]
8. Keep the traffic in the wing and the size of the wing to reasonable levels. A maximum of 20 residents or less is preferable.

Regulations do not always make sense for persons with dementia, who may constitute up to 60 percent of nursing home residents across the country. For example, current regulations require all residents to have wastebaskets and water pitchers in their rooms, to be able to close the doors to their rooms if they want to, to be called by their last name, to have curtains and mirrors in their rooms, and to have their delusional statements corrected with rational ones. As one might expect, since most of these policies and regulations are put together "warehouse-style" to apply to all residents of the facility, whether the policies are therapeutic or not, they actually become abusive and detrimental to many AD residents. For example, due to their disease, AD persons may use wastebaskets for toilets and water pitchers for urinals; they may be injured falling behind closed doors if not supervised; they may smash mirrors, thinking someone else is looking at them; and they may get upset when a staff member "disagrees" with their distorted beliefs rather than the staff using a modified reality orientation and agreeing with a delusion to avoid conflicts.

It is not surprising that such abusive policies exist since non-gerontologists usually develop them. These misguided policies need to be modified and updated. The author has noticed a lack of quality professional guidance in many Alzheimer's disease wings throughout the United States. Few AD wings have certified professional gerontologists providing staff with inservice training.

As stated, family and staff condition AD residents with the constant use of smiles, praise, and hugs to build self-worth. In addition, staff encourages AD residents to do ADLs in a simplified step-by-step fashion, using easy to understand enabling actions toward AD residents in everything they do from dressing to bathing.[2]

In summary, training caregivers of AD persons to change their negative symbol systems creates a sociological metamorphosis, a therapeutic milieu for the AD resident. Staff and family need ongoing training in the nature of disabilities caused by dementias and in cultivating the remaining social skills in persons with dementia. The modified symbolic environment of a low stimulus dementia wing, coupled with new staff behaviors, can encourage positive feelings and interactions with residents.

NOTES

1. Landmarkers are used placing signs with first names of residents in strategic areas, family pictures (note: preferably their parents or siblings since the residents are cognitively back in their childhood and will more readily recognize those pictures) on "biblioboards," colored toilet seats that contrast with the ground below (note: a picture of a toilet is used on the bathroom door), and color-coding resident rooms, etc.
2. Alzheimer's disease has been referred to as an ongoing funeral, and it is believed that AD persons and their loved ones suffer from depression throughout the course of the disease. Therefore, it is important to have positive, easy-going caregivers who encourage them to do as much for themselves as possible.

REFERENCES

Brody, E.M., C. Cole, and M. Moss. Individualizing therapy for the mentally impaired ages. *Social Casework* 132–137, 1973.

Calkins, M.P. Design special care units: A systematic approach. *American Journal of Alzheimer's Care and Research* 2(2):30–34, 1987.

Calkins, M.P. *Design for Dementia: Planning Environments for the Elderly and Confused.* Owings Mills, MD: National Health Publishing, 1988.

Coons, D. Alive and well at Wesley Hall. *Quarterly Journal of Long-Term Care* 121(2):10–14, 1985.

Eisendoofer, C., D. Cohen and C. Preston. Behavior and Psychological Therapies for the Older Patient with Cognitive Impairment. In N. Miller and G. Cohen, eds., *Clinical Aspects of Alzheimer's Disease and Senile Dementia.* New York: Raven Press, 1981.

Hall, G., M.V. Kirshling and S. Todd. Sheltered freedom/An Alzheimer's unit in an ICF. *Geriatric Nursing,* May-June 1986, pp. 132–137.

Hellebrandt, F. A comment: The senile dementia in our midst. *The Gerontologist* 18(1):67–70, 1978.

Hiatt, L. Conveying the substance of images: Interior design in long-term care. *Contemporary Administration* 6:86–89, 1984.

Johnson, C.J. Sociological intervention through developing low-stimulus Alzheimer's wings in nursing homes. *American Journal of Alzheimer's Care and Related Disorders and Research* 4(2):33–41, 1989.

Johnson, C. J. The Sociology of Alzheimer's Wings in Nursing Homes. In E. Clark, J. Fritz and P. Rieker, eds., *Clinical Sociological Perspectives on Illness and Loss.* Philadelphia: The Charles Press, Publishers, 1990.

Lawton, M.P. Sensory deprivation and the effect of the environment on management of the patient with senile dementia. In N. Miller and G. Cohen, eds., *Clinical Aspects of Alzheimer's Disease and Senile Dementia.* New York: Raven Press, 1981.

Lawton, M.P. Environment and other determinants of well-being in older people. *The Gerontologist* 23(4):349–357, 1983.

Moore, R.H. The use of symbolic interaction in the management of Alzheimer's persons: A review of the literature. *American Journal of Alzheimer's Care and Related Disorders and Research* 6(5): 28–33, 1991.

Final indignities: The care of elders with dementia

Jennifer Foote

Maturity News

Our visions of nursing homes are conjured reluctantly, usually from flashes of memory clouded by age or dread. We see them as the last resort of the elderly ill, whose ailments—arthritis, heart disease, cancer or broken bones—are familiar, even inevitable.

They are, we think, the flawed but grimly adequate infirmaries of the very, very old.

That is what we think. But we are wrong.

Today nursing homes and other long-term care facilities are de facto psychiatric wards, overwhelmed by the needs of nearly 1 million elderly residents with Alzheimer's disease and other dementias. The numbers will explode as baby boomers age.

Traditionally focused on medical services, the facilities are failing in many cases to deliver even marginal care to elders with dementia.

In an investigation of institutional care of elderly dementia patients, reporters from Maturity News Service and Newhouse News Service found widespread evidence that ignorance, lack of training and neglect have resulted in the physical and sexual abuse of patients and, in many cases, their deaths.

These patients often are the defenseless targets of long-term care staff who, guided by the belief that a loss of cognitive ability diminishes a person's humanity, dismiss residents with dementia as beyond help and unworthy of care. Other times, patients are victims of staff with criminal records and unchecked violent behavior.

"Nursing homes are now mental institutions where the few patients who get treatment are over-medicated and restrained," says Dr. Barry Rovner, director of geriatric psychiatry at Jefferson Medical College in Philadelphia.

> There are nursing homes that have learned how to help dementia patients, using new research training to cope with their needs. But they are the exception. Many other facilities use overmedication, physical restraint and isolation to cope with dementia patients.

"They are taken care of the way we took care of institutionalized psychiatric patients 150 years ago," Rovner says.

Past horror stories about nursing homes resulted in a sweeping series of reforms in the 1980s—federal laws hailed by advocates as a nursing home resident's Bill of Rights. But measures specifically designed to improve the quality of care for dementia patients have largely failed, leaving the most vulnerable residents with the weakest guarantees of care.

In fact, some changes in the way the federal government subsidizes patient care actually provide nursing homes with clear financial incentives to dump those with dementia, often into mental hospitals where they are more open to attack by stronger patients.

There are nursing homes that have learned how to help dementia patients, using new research and training to cope with their needs and innovations in care to offer a better quality of life.

But they are the exception. Many other facilities use overmedication, physical restraint and isolation to cope with dementia patients, compromising their health and accelerating their mental decline in the process.

"Two out of three nursing home residents have some kind of dementia," says Linda Keegan, a vice president of the American Healthcare Association, the largest organization of long-term care providers.

Nursing home staff "need good practical tools" for dealing with dementia patients, Keegan says. "And we feel they still have a long way to go. I don't think great tools exist for them yet."

Twenty-five percent of all Americans 85 and older already have dementia, according to a 1990 report by the federal Office of Technology Assessment. No other age category is growing as fast; none has a greater vulnerability to brain disease.

In the year 2000, the Census Bureau estimates, there will be 4.6 million people older than 84 in the United States. One study, published in the Journal of American Medicine in 1990, suggests that by 2040, the number of moderately and severely demented patients will quadruple.

Yet the number of long-term care homes is actually decreasing as the fa-

What is the experience of dementia?

Jennifer Foote
Maturity News

The void descends like an airborne anvil. A split-second brainwash and all the givens go at once. The date, the place, the name of the dog.

Hold on to a chair. Look out the window. Search for hints.

It is light outside, but it could be dinner time. It is cold inside, but where is the heat? Today might be the day you make the dinner, but where are the kids?

When the fog doesn't clear, the panic is heart-stopping. If it is morning, you really should brush your teeth. But when you do, you are caught red-handed by the woman you know you love, but who will never want to stay. Not now. Not after she found you rinsing your teeth in a sports jacket at 2:30 in the morning. And what is her name? You know you know it, but where is her name?

She will offer a clue, with a dose of impatience or pity, and you will be you again and she will be your wife. (Of course!) But the revelation, slow to penetrate, hard to keep, will leave the noxious residue of another dark episode, another blight on your brain.

And the dizzy fear, the nausea, takes longer and longer to break.

Lists help. Maps help. Labels, flash cards and Post-Its help—and then they make it worse. Is it an old list? Is it a map to home? A hundred lists can't stop you from going every day to buy legal-size envelopes. Nothing helps you to remember, as you try to bake cookies, if you already added the salt.

Nothing, not locks or window panes or second-floor balconies, can stop you from going to work. Even the sign they put around your neck that says "I retired in 1985" doesn't blunt the urge to get to your desk on time.

When the phone rings, it burbles in the drunken haze that rarely lifts and makes your tongue huge and uncooperative. The older woman who lives in the house (she takes care of you, she is often sad) says, "Answer the phone!" But you move in mud, like you haven't slept for a week.

How do you answer the phone? Your arms feel asleep, dead in the way they do when you try to put them through the tubes in the shirt or use your fingers to put the bumps through the holes in the front.

In time, time lose shape. There is light and dark; both are frightening when you notice. Whole floes of memory break loose and float away. Words, tasks, the identities of people you are supposed to know seem to hemorrhage from your brain.

Piercing the cloudy aspic are the less and less frequent moments when terror, shame and despair flood through a narrowing window of self. Everything precious—memories, relationships, identity—will be lost and you will be a burden, a nub of a person to be humiliated or abandoned by the people who are still at least faintly familiar.

But then the dread goes, too, and you forget that you forget. Left behind in the frayed lattice of recollection are Mom, her fragrance, the name of a co-worker, a Girl Scout song, a whole summer abroad.

You move away; they send you away. Is it camp? Is it school?

Food, tasteless if it isn't sweet, goes in blindly. It comes out, beyond your control. Below you are on fire, pain that makes you call, in fact you are shouting, for Mother, over and over again. On top is choking thirst. But the other children in the school are mad at you, they might hit you, they took your coat. And the teachers whiz by, talking nonsense, douse you in needles of hard water. They are different everyday.

Run away, visit the beach house, let the sea heal waves of pain. No more classes, no more books . . . roll from the stinking white ledge and drop like a stone to freedom.

Drained, depleted, strapped to stop walking, to trap breaths, you feel the vapors of what others are thinking. Noise is ear-splitting. The sameness, the absence of caress, heartbreaking.

Language is gone, your own moaning, your own hands, you, not connected to you.

tution, and when we're in that institution, 60 to 80 percent of us will have some form of senile dementia or other mental illness.

"So there's a good chance that those of us sitting here bemoaning the quality of these services may someday need them."

The three-month Maturity and Newhouse investigation—which included interviews around the country with nursing home ombudsmen, elder law attorneys, families of dementia patients, geriatric psychiatrists, clinical researchers, nurses, aides and others—yielded a frightening roster of inadequacy.

In Illinois, a 61-year-old stroke victim was raped repeatedly over a two-year period by a nursing home aide, who was found to have attacked 10 other women in the home, nine of them Alzheimer's patients. Her pleas for help, according to a suit filed by her husband against the home, were dismissed as symptoms of dementia.

In Philadelphia, two nursing home residents with dementia died of blood poisoning caused by deep, open bedsores. Police there found others living in squalid personal care and boarding homes, with buckets for toilets and C-rations for meals. One dementia patient, police reported, was dumped by a facility in a local emergency room, covered with softball-size bedsores that had rotted to the bone.

In California, an Alzheimer's patient was discovered beaten and in a pool of blood, the crippling brutality a mystery to the nursing home.

Reporters found that many of the abuses, including physical and sexual assault, are committed repeatedly and rarely reported to authorities.

The cases that reach law enforcement authorities through public health or adult protective services agencies rarely are prosecuted successfully because victimized dementia patients often are not considered credible and frequently there are no witnesses to the neglect or assault.

cilities shift to the more lucrative field of short-term or "subacute," care.

"These are devastating findings," says University of Pennsylvania

health economist Dennis Shea, an analyst of national data on nursing homes. "Forty to 60 percent of us will end up in a long term care insti-

Retirement Migration and Economic Development in High-Amenity, Nonmetropolitan Areas

There has been a rapid growth of retired inmigrants in high-amenity, nonmetropolitan areas in the Southeast during the last two to three decades. This article examines the economic impact they have made on these counties and the economic development opportunities they present. Data used in this study were obtained from 350 in-home interviews of households who had moved to these counties for the purpose of retiring.

D. Gordon Bennett

D. Gordon Bennett is Professor of Geography at the University of North Carolina at Greensboro. His research interests include migration and demographic analysis, and his most recent publications are Applied Human Geography *(3rd ed.), (Kendall/Hunt Publishing Co.) and "The Impact of Retirement Migration on Carteret and Brunswick Counties, N.C.," (The North Carolina Geographer).*

During the 1970s, 4 of the 10 most rapidly growing states for the elderly were along the South Atlantic Cost: Florida, South Carolina, North Carolina, and Georgia (Serow & Charity, 1988). Bohland and Rowles (1988) reported that in North Carolina and Georgia, increased numbers of elderly migrants have been associated with the emer-gence of retirement areas beyond the traditional ones in Florida and Arizona. Biggar, Flynn, Longino, and Wiseman (1984) indicated that by 1980 Florida and North Carolina had become the two most popular destinations in the eastern Sunbelt, and Longino, Biggar, Flynn, and Wiseman (1984) stated that these two states were two of the four major receivers of retired inmigrants from nonadjacent states. Glasgow and Reeder (1990) reported that during the 1980s, nonmetropolitan retirement counties continued to grow faster than national, metropolitan, or all nonmetropolitan averages. The purpose of this article is to examine the impact of retirement migration on the economy of seven high-amenity, rapidly growing nonmetropolitan coastal counties in the southeastern part of the United States and to suggest potential economic development possibilities for these areas.

As early as 1975, Barsby and Cox studied the impact of older migrants on state economies. In 1979, McCarthy and Morrison indicated that "Retirement and recreation has emerged as important growth-related (and probably growth-inducing) activities in nonmetropolitan areas" (p. vii). Glasgow (1980) stated that the higher incomes of elderly newcomers to nonmetropolitan retirement communities stimulated demand for goods and services and often growth in sections of the

AUTHOR'S NOTE: This research project was funded by a grant from the Economic Development Administration, by research leave from the University of North Carolina at Greensboro, and by a small grant from the Research Council of UNC, Greensboro. The findings and conclusions are those of the author and do not necessarily reflect the view of the Economic Development Administration. Requests for reprints should be addressed to D. Gordon Bennett, Ph. D., Department of Geography, University of North Carolina, Greensboro, Greensboro, NC 27412.

country that were traditionally below the average in income and services and facilities for the elderly. Aday and Miles (1982) found that young retired migrants were important consumers and tended to be homeowners and to improve the tax base. Summers and Hirschl (1985) found that "retirement income often constitutes a good base for economic development" (p. 13). They also reported that Harmston (cited in Summers & Hirschl, 1985) found in Vandalia, Missouri that for every $1.00 spent locally by retirees an additional $1.22 of local income and business revenue was generated (a multiplier of 2.22).

Comparing the income of retired inmigrants to the overall elderly population, Longino (1985) found that the average income of elderly migrant households in 1979-1980 was nearly 80% higher than that of all older households. Moreover, Glasgow and Beale (1988) stated that retired migrants to nonmetro areas are affluent compared to the indigenous elderly population. Henry, Drabenstott, and Gibson (1987) further noted that of all nonmetropolitan areas, only those primarily dependent on retirement were able to improve their relative incomes between 1973 and 1984.

Several recent studies have added to the understanding of the influence of retired migrants on their destinations. Crown (1988) argued that with the continued aging of the population, retirement migration with be a major factor in economic development. Glasgow (1988) reported that the higher incomes of newcomers stimulate demand for goods and services, particularly in areas with below-average services for the elderly. Longino and Crown (1989) noted that retired migrants to major Sunbelt receiving states were an economic bonanza for less-populated counties with large numbers of elderly newcomers. Longino and Crown (1990) also found that Florida, North Carolina, South Carolina, and Georgia ranked first, fourth, seventh, and ninth in the nation in the net amount of income brought into states by retired inmigrants. Longino (1990) also found that interstate retired migrants to North Carolina counties with appropriate lifestyle settings for amenity-oriented retirees have a positive economic impact. Reeder and Glasgow (1990) noted that, in general, retirement counties benefited county economies, particularly those with a sixth or more of their population being elderly. Cuba and Longino (1991) found that retired migrants to Cape Cod were well educated and financially comfortable. In a Canadian study, Hodge (1991) reported that every two retired inmigrant households generated one job.

Despite these findings, several authors have cautioned that the economic benefits brought by the relatively young retirees who move to retirement areas could become a liability 15 to 25 years later as physical impairments increase the demand for medical facilities and medical costs rise (Crown, 1988; Haas, 1990; Glasgow & Reeder, 1990; Longino, 1990; Longino, Marshall, Mullins & Tucker, 1991; Rosenbaum & Button, 1989). However, Glasgow and Reeder (1990), although cautioning that planners should monitor the impact of their retired migrants as they age, concluded that retirement migration had not been a local fiscal burden but rather a "boon" to the economy. Haas and Crandall (1988) reported that, in fact, the

growth in Medicare patients in rural counties they studied stimulated the health care economy and attracted more physicians to the area.

Longino and Crown (1989) concluded that because of a growing sense that retired inmigrants are an economic benefit to receiving communities "the fear of the gray peril is dying" (p. 28). These authors (1990) also noted that "the apprehension that retired migrants may burden social services targeted to the elderly has never been documented" (p. 788) and that the newcomers use these services less than do the indigenous elderly. Reeder and Glasgow (1990) found that retirement counties spent less on public health and hospitals than did nonmetro counties as a whole and that only with regard to utilities have local governments indicated any strain on finances from rapid retirement migration. Serow (1990) reported that not only do retired migrants improve the local tax and economic base but also demand no more local and state services than do younger local citizens.

During the 1980s, several authors indicated that to better understand the relationship between retirement migration and economic development there was a need for microlevel studies that could use data gathered directly from retirees who had moved into nonmetropolitan areas (Aday & Miles, 1982; Bryant & El-Attar, 1984; Crown, 1985; Longino, 1988; Longino & Biggar, 1982). Two recently published studies on eight western and two eastern North Carolina countries used data collected directly from retired inmigrants. Both studies found that the elderly inmigrants were a positive economic benefit to the economies of the receiving counties (Bennett, 1992; Serow & Haas, 1992).

Method

The data used for this study were collected directly from elderly residents who had moved into these counties for the express purpose of retiring. None of them had worked or been stationed in the military in the country directly before retiring there. The 350 respondents (50 in each country) who completed their personal surveys were selected by using a spatially stratified random-sampling technique (placing a grid over areas on the map identified by planners and realtors as sections to which retired newcomers have moved and selecting 150 ft. by 150 ft. cells at random), so that each retired newcomer household living in these countries had an equal chance of being interviewed. Because the respondents were geographically selected by a weighted random system throughout the county, they were also representative of socioeconomic variations that occur spatially. Local newspapers ran a front-page story about the purpose of the study the day the in-home interviews began. Thus, of the residents contacted for the surveys, fewer than 1 in 50 refused to answer the questionnaire.

The nonmetropolitan areas included in the study were all high-amenity, rapidly growing retirement counties along the southeastern coast of the United States between Morehead City, North Carolina and Vero Beach, Florida (Figure 1). (The

Figure 1.

Study area counties and selected cities in the eastern United States.

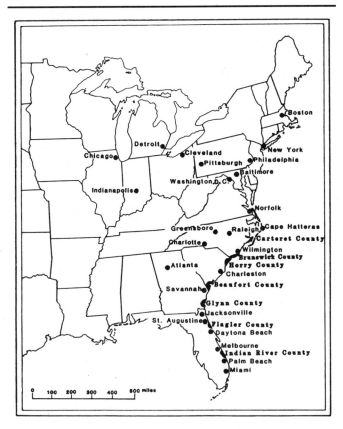

average growth rate for the elderly in these counties in the 1980s was 94%, accounting for 28% of all growth.) The basic geographical and socioeconomic characteristics of the counties in the region were similar, although the areas were not contiguous (Figure 1).

Specific questions on the survey included the amount spent in the county by the retired respondent household on a variety of goods and services. These including housing; utilities; groceries; clothing; car maintenance; meals in restaurants; a variety of recreation/entertainment activities; medicine and medical care; and a variety of major purchases, such as appliances, home furnishings, automobiles, boats, electronics, property, and so on. Various demographic characteristics of the household, such as age, sex, relationship, education, occupation at retirement, and income were also included. In addition, they were also queried about any problems or needs they had.

The basic premises were the retired inmigrants would be of a higher socioeconomic level than the indigenous population, have a positive economic impact on the receiving counties, and represent a large and growing moderate-to-high income market about which businesses were either unaware or to which they had failed to respond adequately. It was hypothesized that as these retired inmigrants continued to age they would *not* significantly lower their purchasing level (ex-

35. Retirement Migration and Economic Development

cept for housing, including basic appliances) and that most would have above-average incomes for the region and thus be major consumers. Chi-square tests were employed to see if expenditures on various goods and services varied either by age or income of the retired inmigrants or by length of residence in the area.

Findings

Characteristics of Retired Migrants

The demographic characteristics of a population can provide an indication of their potential economic—and even noneconomic—contribution to an area. The findings in this investigation of seven nonmetropolitan counties along the southeast coast will be compared with those for retired inmigrants in eight counties of western North Carolina—although one of those counties was metropolitan and sampling techniques and survey instruments were different (Haas & Serow, 1990; Serow & Haas, 1992).

The educational and preretirement occupational levels of the retirees who moved into the nonmetro coastal countries were very high (Table 1). About 36% of those who moved into the region for the sole purpose of retiring had a college diploma (compared to only 18% of all adults—according to the 1990 census of population [Bureau of the Census, 1992]), including about 10% with a graduate degree. Moreover, 73% of males had held professional/managerial positions (including owning their own businesses) immediately before retiring. These high educational and occupational levels were reflected in their annual retirement incomes. The 1989 median household income of the retired inmigrants was approximately $37,000, compared to $27,000 for all households in the region (1990 census of population). About 43% of the retired newcomer households had a yearly income of $40,000 or more (Table 1), compared to only 10% of all elderly in the nation in 1986 (Soldo & Agree, 1988). Although only 30% of retired inmigrants in western North Carolina had annual incomes of $40,000 or more, an Amazing 59% of all retired newcomers in that region had college diplomas, including 27% with a graduate degree (Haas & Serow, 1990).

The persons who had moved to the nonmetropolitan coastal counties to retire were relatively young, with about 36% being under 65 years of age (14%;) and only approximately 13% being 75 years and over. The retired inmigrants in the western North Carolina counties were somewhat older, with 27% under 65 and 22% 75 and over (Haas & Serow, 1990). Slightly over 80% of the retired newcomer households in the nonmetro coastal counties were composed of married couples, and somewhat less than 80% of those in western North Carolina were in this category.

Table 1.

Socioeconomic Characteristics of Retirees

	Seven Nonmetro Counties of Southeast Coast	Eight Counties in Western North Carolina
With college diploma (%)		59
Male	45	
Female	27	
With graduate degree (%)		27
Male	16	
Female	5	
In professional management (%)		N/A
Male	73	
Female	24	
Under 65 years old (%)	36	27
75 years and over (%)	13	22
Married (%)	82	77
Annual household income of $40,000 or more (%)	43	30
Average housing market value	$177,000	$109,000[a]

a. Average sales price of homes purchased in last 3 years (Serow & Haas, 1992).

Expenditures of Retired Migrants

The greatest immediate impact that retired inmigrants make on communities is the purchase of housing. Whereas just over 70% of all housing units in the nonmetro coastal region were owner occupied, over 90% of the retirees who moved into the nonmetro coastal region had bought or built a residence within a year of moving into these counties. One further indication of the impact of these newcomers on the housing economy is that nearly half of these had a new house built rather than just buying what was already available. Moreover, the average market value of the residences of the retired inmigrants was over $175,000 (see Table 1). (This high average was influenced by a few homes being well over $500,000.) The median housing value of slightly under $150,000 is, perhaps, a better indicator because of the many high-priced homes in the survey, with 16% living in homes worth $250,000 or more. These figures compared to a mean of $109,000 and a median of $92,000 for all owner-occupied units in the region, with only 7% being valued at $250,000 or more. Because most of the homes of the retired newcomers had been paid for in cash, the average monthly payment (including taxes and insurance) was only about $420 (Table 2). The average value of retired in-migrant homes in the eight counties of western North Carolina was $109,000 (the same as for all units in the nonmetro coastal region). The average monthly payment of $218 spent by the

elderly newcomers in western North Carolina was far below that of those in the coastal region (Haas & Serow, 1990).

The retired inmigrants spent an average of about $106 a month for utilities (not including telephone/cable) in the seven nonmetropolitan counties (Table 2). This was despite the fact that many did not have public water or sewer service and that the "winter" temperatures were rather mild. Total utilities did not vary latitudinally along the coast but, rather, were influenced by variations in availability of water, sewer, and various heating fuels and by the differences in the rate structures for electricity, natural gas, oil, water, and sewer. Because the average cost of all utilities in the Haas and Serow study (1990) was $152 per month (including nearly $45 for telephone and $12 for cable), it would appear that retired newcomers in western North Carolina spent an average of about $95 a month for heating, cooling, water, and sewer—compared to $106 in the nonmetro coastal counties.

Despite the dearth of retail outlets in the nonmetro coastal counties, 60% of the retired households made a major purchase (car, furniture, electronics, appliances, property, etc.) *in the county,* with over a fifth having spent $10,000 or more—in addition to housing. About 22% of all the households bought motor vehicles within the county, and over 40% of them purchased other durable goods. Major purchases of cars and other

Table 2.

Retiree Expenditures

	Seven Nonmetro Counties of Southeast Coast[a]	Nine Counties in Western North Carolina
Average monthly housing payment (PITI)[b]	$421	$218
Average monthly utilities (exluding telephone/cable)	$106	$95
Annual major purchases (including home furnishing, autos, yard/recreation equipment)	$6,600	$4,220
Annual clothing purchases	$491	$1,324
Average monthly auto maintenance and operating expenses	$76	$148
Average weekly dining out expenses	$42	$27
Average weekly grocery expenses (including alcohol)	$70	$69
Average monthly recreation/entertainment/club expenses	$104[c]	$81
Annual club and organization expenses	$346[d]	$356

a. Within-county only.
b. PITI = principal, interest, taxes, insurance.
c. Including golf, refers to column 1 only.
d. Not including golf, refers to column 1 only.

Table 3.

Chi-Square Probabilities

Household Characteristics	Expenditures			
	Medicine	Clothing	Meals	Golf
Males < 65 and 70+	.070*	.913	.353	.448
Females < 65 & 70+	.068*	.139	.002**	.002**
Household incomes < $20,000 and $40,000+	.920	.008**	.000**	.000**
Lived in county < 6 Yrs and 6++ Years	.753	.746	.176	.587

*Significant at the 0.10 level; **significant at the 0.05 level.

durables averaged nearly $6,600. This was more than 50% greater than the $4,220 figure for western North Carolina (Serow & Haas, 1992).

Clothing bought *within* these seven nonmetro coastal counties was much less than might well be expected, given the annual incomes, major purchases, and housing values. The average annual expenditure was less than $500 per retired household. This was much lower than the more than $1,300 a year spent by retired newcomers in the counties of western North Carolina (Haas & Serow, 1990).

Car operating expenses (gas, oil, maintenance, and repair) in the county of residence averaged over $75 a month in the nonmetro coastal region. Here, again, this was far below the $148 in-county figure for western North Carolina (Haas & Serow, 1990).

The average weekly expenditure for dining out in the county was about $40, and the average weekly grocery bill (excluding alcohol) was $70 for the coastal region. These figures would have been much greater had data for purchases outside the county been included. In several instances, when the retired inmigrants lived closer to better restaurants and grocery stores in adjacent counties, they would travel outside the county for these purchases. Nevertheless, these in-county expenditures still exceeded those of $27 and $69, respectively, in western North Carolina (Haas & Serow, 1990).

The main type of recreational activities on which funds were expended in the nonmetro coastal area were golf and boating. The retired newcomer households spent an average of nearly $50 a month on these two forms of recreation. Although these retired inmigrants rarely went to movies, nearly all had VCRs on which they watched rented films. A large percentage of the women and a considerable proportion of the men were involved in crafts (including woodworking). Gardening was also an activity enjoyed by many. The average monthly expen-

diture on all recreation/entertainment/clubs for these nonmetro counties was $133, compared to $119 in the counties of western North Carolina (Haas & Serow, 1990).

Many people assume that as retirees age they will spend significantly less on consumer items. However, significance tests show that although expenditures for such items as clothing, restaurant meals, and golf were significantly different for high-income and low-income retired inmigrant households, expenditures for most major items purchased did not differ significantly by age of those retirees or by length of time they had lived in the retirement areas (Table 3).

These findings support the conclusion of Elaine Sherman of Hofstra University that the level of affluence determines consumer behavior much more so than does age (cited in Wolfe, 1987). Wolfe believes that it is best "to forget about age and focus on consumer wants and needs" (p. 27).

One exception to the lack of significant variation in spending by age was—as might well be expected—for housing acquisitions, being greater for younger retired inmigrants. Another case where there was a significant difference by age was for expenditures for medicine, being greater for older persons in this group (Table 3). Finally, golf and restaurant dining expenses were significantly greater for younger females than for older ones but expenditures for medicine were significantly less. There were no significant differences for these expenditures by age for males.

Medical expenses are a major concern of many, it not most, of the elderly. The retired inmigrant households averaged spending in their countries over $1,200 a year on doctors, dentists, nurses, and hospitals and nearly $1,000 annually on medicine, or a total of over $2,200 each year. Fortunately, most of these expenses were covered by private health insurance and Medicare. Only about 1 in 50 had to use Medicaid. Serow and Haas (1992) report that retired newcomers in western North Carolina averaged $2,800 annually in medical expenses not covered by insurance, considerably more than in the seven nonmetro coastal counties. In the latter region, the retired inmigrant population was somewhat younger and the lack of sufficient doctors and medical facilities caused many of these retirees to go to either well-known medical centers within the Southeast or to return to their former home doctor and hospital for treatment for potentially serious illnesses.

As Longino and Crown (1989) point out, the economic impact of retired inmigrants has a multiplier effect on business. Thus, in addition to wages for workers providing goods and services directly to these retirees, additional jobs were created to support these workers. In addition, sales, income, and property taxes generated by all those involved supported a higher level and greater variety of public services than would otherwise have been the case. The larger share of tax payments and the relatively lower demand for public services by these retirees resulted in their being a net positive economic influence on the public—as well as on the private—sector.

The computed estimated average annual direct economic impact within the county of residence for each retired inmigrant household was between $37,000 and $38,000; however, about a third of this amount was represented by a one-time residence acquisition. Haas and Serow (1990) reported that in the eight western North Carolina counties "the direct impact of consumption expenditure in the local community amounted to . . . nearly $36,000 per migrant household" and "about 30 percent . . . is accounted for by home purchases" (p. 37). They arrived at a total annual direct and indirect impact per household—with a multiplier of 1.99—of nearly $72,000. If the same multiplier were applied to the nonmetro coastal region, the total annual in-county impact would be approximately $75,000. This figure would certainly have been greater had there been sufficient stores and medical services to meet the total purchasing demand of the retirees who had moved into these counties.

Discussion

Although incomes and expenditures for housing, utilities, major purchases, dining out, groceries, recreation, entertainment, and clubs and organizations were greater for the retired inmigrants in the seven nonmetropolitan coastal counties than for those in the eight western North Carolina ones, amounts spent for clothing and car maintenance and operation were less in the coastal region. One reason for the much lower expenditure on clothing in the coastal region was that of the seven counties only one contained a major department store, and it carried only a limited selection of high-quality ladies wear; moreover, these counties were usually within an hour's drive of a metropolitan center with upscale department stores. The western North Carolina region did contain a small metro area— Asheville—which was much better able to satisfy demand for this item and in which about a third of the respondents lived. In addition, driving time to higher-level department stores from the latter region was greater than for most of the coastal counties.

The much lower expenditure on car maintenance in the coastal region was partly related to the lack of establishments in the individual counties selling and servicing automobiles, but also partly related to the fact that 22% had recently purchased a new car within the county—plus additional ones outside the county—during that year and by far the majority of retired inmigrant households had cars still under warranty. However, nearly all the 19% of retirees in the western North Carolina counties had bought a car during the previous year and most had their automobiles serviced within their county of residence.

Although detailed expenditures outside the seven nonmetropolitan coastal counties were not collected, it was apparent that not only did a large share of those outlays for clothing and car maintenance occur outside the county of residence, but this was also true for automobiles and home appliances and furnishings and to a lesser extent for other items, such as recreation and dining out—and even groceries in some areas.

Over a fourth of the retired inmigrant households in the nonmetro coastal counties felt that either a better (much improved) major department store or a new upscale department store selling better ladies clothing was the type of store most needed in their county. However, this figure does not include the much greater proportion who traveled elsewhere to buy clothing and who wanted to limit the degree of commercial development in their county.

Conclusions

Although both the mountains of western North Carolina and the nonmetropolitan coastal counties of the Southeast are known to be attractive retirement areas, the retired inmigrants in the latter region are more affluent. These newcomers are also much more affluent than the general population of this coastal region.

Certainly, numerous business opportunities are available in the high-amenity, nonmetropolitan coastal counties where recent high inmigration rates of affluent, relatively young retirees have occurred. Most businesses in these areas continue to be oriented to either seasonal tourists or to the traditional low- to moderate-income indigenous population. One of the seven counties studied did not even contain a large discount store and although most did have a low- to middle-level department store—some of which had recently been remodeled, none contained the size and level of store that could not be justified given the market of upper-income retirees, upper-middle- and upper-income entrepreneurs, and high-level tourism. As was stated by several realtors, officials and retirees, any one of many different types of businesses could be successful in these counties because of the imbalance of supply and demand.

After Serow and Haas (1992) completed a detailed analysis of the balance between taxes paid and public benefits required by the retired inmigrants in western North Carolina, they found that these elderly newcomers "represent a strong net increment to the economy of western North Carolina" (p. 213). The even higher incomes and expenditures of the retired inmigrants in the nonmetropolitan coastal counties of the Southeast represent not only a positive financial impact on their areas but also a great potential economic opportunity for entrepreneurial development.

Several authors, as noted earlier, have cautioned that as these retirees age, they might become a financial drain on the local community because of medical and social services needs. There is little, if any, reason to be so concerned about the kind of retiree attracted by these high-amenity coastal counties. Nearly all have excellent private insurance coverage to supplement Medicare. Rather than being a drain on finances, they provide additional funds for medical services for the indigenous poor and stimulate the development of much better medical services than would ever have been possible had they not moved to the region. This supports the conclusion of Haas and Crandall (1988), Glasgow and Reeder (1990), and Longino and Crown (1990).

The benefits brought by retired inmigrants are not limited to purchases, taxes paid, and jobs created but include the fact that over half of them are volunteers in their communities, with three fifths of these unpaid workers providing over 10 hours a month in service. Although much of the volunteer work

was to benefit their own neighborhood, many also provided
assistance to the indigenous poor and elderly through senior
centers, mobile meals, youth tutoring programs, and a wide
variety of other public services. The retired newcomers are
also very active politically—even running for local office in
many cases—in preserving the environment and working to
ensure that tax money is used effectively for better education
and other public needs.

These well-educated retirees who have moved into the region view the low educational levels of many of the retail and
service workers in their areas as a major problem limiting their
own level of living. These older citizens are often viewed as
being against taxes for schools and highways. Nevertheless,
in-depth interviews with retired inmigrants in these seven
counties revealed that they are primarily interested in their tax
money being well spent and will support local educational
taxes if they are convinced the money will be spent wisely.
Although this view was substantiated earlier by Haas and Serow (1990) and Rosenbaum and Button (1989), Button (1992)
recently concluded in a study of Florida that there is a direct
relationship between increasing age and opposition to local tax
proposals, particularly those related to public schools. He cau-
tions that this indicates that retirees as a whole will vote their
own financial interest "to the detriment of younger persons"
(p. 796).

In sum, the retired inmigrants are a net positive
benefit to their new "home" communities, not just in
the dollars they spend but in many additional ways as
well. This supports the conclusion of Longino (1990)
concerning retirement migration to North Carolina
communities that "migrants who concentrate in counties that offer appropriate lifestyle settings for amenity
migrants will have an overall positive economic impact
on the locality" (p. 401). Indeed, both this nonmetro
coastal study and the one by Haas and Serow confirm
that this is the case.

During the past two to three decades, the number and
proportion of the elderly in America has grown rapidly and
the rate of retirement migration to these high-amenity areas
has been great. Serow and Haas (1992) have cautioned that
the number of elderly "will more or less be on a plateau .
. . until the baby boomers . . . begin to reach retirement age
about 2010" (p. 213) and that this will increase the competition for these inmigrants. Unless a major economic catastrophe befalls the new retirees during the next 15 years, the
dearth of elderly inmigrants should not be a major problem.
Indeed, whatever level of retirement inmigration to these
areas below that of recent decades might occur—if any, a
somewhat reduced rate of influx of newcomers could be
beneficial in the short term by giving these counties and
their communities the time needed to "catch-up" with the
expansion of roads, water, and sewer and other services that
have often been overwhelmed by the rapid influx of both
retirees and working-age people. The level of inmigration
into these high-amenity coastal areas, however, will likely
be limited as much by the scarcity of developable land in

35. Retirement Migration and Economic Development

a region with a high percentage of wetlands as by the number
of people reaching retirement age.

Nevertheless, given the large population living in the northeastern quarter of the nation, the number of affluent elderly
desiring to secure their "place in the sun" is likely to far
exceed the amount of desirable space remaining in these
areas. Moreover, as the limited supply of more desirable
space is sought after by the preretirement investors—those
55 and above, who will increase by about 65% between
2000 and 2030 (estimated from Soldo & Agree, 1988, p.
7)—the price of land will escalate, thus attracting an even
higher-income clientele. This will provide a growing affluent market, not only for goods sought for this age group
(homes, furnishings, autos, appliances, mature clothing,
etc.) but also for toys and clothing for the grandchildren for
whom retirees especially like to shop.

References

Aday, R. H., & Miles, L. A. (1982). Long-term impacts of rural migration of the elderly: Implications for research. *The Gerontologist, 22,* 331–336.
Barsby, S., & Cox, D. (1975). *Interstate migration of the elderly: An economic analysis.* Lexington, MA: D. C. Heath.
Bennett, D. G. (1992). The impact of retirement migration on Carteret and Brunswick Counties, N.C. *North Carolina Geographer, 1,* 25–38.
Biggar, J. C., Flynn, C. B., Longino, C. F., Jr., & Wiseman, R. F. (1984). Sunbelt update. *American Demographics, 6,* 22–25, 37.
Bohland, J. A., & Rowles, G. D. (1988). The significance of elderly migration to changes in elderly population concentration in the United States: 1960–1980. *Journal of Gerontology, 43,* 145–152.
Bryant, E. S., & El-Attar, M. (1984). Migration and redistribution of the elderly: A challenge to community services. *The Gerontologist, 24,* 634–640.
Bureau of the Census. (1992). 1990 census of population and housing: Summary social, economic, and housing characteristics. 1990 CPH-5-11, 35, 42. Washington, DC: U.S. Government Printing Office.
Button, J. W. (1992). A sign of generational conflict: The impact of Florida's aging voters on local school tax referenda. *Social Science Quarterly, 73,* 786–797.
Crown, W. H. (1985). Measuring the economic impacts of aged migration. In C.F. Longino, Jr. (Ed.) *Returning from the Sunbelt* (pp. 22–31). New York: Columbia University, Brookdale Institute on Aging and Adult Human Development.
Crown, W. H. (1988). State economic implications of elderly interstate migration. *The Gerontologist, 28,* 533–539.
Cuba, L., & Longino, C. F., Jr. (1991). Regional retirement migration: The case of Cape Cod. *Journal of Gerontology: Social Sciences, 46,* 533–542.
Glasgow, N. (1980). The older metropolitan migrant as a factor in rural population growth, In A. J. Sofranko & J. D. Williams (Eds.), *Rebirth of rural America: Rural migration in the Midwest* (pp. 153–170). Ames, IA: North Central Center for Rural Development.
Glasgow, N. (1988). *The nonmetro elderly: Economic and demographic status.* (Report prepared for the U.S. Department of Agriculture, Economic Research Service, Rural Development Report No. 70). Washington, DC: U.S. Department of Agriculture.
Glasgow, N., & Beale, C. F. (1988). Rural elderly in demographic perspective. *Rural Development Perspectives, 2,* 22–26.
Glasgow, N., & Reeder, R. J. (1990). Economic and fiscal implications of nonmetro retirement migration. *Journal of Applied Gerontology, 9,* 433–451.
Haas, W. H., III. (1990). Retirement migration: Boon or Burden? *Journal of Applied Gerontology, 9,* 387–392.
Haas, W. H., III, & Crandall, L. A. (1988). Physicians' view of retirement migrants' impact on rural medical practice. *The Gerontologist, 28,* 663–666.
Haas, W. H., III, & Serow, W. J. (1990). *The influence of retirement inmigration on local economic development* (Final report to the Appalachian Re-

gional Commission, No. 89–48NC–10269–89–1–302–0327). Asheville, NC: North Carolina Center for Creative Retirement.

Henry, M., Drabenstott, M., & Gibson, L. (1987). Rural growth slows down. *Rural development Perspectives, 3,* 25–30.

Hodge, G. (1991). The economic impact of retirees on smaller communities: Concepts and findings from three Canadian studies. *Research on Aging, 13,* 39–54.

Longino, C. F., Jr. (1985). Returning from the Sunbelt: Myths and realities of migratory patterns among the elderly. In Longino (Ed.), *Returning from the Sunbelt* (pp. 7–21). New York: Columbia University, Brookdale Institute on Aging and Adult Human Development.

Longino, C. F., Jr. (1988). The gray peril mentality and the impact of retirement migration. *Journal of Applied Gerontology, 7,* 448–455.

Longino, C. F., Jr. (1990). Retirement migration streams: Trends and implications for North Carolina communities. *Journal of Applied Gerontology, 9,* 393–404.

Longino, C. F., Jr., & Biggar, J. C. (1982). The impact of population redistribution on service delivery. *The Gerontologist, 22,* 153–159.

Longino, C. F., Jr., Biggar, J. C., Flynn, C. B., & Wiseman, R. F. (1984). *The retirement migration project* (Final report to the National Institute on Aging.) Coral Gables, FL: University of Miami, Center for Social Research on Aging.

Longino, C. F., Jr., & Crown, W. H. (1989). Old money. *American Demographics, 11,* 28–31.

Longino, C. F., Jr., & Crown, W. H. (1990). Retirement migration and interstate income transfers. *The Gerontologist, 30,* 784–789.

Longino, C. F., Jr., Marshall, V. W., Mullins, L. C., & Tucker, R. D. (1991). On the nesting of snowbirds: A question about seasonal and permanent migrants. *Journal of Applied Gerontology, 10,* 157–168.

McCarthy, K. F., & Morrison, P. A. (1979). *The changing demographic and economic structure of nonmetropolitan areas in the United States* (Report No. R-2399-EDA). Santa Monica, CA: RAND.

Reeder, R. J., & Glasgow, N. (1990). Nonmetro retirement counties' strengths and weaknesses. *Rural Development Perspectives, 6,* 12–17.

Rosenbaum, W. A., & Button, J. W. (1989). Is there a gray peril?: Retirement politics in Florida. *The Gerontologist, 29,* 300–306.

Serow, W. J. (1990). Economic implications of retirement migration. *Journal of Applied Gerontology, 9,* 452–463.

Serow, W. J., & Charity, D. A. (1988). Return migration of the elderly in the United States: Recent trends. *Research on Aging, 10,* 155–168.

Serow, W. J., & Haas, W. H. III (1992). Measuring the economic impact of retirement migration: The case of western North Carolina. *Journal of Applied Gerontology, 11,* 200–215.

Soldo, B. J., & Agree, E. M. (1988). America's elderly. *Population Bulletin, 43,* 3–51.

Summer, G. F., & Hirschl, T. A. (1985). Retirees as a growth industry. *Rural Development Perspectives, 1,* 13–16.

Wolfe, D. B. (1987). The ageless market. *American Demographics, 9,* 27–29. 55–56.

Caring for Aging Loved Ones

Jackie Fitzpatrick

JACKIE FITZPATRICK is a freelance writer for *The New York Times, The Boston Globe, Quinnipiac Magazine, The Hartford Courant's Northeast Magazine* and numerous other publications, as well as a columnist for the *Connecticut Post*. Fitzpatrick is also a fiction writer completing her first novel, which traces the story of three generations of women in one family.

With today's longer life expectancies and increasingly aging population, chances are you will be called on some day to care for a frail loved one. By the year 2000, an estimated 35 million Americans will be age 65 or over. Elders' needs account for almost a third of all healthcare expenditures. More than six million seniors need assistance with daily living skills, and most of that help comes from relatives.

Alan P. Siegal, M.D, director of Geriatric and Adult Psychiatry in Hamden and author of *Forget Me Not: Caring For and Coping With Your Aging Parents,* estimates about 80 percent of elder care is provided by family members, primarily wives, daughters and daughters-in-law.

Caregiving, however, can be a positive rather than a painful experience if you plan ahead and discuss the situation with the elder and other relatives before a crisis occurs. "The whole family needs to sit down together with the parent or grandparent and talk things through," says Lea Nordlicht Shedd, who practices elder law in Hamden.

Geriatric assessment
If you suspect an elder needs help, take the person to a geriatrician, a medical doctor who specialized in elder care and can assess the situation, initiate treatment, suggest appropriate care and help the family create a care plan for the future. At the Senior Assessment Center at the Hospital of Saint Raphael, a geriatrician, nurse and social worker assess a patient's health and his or her functioning level, in terms of their ability to perform daily living activities (bathing, dressing, cooking, shopping or housekeeping).

"We don't look so much at a medical diagnosis, but rather at how well an older person functions on his or her own," says John Merritt, M.D., a board-certified geriatrician and director of Saint Raphael's Senior Assessment Center. "There can be subtle changes; maybe the person can no longer handle finances and his or her memory slowly begins to fail. Families don't often do anything until there is a crisis. Then comes the question: What are we going to do with Mom or Dad as his or her functioning begins to fail?"

The geriatric assessment team also looks for signs of depression, which plagues many seniors and can sometimes be confused with dementia. "A high percentage of elderly persons see marked improvement when treated with a combination of anti-depressant medication and therapy, as long as they

are properly medicated," says Siegal, who also is medical director at the Alzheimer's Resource Center in Southington and an attending psychiatrist at the Hospital of Saint Raphael. Siegal is board certified in adult psychiatry, neuropsychiatry and geriatrics.

The next step is creating a care plan for the elderly person, which could include numerous options: moving in with relatives; moving to a nursing home; assisted living arrangements; getting help from a home healthcare agency so the person can continue living independently; or utlizing adult day centers.

"Caregiving can take an emotional, physical and financial toll," says Merritt, "so people need to weigh their options accordingly."

At home with family
Many families, like the Adantes, decide to care for their frail elder themselves.

Lucy Adante's parents moved into her house almost three years ago, after her father was diagnosed with Parkinson's disease. He later developed cancer and congestive heart failure. In the midst of her father's illness, Adante noticed her mother's memory failing. She was later diagnosed with Alzheimer's disease. Her mother's condition worsened after her husband died. Adante says she willingly cares for her mother, but the situation has taken its toll on her family, especially her four children.

"I want to care for my mother. I love her. But it's so hard," says Adante.

Gerry Smith moved in with her parents when it became apparent they could no longer care for themselves. Her mother had lymphoma and now suffers from shingles and the after-effects of a torn rotator cuff. Her father, who has Parkinson's disease, is temporarily in a nursing home because he is fighting a serious infection. Smith works full-time, visits her father daily and takes care of her mother.

"My parents lived their lives doing so much for everyone. They were active, going all the time, caring for people. I made my mind up a long time ago that I was going to care for them in their old age," she says. "I'm happy to do what I'm doing, but it can be very exhausting."

caring for the caregiver

No matter how much a person wants to provide loving care for a spouse or parent, caregivers need respite and support. About 30 percent of all caregivers of elderly are so overwhelmed they turn to alcohol or anti-anxiety medication. Elder abuse is another sad fact, often stemming from the stress in the care situation, geriatric specialists say.

The golden years often aren't very golden, says Sara Trachten, executive director of the Alzheimer's Association of South Central Connecticut. "Couples in their 50s and 60s who were working, traveling, and active in their church and with their grandchildren suddenly find themselves at home with an elderly parent or spouse," she says. "It can be isolating and frustrating. People feel full of guilt no matter how much care they're giving."

Fortunately, many community resources exist to help older adults and families caring for elderly loved ones, whether it's a support group, respite care, help with finances or assitance in locating a good program. The Senior Services Department at the Hospital of Saint Raphael, for example, offers a variety of programs. "We provide assistance in several important ways," says Harry Rosenberg, LCSW, manager of Senior Services. "We tend to do an overall assessment of the needs of the person and suggest ways to meet those needs." (See "A Resource Guide for Elders and Caregivers" on next page for a list of community and Hospital resources.)

Caregivers also need to prod other siblings to pitch in, even if they live far away, says Siegal. For example, ask the long-distance relative to pay for two weeks of respite care so the caregiver can get a break. If the sibling balks, says Siegal, "Tell him or her Mom will be on a plane to Chicago. You'd be surprised how fast he or she says 'and who do I make the check out to?'"

Nursing homes

"It's necessary to put Mom in a nursing home." It is a simple sentence of just nine words. Yet it is one of the most difficult sentences to say because the decision to place a loved one in a nursing home is fraught with expectations, guilt and concern. The decision often comes after long debate or in the midst of a crisis when someone is caring for a frail elderly person.

Many families turn to nursing homes after they have exhausted all other alternatives, says David Hunter, administrator of The Mary Wade Home in New Haven. "We find that families have done everything possible for the patient. But they are working people and they can't do it any longer." Adds Kim Czepiga, executive director of Saint Regis Health Center in New Haven, a nursing home affiliated with the Saint Raphael Healthcare System: "We work with families during the admissions process and they talk to us through their tears."

While some family members feel guilty about placing an elder in a nursing home, many also feel relief knowing the person isn't socially isolated and is receiving care from professionals, says Czepiga. At Saint Regis, residents receive care by geriatricians, geriatric nurses, social workers, recreation therapists, and physical, occupation and speech therapists. The facility has a restorative care program in its sub-acute care units and two units for long-term skilled nursing care.

Loretta Sullivan of New Haven found it necessary to place her 88-year-old mother in Saint Regis because her memory was failing and she could not care for herself. "One of the most difficult things is accepting that you are turning someone you love over to the care of others on a 24-hour basis," says Sullivan. "It's a challenge for the facility and the family to keep a dialogue going so the elderly person gets the best integrated care possible."

Becoming familiar with the nursing homes in your area before the need arises can alleviate some stress. "The best scenario is when the family is involved with the elder through the whole decision-making process, prior to placement and prior to crisis," says Andrew Krochko, the administrator of Harborview Manor in West Haven. "Nobody likes to think, 'Let's take a Sunday drive and look at nursing homes because you might need one two years down the road.' But it can be helpful." (For help with choosing the right nursing home, turn to page 200.)

While it is a hard decision, a nursing home can be a healthy and safe setting for people who require constant care and are unable to perform activities of daily living, or for a person who has suffered a serious stroke or has Alzheimer's disease, experts say.

"It's a big step," says Hunter. "People are basically giving over the bulk of the care of their loved one." But relatives can still take part in their loved one's life once they are in a nursing home. "It can be a very positive experience," he says.

Assisted living communities

Assisted living arrangements refer to a variety of facilities that provide room and board for independent elderly residents. These facilities range from modest homes in residential neighborhoods to luxury complexes in park-like settings. Unlike nursing homes, assisted living communities do not provide round-the-clock, skilled nursing care, so these facilities may not be appropriate for elders who require a great amount of medical attention and supervision. Some assisted living facilities, however, do offer limited healthcare services on the premises.

Although the level of services provided may vary, assisted living communities all share a common goal: enabling people to live as active and independent a life as possible.

At the Four Corners Rest Home in

Milford, residents are almost one of the family. "It's like anyone else's home, except that we have 19 people living downstairs," says Ron Miller, Four Corners' manager, who lives at the home with his wife, two daughters, a dog and several birds.

"One of the most important things we offer is companionship," Miller says. This sense of community can be a morale booster, since many older adults feel isolated from their families. Miller says that an assisted living facility can help fill that void. "This environment really changes their lives around," he says.

Larger facilities, such as Tower One/Tower East in New Haven, provide close companionship and a wide range of activities and programs, including Project ElderCare, a Hospital of Saint Raphael program that offers on-site healthcare services to the eldelry.

"Our philosophy is to do whatever is needed to maintain our residents' independence," says Dorothy Giannini-Myers, executive director at Tower One/Tower East.

At The Gables at Guilford, residents live in one- or two-bedroom apartments. "We have a close community," says Jane O'Brien, one of The Gables' managers. "We offer independent living, but with the oversight that busy families can't always provide. Living here reduces a number of risks. If something happens, help is never far away." Resident managers and co-managers live on the premises and are available 24 hours a day. Each apartment has pull-cords tied into an emergency response system.

Home care

Today, more elderly people are remaining in their own homes where they can maintain social and family ties thanks to home healthcare agencies.

The term home care covers a range of services, including homemakers who help with personal grooming, housekeeping and shopping; registered nurses who provide skilled nursing care such as inserting feeding tubes, catheters and breathing devices; and physical, occupational and speech therapists who provide specialized care. Home healthcare is one of the fastest growing service industries in the

A Resource Guide for Elders and Caregivers

The Alzheimer's Association of South Central Connecticut in Hamden offers information and support groups. 203-230-1777.

The Alzheimer's Resource Center in Southington. 860-628-9000.

Community Action Agency of New Haven offers free transportation for elders who need rides to their physicians' office or for shopping, people need to fill out an application. 203-387-8033.

Connecticut Department of Social Services, Elderly Division, provides information and referrals. 800-443-9946

The Senior Assessment Center at the Hospital of Saint Raphael includes an interdisciplinary team of experts who specialize in assessing and diagnosing elders, provide practical and emotional support to families and refer patients to community resources. 203-789-3989

The Hospital of Saint Raphael's **Senior Services Department** offers a variety of programs:

• **Outreach to Older Adults.** Assistance for primary caregivers, elders and their families, including educational information; help with utilities, Medicare and Medicaid; and an outreach worker to answer questions and provide referrals. 203-789-3275

• **CareCard.** A free health, fitness, education and recreation program for people ages 55 and older. Members receive discounts at selected area stores, at Saint Raphael's Better Health pharmacy on prescriptions with free mail order service, and on programs and courses listed in the HealthLink calendar. 203-789-3777

• **Lifeline.** A 24-hour personal emergency response system that summons help at the touch of a button. 203-789-3702

• **American Parkinson's Disease Association Information and Referral Center.** A statewide program for people with Parkinson's disease, their families, friends and health-care providers. 203-789-3936

Infoline, a resource and referral service, provides information on a variety of elder-related issues, including nursing homes, home healthcare agencies, assistance programs to pay fuel bills, transportation services, meal programs, respite care and adult day centers. Ask to speak with infoline's elderly specialist. 203-867-4150

Interfaith Volunteer Caregivers provides respite care. 203-230-8994

Meals on Wheels brings meal to homebound individuals. 203-387-5026

The National Well Spouse Foundation, which has a chapter in Southbury, helps people who are caring for frail spouses. 203-262-0666

"The Ombudsman Program" in the Connecticut Department of Social Services investigates reports of elder abuse or neglect in homes (203-789-6913) and in nursing homes (203-789-7508).

For other resources, check your phone book under the headings adult day care centers, home health services and nursing homes.

Choosing a nursing home

Families should select a nursing home with the same care they choose day care for a child or a college for a teenager, eldercare experts say. Here are a few things to consider:

Read the state inspection report (also called the state survey) on the facility. The report, which should be posted, details deficiencies and violations of federal law involving health, safety, and quality of life and described incidents that shed light on how a facility treats its residents. Federal guidelines require nursing homes to make their latest inspection report available and readily accessible to residents and the public. Kim Czepigo, executive director of Saint Regis Health Center, says she would be skeptical of a nursing home director who refuses to share the report.

Inspect the facility for yourself before placing a relative there, no matter how good the inspection report may be. Visit unannounced at different times of the day and week. Talk with residents and staff; watch and listen.

Make sure the facility and the residents are clean. Czepigo says a nursing home should be as odor-free as possible. Residents should be clean, well-dressed and well-groomed.

Focus on the quality of care patients receive, rather than outward appearances such as the decor and furnishings, Look for evidence that residents are well cared for. Is staff concerned about a patient's dignity? Are there activities—games, concerts, exercise classes, religious services—to entertain patients? Are restraints used? Federal law prohibits facilities from using restraints unless medically justified or ordered by a physician.

Look for safety hazards such as mops and brooms propped against hand rails—all potential hazards for people with unsteady gaits or poor eyesight.

Observe the attitude of the staff. Does the staff warmly interact with residents? Does the nursing home feel like a positive place? Is the facility properly staffed to accommodate the needs of residents?

If possible, visit at mealtime and taste the food, checking for nutritional value. Note if the staff is available to help residents who cannot feed themselves. Staff should be encouraging residents to eat in the dining room, whenever possible, because it promotes much-needed socialization.

Are care plans for patients properly developed and implemented? When a person enters a nursing home, the facility is required to draft a care plan that outlines such things as nutrition requirements, physical and speech therapy, range-of-motion exercises, appropriate activities and other specifications. It's usually up to the family to make sure these are carried out. Range-of-motion activities are important because they prevent muscle atrophy. Staff should be walking residents or helping them to move their arms and legs. Likewise, staff should work with the family to implement a program to help residents maintain continence when appropriate.

Once you have found a good nursing home, don't hesitate to compliment the staff for doing a good job. And speak up when a problem does arise so the matter can be resolved quickly.

nation and the fastest growing component of personal health care.

Technological advances have enabled people to receive sophisticated medical care without having to come to a hospital or physician's office, says Guy J. Tommasi Jr, vice president, planning and development for OMNI Home Health Services, Inc. in Wallingford. Home healthcare professionals also provide respite for caregivers who have brought their frail loved one into their home.

The Hospital of Saint Raphael has established a homecare network to help discharged patients who require home healthcare during their recuperation. The Hospital also has an affiliation with the Regional Visiting Nurses Agency in Hamden.

Home care is not necessarily a cheaper alternative to nursing homes, if a patient requires a great deal of nursing care, reports the Connecticut Association for Home Care. If you do rely on home healthcare professionals, relatives should check-in on the elder periodically, coordinate services and monitor the person's condition.

Adult day centers

Adult day centers offer elders socialization with their peers and others, plus give them access to a variety of recreation, education, social and nutrition programs. Some centers also provide limited healthcare services. Families, particularly people who work and can't tend to a parent or spouse all day, can rest assured knowing their loved ones are safe during the day.

"At first, some families bring a parent for only a day or two a week. Then they see how well the person is doing, how much fun he or she is having, and they come more often," says Doreen Mosko, director of nursing at the Clelian Adult Day Center in Hamden. The center offers many services, including nutritional meals, recreation and an intergenerational program where nursery school youngsters interact with elders. Students from nearby Sacred Heart Academy also spend time at the center.

"People age faster when they're isolated, inside watching television alone all day," says Mosko. "We encourage people to use their social skills. They feel better about themselves."

Marilyn Kennedy runs a support group for caregivers at the East Shore Regional Adult Day Center in Branford. "My group just likes to sit and talk," she says. "They become close, like a family; we're concerned for each other. If someone doesn't come to a meeting, we'll call to be sure everything is all right. They can share their feelings because they're with people who know exactly what they're going through. They draw strength from each other."

practical matters
Geriatric specialists recommend a family consult a lawyer familiar with elder law to discuss financial and medical matters because every family's situation is unique.

Finances are a factor in all caregiving decisions, especially since Medicare, the primary source of health insurance for most elderly, will not cover everything. Nursing home care can cost up to $70,000 a year and the cost of adult day centers and home

healthcare professionals can add up as well. A lawyer can review what Medicare and Medicaid will cover, plus provide information about other available assistance programs.

Attorney Shedd says families should see a lawyer about drafting legal documents known as advance directives and establishing someone to have the power of attorney to act on the person's behalf in financial matters and serve as a health care agent for medical matters.

"It can save so much heartache if this is done early," she says.

"Advance directives" allow people to choose the type of medical treatment they want or do not want in case they become incapacitated. Advance directives include living wills, a durable power of attorney and a healthcare agent. The living will specifies the kinds of life-prolonging medical treatments that should or should not be administered, such as cardiopulmonary resuscitation, a life-supporting respirator or nourishment.

The durable power of attorney for healthcare decisions is a legal docu-

ment which names a person, usually a family member or trusted friend, to make limited medical decisions if you cannot make them yourself. They can assure that your wishes about specific medical treatments you want or do not want — other than life support decisions — are honored.

A healthcare agent is a person authorized, in writing, to convey your wishes concerning the withholding or withdrawal of life support systems, in case you are unable to communicate your wishes about medical care.

valuing life
Caregivers who have children are providing important lessons to the younger generation, says Siegal. "What kind of a message are you giving your child if you always say, 'I can't get to Grandma's this weekend. I'm just too busy,'" he says. Time spent with a grandparent or great-grandparent offers enrichment and an opportunity for a child or young adult to see the value of human life, old or young. "We all aspire to grow old," he says.

Social Policies, Programs, and Services for Older Americans

It is a political reality that older Americans will be able to obtain needed assistance from governmental programs only to the degree that they are perceived as politically powerful. Political involvement can range from holding and expressing political opinions, voting in elections, participating in voluntary associations to help elect a candidate or party, and holding political office.

Research has indicated that older people are just as likely as any other age group to hold political opinions, are more likely than younger people to vote in an election, are about equally divided between Democrats and Republicans, and are more likely than young people to hold political office. Older people, however, have shown little inclination to vote as a bloc on issues affecting their welfare. In the past, senior activists, such as Maggie Kuhn and the leaders of the "Gray Panthers," have encouraged senior citizens to vote as a bloc, but so far they have not been successful in convincing them to do so.

Gerontologists have observed that a major factor contributing to the increased push for government services for the elderly has been the publicity on their plight generated by such groups as the National Council of Senior Citizens and the American Association of Retired Persons. The desire of adult children to shift the financial burden of aged parents from themselves onto the government has further contributed to the demand for services for the elderly. The resulting widespread support for such programs has almost guaranteed their passage in Congress.

Now, for the first time, there are groups emerging that oppose increases in spending for services for older Americans. Requesting generational equity, some politically active groups argue that the federal government is spending so much on older Americans that it is depriving younger age groups of needed services.

The articles in this section discuss the rising cost of health care and senior services for older Americans. In "Canada's Health Insurance and Ours: Real Lessons, Big Choices," the authors compare Canada's health care program with U.S. health care to determine which is best. With the ever-escalating costs of American health care, many are seeking solutions to what is perceived as a crisis.

Marc Freedman, in "Senior Citizens: A New Force in Community Service," advocates for a greater use of senior volunteers in the community. He argues that seniors bring reliability, dependability, and discipline to vital community services. Then, in "Does Getting Old Cost Society Too Much?" Paul Krugman questions whether the future holds dramatic reductions in Medicare coverage or the emergence of a medical welfare state.

"The Unquiet Future of Intergenerational Politics," by Walter Rosenbaum and James Button, examines communities with very large elderly populations to determine whether this factor increases or decreases generational conflict. An individual's negative attitude toward older persons may be directly related to the size of the aging population in their community.

The final unit article, "Less Medicare, More Magic" by Max Frankel, addresses the popularity of Social Security, Medicare, and Medicaid benefits. These government programs are granted universally to everyone—the rich and the poor. According to Frankel, any attempts to limit the programs to the poor would destroy public support, and the magic would be lost.

Looking Ahead: Challenge Questions

What new programs should the federal government institute in the next five years to assist older Americans?

What service programs for senior citizens could be more efficiently handled by state and local governments than by the federal government? Give some examples.

Do you think that the elderly are often abused in the name of protection? Explain why or why not.

Do you believe that the federal government is investing too much in social services for older Americans? Defend your answer.

UNIT 8

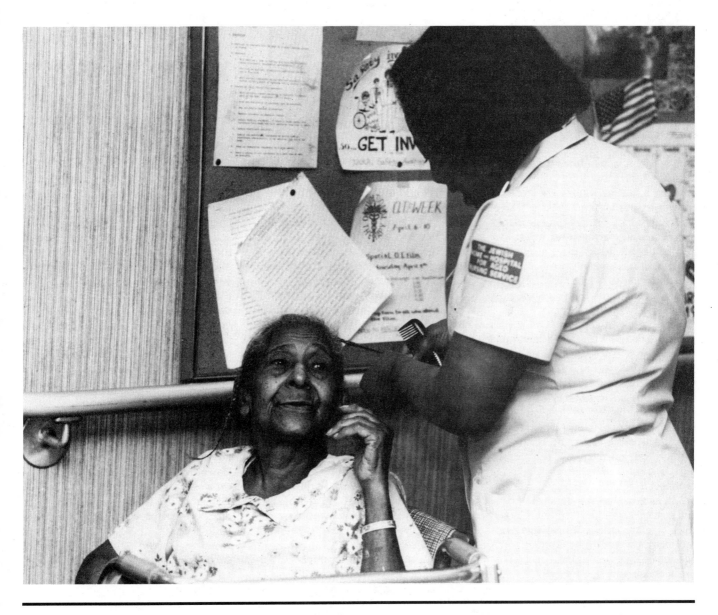

Canada's Health Insurance & Ours:
Real Lessons,
Big Choices

**Theodore R. Marmor and
Jerry L. Mashaw**

(Theodore R. Marmor is professor of public management at the Yale University School of Organization and Management. Jerry L. Mashaw is Gordon Bradford Tweedy Professor Law and Organization at Yale University Law School.)

As medical costs escalate and more Americans find themselves without insurance, Canada's approach to financing health care has taken center stage in the debate in the United States. Congressional committees have invited Canadian experts to testify. Political organizations have sent parades of representatives on crash study tours to Canada. Television networks, National Public Radio, major national newspapers and *Consumer Reports* have done stories on Canadian national health insurance.

Canada's health system raises three separable issues for the United States: Does Canada really have an exemplary medical care system worth importing? Is Canada's program politically feasible in the United States? Can we successfully adapt it?

Canada's National Health Insurance
Canada's ten provinces provide health insurance. The federal government conditionally promises to repay each province a substantial portion of the costs of all necessary medical care, roughly 40 percent. The federal grant is available as long as the province's health insurance program covers all citizens, has conventional hospital and medical care and has no limits on services or extra charges to patients. Each province must recognize the others' coverage and be under control of a public, nonprofit organization.

Annual negotiations between provincial governments and providers of care determine hospital budgets and physicians' fees. As in the United States, most hospitals are nonprofit community institutions.

Unlike U.S. hospitals, they never worry about itemized billings; they receive their budget in monthly installments. Budgets are adjusted each year for inflation, new programs and changes in their volume of services.

As in the United States, physicians practice in diverse individual and group settings, and most are paid on a fee-for-service basis rather than salary. Provincial medical associations determine the structure of a binding fee schedule and negotiate with governments, usually on an annual basis, a percentage increase in the total pool of money budgeted for physicians.

In most provinces, if the fees billed to the provincial insurance fund exceed the budget ceiling, the government grants less than it otherwise would at the next round of negotiations. Escalating physician costs —largely because of increases in procedures per patient—have led most Canadian provinces to explore more explicit limits on total payments to physicians.

As Figure 1 shows, growth patterns of Canadian and U.S. health care expenditures were nearly identical until 1971, when Canada implemented its national insurance plan. Then U.S. health expenditures rose considerably faster, to increase health-care spending from 9 percent of the total goods and services in the economy to 12 percent.

A good system should provide high quality care, timely treatment, good working conditions for health care professionals and other workers, and ultimately a satisfied and healthy citizenry. On these questions, it is time to separate myth from fact.
Myth 1. *National Health Insurance leads to bureaucratic red tape and high administrative costs.*
Canada's national health insurance is a federal plan that the pronvinces administer. Canada's doctors and hospitals receive all payments from a provincial ministry. They don't have to keep track of eligibility requirements or definitions of insured services in hundreds of insurance plans. Canadian patients never have to file claims. Americans, by contrast, file multiple, complicated claims.

Because of the simplicity of the Canadian system, administrative costs are negligible by American standards. The gap between U.S. and Canadian administrative costs has been widening steadily since Canada completed its program. (See Figure 2.)
Myth 2. *NHI interferes with the doctor-patient relationship.*
An increasing number of companies trim health care costs by adopting alternatives such as health maintenance organizations or preferred provider organization. In Canada, citizens have no restrictions on their choice of physicians; physicians do not have to obtain approval from administrators for treatment they recommend. If freedom of choice is the deciding criterion for many people, it actually works in favor of the Candadian model.
Myth 3. *NHI leads to long treatment queues.*
Every country has waiting lists for elective procedures, sometimes even essential ones. Americans treated in hospital emergency rooms, particularly in big cities, often have to wait hours for critical care.

Overall rates of hospital use per capita are considerably higher in Canada than in the United States. Yet there have developed long waiting lists for some services, particularly for open-heart surgery, and magnetic resonance imaging—the newest radiological procedure for diagnosis.
Myth 4. *NHI lowers the quality of medical care.*
[S]ome expensive, high-technology items are less available in Canada than in the United States, It is unclear, however, whether the rates of investment in such technologies in the United States represent a standard for judging other countries.

From *The National Voter*, April/May 1991, pp. 10-11. Adapted from *The American Prospect*, Fall 1990. © 1990 by Theodore M. Marmor. Reprinted by permission of the author.

Analysts believe the United States has overinvested and overused some technologies. Canada has a full range of high technology facilities, but there is considerably less abundance and little competition for market share.

If we define quality by some measure that reflects effectiveness of treatment and respect and consideration shown to all patients—not just the affluent and insured—America ranks lower than other countries in the West, including Canada, that have national health insurance.

According to a ten-nation survey published in *Health Affairs*, Canadians are the most satisfied and Americans the least satisfied with their country's health care system. While only 10 percent of Americans surveyed say their health system functions "pretty well," 56 percent of Canadians thought their health care system works well. Eighty-nine percent of Americans say their system needs "fundamental changes" or "complete rebuilding."

Figure 1. Health Expenditures in the United States and Canada as Percent of Gross National Product. Vertical dotted line indicates 1971 when Canada enacted its National Health Insurance.

Myth 5. *NHI leads to rationing.*
Critics warn that Canada "rations" medical care. If by rationing they simply mean limiting services, every country in the world rations health care.

The United States limits services by ability to pay and shows significant differences in access to health care by race, class, and employment circumstances. By contrast, Canada and most other developed coun-

tries attempt to provide more uniform access to the entire population. Medical care depends more on a professional assessment of need than on insurance status.

Because Canadians have free choice of physician, they do not have to worry about rationing. While the rationing choices of an American HMO are private, Canada's choices about spending on hospitals and other health services are publicly debated and democratically decided.

Myth 6. *NHI causes an exodus of physicians.*
Canadian physicians were coming to the United States long before Canada introduced national health insurance. Emigration did not increase significantly afterwards. The ratio of physicians to population has steadily increased and actually grown closer to the U.S. level. In 1987 we had 234 doctors per 1,000 people, while Canada had 216.

Is It Politically Feasible Here?
The public wants broadened, simplified and stable coverage at reasonable out-of-pocket cost. Firms want to reduce their costs of insuring employees and, at the very least, to avoid paying for the health insurance of the unemployed and uninsured.

Although movement toward something

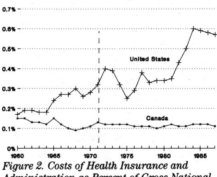

Figure 2. Costs of Health Insurance and Administration as Percent of Gross National Product.

like Canadian national health insurance may appear a large step, most pieces needed for a state insurance program already

are in place. What would it take to make the Canadian model work in the United States? We see two elements:

● Canadians in each providence are insured on the "same terms and conditions."
● Canadians lodge financing responsibility in a ministry of health or its equivalent. It creates more leverage in bargaining with providers.

Modified Universalism
Every Canadian belongs to the same provincial health insurance plan as his neighbor and enjoys the same coverage under the plan. To maintain "equal terms" of access, Canadian doctors have been barred since 1984 from charging patients anything above the government's fee schedule. In these respects, Canada is probably more egalitarian than any other comparable industrial democracy.

Great Britain concentrates financial responsibility in the national ministry of health. Sweden does so in each of its county councils. The lesson for the United States is that there are options.

The more difficult question is whether Canada's public financing and direct government administration are required for political accountability. Public financing makes Canadian outlays for health care highly visible.

Call for Challenge of Status Quo
In the United States of the 1990s, the crucial political problem facing national health insurance advocates may not be the clout of the health insurance industry but the public's hostility toward increased taxes.

Financing medical care out of general tax revenues, as in Great Britain and Canada, seems to reinforce constraints on medical inflation.

The message conveyed to the American public since 1975—that less reliance on government is the key to controlling medical costs—needs to be challenged. That is partly why the Canadian example has become so important.

LIFE IN AMERICA

SENIOR CITIZENS:
A New Force in
Community Service

*With retirees living longer and generally enjoying better health,
many are seeking ways to provide their experience and expertise
in a wide range of programs.*

by Marc Freedman

AS THE BABY BOOM generation approaches retirement and life expectancy continues to increase, the U.S. finds itself in the midst of a demographic revolution. The senior population is twice what it was in 1960 and is expected to double again over the next 30 years. By the middle of the 21st century, seniors will outnumber children and youth for the first time. Few other changes are likely to exert as great an influence on society in the coming decades.

For the most part, the aging of American society is portrayed as a source of impending strife, with new strains on families, social services, and intergenerational relations. While this transformation presents real challenges, it brings new opportunities as well. The U.S. today possesses not only the fastest growing, but the largest, best-educated, and most vigorous collection of older adults in

Mr. Freedman is Director of Special Projects, Public/Private Ventures, Philadelphia, Pa.

its history. In fact, the senior population may represent the country's sole increasing natural resource.

How might the productive and humanitarian potential of this resource be harnessed at a juncture when unmet needs in education, health care, public safety, the environment, and other essential areas are extensive and urgent? National service offers a particularly appealing vehicle for engaging seniors to respond to pressing needs. Many older Americans are in a position to make the major life commitment—ranging from half- to full-time work for at least one year—that defines national service.

The rationale for senior participation in national service centers on three overlapping and complementary objectives: alleviating the country's pressing domestic problems; enhancing the personal development of participants; and bolstering the nation's flagging sense of community.

In the context of America's considerable

unmet needs, seniors represent hope not only because they are numerous, but because they are potentially available. Increased longevity and early retirement means they are spending a greater proportion of their lives in post-retirement—for many, one-third of their lives. Studies show that retirement frees substantial amounts of time—an average of 25 hours per week for men and 18 hours for women—and that most is spent either watching television or doing housework.

There also are indications that older adults are looking for opportunities to serve. A study sponsored by the U.S. Administration on Aging found that 14,000,000 Americans over the age of 65 (37.4% of the senior population) might be willing to come forward if asked, while 4,000,000 current volunteers indicate they would like to give more time. Forty percent of those surveyed say the government should be doing more to promote service opportunities.

From *USA Today Magazine*, January 1997, pp. 54-57. © 1997 by the Society for the Advancement of Education. Reprinted by permission.

Older adults may be particularly appropriate for national service assignments. They are experienced workers, family members, and citizens, among other things, and therefore are a rich repository of the social capital required by young people to make the transition to adulthood. Studies of older workers and volunteers further suggest that seniors bring reliability, dependability, and discipline to responsible assignments.

For many, retirement means a jarring transition from engagement to disengagement, from productivity to idleness. Fifty-five percent of elder respondents to a Louis Harris Poll lamented the loss of usefulness after retirement. Isolation and lack of purpose have been shown to increase seniors' risk of deterioration, illness, and death. Conversely, productive engagement and strong social networks contribute to prolonged mental and physical health. A 25-year National Institute of Mental Health study found, for example, that "highly organized" activity is the single strongest predictor, other than not smoking, of longevity and vitality.

Service provides opportunities for engagement, activity, acquaintanceship, and growth. According to sociologist Erik Erikson, service can meet a deeper need as well, satisfying the impulse toward generativity—the instinctual drive to pass on to the next generation what an individual has learned from life. The final challenge of life, he maintains, involves coming to terms with the notion, "I am what survives of me."

In the 1980s, Americans began hearing about the prospect of coming generational conflict, sparked by the contention that seniors were depriving the country's children and youth of their fair share in a political process dominated by elder interests. This argument usually is overstated, but there can be no doubt that, in a society divided by class, race, and sex, tensions between the generations exist as well. In the absence of cross-generational contact and engagement, these tensions might worsen as the demographic composition of society continues to shift.

National service for seniors—particularly intergenerational efforts—provide a potential antidote to these tensions. Indeed, there is evidence suggesting just such an effect. In the early 1980s, for instance, Miami aggressively began pursuing elder school volunteers, who then became the linchpin in a campaign for passage of a billion-dollar school bond issue.

Engaging seniors through service can contribute to preserving the essential features of civil society, which, many have concluded, is unraveling. In this context, the idea of senior service is compelling, in the words of anthropologist Margaret Mead, "as a way to restore a sense of community, a knowledge of the past, and a sense of the future."

While compelling in the abstract, the idea

of senior service by no means is an untested notion. Beginning three decades ago and proceeding in fits and starts, a partial system of national service for seniors has developed in this country. This experience offers rich lessons for policy and programs.

In spring, 1963, Pres. John F. Kennedy delivered his most important speech on aging, decrying the "wall of inertia" standing between old people and their communities. In response, Kennedy urged the establishment of a National Service Corps, a domestic equivalent of the Peace Corps, that would provide opportunities for community service involving both the elderly and the young. The President's call was an invitation, in Attorney General Robert F. Kennedy's words, to "millions of older and retired people whose reservoir of skill and experience remains untapped."

The National Service Corps proposal to engage a wide swath of older Americans never made it out of Congress, and with its demise went an encompassing vision of senior participation in national service that remains unfulfilled today. In 1965, however, a more limited incarnation of senior service emerged when Pres. Lyndon Johnson announced Federal funding for a new set of programs engaging low-income seniors in community service. The most prominent new efforts were the Foster Grandparent and Green Thumb programs, both administered originally by the Office of Economic Opportunity (OEO) and paying participating seniors stipends equivalent to the minimum wage. Foster Grandparents paired seniors one-to-one with children and youth who were disadvantaged or disabled, while Green Thumb, sponsored by the National Farmers Union, engaged older adults in highway beautification and other community service projects.

Over time, the Foster Grandparent Program moved to the Department of Health, Education and Welfare, eventually becoming part of the Federal volunteer service agency ACTION in 1971. Green Thumb, meanwhile, moved from OEO to Department of Labor jurisdiction and, in the process, developed greater emphasis on public service employment and job placement. It was joined by projects administered by the National Council on the Aging, National Council of Senior Citizens, American Association of Retired Persons, and other leading organizations—all of which eventually became the Senior Community Service Employment Program, Title V of the Older Americans Act. In 1973, the Senior Companion Program, based on a model similar to Foster Grandparents and also lodged in ACTION, was started to provide one-to-one support to frail elders.

Today, these programs engage 100,000 older Americans in year-round, intensive, stipended community service of 20 hours per week. While other Federally funded ini-

tiatives, such as the Peace Corps, VISTA, and RSVP, involve older adults in projects requiring the commitment associated with service, the overwhelming majority of current opportunities are concentrated in the Foster Grandparent, Senior Companion, and Title V initiatives.

Lessons from experience

Examining the experience of established and incipient efforts provides a valuable perspective on the promise, limitations, and future directions for national and community service involving seniors.

● Seniors can provide essential community service. Evidence of the important contribution of seniors in Federally funded service programs is chronicled in more than 70 studies over 30 years. The vast majority of this research, focused on the Foster Grandparent and Senior Companion programs, suggests substantial benefits both to individual clients and host agencies, indicating that seniors fill significant service gaps, provide complementary skills to staff and other volunteers, and are stable and long-lasting participants.

● Seniors can benefit through serving. The motive driving senior service appears to be less altruism than a strong and straightforward desire for structure, purpose, affiliation, growth, and meaning. There is evidence from program evaluations and other research suggesting that older participants derive these benefits from the service experience. One study finds, for instance, that participants experience "increased self-esteem, renewed feelings of health and vigor, and new and satisfying social relationships with peers."

● Low-income seniors can play an important role in service. The vast majority of existing service programs enroll low-income seniors, most of them women and many minorities. The efforts of the past three decades demonstrate that these low-income individuals—the group most likely to be overlooked and undervalued for their assets—can make a substantial contribution to their communities and can benefit in the process.

● Government can enable senior service. The current roster of service programs operates on a national scale, involving more than 1,000 projects and 100,000 participants. They demonstrate the important enabling role government can play in the service arena by stimulating, supporting, and sustaining service efforts through providing ongoing infrastructure, and doing so without suffocating civic spirit or compromising local control. The experience of these programs also highlights their political resilience. They have navigated seven administrations, Democratic and Republican, while building bipartisan support along the way.

● Implementation is crucial. Effective senior service requires sturdy infrastructure not only at the policy level—as reflected in the government's ongoing enabling role—but at the program level as well. An overarching lesson of the past three decades' experience in this arena is that program implementation is essential. Experience to date provides increased sophistication in this arena and a set of lessons concerning the best program practices for training, recruitment, compensation, and supervision.

● Senior service is not cheap. It is not practical simply to call for participants, parcel them out, and hope for the best. Responsible programming costs money, notably for adequate staffing and supervision. At present, the annual Federal cost for the Foster Grandparent Program is $65,800,-000 ($3,508 per slot); the Senior Companion Program, $29,000,000 ($3,723 a slot); and the Senior Community Service Employment Program, $390,000,000 ($6,053 per slot). The lower cost per slot of the first two programs is attributable primarily to differences in compensation. The Foster Grandparent and Senior Companion programs pay a tax-exempt stipend of $2.45 per hour, while the Senior Community Service Employment Program provides taxable compensation pegged to the minimum wage.

● Critical mass is missing. While the absolute numbers involved in senior community service are impressive, these efforts remain small, scarce, and scattered at the ground level. Only about one-quarter of one percent of seniors are involved nationally, in contrast to the roughly five percent of the eligible population engaged in the Depression-era Civilian Conservation Corps. The Foster Grandparent and Senior Companion programs are available in just a small fraction of the counties and have long waiting lists of interested participants.

● Program limitations exist. First, very few men participate in the programs—11% of Foster Grandparents, 15% of Senior Companions, and 34% in the Senior Community Service Employment Program are male. Second, by law, these efforts are restricted to low-income individuals, screening out many working- and middle-class seniors—including large numbers on fixed incomes that still put them slightly above the eligibility line. Third, available assignments tend to be caregiving, delivering Meals on Wheels, or providing support services—offerings that do not begin to approximate the wider variety of tasks seniors might contribute.

● Obstacles and questions remain. Despite progress, a cultural ambivalence about older adults as serious, capable, and productive citizens and service-providers persists. At the organizational level, underutilization of seniors in service assignments is a serious problem, ranging from being ignored through being placed in assignments that do not make full use of their skills and abilities. Host agency personnel often are overwhelmed with other duties, lack training in working with seniors in service roles, or are concerned that elders will impinge on their turf or even displace regular staff. Indeed, knowledge is lacking about many key issues related to senior service, including displacement and cost-effectiveness. Over the past 30 years, a great deal has been accomplished in senior service, constructing the rudiments of a national service system for older Americans and developing an understanding about what it takes to put senior service into action. These accomplishments notwithstanding, the gap between promise and practice remains substantial.

In many ways, the nation still is subsisting on innovations dating back to the War on Poverty. The great triumph of this legacy is the involvement of low-income seniors in essential community service; the great limitation can be found in the absence of opportunities for the vast remainder of the senior population.

Today, with national service in the public mind, there is an opportunity to re-examine this legacy, to build on the achievements of the 1960s while preparing for the circumstances of the 2020s. A central task is to close the senior service gap, not only out of a desire to meet current needs, but to produce what historian Peter Laslett calls an "institutional inheritance" for the coming wave of older Americans.

In moving forward, an effort should be made to engage a wider range of older adults (in terms of education, income, and sex), provide an expanded menu of service roles (within existing programs and through new opportunities), and create mechanisms for meeting essential community needs while stimulating the growth and development of participants. A system should be created that provides opportunities at a variety of levels—not merely the chance to volunteer a few hours a week (where immense progress has been made over the past generation), but to serve in well-developed half- and full-time opportunities. If these efforts were linked effectively, interested seniors might be in the position to move in and out of various options, perhaps serving half time or more for a year or two, then making the transition to assignments requiring a less encompassing commitment.

Throughout, these efforts should be anchored in a vision of senior service that is substantially, though not exclusively, intergenerational, involving not only opportunities for seniors to serve the younger generation, but to serve side by side with youth for the good of the community. A reasonable goal for these efforts would be creation of high-impact, well-crafted senior service opportunities for one percent of the senior population, or approximately 500,000 adults 65 years and older, by 2020. The Federal cost for this undertaking would be about $3,000,000,000 in current dollars (at an average per-senior cost of $6,000 for half-time service, a figure reflecting additional investment in strengthening program practices). In return, communities would receive 500,-000,000 hours of annual elder service.

Strategic planning

An incremental strategy in pursuing this objective is prudent. Current slots should be expanded from 100,000 to 150,000 over the next five years, then steadily built toward one percent of the population, and that proportion maintained as the older adult cohort increases in size. Achieving this vision for senior service in America will require progress on the following fronts:

Strengthen the three programs currently providing the vast majority of senior service opportunities. First, expand the Foster Grandparent and Senior Companion Programs. Five years after the Foster Grandparent Program was created, the Senate Special Committee on Aging, citing the program's record of achievement, called for an increase in its size to 60,000. A quarter-century later, the initiative barely is one-third this size, and the Foster Grandparent and Senior Companion programs combined enroll just over half this number. Meanwhile, the vast need for caregiving for children and youth on one hand, and older adults and the ailing on the other—as well as the track record of these programs—strongly support dramatic expansion.

Second, re-examine the service dimension of the Senior Community Service Employment Program. Much effort over the past decade has been spent fortifying its job transition aspect. Interviews with participants, program operators, and national officials suggest that the community service component of Title V might benefit from revamping. Currently, at least two informal strands exist within this program. One primarily serves younger enrollees who join for help in returning to unsubsidized jobs. The second, much larger strand serves "career enrollees," those who essentially have stopped looking for unsubsidized work and most likely will remain in subsidized community service placements in nonprofit and public agencies for substantial periods. This second strand should be bolstered to raise the priority, quality, and level of service performed, enabling participants to provide the greatest possible contribution to their communities.

Embark on a period of innovation and experimentation. Engage male seniors, a group that has been reluctant to participate in existing efforts. In addition to making the Foster Grandparent and Senior Companion programs more attractive to this group, establishing new program areas such as environmental work, apprenticeship efforts, and professional services might draw a greater proportion of men.

Secure the participation of seniors living above poverty circumstances. A variety of routes toward this goal might be pursued. For example, a portion of expanded Foster Grandparent and Senior Companion slots might be freed from income guidelines entirely. Another option is to develop a high-intensity, stipended, half- to full-time track within the Retired and Senior Volunteer Program, which currently is open to participation regardless of income, but is oriented toward assignments involving two to four hours of uncompensated voluntarism a week.

Develop intergenerational programs in which seniors and youth serve jointly. It is necessary to explore partnerships, for instance, between senior service and youth service efforts, including opportunities for seniors and youth to serve side by side in the new AmeriCorps initiative. The concept of an intergenerational service corps equally balanced between senior and youth participants should be explored.

Conduct experiments involving a variety of compensation and program strategies. It would be useful to compare, for example, the different effects of tax-exempt, sub-minimum wage stipends and taxable stipends at the minimum-wage level and higher. Alternative forms of compensation such as service credits, health benefits, long-term care credits, or even property tax relief might be explored, along with a variety of strategies in such areas as training, supervision, and support.

Build infrastructure at the national and local levels. Establish a national center for senior service. A new entity is needed capable of providing muscle to a set of essential—and long-neglected—marketing, technical assistance, demonstration, and research functions designed to raise the level of knowledge, awareness, and implementation of senior service across the country. While some of these functions might be carried out internally by the Corporation for National and Community Service, the creation of a not-for-profit intermediary organization probably is preferable. This institution should be established through collaboration by the Corporation and private sponsors, including foundations and major organizations for the aging.

Create mechanisms at the local level to give visibility and meaning to the senior corps concept. Such local mechanisms, which well might evolve out of existing structures, would act as a single point of entry for older adults; perform local marketing among seniors and others in the community; conduct training for seniors involved in community service; develop the capacity of community agencies to use the talents of seniors; promulgate new initiatives designed to meet local needs; and provide opportunities for contact among elders participating in different programs.

Moving forward with this agenda promises potential benefits not only to recipients of service and participating seniors, but to society at large. Anchored on sturdy institutional moorings, senior service might help to create a more generative society, dedicated to posterity, striving to extend Erik Erikson's "I am what survives of me" until it becomes the defining outlook of a generation.

The Economics of the Boom

Does Getting Old Cost Society Too Much? All the scary talk about medical costs misses the point. The money is mostly well spent; the hard question is where to set limits—and for whom.

By Paul Krugman

BACK IN THE EARLY 1980'S, BEFORE most of us had ever heard of the Internet, science-fiction writers like Bruce Sterling invented a genre that came to be known as cyberpunk. Its protagonists were usually outlaw computer hackers, battling sinister multinational corporations for control of cyberspace (a term coined by another sci-fi novelist, William Gibson). But in his 1996 novel, "Holy Fire," Sterling imagines a rather different future: a world ruled by an all-powerful gerontocracy, which appropriates most of the world's wealth to pay for ever more costly life-extension techniques. And his heroine is, believe it or not, a 94-year-old medical economist.

When the novel first came out, it seemed that Sterling was behind the curve. Public concern over medical costs peaked about four years ago, then dropped off sharply. Not only did the Clinton health care plan crash and burn, but the long-term upward trend in private medical costs also flattened, as corporations shifted many of their employees into cost-conscious H.M.O.'s. Even as debates over how to save Social Security make headlines, few question budget plans by Congress and the Administration, which assume, while being systematically vague about the details, that the growth of Medicare can be sharply slowed with few ill effects. With remarkable speed, in other words, we have gone from a sense of crisis to a general belief that the problem of health costs will more or less take care of itself.

But in recent months, there has been a flurry of stories with the ominous news that medical costs are on the rise again. Suddenly, our recent complacency about health care costs looks as unjustified as our previous panic. In

Paul Krugman is a professor of economics at the Massachusetts Institute of Technology. His most recent article for the Magazine, "New Math, Same Story," appeared in January.

fact, both the panic and the complacency seem to stem from — what else? — a misdiagnosis of the nature of the problem.

Over the last generation, the U.S. economy has been digitized; it has been globalized; but just as important, it has become medicalized. In 1970 we spent 7 percent of our gross domestic product on medical care; today the number is twice that. Almost 1 worker in 10 is employed in the health care service industry; if this trend continues, in a few years there will be more people working in doctors' offices and hospitals than in factories.

So what? As Joseph Newhouse, a Harvard health economist, put it, "Neither citizens nor economists ... are especially concerned about rapid growth in most sectors of the economy, like the personal computer industry, the fax machine industry or the cellular phone industry." Yet where the growth of other industries is usually regarded as a cause for celebration, the growth of the medical sector is generally regarded as a bad thing. (Not long ago, an article in The Atlantic Monthly even proposed a measure of economic growth that deducts health care from the G.D.P., on the grounds that medical expenditures are a cost, not a benefit.) Indeed, the very phrase "medical costs" seems to have the word "bloated" attached to it as a permanent modifier: we are not, everyone agrees, getting much for all that money.

Or are we? There is, of course, some truth to what Newhouse calls the "cocktail party story of excessive medical spending." Traditional medical insurance gives neither doctors nor their patients an incentive to think about costs; the result can be what Alain Enthoven, a health care reform advocate, calls "flat of the curve" medicine, in which doctors order any procedure that might possibly be of medical value, no matter how expensive. Reintroducing some incentives can produce important savings.

In 1983, for example, Medicare replaced its previous policy of paying all hospital costs with a new policy of paying hospitals a lump sum for any given procedure. The result was an immediate sharp drop in the average number of days in the hospital, with no apparent adverse medical effects. But after that one-time saving, the cost of hospitalization began rising again. There is, in fact, a clear rhythm in the health care industry. Every once in a while, there is a wave of cost-cutting moves — fixed fees for Medicare, replacing traditional insurance with H.M.O.'s — that slows the growth of medical expenses for a few years. But then the growth resumes.

WHY CAN'T WE SEEM TO KEEP the lid on medical costs, for older adults and for everyone else as well? The answer — the clean little secret of health care — is simple: we actually do get something for our money. In fact, there is a consensus among health care experts that the main driving force behind rising costs is neither greed nor inefficiency nor even the aging of our population but technological progress.

Medical expenditures used to be small, not because doctors were cheap or hospitals were well managed but because there was only so much medicine had to offer, no matter how much you were willing to spend. Since the 1940's, however, every year has brought new medical advances: new diagnostic techniques that can (at great expense) identify problems that could previously only be guessed at; new surgical procedures that can (at great expense) correct problems that could previously only be allowed to take their course; new therapies that can (at great expense) cure or at least alleviate conditions that could previously only be endured. We spend ever more on medicine mainly because we keep on finding good new things that (a lot of) money can buy.

It is often argued that the share of our national income that we devote to health care cannot continue to rise in the future as it has in the past. But why not? An old advertising slogan asserted that "when you've got your health, you've got just about everything." Sterling's sci-fi protagonist goes through an implausible procedure (albeit one based on an extrapolation of some real medical research) that restores her youth; who would not give most of their worldly goods for that? Even barring such medical miracles, it is not hard to imagine that some day we might be willing to spend, say, 30 percent of our income on treatments that prolong our lives and improve their quality.

Some economists therefore argue that we should stop worrying about the rise in medical costs. By all means, they say, let us encourage some economic rationality in the system — for example, by eliminating the bias created by the fact that wages are taxed but medical benefits are not — but if people still want to spend an ever-growing fraction of their income on health, whether for older adults or for all Americans, so be it.

But matters are not quite that simple, for medicine is not just like other goods.

The most direct difference between medicine and other things is that so much of it is paid for by the Government. In most ad-

---

Any religion that doesn't deal with death
realistically is not worth its salt.
Rembert G. Weakland, 69
Archbishop of Milwaukee

Getting old is not for sissies. One of the priests told me the other day of a woman who was complaining about her pain. He told her that she should remember Jesus and His suffering, and she shot back, "Yeah, but He didn't live long enough to feel the pain of rheumatism." It's like any machine that ages. There's a lot more suffering than I imagined, but we've got to learn to take that pain and still be cheerful. I met an elderly woman the other day who said that she lives every day as if it were a gift. I think this is helpful. Thinking this way helps us to live each day fully.

People of my generation are concerned with mortality. So many Americans watched as Cardinal Bernardin faced his mortality. His holiness was so attractive to people because it drew from our tradition of human dignity. I think we were all edified by his acceptance of death as a friend and not an enemy. Any religion that doesn't deal with death realistically is not worth its salt.

Medical expenditures used to be small, not because doctors were cheap, but because there was only so much medicine had to offer, no matter how much you were willing to spend.

vanced countries, the Government pays for most medical care; even in free-market, anti-government America, the public sector pays for more than 40 percent of medical expenditures. This in itself creates a special problem. It is not at all hard to see how the American economy could support a much larger medical sector; it is, however, very hard to see how the U.S. Government will manage to pay for its share of that sector's costs.

When Cassandras like Pete Peterson, the former Commerce Secretary, present alarming numbers about the future burden of baby boomers on the budget, it turns out that only part of that prospective burden represents the sheer demographic effects of an aging population: forecasts of rising medical costs account for the rest. Despite the aging of our population, the Congressional Budget Office projects that in 2030, Social Security payments will rise only from their current 5 percent of G.D.P. to about 7 percent — but it projects that Medicare and Medicaid will rise from 4 percent to more than 10 percent of G.D.P. (Some people dismiss such forecasts: they point out that these projections also imply an enormous increase in private health care costs, perhaps to as much as 15 to 20 percent of G.D.P. That, they insist, is just not going to happen. But why not?)

SOME MIGHT THEN SAY THAT THE answer is obvious: we must abandon the idea that everyone is entitled to state-of-the-art medical care. (That is the hidden subtext of politicians who insist that Medicare is not being cut — that all they are doing is slowing its growth.) But are we really prepared to face up to the implications of such an abandonment?

We have come to take it for granted that in advanced nations almost everyone can afford at least the essentials of life. Ordinary people may not dine in three-star restaurants, but they have enough to eat; they may not wear Bruno Maglis, but they do not go barefoot; they may not live in Malibu, but they have roofs over their heads. Yet it was not always thus. In the past, the elite were physically superior to the masses, because only they had adequate nutrition: in the England of Charles Dickens, the adolescent sons of the upper class towered an average of four inches above their working-class contemporaries. What has happened since represents a literal leveling of the human condition, in a way that mere comparisons of the distribution of money income cannot capture.

There is really only one essential that is not within easy reach of the ordinary American family, and that is medical care. But the rising cost of that essential — that is, the rising cost of buying the ever-growing list of useful things that doctors can now do for us — threatens to restore that ancient inequality with a vengeance.

Suppose that Lyndon Johnson had not signed Medicare into law in 1965. Even now there would be a radical inequality in the prospects of the elderly rich and the ordinary older citizen; the affluent would receive artificial hip replacements and coronary bypasses, while the rest would (like the elderly poor in less fortunate nations) limp along painfully — or die.

The current conventional wisdom is that the budget burden of health care will be cured with rationing — the Federal Government will simply decline to pay for many of the expensive procedures that medical science makes available. But what if, as seems likely, those procedures really work — if there comes a time when those who can afford it can expect to be vigorous centenarians, and perhaps even buy themselves smarter children, while those who cannot can look forward only to the biblical threescore and 10. Is this really a tolerable prospect?

There is, some might say, no alternative. But of course there is. It is possible to imagine a society that taxes itself heavily to provide advanced medical care to everyone and that rations care not by wealth but by other criteria. (Bruce Sterling's imaginary future is ruled by "the polity," a nanny state that rewards not wealth but personal hygiene: society takes care of those who take care of themselves.)

Such an outcome sounds unthinkable in the current political climate, which is dominated by a low-tax, anti-government ideology. But history is not over; ideologies may change. For all we know, the future may belong to the medical welfare state, a state whose slogan might be "From each according to his ability, to each according to his needs."

Empirical studies of political opinion and behavior about national issues affecting the aging
have not revealed the intergenerational conflicts often predicted in recent decades. Using
public opinion studies of attitudes about the aging at the community level in Florida, this study
does identify significant cleavages in attitude and belief between generations, suggesting
intergenerational political conflict may be likely in the future. The research implies the most
important source of this conflict may be the community level and the "image" of the aging
that is developing among younger community residents.
Key Words: Retirement politics, Community politics, Aging and politics, Aging and voting,
Political gerontology, Generational conflict, Generational politics

The Unquiet Future of Intergenerational Politics

Walter A. Rosenbaum, PhD,
and James W. Button, PhD

Department of Political Science, 3324 Turlington Hall, University of
Florida, Gainesville, FL 32611. Correspondence should be addressed to
Walter A. Rosenbaum, PhD, at the above address.

For almost two decades, social commentators have been predicting a political confrontation between old and young Americans that has not materialized. Now, many observers cite empirical studies to demonstrate that a generational conflict is unlikely. This revisionist interpretation seems premature. Evidence of generational tension has been elusive, we think, in part because investigators have often looked in the wrong place for the wrong thing. If one turns to intergenerational stereotypes and attitudes — to the mutual images that contemporary generations hold of one another — social, economic and political dissonance does appear. And it appears at the community level, within the context of local government and politics.

We have found the data suggestive of these conclusions largely in the contemporary images and attitudes that old and young elicit from each other in Florida, an especially advantageous setting for an intergenerational study. In the Sunshine State, where almost 1 in 5 residents has reached retirement age (the highest proportion in the nation), generational relationships and their social consequences are thrown into particularly sharp relief and continually examined through politics, the media and daily civic life. With this large retirement population, moreover, Florida is frequently presumed to be an augury of graying America, the state where political and economic transformations implicit in the demographic aging of the U.S. population will be foreshadowed.

The perceptual foundations of generational political relationships have been relatively unexplored. Instead, public policy preferences and issue concerns have been the customary social barometers for generational conflict. Attitudes and stereotypes, however, should be especially important when intergenerational politics is discussed because, as many commentators have observed, it is the social image of the aging as much as any other social attribute that has fortified the elderly's political status. America's aging, as Roger Cobb and Charles Elder have aptly observed, have enjoyed a "peculiar potency" and "a special legitimacy" as claimants for budgetary priority in the political struggle for governmental resources (Elder & Cobb, 1984). To many observers, like gerontologist Eric Kingson, a deterioration in the public image upon which the political privilege of the aging is grounded is a bellwether of generational tension. "The budgetary politics of recent years," he has warned, "have placed the elderly interest-groups and elder advocates on the defensive, threatening . . . to reduce their legitimacy and [to] change the perception of the elderly population as a group deserving of government support" (Kingson, 1988, p. 771). The contemporary literature on generational conflict, in fact, is rich in assumptions about the social perceptions and attitudes that incite or perpetuate generational tensions. Since our survey protocols are largely derived from these studies, it will be helpful to review briefly those aspects most important in shaping the substance and administration of the survey questionnaire.

Age, Social Imagery and Generational Conflict

Generational amity has prevailed during the last several decades in defiance of the many jeremiads predicting its collapse as far back as 1951 (Longman, 1987). These predictions, increasing notably in the last 20 years, have awakened substantial concern among public advocates and organizational representatives for the elderly. Throughout the 1970s a variety of observers, from academic gerontologists to political advocates of the aging, began to warn about a real, or potential, rise in resentment toward the aging as a result of their growing entitlements and political power (Longman, 1987; Schuck, 1979).

Dark prophecies of generational discontent, feeding on assumptions about the deteriorating social image of the aging, multiplied through the 1980s. The aging population was growing bigger and, said many critics, much greedier (Barnes, 1991; Huddy, 1989; Reeves, 1988; Tolchin, 1988). It seemed to many observers that older Americans had truncated Reaganomics to a single political principle — me first! — which they celebrated for a decade in their ferocious determination to expand already generous entitlements. The 1980s were also years of large, inflating federal deficits and diminishing federal spending for youth — the politically volatile ingredients perhaps sufficient to ignite a generational confrontation.

From Needy to Greedy Old

The new imagery of the aging was a composite of several qualities that suggested the design of this study's survey questionnaire. Many commentators saw in an expanding older population the foreshadow of a political gerontocracy forged from the aging's political power. "You're going to have [a society] ruled by old people," warned one business consultant in a major metropolitan newspaper, popularizing an idea already gaining public attention elsewhere (Philadelphia Inquirer, 1989; see also Grubb & Lazerson, 1982; Oberhofer, 1989; Petersen, 1991; Walker, 1990). In a more scholarly manner, Alan Pifer alerted readers of the *Annals of the American Academy* a few years earlier about the potential political problem in an enlarging older population: "... public officials, because of the voting strength of the elderly, may direct too much money in their direction, and too little towards other groups that lack voting strength" (Pifer, 1986; see also Hudson, 1980; and Hudson, 1978).

The provocative contrast between the aging's steadily enlarging share of the federal budget and the diminishing entitlements of the young also caused many commentators to warn of a political backlash. The entitlement gap emerged as a national issue in 1984 when Samuel Preston's *Scientific American* article reported a decline in health and education levels of American children and noted that the proportion of children in poverty was vastly greater than the proportion of the elderly poor and federal expenditures for the aging vastly exceeded that for children (Preston, 1984a). The media repeated and amplified this theme (Preston, 1984b). By 1991, a *Business Week* article posed the provocative question "Is Uncle Sam Shortchanging Young Americans?" and answered in the affirmative (Bernstein, 1991).

The decade's apotheosis in scholarly polemics against the federal budget's generational inequities was Phillip Longman's 1987 book *Born To Pay*, a longer version of his earlier, widely discussed *Atlantic Magazine* article. "So long as the wealthy elderly demand, in addition to return on their capital, to be provided with across-the-board old age subsidies," warned Longman, "the resentment of the young in general can only increase..." (Longman, 1987, p. 32). Despite evidence that social welfare during the 1980s was no zero-sum game in which the young were losing to the elderly (Jencks & Torrey, 1988), and Social Security would not necessarily discriminate against future generations (Aaron, 1989), arguments to the contrary continued to receive considerable media attention.

With increasing frequency during the 1980s, the aging were also portrayed in the media as self-indulgent and self-absorbed, as in a 1988 *Fortune* article on the American Association of Retired Persons (AARP): "Think of the American Association of Retired Persons as grandfather, very big and very rich ... When grandfather taps his knife on the water glass, as he is doing now, everyone at the table pays attention. It could be the start of an expensive new project, and everyone else might have to give up at least a second helping of dinner" (Smith, 1988, p. 96). Apparently, grandfather (and grandmother) were quite comfortable with their newly affluent aspect. Phillips quotes an AARP media kit of the mid-1980s: "50 & Over people ... They've got clout! Affluent ... Aware ... Active Buyers with over $500 billion to spend ... They're spending on self-fulfillment *now* ... rather than leaving sums behind."

Will There Be A Backlash?

The generational equity issue continues to worry many advocates and representatives for the aging. In 1986, The Gerontological Society of America published a major study, *Ties That Bind: The Interdependence of Generations*, intended to refute the growing literature on generational inequities while emphasizing the mutual dependence of American generations (Kingson, Hirshorn & Harootyan, 1986; see also Kingson, 1988).

Belatedly, the AARP initiated publicity and programs to defuse the generational equity issue and to refute the notion of generational conflict. Many advocates for the aging, like Ron Pollack, the Executive Director of Families United for Senior Action Foundation, believe the aging have already sustained significant political damage from their new stereotype (Skinner & Kinney, 1991). Reviewing the politics of the 1980s, gerontologist Fernando Torres-Gil recently concluded that the causes and consequences of generational conflict might be exaggerated, but "Despite the efforts of gerontologists to discount the generational conflict thesis ... tensions are increasing between generations..." (Torres-Gil, 1992, p. 87).

The Elusive Evidence of Generational Conflict

Apprehension about generational antagonisms would seem ill-founded if one examined only the generational policy preferences upon which most empirical studies of generational conflict currently depend. Generally, these studies gauge the intensity of generational conflict by examining: (a) public policy preferences or attitudes about public policy which are widely shared within age groupings and, especially, that create significant cleavages between older and younger age cohorts; or, (b) voting patterns among the aging which distinguish them from younger voters or suggest significant issue cleavages across generations. These studies usually focus upon age-related policies such as Social Security, entitlement formulas, the generational equity of federal budget allocations and, less frequently, the degree of issue preference and consensus among the aging.

Policy Studies

Studies of policy preferences among generations, with few exceptions, provide scant evidence of intergenerational conflict, even over policies most likely to incite tension. Cook and Barret's 1986 study of public attitudes toward Social Security, for instance, found "few differences in supportiveness across age groups" and "little evidence" of diminishing support among younger Americans (Cook and Barret, 1988, p. 354). Other policy studies generally support the conclusions reported by Michael Ponza and his co-authors in their review of the University of Michigan's 1973 and 1986 General Social Surveys. "Taken as a whole," they conclude, "the results provide no support whatsoever for the 'cohort' view . . . that the elderly favor redistributive transfers away from low-income families with children and toward low-income families of their own age group." Moreover, ". . . lobbying efforts for programs that benefit the elderly are successful because they are consistent with the willingness of individuals in *all* age groups to support the elderly" (Ponza, Duncan, Corcoran, & Groskind, 1989, pp. 6–7; see also Day, 1990, p. 61; and Campos, 1986).

Studies focused on attitudes among the aging concerning almost all age-related policy issues generally uncover no mind-set common to the aging. Political scientists Laurie Rhodebeck and Roy Fitzgerald, for instance, examined political attitudes among the aging reported in seven National Election Studies conducted by the University of Michigan's Survey Research Center between 1972 and 1986. "The cumulative evidence," they conclude, "still points toward lack of unambiguous group-oriented interests among older Americans. . ." (Rhodeback & Fitzgerald, 1989, pp. 6–7; see also Beck & Dye, 1982).

Voting Studies

Studies of candidate and party preference among the aging, like policy studies, seldom reveal significant associations between age and voting choice that cannot be explained by other socioeconomic factors such as income, occupation or race. Even when an age-based voting pattern has been identified, it is apparently transient (Freiman & Grasso, 1982; see also Day, 1990; Foner, 1972; Rhodebeck & Fitzgerald, 1989; Schmidhauser, 1970).

But what about local education? Here, the elderly bear a distinctive stigma. The aging, so runs a common indictment, incite generational animosities by their pervasive hostility to local school bond referenda, tax increases or other pocketbook measures to support the schools. The elderly's "anti-education" bias, in fact, is a verity to many local public officials. The evidence supporting this "anti-education" assumption, however, is meager and inconclusive. Recent studies by Mullins and Rosentraub, and by Haas and Preston, for example, suggest that an increase in the size of retirement populations may have a positive effect on local government spending for education (Mullins & Rosentraub, 1990; see also Haas, 1989; and Haas & Serow, 1991). In contrast, Button's recent study of voting by the elderly in Florida local school bond elections suggests that the aging often — but not always — vote against local school bonds (Button, 1992). The pervasive "anti-education" bias among aging has yet to be persuasively demonstrated (Button & Rosenbaum, 1989).

Beyond Issues and Voting: Exploring Images and Stereotypes

Studies of issue preferences and voting patterns within or between generations provide little insight concerning development and change in the social and political image of the aging. Moreover, issue and voting studies have given little attention to the quality of generational relationships evolving at the local level, especially within communities where the young and old are daily, intimately brought into contact through the most ordinary civic rituals.

Sociopolitical image, however, is explicitly and implicitly a matter of enormous concern to scholars and social commentators writing about current intergenerational tensions. A sensitivity to stereotype and image as a potential source of generational tension is sensible, even essential. It reflects an awareness, well established in sociology and social psychology, that group attitudes and group beliefs about social reality are often the grounding and inspiration for social action. Equally important, attitude, belief or stereotype are often the *precursors* to action, the early warnings of imminent social events, the barometers of social change that may tell us that change is possible, or probable, even though the character and import of such change may be unclear. As sociologist Peter Berger observes, the transformation of social image foreshadows the fact of social change: ". . . when we look at revolutions, we find that the outward acts against the old order are invariably preceded by the disintegration of inward allegiance and loyalties. The images of kings topple before their thrones do" (Berger, 1963, p. 51). In short, the quality of intergenerational attitudes and stereotypes manifest today may open a window upon the future or, at the very least, alert us that social change may be imminent even before — perhaps long before — it becomes manifest.

An interest in social image and stereotype as a precursor of generational conflict led to our 1990–1991 Florida public opinion study which explored differences in generational perceptions about the character of the aging and their impact upon communities in which they reside. This study also replicates portions of our 1986 survey concerning attitudes toward the aging among Florida's local government officials and includes, as well, several questions addressed to the Florida public by another survey more than a decade ago (Burton & Rosenbaum, 1990). Thus, we can compare, at least tentatively, generational stereotypes among the public and its local officials and also examine the congruity between this recent study and earlier measures of generational relationships in Florida.

The Florida Survey

In November of 1990 and 1991, 9 items concerning community images and activities associated with the aging were included in the Florida public opinion poll, conducted monthly by the University of Florida's Bureau of Economic and Business Research (BEBR). The BEBR telephone poll, involving a variety of political or economic issues, is periodically taken among a random sample of the Florida public and includes standard information about the socioeconomic characteristics of respondents. The sample populations interviewed in November of 1990 and 1991 were representative of Florida citizens along basic demographic dimensions (age, gender and race) and the sample sizes (535 in 1990 and 556 in 1991) provided an acceptable confidence interval for all estimates (± 4%). We were primarily concerned with the extent of agreement *within* age categories and disagreement *between* age categories on the items intended to probe generational differences.

The Questions

Five of the survey questions concerned the respondents' beliefs about the political behavior of the aging and their impact upon the local community. Two of these questions in 1990 related to the impact the aging might have on the local community (abbreviations for all variables are in brackets). Respondents were asked the extent to which they agreed with these statements:

The economic benefits brought to my community by older residents do not compensate for the burden they place upon local government. [GOVBURDEN]

Older residents generally help to improve the quality of life in my community. [QUALIFE]

A third item, used only in the 1991 survey, replicated a question used by Douglas St. Angelo in his 1980 survey of attitudes toward the aging in Florida (St. Angelo, 1981):

Do senior citizens in your area have too little political power, too much political power, or about the right amount of political power? [SENPOWER]

Two additional items in the 1990 survey concerned agreement with statements about the political behavior of the aging and its generational impact:

Older persons in my community tend to oppose paying for local public services which do not directly benefit them. [OPPGOVSV]

When older residents in my community advocate government policies that benefit themselves, this often creates political opposition from younger residents. [YOUNGOLD]

Two other questions, the first (originally a Gallup Poll item) used in both surveys and the second in 1990 only, concerned support for the local schools and for local economic growth (Gallup, 1978):

Suppose the local public schools said they needed much more money. As you feel at this time, would you vote to raise taxes for this purpose, or would you vote against raising taxes for this purpose? [EDVOTE]

I think continued economic growth is good for my community. [ECOGROW]

The final two questions in the first survey, adapted from an Eagleton Institute Poll, involved the amount of time spent by the respondents in voluntary local activities — a community service often attributed especially to the aging (Eagleton Institute of Politics, 1987):

Some people get involved in local affairs through donating their time to voluntary organizations — that is, working for no pay for non-profit groups or charity. In the last 12 months, have you volunteered time to any non-profit groups or charities? [CHARITY]

[If 'Yes'] About how many hours in an average month do you do volunteer work for these kinds of organizations? [HOURS]

Generational Consensus and Cleavages

Responses to each of these items concerning the local impact of the aging are presented in Table 1.

The responses to several of these items reveal important, and possibly contentious, differences between age cohorts in their evaluation of the aging. While a substantial majority of each age group believed the aging were generally an economic benefit to their community, about 42% of the younger respondents (those less than 55 years old) did agree with the contrary statement that the aging did not bring benefits to their community that compensate "for the burdens they place on local government." Moreover, about 25% of the older respondents concurred in this negative verdict. (That fully one-fourth of the older respondents may thus be stigmatizing themselves as a community burden is a remarkable statistic worth further study.) Although a clear majority of the age groups also agreed that older residents "generally help to improve the quality of life in my community," slightly more than a third (35%) of younger respondents did not agree that older residents improved their community's quality of life, compared with only 10% of the older respondents. Even on the issue of the aging's political power, where only a small minority of each age group believed that seniors had too much political power, the difference in responses between young and old was notable. Thus, on these items, the response patterns

Table 1. Beliefs About the Local Community Impact of the Aging

Item		Percent of respondents		
		All	<55	55+
"The economic benefits brought to my community by older residents do not compensate for the burden they place upon local government." [GOVBURDEN]	Strongly disagree	4	4	6
	Disagree	51	47	59
	Don't know	9	7	10
	Agree	32	38	23
	Strongly agree	4	4	2
	(n =)	(491)	(306)	(146)
	T-value = .38, df = 450, p = .71			
"Older residents generally help to improve the quality of life in my community." [QUALIFE]	Strongly disagree	1	1	—
	Disagree	26	34	10
	Don't know	6	4	9
	Agree	62	57	70
	Strongly agree	6	4	11
	(n =)	(497)	(310)	(150)
	T-value = 3.46, df = 458, p = .00			
"Older persons in my community tend to oppose paying for local public services which do not directly benefit them." [OPPGOVSV]	Strongly disagree	1	1	2
	Disagree	36	33	42
	Don't know	12	12	10
	Agree	47	48	46
	Strongly agree	4	6	1
	(n =)	(495)	(311)	(148)
	T-value = −1.15, df = 457, p = .25			
"When older residents in my community advocate government policies that benefit themselves, this often creates political opposition from younger residents." [YOUNGOLD]	Strongly disagree	—	—	—
	Disagree	34	34	30
	Don't know	10	8	15
	Agree	51	52	55
	Strongly agree	4	6	1
	(n =)	(492)	(309)	(148)
	T-value = 2.23, df = 455, p = .03			
"Do senior citizens in your area have too little political power, too much political power, or about the right amount of political power?" [SENPOWER]	Too little	30	29	33
	Right amount or don't know	56	55	58
	Too much	14	17	9
	(n =)	(531)	(350)	(181)
	T-value = 1.21, df = 529, p = .24			
"Suppose the local public schools said they needed much more money. As you feel at this time, would you vote to raise taxes for this purpose, or would you vote against raising taxes?" [EDVOTE]	For taxes	47	47	49
	Don't know	4	2	8
	Against taxes	49	51	43
	(n =)	(496)	(310)	(152)
	T-value = .91, df = 441, p = .36			
"I think continued economic growth is good for my community." [ECOGROW]	Strongly disagree	—	—	—
	Disagree	7	5	9
	Don't know	3	3	2
	Agree	73	73	73
	Strongly agree	18	19	17
	(n =)	(495)	(311)	(151)
	T-value = −1.11, df = 460, p = .27			
"Some people get involved in local affairs through donating their time to voluntary organizations — that is working for no pay for non-profit groups or charity. In the last 12 months, have you volunteered time to any non-profit group or charities?" [CHARITY]	Yes	40	42	39
	No	60	58	61
	(n =)	(498)	(313)	(152)
	T-value = −.62, df = 463, p = .53			
"How many hours in an average month do you volunteer work for these types of organizations?" [HOURS]	Average	16	12	23
	(n =)	(180)	(112)	(67)
	T-value = −2.07, df = 171, p = .04			

Note. Not all percentages equal 100 due to rounding.

often appear to suggest significant generational differences in perception concerning the local impact of the aging.

The most surprising response patterns, however, involve the three items concerned with the aging's attitude about local government services. A majority, or near majority, of *both* age groups agreed with statements that the aging did not want to pay for local services benefitting others and did incite the opposition of younger citizens when they promoted policies to their own advantage. However, younger citizens were more likely to agree with these items than the aging, and the differences on one of these items [YOUNGOLD] were statistically significant. Responses to the third statement, a measure of the respondent's willingness to support increased local school taxes, indicate that a majority in *both* age groups was unwilling to support new taxes or was undecided. These latter responses suggest that while the aging may, as often supposed, resist school taxes, they are not radically different (even statistically) in this respect than younger community residents — which is not often supposed.

The remaining items concerning involvement in local volunteer activities also entail a surprise. The aging, it appears, are no more involved in volunteer work than are younger community members, although the older volunteers tend to serve more hours than younger persons. Thus, approximately 40% of both age groups report some voluntary work, yet this does not seem a notably large proportion of the aging in light of assertions that the aging are distinguished by their community volunteerism.

The Public Mind Mirrored: Elite Images of the Aging

Three items used in the BEBR survey were also used in an earlier study, previously described, concerning beliefs about the aging among Florida's state and local officials (Rosenbaum & Button, 1989). Comparing these surveys further clarifies the extent to which stereotypes of the aging have diffused among Florida's population and, more importantly, have affected perceptions of the political elite. In Table 2 the earlier responses of Florida public officials are compared with the public's BEBR survey response to three common survey items.

A similar, and very substantial, proportion of the public and the officials concurred in two statements critical of the aging and conducive to generational tensions. More than a majority of both groups agreed with the statement that the aging opposed

local services not beneficial to them and approximately a third in each group agreed that the aging were more burden than benefit to the local community. The final item, concerning local generational cleavages incited by the aging, elicited somewhat different responses: a majority of citizens agreed with this statement compared with a third of the officials. While state and local officials were more divided on this matter than were their constituents, fully one in three — a significant proportion — agreed with the public majority. Thus, on one questionnaire item, attitudes and stereotypes conducive to generational conflict seemed to be widely shared between the political elite and the public. On the second item, a substantial minority of both groups seemed to share such opinions and, on a final item, more than half the public officials and a third of the Florida public concurred in opinions critical of the aging. These responses seem to imply that generational tensions, though far from crisis proportions, are nonetheless real in Florida's communities. In particular, many community leaders — those most strategically placed to influence public policies within the state — appear susceptible to the new, negative imagery of the aging as the average citizen.

The Social Correlates of Attitudes About the Aging

Using socioeconomic and demographic information about respondents in the BEBR survey, we attempted to evaluate, in a preliminary way, several plausible social explanations for differing perceptions of the aging among the sample population. It seemed to us that antipathy toward the aging: (a) might result from resentment of their perceived new economic status and therefore would relate inversely to the economic status of respondents; (b) might increase among younger persons as the size of the

Table 2. Citizen and Public Officials' Responses to Survey Questions About the Aging

Item	Response	Percent of respondents	
		BEBR survey	State and local officials
"The economic benefits brought to my community by older residents do not compensate for the burden they place upon local government."	Strongly disagree	4	37
	Disagree	51	26
	Don't know	9	5
	Agree	32	26
	Strongly agree	4	6
	N =	491	253
"Older persons in my community tend to oppose paying for local services which do not directly benefit them."	Strongly disagree	1	13
	Disagree	36	31
	Don't know	12	3
	Agree	47	38
	Strongly agree	4	16
	N =	495	252
"When older residents in my community advocate government policies that benefit themselves, this often creates political opposition from younger residents."	Strongly disagree	—	27
	Disagree	34	33
	Don't know	10	7
	Agree	51	29
	Strongly agree	4	4
	N =	492	252

Note. Not all percentages equal 100 due to rounding.

aging population in a respondent's community grows; (c) might relate inversely to a respondent's own age; and (d) might indicate lack of information, education, social awareness or other cognitive qualities associated with diminished social or economic status.

Socioeconomic data acquired for each respondent included age, sex, race, education, years of Florida residence, and income. Additionally, we obtained data concerning the population growth rate between 1980–1990 and the proportion of the population aged 65 + for each respondent's county, as well as the respondent's current voter registration status and political party affiliation. A multiple regression analysis was utilized in which each of the 9 BEBR items previously described was treated as a dependent variable and the respondent's socioeconomic and demographic characteristics were classified as independent variables. Among the independent variables, only education and income were highly intercorrelated. To resolve this problem of multicollinearity, we used only education as a measure of socioeconomic status in the regression equations. Our primary concern was to learn if the resulting statistics were consistent with any of the explanatory theories we have described. The results of this statistical analysis are summarized in Table 3.

The most important information in Table 3 involves the first 4 dependent variables — the attitude items concerning the community impact of the aging. *The one variable most consistently, significantly related to critical attitudes toward the aging was the proportion of aging (65+) in the population of the respondent's county.* Stated differently, antipathy toward the aging appeared to grow within counties concurrently with the growth of the older population. (The average proportion of the aging in counties surveyed was 19% with a range of 8 to 35%.) Moreover, when the survey population was divided into older groups (55+) and younger (less than 55), the relationship between the size of the older population within the respondent's county and critical attitudes toward the aging was much more significant for the younger survey group.

This contextual variable also was significantly associated with responses to the question on the second survey concerning the political power of the aging (SENPOWER). Among all respondents, those expressing a belief that the aging had "too much" political power were likely to come from counties where the average proportion of aging was significantly larger than that for the respondents who believed the aging had "too little" political power (the respective county averages for the aging were 20%

Table 3. Regression Results for Items in the BEBR Survey[a]

Independent variables	Dependent variables[b]								
	GOVBURDEN	QUALIFE	OPPGOVSV	YOUNGOLD	SENPOWER	EDVOTE	ECOGROW	CHARITY	HOURS
Age	−.012**	.016**	−.009**	−.004	−.019*	−.430	−.002	.052	.267
	(.003)	(.003)	(.003)	(.002)	(.009)	(.267)	(.002)	(.280)	(.158)
Sex (1 = male) (2 = female)	−.278**	.116	−.218*	−.305**	−.882**	−.360	−.106	−.396	−1.21
	(.102)	(.092)	(.099)	(.096)	(.327)	(.290)	(.066)	(.304)	(5.22)
Race (1 = white) (2 = non-white)	.247	.023	−.270	−.056	−1.23*	−.111	.056	1.40*	−6.20
	(.195)	(.174)	(.190)	(.181)	(.599)	(.529)	(.125)	(.710)	(12.7)
Education	−.049*	−.010	.003	−.067**	.109	−.659	.025	−2.33**	.573
	(.024)	(.021)	(.024)	(.022)	(.070)	(.632)	(.015)	(.745)	(1.20)
Years of residence	.004	−.005	.007*	−.000	−.048	.185	−.000	−.137	.390*
	(.003)	(.003)	(.003)	(.003)	(.399)	(.097)	(.002)	(.110)	(.161)
Population growth	−.000	−.000	−.000	−.000	−.005	.091	−.002	.085	.010
	(.002)	(.002)	(.002)	(.002)	(.009)	(.157)	(.001)	(.167)	(.096)
% 65 +	.002**	−.003**	.003**	.001*	.076**	−.177	−.000	.163	.013
	(−.000)	(−.000)	(−.000)	(−.000)	(.024)	(.251)	(−.000)	(.266)	(.038)
Voter registration (1 = No; 2 = Yes)	−.003	.134	.068	.136	—[c]	−.563	.087	−1.18**	.358
	(.124)	(.111)	(.121)	(.115)		(.374)	(.080)	(.432)	(7.27)
Party ID (1 = Dem.; 2 = Ind.; 3 = Rep.)	.012	−.048	−.026	−.121	−.150	−.056	−.062	−.073	5.03
	(.067)	(.061)	(.066)	(.063)	(.213)	(.229)	(.044)	(.238)	(3.20)
R^2 =	.08	.09	.06	.06	.07	[d]	.04	[d]	.10

[a]Unstandardized regression coefficients are listed; standard errors are in parenthesis.

[b]For the first 5 dependent variables and for ECOGROW, "strongly agree" is coded 4. For EDVOTE, "for raising taxes" is coded 1, and for CHARITY "yes" is coded 1.

[c]Voter registration status not asked in 1991 survey.

[d]R^2 not reported because logit regression analysis was used for this dichotomous dependent variable.

*$p < .05$; **$p < .01$.

and 17%). Among the respondents under age 55, the same contrast was apparent and the disparity between the proportions of the county aging populations even larger (20% and 16%). Thus, the data offer support to the assumption that generational conflict may arise, and intensify, as the proportion of aging increases at local levels.

The second respondent attribute to be significantly associated with antipathy toward the aging was the respondent's age. Age was associated with 4 of the 5 attitude items, and this finding seems consistent with the idea that generational cleavages may account for growing hostility toward the elderly. This finding is especially noteworthy because it confirms a similar conclusion reached more than a decade ago in Douglas St. Angelo's study of public perceptions about the aging in 10 representative Florida counties (St. Angelo, 1981).

More puzzling is the correlation between sex and benign perceptions of the aging. On 4 of the attitude items relating to the aging (GOVBURDEN, OPPGOVSV, YOUNGOLD and SENPOWER), women were much more likely than men to evaluate the aging and their civic activities favorably. Any explanation is speculative because the literature on political gerontology is silent about such a gender issue. One or two explanations seem plausible. Since women constitute a large proportion of the aging — a proportion that grows steadily with advancing age — the gender association may reveal a natural empathy between women of all ages toward a population perceived as predominately female and variously handicapped. The gender association may also reveal another psychological dimension of the nurturing and caretaking role which women so often assume in American society (Gilligan, 1982; Welch & Hibbing, 1992).

The data in Table 3 related to the remaining dependent variables are noteworthy for what does *not* appear. There is no significant statistical association (controlling for other variables) between age, or any other respondent attribute, and propensity to oppose an increase in local school taxes — an apparent refutation of the "anti-education" bias attributed to older persons. In the first BEBR survey, both the younger and older groups were divided about equally over additional taxes for education, with a slightly larger proportion of the older respondents (49%) than younger (47%) supporting more taxes. So anomalous did this finding seem that we repeated the item on the second BEBR poll with very similar results. When other variables are controlled, however, age is not statistically significant. Thus, the aging are no more willing than younger respondents to favor or to oppose increased taxes for education. Equally unexpected was the finding that neither voluntary community service nor the amount of such service was associated with age when other variables were controlled. Contrary to another assumption about older Americans, they do not appear to be more involved in community service than their younger neighbors.

The relationship between socioeconomic status

and hostility toward the aging is inconclusive in our data. Education, our measure of socioeconomic status and social awareness, was significantly related with negative perceptions of the aging on only 2 (GOVBURDEN, YOUNGOLD) of the 5 survey items directly involving such attitudes.

Discussion and Conclusion

Does Florida epitomize in any important way the political status of the aging elsewhere? Florida's aging, as demographer Brad Edmundson has observed, have reached a socioeconomic stage that an increasing number of older persons will reach in the future elsewhere and, for American business, the social styles and values of Florida's aging have become reliable indicators of national trends among the aging (Edmundson, 1987). Most important politically, Florida is on the leading edge of a profound urban demographic transformation in which the aging will become an increasingly large proportion, or a majority, of many communities and political constituencies. "Florida may not be the blueprint for the nation's future," notes Edmundson, but it "tells us what society looks like when age, not youth, is in charge" (Edmundson, 1987, p. 69). Thus, Florida suggests not only qualities of a civic culture in which the aging are "in charge" politically but also how this transformation may be greeted by those not empowered.

The most significant finding in our survey is the very substantial proportion of younger respondents, ranging from roughly a third to more than half this group, who agreed to a variety of statements suggesting that older residents in their county or city were variously an economic burden, an economically selfish voting bloc, a generationally divisive influence, or an unconstructive community element. Moreover, these proportions closely resembled responses we received a few years earlier to a similar survey of Florida's state and local public officials. These findings imply no imminent eruption of generational conflict. Indeed, we often found complimentary and beneficial images of the aging widely shared between the generations when, for instance, they agreed that older persons had "about the right amount of political power." But we also found a widely distributed, latent disaffection with the aging's community impact and civic behavior. The social breadth and depth of this negative image suggests that it ought to be considered at least as typical of the aging's community stereotype as more complimentary images.

Another important aspect of our findings is the statistically significant association between critical appraisals of the aging and the size of the aging population in the respondents' home counties. Generally, the respondents most likely to express critical views about the aging's civic impact came from the counties with the larger proportion of older residents. This relationship was especially noteworthy among the younger survey group (those under age 55).

Our findings challenge several articles of political faith among the public and their local officials. Our responses suggest that the aging may be no more likely than younger community residents to oppose new school taxes and that younger residents are themselves almost evenly divided (not strongly agreed) about supporting such taxes. Additionally, the older respondents in our survey were not significantly more involved in voluntary community activities than younger ones.

These findings beg the question of why generational tensions do not appear with similar clarity in the studies previously reviewed. One persuasive answer, we believe, is that the public policy questions do not usually ask whether respondents believe the older beneficiaries of entitlement programs need or deserve them. Also, the generational tensions we have observed may arise only in a community context, in relation to local issues, or arise at the local level first. Generational cleavages over national policies may gradually evolve if beliefs in the legitimacy of the aging's claims on entitlements, or other negative stereotypes of the aging, persist longer, as Cook and Barret suggest could happen in the case of Social Security (Cook & Barret, 1988).

Most importantly, we believe these survey findings should reinvigorate the debate over the eminence of generational conflict in America. It is notable, we think, that the critical appraisals we have documented among so many of Florida's younger residents arise at the *community* level, where respondents are often brought into daily, sustained relationship with the aging through the normal events of civic life. Here, where elderly persons are no abstraction but a daily reality, seen and heard, critical cross-generational antagonisms have evolved and persisted. Moreover, our data imply that this community-level antipathy to the aging among the younger population may be expected to increase as the size of the local aging population grows. One provocative implication of these data is that greater contact between generations in civic life arising from the increasing size of the aging population in America's cities and counties may exacerbate generational tensions and nationalize them as the aging become more prominent across the nation.

Moreover, the criticism of the aging we often encountered among younger persons was generalized and diffuse, unanchored to specific community acts or events. This strongly suggests a "standing verdict" among many younger Floridians, a propensity to perceive the aging and their behavior in critical, uncomplimentary terms. If a deteriorating image of the aging precedes a declining political status, then the unattractive images of the aging we have often documented would seem to bespeak an image degeneration that might anticipate, or promote, generational conflict. This image transformation seems analogous to a pattern that Torres-Gil suggests could be a provocation of generational tensions: change from an image of the aging as poor and needy with the "automatic legitimacy" implied for their political claims to an image as "selfish and concerned only with personal pension and income benefits" (Torres-Gil, 1992, pp. 76, 87). In short, we think there is good

reason for continuing concern about generational tensions in the U.S.

References

Aaron, H. J., Bosworth, B. P., & Burtless, G. T. (1989). *Can America afford to grow old?* Washington, DC: Brookings Institution.

Barnes, J. (1991). Age old strife. *National Journal, 4* (January 26, 1991), 216–219.

Beck, P. A., & Dye, T. R. (1982). Sources of public opinion on taxes: The Florida case. *Journal of Politics, 44,* 172–182.

Berger, P. (1963). *Invitation to sociology.* Garden City, NY: Doubleday.

Bernstein, A. (1991). Is Uncle Sam shortchanging young Americans? *Business Week* (August 18), 85.

Button, J. W. (1992). A sign of generational conflict: The impact of Florida's aging voters on local school and tax referenda. *Social Science Quarterly, 73,* 786–797.

Button, J. W., & Rosenbaum, W. A. (1989). Seeing gray: School bond issues and the aging in Florida. *Research on Aging, 11,* 158–173.

Button, J. W., & Rosenbaum, W. A. (1990). Gray power, gray peril, or gray myth?: The political impact of the aging in local sunbelt politics. *Social Science Quarterly, 71,* 25–38.

Campos, C. D. (1986). *Political priorities of older Americans.* Paper delivered at the Annual Meeting of the Midwest Political Science Association, Chicago, April 10–12.

Cook, F. L., & Barrett, E. J. (1988). Public support for social security. *Journal of Aging Studies, 2,* 339–356.

Day, C. L. (1990). *What older Americans think: Interest groups and aging policy.* Princeton, NJ: Princeton University Press.

Edmundson, B. (1987). Is Florida our future? *American Demographics, 9,* 38–44.

Eagleton Institute of Politics (1987). *Eagleton Poll.* New Brunswick, NJ: Rutgers University.

Elder, C. D., & Cobb, R. W. (1984). Agenda-building and the politics of aging. *Policy Studies Journal, 13,* 115–130.

Foner, A. (1972). The polity. In M. W. Riley, M. Johnson, & A. Foner (Eds.), *Aging and society: A sociology of age stratification, Vol. 3.* New York: Russell Sage Foundation.

Freiman, M. P., & Grasso, P. G. (1982). Budget impact and voter response to tax limitation referenda. *Public Finance Quarterly, 10,* 49–66.

Gallup, G. H. (1978). *The Gallup poll: Public opinion 1972–77.* Wilmington, DE: Scholarly Resources, Inc.

Gilligan, C. (1982). *In a different voice.* Cambridge, MA: Harvard University Press.

Grubb, W. N., & Lazerson, M. (1982). *Broken promises: How Americans fail their children.* New York: Basic Books.

Haas, W. H. (1989). *The gray peril?: Implications for politics, health and service delivery.* Paper presented at the Conference on Migration and Elderly Population Change in Appalachia: The 1980s and Beyond. Asheville, NC.

Haas, W. H., & Serow, W. J. (1991). *An exploratory study of retirement migration decision making.* Research Report to the Appalachian Regional Commission.

Huddy, L. (1989). *Political attitudes in an aging society: Raising the specter of generational conflict.* Paper presented at the annual meeting of the Midwest Political Science Association, Chicago, IL.

Hudson, R. B. (1978). The 'graying' of the federal budget and its consequences for old-age policy. *The Gerontologist, 18,* 428–440.

Hudson, R. B. (1980). Old-age politics in a period of change. In E. F. Borgatta & N. G. McCluskey (Eds.), *Aging and society.* Beverly Hills: Sage.

Jencks, C., & Torrey, B. B. (1988). Beyond income and poverty: Trends in social welfare among children and the elderly since 1960. In J. L. Palmer, T. Smeeding, & B. B. Torrey (Eds.), *The vulnerable.* Washington, DC: Urban Institute Press.

Kingson, E. R., Hirshorn, B. A., & Harootyan, L. K. (1986). *Ties that bind: The interdependence of generations.* Cabin John, MD: Seven Locks Press.

Kingson, E. R. (1988). Generational equity: An unexpected opportunity to broaden the politics of aging. *The Gerontologist, 28,* 765–772.

Longman, P. (1985). Justice between generations. *Atlantic Monthly, 255,* 73–81.

Longman, P. (1987). *Born to pay.* Boston: Houghton Mifflin Co.

Mullins, D. R., & Rosentraub, M. S. (1990). *Migrating dollars?: Elders, taxes and local budgets.* Special Issues Report No. 7, Heartland Center on Aging, Disability and Long Term Care, School of Public Administration and Environmental Affairs, Indiana University, South Bend, Indiana.

Oberhofer, T. (1989). The cultural discount rate, social contracts, and intergenerational tension. *Social Science Quarterly, 70,* 858–869.

Palmer, J. L, Smeeding, T., & Boyle, B. T. (1988). *The vulnerable.* Washington, DC: Urban Institute Press.

Petersen, J. E. (1991). All those goodies for the elderly, have they gone too far? *Governing, 4,* 79.

Philadelphia Inquirer (1989). February 1, pp. 1A, 4A.

Pifer, A. (1986). The public response to population aging. *Daedalus, 115*, 373–380.

Ponza, M., Duncan, G. J., Corcoran, M., & Groskind, F. (1988). The guns of autumn: Age differences in support for income transfers to the young and old. *Public Opinion Quarterly, 52*, 441–463.

Preston, S. H. (1984a). Children and the elderly. *Scientific American, 251*,

Preston, S. H. (1984b). Children and the elderly: Divergent paths for America's dependents. *Demography, 21*, 435–457.

Reeves, R. (1988). Seniors are wielding more clout. *Gainesville Sun*, March 23.

Rhodeback, L. A., & Fitzgerald, R. E. (1989). *The Politics of greed?: The dynamics of public opinion among the elderly*. Paper prepared for presentation at the Annual Meeting of the Midwest Political Science Association, Chicago, April 13–15.

Rosenbaum, W. A., & Button, J. W. (1989). Is there a 'gray peril?': Retirement politics in Florida. *The Gerontologist, 29*, 300–306.

St. Angelo, D. (1981). *Are senior citizens the next backlash target?* Paper presented at the Annual Meeting of the Midwest Association for Public Opinion, Chicago, October 24.

Schmidhauser, J. R. (1970). The elderly in politics. In A. M. Hoffman (Ed.), *The daily needs and interests of older people*. Springfield, IL: Charles C Thomas.

Schuck, P. H. (1979). The graying of civil rights law: The Age Discrimination Act of 1975. *Yale Law Journal, 89*, 27–93.

Skinner, M., & Kinney, L. (1991). 'We have a right to be heard.' *Gainesville Sun*, July 14, 6–7 (Supplement).

Smith, L. (1988). The world according to AARP. *Fortune, 117*, 96–98.

Tolchin, M. (1988). Aid to elderly divides young, old and politicians. *New York Times*, December 23.

Torres-Gil, G. (1992). *The new aging*. New York: Auburn House.

Walker, A. (1990). The economic 'burden of the aging' and the prospect of intergenerational conflict. *Ageing and Society, 10*, 377–396.

Welch, S., & Hibbing, J. (1992). Financial conditions, gender and voting in American national elections. *Journal of Politics, 54*, 197–213.

MAX FRANKEL

Less Medicare, More Magic

THE PROMISE OF BENEFITS FOR ALL, NEEDY OR NOT, WILL SAVE SOCIAL SECURITY.

THE SERIOUS JOURNALS ARE FULL of alarms about a budgetary crisis that threatens to sink America in perhaps 20, maybe 30, surely 50 years. They say that I, as one of the elderly, am a major cause of the impending catastrophe. I am accused of bleeding the Government by claiming a richer pension and health insurance than my contributions would have earned from an insurance company. And I am accused of producing so many boomer children that *their* retirements with similar benefits will surely deplete the Treasury.

Duly shamed, I am struggling to help shape a remedy. I have absorbed Peter Peterson's "Will America Grow Up Before It Grows Old?" in hardcover and newsprint and scores of reactions: Paul Krugman's rave (and recantation) on the Web; critiques by John Judis in The New Republic and John Cassidy in The New Yorker; caveats from Herbert Stein in The Wall Street Journal and a ream of Op-Ed essays in The Washington Post and The New York Times. I've come through a dense semantic fog.

Plainly, the Social Security payroll taxes exacted from me and my boss by the Federal *Insurance Contributions* Act of 1935 (F.I.C.A.) were never handled as "insurance contributions" to any "trust fund." The taxes were simply mingled with Treasury revenues and spent not only for pension and Medicare payments to my parents but also on highways, moon shots, drug busts and jungle wars. Similarly, the retirement benefits now owed to me are being paid, along with all other Government expenses, with all the taxes drawn from the working population.

So while Social Security and Medicare masquerade as capitalistic insurance schemes, they serve the socialistic function of redistributing wealth, from the energetic young to the retired old. And the popularity of those programs, I am convinced, is sustained by this duplicity. By covering almost all the elderly, irrespective of need, they have avoided the stigma that attaches to other redistributions, like welfare and Medicaid. The young have borne a growing burden because they were assured their turn to benefit would come. The old have cashed their checks with no trace of guilt because they've been led to believe they are only drawing down their own investments.

"The resulting consensus about the system is its magic," said Arthur Okun, the late Great Society economist; the fiction of earmarked contributions "serves mainly to preserve pride" while actually fulfilling a "right to survival." But he wrote 20 years ago. Now Peterson and other hardheaded analysts condemn Okun's consensus as a cruel Ponzi scheme, a promise of entitlements that threaten to bankrupt the nation. Whereas every person over 65 is currently supported by the taxes of five working people, the rapid aging of the population, they warn, means that every retiree in 2030 can expect support from only three.

That bleak prospect assumes that Medicare outlays will continue to grow much faster than the general cost of living and go on claiming two of every three Government dollars paid to the elderly. Yet though we old folks run up huge hospital and nursing bills in the last years of life, Americans have only begun to discover how to reduce medical costs. I don't think we should bet against our learning to live more healthily and to age less expensively.

Still, the number of the aged will soon explode, and they will live longer than ever before. The sooner we cover their deficits the less painful the retrenchment. All the available remedies involve some increase in payroll deductions—either modest tax increases or genuine contributions to annuity schemes. And all the experts urge assorted caps and cutbacks in Social Security and Medicare allowances, with new efforts to steer benefits away from the affluent toward the needy. There are suggestions to raise the retirement age past the already scheduled increase from 65 to 67. There are responsible plans to reduce the cost-of-living increases in Social Security pensions and to withhold benefits from retirees with sizable earnings or investments. And there are many ideas for making most of the elderly pay a larger share of their medical expenses.

My greatest concern, however, is not for the economics of the remedy, but for the ecumenism of its design. I want to preserve Arthur Okun's magical consensus—and the psychic income that the liberated young

have derived for half a century from the independence of the old.

"My mother thanks you," I said to Lyndon Johnson after he signed Medicare into law in 1965.

"No," he replied, "It's *you* who should be thanking me."

AS PETERSON AND OTHER CONSERVATIVES urge, Congress could invoke the specter of bankruptcy to impose forced savings on future generations and to ration payments to the elderly with a means test that would eventually pay benefits only to the "truly needy." But as we know from Medicaid, a means test will have two deplorable consequences. It will tempt the nonneedy to shed their assets to qualify for benefits, as many have done to get Medicaid coverage in nursing homes. And it will stigmatize all aid to the elderly poor as "welfare," depriving them of significant political support.

The only effective way to favor the poor without robbing them of dignity and public favor is to preserve the universality of Social Security—and to quietly reclaim moneys from the affluent by progressively taxing their medical and pension benefits.

One other image in this discussion urgently needs repair. It is destructive to stir up intergenerational warfare. That would occur if a powerful voting bloc of the elderly were pitted against an angry younger population. But there is no profit for either side in such a war. If the elderly emerged with wildly excessive benefits, they would only succeed in devaluing the currency in which they are ultimately paid. And if the young reneged on too many promised benefits, they would only inherit the burden of their parents' distress and feel compelled to support them in other ways.

Cut back on Medicare. But keep the magic.

Index

abstinence, sexual, 41
active life expectancy, 29
activities of daily living (ADLS), 185
activity director, 184, 198
adenosine triphosphate (ATP), 36
adult day care centers, 200
adult protective service agencies, 188
advance directives, 169, 170, 176, 201. *See also* durable power of attorney; living wills
affluent elderly households, 111
age discrimination complaints, 78
Age Discrimination in Employment Act, 78
age discrimination, in Sweden, 151
Age of Integrity, 74, 75
ageism: as prejudice, 81; as worst part of getting older, 69
age-sizing versus downsizing, 80
aging: attitudes toward, 94–97; and beliefs, 96; characteristics associated with, 13–14; children's attitudes toward, 81–86; economics of, 147–159; and men and women, differences in, 61; and new capacities, 97; physiological, 14, 17; positive aspects of, 17, 94–97; process, "program" versus "error," 10; problems of, 113; requirements for, 19; result of disease, 16; in rodents, 14; successful, 10, 16–18, 27; survival of the fittest and, 16, 23; variations in, 10; and voting, 214, 215
aging and voting, 214, 215
"aging in place," 155–156
aging of baby boomers, 112
aging populations, spending cuts and, 159
aging, positive aspects of, 67–70
aging research: and change, 14; confounding in, 14; difficulty of longitudinal studies in, 14; lack of good data before 1958, 9; and relocation, 65; versus study of disease, 16, 21
altruism, in families, 47. *See also* generational transfers of wealth
Alzheimer's disease, 16; EEGs in, 16; and elder abuse, 123; and ibuprofen, 10; and inflammation, 10; mortality from, 24; new treatments for, 24, 25; not a natural part of aging, 16; residential treatment for, 184–186, 187–188
ambulance, 170
American Association of Retired Persons (AARP), 207
anti-euthanasia passports in the Netherlands, 164
Area Agencies on Aging, 170
artificial nutrition, and hydration, 170
assisted death, 162–168
assisted living communities, 198–199
attitude(s): and beliefs, 82; of nursing home staff, 200; resistant to change, 81; toward aging, 94–97
average life expectancy: of baby boomers, 21; increased, 27, 28, 46; in Japan, 48; in 1900, 23; in 1970, 23; in 2050, 14; by 2020, 20; by 2040, 24; by 2050, 46; of 20-year-olds, 49
average life span: in 1990, 9; of some animals, 14; species maximum, 26; for women in 1900, 14

baby boomers, 21, 50, 57
Baltimore Longitudinal Study of Aging: discussion, 1–12; mission, 10; participants, 9; productivity of participants, 12; world class medical work-up of, 9
blue collar workers, 145
boating, 193
"bottom line," 168. *See also* medical cost containment
burial customs, history of, 172–174
business opportunities, 194
busy ethic, 128–133

caloric intake, for human beings, appropriate, 37
caloric restriction, 26, 32–37
Canadian national health insurance: political accountability for, 205; myths of, 205
Canadian seniors, 90–93
cancer: and caloric restriction in mice, 34; and personality's contribution to onset of, 31; and sexuality, 44
care plan, for elderly persons, 197–201
caregiver(s): child functioning as, 62; in Japan, 155; men as, 65; primary, family as, 169–171; professional, 170; training of, 184–186, 187. *See also* respite care
caregiving, assessments toward, 197
caregiving, pre-crisis discussion of, 197
cemeteries, architecture of, 172–174
Chaos Theory, 18–19
child functioning as a caregiver, 62
childrearing. *See* grandparents
children's concerns about growing old, 82
Children's Views of Aging (CVoA), 83–86
clutch, need to, 185
community, impact of aging on, 216–222
community politics, 216–218, 219
community, sense of, 199
companionship, 199
competency, 170
conditioning actions, 184
Confucian concept of care of elderly, 53
conscious aging, 95
consumer behavior, and affluence, 193, 194
consumer items, expenditures for, 193, 194
continuity theory, 135, 136
coping styles, Types A and C, 31
coresidence, 101
crafts, 193
cremation, 174
criminal records, nursing home staff with, 187
"crisis theory," 135
Cruzan opinion, 170

daily routines, 63–64
death planning, 177. *See also* patients' wishes
death rates. *See* mortality
death with dignity, 169–171
dehydration, 17
dementia: and confusion with depression, 197; environments for patients with, 184–186; percentage of nursing-home residents with, 185; subjective experience of, 187; treatment of, 187–188

denial of aging, 95
department stores, needed in communities, 194
depression: and confusion with dementia, 197; and euthanasia, 168; in retirees, 134, in retirees and workers, 139
diabetes, 44
diet: and antioxidant vitamins, 22, 26; caloric restriction untested in humans, 35; plant-based, 21, 23; vegetables and fruit, 26. *See also* caloric restriction
differences in aging, in men and women, 61–66. *See also* sexuality
dignity, 177
dining out, 193
disability: changes in sexuality due to, 41; in late-late life, 62; and limitations, 108–110, 111
disease: causes of, 17; and heredity, 48; postponement of (in rodents), 33
Do Not Resuscitate (DNR) order, 170
doctor-patient relationship, 162, 165, 167, 168, 204
doctors as public servants in the Netherlands, 163
durable power of attorney, 170, 201
Dutch Health Ministry, 164
Dutch Patients' Association, 164, 167
Dutch Voluntary Euthanasia Society, 164
dying, cost of, 177

early retirement, 60
economic growth, contribution of elderly towards, 189–190
elder abuse, 121–125
elder law, 201
elder mistreatment. *See* elder abuse
Elderhostel, 58, 59
elderly: in Canada, 92; demographics of, 206; migration of, 189–196; and relocation, 65; resilience of, 19, 22; and school, 59, 60; sources of information about, for children, 84; status of, in history, 51; and travel, 59. *See also* elderly populations
elderly populations: most rapidly growing, 189–196; percentage of, in nursing homes, 49; with self-care limitations, 109; suburban, 108
emergency medical service (EMS), 170
endorphins, discovery of, 30
entitlement programs, and increase in elderly, 46–50
euthanasia: acceptability of, 162; consensus about, 163, 168; criteria for, in the Netherlands, 165; and individual choice, 163; legality of, 162; nature of, 167; in the Netherlands, 162–168; of newborns, 166–167; regulation of, 163; as a right, 167; unreported cases of, in the Netherlands, 163; versus "life-terminating treatment," 165
experience, 89

family physician as advocate, 31
fear of aging, 96
feeding tube, 175–176, 199
financial impact, of elderly, 189–196

Credits/Acknowledgments

Cover design by Charles Vitelli.

1. The Phenomenon of Aging
Facing overview—© 1997 by Cleo Freelance Photography. 11—© 1997 by The Image Bank.

2. The Quality of Later Life
Facing overview—© 1997 by PhotoDisc, Inc.

3. Societal Attitudes toward Old Age
Facing overview—United Nations photo by F. B. Grunzweig.

4. Problems and Potentials of Aging
Facing overview—© 1997 by PhotoDisc, Inc.

5. Retirement: American Dream or Dilemma?
Facing overview—© 1997 by PhotoDisc, Inc.

6. The Experience of Dying
Facing overview—Photo by Louis P. Raucci.

7. Living Environments in Later Life
Facing overview—United Nations photo by G. Palmer

8. Social Policies, Programs, and Services for Older Americans
Facing overview—United Nations photo by John Isaac.

PHOTOCOPY THIS PAGE!!!*

ANNUAL EDITIONS ARTICLE REVIEW FORM

■ NAME: _____ DATE: _____

■ TITLE AND NUMBER OF ARTICLE: _____

■ BRIEFLY STATE THE MAIN IDEA OF THIS ARTICLE: _____

_____

■ LIST THREE IMPORTANT FACTS THAT THE AUTHOR USES TO SUPPORT THE MAIN IDEA:

_____

_____

_____

_____

■ WHAT INFORMATION OR IDEAS DISCUSSED IN THIS ARTICLE ARE ALSO DISCUSSED IN YOUR TEXTBOOK OR OTHER READINGS THAT YOU HAVE DONE? LIST THE TEXTBOOK CHAPTERS AND PAGE NUMBERS:

_____

_____

_____

_____

_____

■ LIST ANY EXAMPLES OF BIAS OR FAULTY REASONING THAT YOU FOUND IN THE ARTICLE:

_____

_____

_____

_____

■ LIST ANY NEW TERMS/CONCEPTS THAT WERE DISCUSSED IN THE ARTICLE, AND WRITE A SHORT DEFINITION:

_____

_____

_____

_____

We Want Your Advice

ANNUAL EDITIONS revisions depend on two major opinion sources: one is our Advisory Board, listed in the front of this volume, which works with us in scanning the thousands of articles published in the public press each year; the other is you—the person actually using the book. Please help us and the users of the next edition by completing the prepaid article rating form on this page and returning it to us. Thank you for your help!

ANNUAL EDITIONS: AGING 98/99
Article Rating Form

Here is an opportunity for you to have direct input into the next revision of this volume. We would like you to rate each of the 41 articles listed below, using the following scale:

1. **Excellent: should definitely be retained**
2. **Above average: should probably be retained**
3. **Below average: should probably be deleted**
4. **Poor: should definitely be deleted**

Rating	Article	Rating	Article
	1. A Study for the Ages		24. Does Retirement Hurt Well-Being? Factors Influencing Self-Esteem and Depression among Retirees and Workers
	2. Toward a Natural History of Aging		
	3. How to Live to 100		25. Rethinking Retirement
	4. Why We Will Live Longer . . . and What It Will Mean		26. The Economics of Ageing
	5. The Mind Connection		27. Euthanasia's Home: What the Dutch Experience Can Teach Americans about Assisted Suicide
	6. Caloric Restriction and Aging		
	7. Sexuality and Aging: What It Means to Be Sixty or Seventy or Eighty in the '90s		28. Euthanasia in the Netherlands
			29. Going Home to Die
	8. Live Long and Prosper?		30. Ashes to Ashes, Dust to Dust: Is There Any Future for Cemeteries?
	9. Roles for Aged Individuals in Post-Industrial Societies		
			31. The American Way of Dying
	10. The Age Boom		32. The Story of a Nursing Home Refugee
	11. Men and Women Aging Differently		33. A Proposal for Minimum Standards for "Low-Stimulus Alzheimer's Wings" in Nursing Facilities
	12. Getting Over Getting Older		
	13. New Passages		
	14. On the Edge of Age Discrimination		34. Final Indignities: The Care of Elders with Dementia
	15. Children's Views on Aging: Their Attitudes and Values		35. Retirement Migration and Economic Development in High-Amenity, Nonmetropolitan Areas
	16. What Doctors and Others Need to Know: Six Facts on Human Sexuality and Aging		
			36. Caring for Aging Loved Ones
	17. Amazing Greys		37. Canada's Health Insurance and Ours: Real Lessons, Big Choices
	18. Learning to Love (Gulp!) Growing Old		
	19. Three Phases in the History of American Grandparents: Authority, Burden, Companion		38. Senior Citizens: A New Force in Community Service
	20. American Maturity		39. Does Getting Old Cost Society Too Much?
	21. My Mother Is Speaking from the Desert		40. The Unquiet Future of Intergenerational Politics
	22. Understanding Elder Abuse and Neglect		41. Less Medicare, More Magic
	23. The Busy Ethic: Moral Continuity between Work and Retirement		

(Continued on next page)

ABOUT YOU

Name _____ Date _____

Are you a teacher? ❑ Or a student? ❑

Your school name _____

Department _____

Address _____

City _____ State _____ Zip _____

School telephone # _____

YOUR COMMENTS ARE IMPORTANT TO US !

Please fill in the following information:

For which course did you use this book? _____

Did you use a text with this *ANNUAL EDITION*? ❑ yes ❑ no

What was the title of the text? _____

What are your general reactions to the *Annual Editions* concept?

Have you read any particular articles recently that you think should be included in the next edition?

Are there any articles you feel should be replaced in the next edition? Why?

Are there any World Wide Web sites you feel should be included in the next edition? Please annotate.

May we contact you for editorial input?

May we quote your comments?

ANNUAL EDITIONS: AGING 98/99